A CENTURY OF COURTS

A century of courts

The Courts of Justice Act 1924

NIAMH HOWLIN
EDITOR

FOUR COURTS PRESS
in association with
THE IRISH LEGAL HISTORY SOCIETY

Set in EhrhardtMT Pro 10.5pt/12.5pt by
Carrigboy Typesetting Services for
FOUR COURTS PRESS LTD
7 Malpas Street, Dublin 8, Ireland
www.fourcourtspress.ie
and in North America for
FOUR COURTS PRESS
c/o IPG, 814 N Franklin St, Chicago, IL 60610

© the various contributors and Four Courts Press 2024

References to this publication should cite the publisher as Four Courts Press
in association with the Irish Legal History Society.

A catalogue record for this title is available
from the British Library.

ISBN 978-1-80151-137-7

All rights reserved. No part of this publication may be reproduced,
stored in or introduced into a retrieval system, or transmitted, in any form
or by any means (electronic, mechanical, photocopying, recording, or otherwise),
without the prior written permission of both the copyright
owner and publisher of this book.

Printed in England
by CPI Antony Rowe Ltd, Chippenham, Wilts.

Contents

LIST OF ILLUSTRATIONS		vii
LIST OF ABBREVIATIONS		viii
NOTES ON CONTRIBUTORS		ix
ACKNOWLEDGMENTS		xiii
1	Reflecting on a century of Irish courts *Niamh Howlin*	1
2	Ireland in 1924: the historical context *Diarmaid Ferriter*	11
3	The Dáil courts and opposition to the Courts of Justice Act 1924 *Thomas Mohr*	22
4	The 'judicial interregnum', 1922–4: the new Constitution in the old courts *Maurice G. Collins*	33
5	Comfortably housed? The law courts at Dublin Castle, 1923–31 *Evan McGuigan*	50
6	Establishing judicial independence *Bláthna Ruane*	62
7	A balanced judiciary: the early appointments to the Superior and Circuit Courts *Robert D. Marshall*	72
8	The introduction of a retirement age for judges *Daire Hogan*	84
9	Remuneration of judges under the 1924 Act *Laura Cahillane*	92
10	'On the fly and on the sly': a District Court in action *Niamh Howlin*	105
11	The District Court, 1924–2024: 'big bang' 100 years on *Paul Kelly*	116
12	'Illegal, immoral and unpatriotic': cross-border smuggling and the courts *Lynsey Black and Danielle C. Jefferis*	128

Contents

13	'Twenty-six high courts': the Circuit Court, decentralisation and its opponents, 1924–34 Kevin Costello	145
14	The expanding role of the Circuit Court judge Patricia Ryan	156
15	The role of the president of the High Court David Barniville	165
16	Who would be a chief justice? Donal O'Donnell	183
17	The Supreme Court and the winter of 1936–7 Gerard Hogan	203
18	Where were the women? Niamh Howlin and Mark Coen	213
19	The Courts of Justice Act 1924 and the Irish language in the courtroom Úna Ní Raifeartaigh and Róisín Á. Costello	234
20	Section 29 of the Courts of Justice Act 1924 and the certification process: a long-lasting legacy Hilary Biehler	249
21	Appeal routes in Northern Ireland Brice Dickson	258
22	The Courts of Justice Act in comparative perspective Donal K. Coffey	269
23	'A new order in this country': symbolism and the new courts Mark Coen	278
APPENDICES		293
BIBLIOGRAPHY		301
TABLE OF STATUTES		321
INDEX		327
THE IRISH LEGAL HISTORY SOCIETY SERIES		347
THE IRISH LEGAL HISTORY SOCIETY		348

Illustrations

appear between pp 146 and 147.

1. Hugh Kennedy and Lord Glenavy, early 1920s.
2. 'New Irish Courts', 1924.
3. The new judges arriving at Dublin Castle, 1924.
4. Christmas card sent by Hugh Kennedy from Dublin Castle.
5. Dun Emer Guild design for robes for Circuit Court judges.
6. Dun Emer Guild design for robes for Supreme Court judges.
7. Charles Shannon designs for the District Court and the Central Criminal Court.
8. Charles Shannon design for the High Court.
9. District judges in 1926 wearing new robes.
10. Hugh Kennedy holding his wig.
11. Chief justice's seal.
12. 'Man Overboard'. Cartoon by Gordon Brewster regarding the Courts of Justice Act 1925.
13. 'Kennedy Chief Justice'. Cartoon by Isa Macnie.
14. A Century of Courts conference logo, depicting both Dublin Castle and the Four Courts.
15. Tralee courthouse with cannon.
16. Monaghan courthouse.
17. Cavan courthouse before the removal of its coat of arms.
18. An Post stamp commemorating the Courts of Justice Act 1924.

Abbreviations

App.	Appendix
AIC	Army Inquiry Committee
att. gen.	attorney general
BL	Barrister at law/British Library
BMH	Bureau of Military History
Deb.	Debates
Dept.	Department
DIB	*Dictionary of Irish biography, online edition*
D.U.L.J.	*Dublin University Law Journal*
EHRR	European Human Rights Reports
Govt.	Government
HC	High Court
I.L.T.&S.J.	*Irish Law Times and Solicitors' Journal*
ILRM	Irish Law Reports Monthly
Ir. Jur.	*Irish Jurist*
IMA	Irish Military Archives
IR	Irish Reports
KC	King's Counsel
Memo.	Memorandum
Min.	Minister
MSPC	Military Service Pensions Collection
NAI	National Archives of Ireland
NICA	Northern Ireland Court of Appeal
N.I.L.Q.	*Northern Ireland Legal Quarterly*
NLI	National Library of Ireland
obit.	obituary
OPW	Office of Public Works
Oxford DNB	*Oxford dictionary of national biography*
PC	Privy Council
PRONI	Public Record Office of Northern Ireland
RUI	Royal University of Ireland
SC	Supreme Court/senior counsel
Sec.	secretary
TCD	Trinity College Dublin
TD	Teachta Dála
TNA	The National Archives (UK)
UCD	University College Dublin
UCDA	University College Dublin Archives
WLR	Weekly Law Reports
WRC	Workplace Relations Commission
ws	witness statement

Contributors

DAVID BARNIVILLE has held the office of president of the High Court since July 2022.

HILARY BIEHLER has practised as a barrister and is professor of public law in Trinity College Dublin. She has written extensively in the fields of equity and the law of trusts, civil procedure and administrative law.

LYNSEY BLACK is an assistant professor in the School of Law and Criminology, Maynooth University. She researches in the areas of gender and punishment, postcolonial and historical criminology, and Northern Ireland. She is principal investigator on the Irish Research Council starting laureate award CONSPACE ('Contested space: penal nationalism and the Northern Ireland Border). In 2022 she published *Gender and punishment in Ireland: women, murder and the death penalty, 1922–64* (Manchester, 2022).

LAURA CAHILLANE is an associate professor in the School of Law, University of Limerick. Her research interests lie in the areas of constitutional law, legal history and judicial studies. She is a frequent contributor to the media and has advised the Oireachtas on law reform on a number of occasions. Her work has been cited several times in the Dáil and the Seanad, by the Irish superior courts and UK parliamentary briefings, among others. She is editor-in-chief of the *Irish Judicial Studies Journal*.

MARK COEN is an associate professor in law at the Sutherland School of Law at University College Dublin. His main research interest is in contemporary and historical criminal trials. His research on trial by jury in twentieth-century Ireland has been published in the *Law and History Review*, the *American Journal of Legal History* and *law&history*. He is the editor of *The Offences Against the State Act at 80: a model counter-terrorism act?* (Oxford, 2021) and co-editor of *A Dublin Magdalene laundry: Donnybrook and Church-State power in Ireland* (London, 2023).

DONAL K. COFFEY is an assistant professor in Maynooth University where he lectures on legal history and public law. He is also an affiliate researcher at the Max Planck Institute for Legal History and Legal Theory in Frankfurt am Main. He has published two volumes on Irish constitutional history in the 1930s: *Drafting the Irish Constitution, 1935–1937* (London, 2018) and *Constitutionalism in Ireland, 1932–1938* (London, 2018). In 2024, he co-edited a volume with Laura Cahillane entitled *The centenary of the Irish Free State Constitution* (London, 2024).

MAURICE G. COLLINS practised as a barrister before being appointed as a judge of the Court of Appeal in 2019. In 2020, he was appointed a part-time commissioner of the Law Reform Commission and continues to hold that position. He was appointed to the Supreme Court in 2022.

KEVIN COSTELLO is an associate professor at University College Dublin, where he teaches legal history. He has research interests in aspects of British and Irish legal history, and, in particular, the history of administrative law 1600 to 1900. His monograph, *The court of Admiralty of Ireland, 1575–1893* (Dublin, 2011), was published by the Irish Legal History Society in 2011.

RÓISÍN Á. COSTELLO is an assistant professor of EU and international law at Trinity College Dublin and a practising barrister. Róisín works on EU law, privacy and data protection and minority language rights and has published chapters and articles on the role of the Irish language in all-island constitutional dialogues, and under the 1922 Constitution.

BRICE DICKSON is emeritus professor of international and comparative law at Queen's University Belfast. Among his recent publications are *The Irish Supreme Court* (Oxford, 2019), *Law in Northern Ireland* (Oxford, 2022), *International human rights monitoring mechanisms: a study of their impact in the UK* (Cheltenham, 2022) and, with Conor McCormick, *The Court of Appeal in Northern Ireland* (Bristol, 2024).

DIARMAID FERRITER is full professor and chair of modern Irish history at University College Dublin and author of numerous books, including *The transformation of Ireland 1900–2000* (London, 2004), *Judging Dev* (Dublin, 2008), *Ambiguous Republic: Ireland in the 1970s* (London, 2012), *Between two hells: the Irish Civil War* (London, 2021) and *The revelation of Ireland: 1995–2020* (London, 2024). He is a regular television and radio broadcaster and a weekly columnist with the *Irish Times*. In 2019 he was elected a member of the Royal Irish Academy.

DAIRE HOGAN is a solicitor and author of *The legal profession in Ireland, 1789–1922* (Dublin, 1986). He is a former president of the Irish Legal History Society, and has co-edited and contributed to a number of its publications, most recently (with Patrick Maume) *The reminiscences of Ignatius O'Brien, lord chancellor of Ireland 1913–1918* (Dublin, 2021).

GERARD HOGAN was appointed to the Supreme Court in October 2021.

NIAMH HOWLIN is an associate professor at the Sutherland School of Law, University College Dublin. She sits on the Council of the Irish Legal History Society and on the Irish Manuscripts Commission. Her books include *Juries in Ireland: laypersons and law in the long nineteenth century* (Dublin, 2017); *Barristers in Ireland: an evolving profession since 1921* (Dublin, 2023); *Law and the family in Ireland 1800–1950* (London, 2017); *Law and religion in Ireland, 1700–1970* (London, 2021) (both with Kevin Costello), and *Confluences of law and history: Irish Legal History Society discourses, 2011–2021* (Dublin, forthcoming) (with Felix M. Larkin).

DANIELLE C. JEFFERIS is a doctoral researcher in the School of Law and Criminology at Maynooth University. Her research focuses on the law and policy of crime control in Irish border regions and the experience of border living. She is a US-trained lawyer and academic with further research experience in constitutional law, punishment, and critical race theory.

PAUL KELLY is a graduate of University College Dublin and Northumbria University. He was enrolled as a solicitor in 1979 and worked in Arthur Cox before setting up his own legal practice in Co. Kildare. He has presented papers in a variety of contexts on such areas as restorative justice, legal procedures and case management and he served as president of the Kildare Solicitors Bar Association. Paul Kelly was appointed to the bench in 2010, and has held the office of president of the District Court since 2021.

ROBERT D. MARSHALL is a retired solicitor and a former president of the Irish Legal History Society (2012–15). He is a priest in the Anglican tradition and registrar of both the United Dioceses of Dublin and Glendalough, and of the Court of the General Synod of the Church of Ireland. He contributed a number of entries on judicial personalities of the early twentieth century in the *Dictionary of Irish biography*, and has published chapters in edited collections on Church history, legal biography and the Land War. He is a member of the Historical Studies Committee of the Royal Irish Academy.

EVAN McGUIGAN is an historian and a former guide and information officer for the Office of Public Works at Dublin Castle. He curated the 'Delivering Justice: the Law Courts at Dublin Castle' exhibition and has also previously worked at the National Museum of Ireland.

THOMAS MOHR is an associate professor at the School of Law, University College Dublin. He is vice president of the Irish Legal History Society and book review editor of the *Irish Jurist*, Ireland's oldest law journal. His publications on Irish legal history range from medieval Gaelic law to the law of the independent Irish state in the twentieth century. His latest books are *Guardian of the Treaty – the Privy Council appeal and Irish sovereignty* (Dublin, 2016) and, as editor with Dr Peter Crooks, *Law and the idea of liberty in Ireland: from Magna Carta to the present* (Dublin, 2023).

ÚNA NÍ RAIFEARTAIGH is a judge of the European Court of Human Rights. She was previously a judge in the Court of Appeal (2019–24) and the High Court (2016–19) where she dealt with cases in a wide variety of legal fields, including public and constitutional law, the Hague Convention on the Civil Aspects of International Child Abduction, EU law, ECHR law, criminal law, and private civil law. Prior to becoming a judge she worked as a barrister from 1993–2016, becoming a Senior Counsel in 2009, specializing in criminal law where she worked extensively in the Central, Special and Circuit Criminal Courts, including the prosecution of trials arising out of the collapse of Anglo Irish Bank in the period 2011–16. She also undertook a variety of other types of work including public law and public inquiry work, having acted before the Commission to inquire into Child Abuse (the 'Ryan' inquiry); an inquiry into alleged misconduct by the Garda Siochana Ombudsman Commission; and the 'Curtin inquiry' (and associated court proceedings) concerning the procedures relating to the removal of a judge from office. She started her career in the Law Reform Commission and in Trinity College Dublin, where she was Reid Professor of Criminal Law, Criminology and Penology.

DONAL O'DONNELL was appointed the 13th chief justice of Ireland on 11 October 2021. Born in Belfast, he was educated at University College Dublin, The Honorable Society of King's Inns, and the University of Virginia. He was called to the Bar of Ireland in 1982 and to the Bar of Northern Ireland in 1989. He was admitted to the Inner Bar of Ireland in 1995 and appointed a judge of the Supreme Court in January 2010. He was a council member of the Irish Legal History Society from 2018 to 2021 and is now a joint patron of the society. He is also an honorary member of the Society of Legal Scholars, a Bencher of King's Inns and an Honorary Bencher of Lincoln's Inn.

BLÁTHNA RUANE is a senior counsel, who has written widely on the constitution, law and legal history. She is an adjunct professor of law at the Sutherland School of Law at University College Dublin.

PATRICIA RYAN is the president of the Circuit Court.

Acknowledgments

On 12 April 2024, exactly one hundred years after its enactment, the Courts of Justice Act 1924 was commemorated at an event in Dublin Castle, the venue for the Dublin courts in the 1920s. The event included a multimedia exhibition, guided tours, a musical performance and, of course, a series of talks which form the foundation for this collection of essays. This has been a successful collaboration between University College Dublin, the Irish Legal History Society and the Courts Service. As such, there are quite a number of individuals and organisations to whom gratitude is owed.

The Council of the Irish Legal History Society has been very supportive of this project, with members contributing chapters, supporting the Dublin Castle event and even promoting the event and the centenary on the airwaves. Robert Marshall, as well as contributing a chapter and coordinating the Society's presence at the Dublin Castle event, chairs the Society's Publications Committee and is one of the Joint Treasurers. I would also like to thank the outgoing president of the Society, John Gordon, for his support and enthusiasm.

UCD's involvement in this project has been multifaceted. Thank you to the UCD Sutherland School of Law, the UCD Decade of Centenaries fund and the UCD Legal History Group for supporting this project. Thank you to the colleagues who have contributed chapters, as well as those who attended the event in Dublin Castle. I am very grateful to Kate Manning, principal archivist at the UCD Archives, and Catherine Bodey from the UCD Library, for putting together a visually impactful exhibition featuring designs for judicial robes in the 1920s. Thanks also to the UCD law students who helped out at that event: Robin Jowett; Kylie Shi; Sophia Panagopoulos; Robert Grendon; Charlotte Doyle; Caoimhín Jiao and Pema-Lhamo Fitzsimons. Laura McLoughlin provided administrative support.

From the Courts Service, I thank Avril Brady from the Judicial Support Unit for her help organising the Dublin Castle event; Alan Baker from the Communications and Media Unit for his help sourcing images for the Judicial Robes exhibition, and Denis Burke for designing such an evocative logo for the centenary. I also wish to thank Sarahrose Murphy, Lucy Rowan and Rebecca Murphy from the Office of the Chief Justice. The CEO of the Courts Service, Angela Denning, was very supportive of the event and gave the opening remarks on the day. The Office of Public Works provided us with an excellent venue, and Christine Ng, Stephen Ellis and Dee Rogers ensured that everything ran smoothly.

The Dublin Castle event was greatly enhanced by the guided tours provided by Evan McGuigan; the music performed by Teresa O'Donnell; the exhibition panels by my colleagues in the UCD Library; by the Pathé footage and by the original artwork lent by court artist Mike O'Donnell. An Post issued two stamps to commemorate both the Courts of Justice Act 1924 and the Ministers and Secretaries Act 1924 and attendees at Dublin Castle were provided with commemorative stamped cards and first day covers. I am very grateful to Aileen Mooney and Brona McDonagh in particular.

I am grateful to the members of the 1924 Centenary Committee: Ms Justice Iseult O'Malley, Mr Justice Gerard Hogan, Mr Justice Maurice Collins, Ms Justice Caroline Costello, Mr Justice Cian Ferriter, Judge Martin Nolan and Judge Gráinne Malone. Chaired by Chief Justice Donal O'Donnell, this committee has put together a series of events to mark the centenary of the Courts of Justice Act 1924. I would like to give particular thanks to the chief justice for supporting this initiative in several ways, not least by contributing a chapter to this volume.

I thank each of the contributing authors for engaging with this project. It has been a pleasure to work with legal practitioners and academics who produce high-quality original scholarship, not to mention delivering all that was asked of them and adhering to deadlines – often unheard of with such collaborative projects. Thank you also to Alex Casey for helping to prepare the bibliography, and to Julitta Clancy for the indexing. I am also grateful to the National Library of Ireland; UCD Archives; the Courts Service, Brian O'Donnell; British Pathé; An Post and the Daily Mirror for allowing us to use their images, and I am grateful to the Irish Architectural Archive for permission to use the cover image from the T.J. Byrne collection.

As ever, thank you to Four Courts Press for producing another handsome volume for the Irish Legal History Society. Martin Healy, Martin Fanning and Anthony Tierney have been a pleasure to work with.

Finally, thank you to Robert, Louise and Neasa for their love and support.

CHAPTER ONE

Reflecting on a century of Irish courts

NIAMH HOWLIN*

The 1922 Free State Constitution provided for 'courts of first instance and a court of final appeal to be called the Supreme Court.' However, the detail as to how these courts would operate and function was left to legislation. Recent years have seen renewed scholarly reflection on and analysis of the Treaty negotiations and the drafting of the 1922 Constitution.[1] This book picks up the narrative thread to explore what happened next. During the debates on the Constitution, Minister for Home Affairs Kevin O'Higgins expressed his intention to form a committee to examine existing legal systems and structures, and 'to evolve an entirely new judicial system, which will supersede both the British courts and the Dáil courts ... absorbing whatever is best in both of these systems.'[2] In early 1923 the Judiciary Committee[3] was

---

* Associate professor at the Sutherland School of Law, University College Dublin.
1 Notable recent publications are Laura Cahillane and Donal Coffey (eds), *The centenary of the Irish Free State Constitution: constituting a polity?* (London, 2024); Thomas Mohr, 'Dismantling the Anglo-Irish Treaty: removing the oath and the repugnancy clause from the Constitution of the Irish Free State' in Niamh Howlin and Felix M. Larkin (eds), *Confluences of law and history: Irish Legal History Society discourses, 2011–2021* (Dublin, forthcoming); Thomas Mohr, 'Irish newspapers and the creation of the 1922 Constitution of the Irish Free State', *Comparative Legal History*, 11:2 (2023), 186–225; Thomas Mohr, 'Religious minorities under the Constitution of the Irish Free State, 1922–1937', *American Journal of Legal History* 61:2 (2021), 235–272. Earlier scholarship on the 1922 Constitution includes Laura Cahillane, *Drafting the Irish Free State Constitution* (Manchester, 2016); Thomas Mohr, 'The rights of women under the Constitution of the Irish Free State', *Ir. Jur.*, 41 (2006), 20–59. The centenary was also marked by a number of events during 2021 and 2022 including a dramatic re-enactment of the drafting, available to watch on YouTube at www.youtube.com/watch?v=T8t6WYaWrmM (a joint endeavour by the National Archives of Ireland and the Courts Service); a conference at the Shelbourne hotel where the Constitution was drafted (organised by Donal Coffey and Laura Cahillane) and a major two-day national conference marking the foundation of the State also available to watch on YouTube: www.youtube.com/playlist?list=PLHKVjBSDqMB6aa4LcEkJCa73CeuGB_305 (hosted by University College Dublin).
2 *Dáil Éireann deb.*, vol. 1, col. 20 (10 Oct. 1922).
3 The members of the committee were: James Campbell, Lord Glenavy (former lord chancellor); Charles O'Connor (master of the rolls; subsequently appointed to the Supreme Court); Hugh Kennedy KC (law officer; subsequently first attorney general and first chief justice); Judge William Johnston KC (County Court judge; later a judge of the High and Supreme Courts); Timothy Sullivan KC (subsequently appointed the first president of the High Court); James Creed Meredith KC (president of the Dáil Supreme Court;

duly established, in the words of President William T. Cosgrave, 'to advise the government on matters judicial'. Its terms of reference were

> To advise the Executive Council of Saorstát Éireann in relation to the establishment, in accordance with the Constitution, of courts for the exercise of judicial power and the administration of justice in Saorstát Éireann, and the setting up of the offices and other machinery necessary or expedient for the efficient conduct of legal business.[4]

In a letter to each of the committee members, probably penned by Attorney General Hugh Kennedy, Cosgrave wrote:

> In the long struggle for the right to rule in our own country there has been no sphere of the administration which impressed itself on the minds of our people as a standing monument of alien government more than the system, machinery and the administration of law and justice, which supplanted in comparatively modern times in the laws and institutions till then a part of the living national organism. The body of laws and the system of judicature so imposed upon this nation were English (not even British) in their seed, English in their growth, English in their vitality. Their ritual, their nomenclature were only to be understood by the student of the history of the people of Southern Britain. A remarkable and characteristic product of the genius of that people the manner of their administration prevented them from striking root in the fertile soil of this nation.
>
> Thus, it comes that there is nothing more prized among our newly won liberties than the liberty to construct a system of judiciary and administration of law and justice according to the dictates of our own needs and after a pattern of our own designing.[5]

Chaired by Lord Glenavy, the committee met for the first time on 2 February 1923 and produced a report on 23 May 1923. It was presented as a unanimous report, with the committee remarking 'we have not thought it necessary to set out the reasons on which our recommendations are made'.[6] Running to about seventeen pages, it sketched out a proposed new system and

subsequently appointed to the High Court); Patrick J. Brady (solicitor and former chair of the Incorporated Law Society of Ireland); Cahir Davitt BL (judge of the Dáil Supreme Court; later president of the High Court); William Hewat (president of Dublin Chamber of Commerce and subsequently a TD); Louis Walsh (solicitor, district justice); John O'Byrne BL (previously a legal adviser to the Dáil delegation in the Anglo-Irish Treaty negotiations; later attorney general and a judge of the High and Supreme Courts), and Henry Murphy (former Crown solicitor for Monaghan). Micheal Smithwick BL was secretary to the committee.
4 *Report of the Judiciary Committee* (Dublin, 1923), p. 9.
5 Ibid., pp 4–5. Also referred to as the Glenavy Committee, after its chair. The message, language and authorship of this letter is referred to in several chapters of this book.
6 Ibid., p. 26.

contained recommendations for the establishment and operation of a new hierarchy of courts. This was, in the words of Cosgrave, a 'big and important matter'.[7] The Courts of Justice bill 1923 was published in July and after much debate in both houses of the Oireachtas, the Courts of Justice Act 1924 was signed into law the following April and commenced later that summer.

The 1924 Act was an important piece of constitutional legislation, putting flesh on the bones of articles 64–72 of the 1922 Constitution. As Robert Marshall explains, the term 'constitutional statute' 'distinguishes those statutes which fleshed out the institutions of the new state from regulatory statutes intended to govern everyday life'.[8] It established the basic structure of our courts system, which has endured for a century with only the addition of one new court, the Court of Appeal, in 2014. As will be seen in the chapters which follow, the 1924 Act contained both innovations and continuations.

Article 75 of the Constitution provided for the continuing jurisdiction of the existing courts on a transitional basis, and justice continued to be administered. In January 1922 the new Provisional Government issued a proclamation directing that 'all law courts ... [and] judges ... hitherto acting under the authority of the British government shall continue to carry out their functions unless and until pending the Constitution of the Parliament and government of Saorstát na hÉireann'.[9] Maurice Collins focuses on what happened during the 'judicial interregnum' of 1922–4,[10] the period between the adoption of the Free State Constitution and the enactment of the Courts of Justice Act. As he observes, '[t]he former Crown courts might not have had the confidence or affection of the people, or even of the government but they persevered with their task nonetheless'.[11] At the other end of the hierarchy of courts, it is worth noting that the District Court, in fact, predates the Courts of Justice Act 1924,[12] with temporary district justices having been appointed first under the Provisional Government (Transfer of Functions) Order 1922 and then under the District Justices (Temporary Provisions) Act 1923.

It is important to recognise that the 1924 Act was not passed in a vacuum. Diarmaid Ferriter sets the scene for subsequent analysis of the Act by describing the state of the country and the general mood in 1924.[13] Poverty and post-conflict trauma sat alongside the thorny issues of the Border and demobilised soldiers, while an ambitious legislative state-building programme got underway. As well as a new courts system, the government was preoccupied

7   Cosgrave to Glenavy, 11 June 1923, ibid., p. 8.
8   Robert D. Marshall, 'A balanced judiciary: the early appointments to the superior and Circuit courts'.
9   See Maurice Collins, 'The "judicial interregnum", 1922–4: the new Constitution in the old courts'.
10 Ibid.
11 Ibid.
12 Niamh Howlin, '"On the fly and on the sly"'.
13 Diarmaid Ferriter, 'Ireland in 1924: the historical context'.

by the establishment of a new civil service, the Land Commission, electricity, local government, the reconstruction of government and the reform of licencing laws.[14] Bláthna Ruane explores the background to the establishment of judicial independence in 1924,[15] while Thomas Mohr evaluates the new courts' relationship to the popular Dáil courts. He notes that the Dáil courts continued to have influence even after their abolition in 1922;[16] indeed, the Judiciary Committee had received proposals to 'either revive or in some way replicate the structure of the Dáil court system'.[17] Mohr also addresses some of the misgivings regarding the new legal regime. Those who opposed the Anglo-Irish Treaty, he observes, 'challenged the 1924 Act through its association with the 1922 Constitution.'[18] In a similar vein, Kevin Costello examines the Irish Bar's opposition to aspects of the legislation, specifically the move towards the decentralisation of justice.[19] While some of these controversies were no doubt grounded in concerns over access to justice and the rule of law, there was also an element of self-interest, as Costello explains.

There were lingering echoes of the Revolution following the passing of the 1924 Act, particularly in the lower courts, as demonstrated by Lynsey Black and Danielle Jefferis.[20] They point out that the introduction of a customs barrier imposed a new legal reality on border communities and the District Court was the forum for hearing the new smuggling cases. Evan McGuigan reminds us that in the capital, the courts sat in Dublin Castle for their first few years following the destruction of the Four Courts.[21] Indeed, courts around the country sat in a variety of multi-use venues in the early years of the Free State.[22] One aspect of the Revolution that fell into abeyance after the passing of the 1924 Act was role played by women in the administration of justice. Although several women, notably members of Cumann na mBan, served as judges in the Dáil Parish and District Courts,[23] no women were appointed to the benches of new courts for several decades.

A common theme in the chapters dealing with the District, Circuit, High and Supreme Courts is their jurisdictional expansion, accompanied by

14 Ibid.
15 Bláthna Ruane, 'Establishing judicial independence'.
16 Thomas Mohr, 'The Dáil courts and opposition to the Courts of Justice Act 1924'.
17 Ibid.
18 Ibid.
19 Kevin Costello, '"Twenty-six high courts": the Circuit Court, decentralisation and its opponents, 1924–34'.
20 Lynsey Black and Danielle Jefferis, '"Illegal, immoral and unpatriotic": cross-border smuggling and the courts'. See also Niamh Howlin, '"On the fly and on the sly": a District Court in action'.
21 Evan McGuigan, 'Comfortably housed? The law courts at Dublin Castle, 1923–31'.
22 Indeed, due to the destruction and unavailability of court buildings, in 1922 a decree was passed 'to enable certain courts of quarter sessions and civil bill courts to be held in towns other than those in which they are usually held.' Provisional Government (Courts - Emergency Provisions) Decree no. 9, 1922, in *Iris Oifigiúil*, 3 Oct. 1922.
23 Niamh Howlin and Mark Coen, 'Where were the women?'

necessary increases in the number of judges. Gerard Hogan brings the narrative almost up to the 1937 Constitution in his examination of the Supreme Court's expansion from three to five members.[24] Of course, increases in the number of judges have been necessitated by a growing population and we have lagged behind our European neighbours in this regard.

Gerald Horan, in a contemporaneously published book, described the new Circuit Court as 'the central feature of the whole scheme. These courts, eight in number, sitting almost continuously, exercise a jurisdiction vastly more extensive than the former county courts.'[25] Kevin Costello[26] and Patricia Ryan[27] address the early years and evolution of this court in their respective chapters. Costello makes the point that the Circuit Court, a court of shopkeepers and debt collection, was not the busiest forum in the new system; this title belonged to the District Court. As Horan noted, the District Court took over 'the minor jurisdiction of the former county courts and the judicial functions of the former magistrates and justices of the peace.'[28] Paul Kelly's chapter illustrates how the work of the District Court has changed over the past century, as a result of both legislative and social developments.[29] It remains the court where members of the public are most likely to engage with the justice system.

While the offices of president of the Circuit Court[30] and president of the District Court[31] were later innovations, the offices of chief justice and president of the High Court were established by the 1924 Act.[32] David Barniville and Donal O'Donnell examine the multifaceted and ever-expanding role played by these office-holders. Barniville points out that since 1924, the president of the High Court has assumed responsibility for the solicitors' profession, as well as several other statutorily regulated professions.[33] Wardship jurisdiction was originally vested in the chief justice, until its transfer to the president of the High Court in 1936.[34] O'Donnell describes this as 'the only example of a statutory *reduction* in the tasks to be performed by the chief justice since the foundation of the State.'[35] Bodies such as the Courts Service, the Judicial Appointments Advisory Board, and the Judicial Council have added considerably to the workloads of both office-holders,[36] and O'Donnell also

24 Gerard Hogan, 'The Supreme Court and the winter of 1936–7'.
25 Gerald Horan, *The Courts of Justice Act, 1924 (Saorstát Éireann)* (Dublin, 1924), p. vi.
26 Costello, '"Twenty-six high courts"'.
27 Patricia Ryan, 'The expanding role of the Circuit Court judge'.
28 Horan, *Courts of Justice Act*, p. vi.
29 Paul Kelly, 'The District Court, 1924–2024: "big bang" 100 years on'.
30 The Courts of Justice Act 1947, s. 9(1).
31 The Courts (Establishment and Constitution) Act 1961, 5(2)a.
32 Sections 4 and 5.
33 David Barniville, 'The role of the president of the High Court.'
34 Courts of Justice Act 1936, s. 9.
35 Donal O'Donnell, 'Who would be a chief justice?'
36 See Appendix 5 for lists of former presidents of the various courts and former chief justices.

points to various committees and organisations, both domestic and international, which require the chief justice's involvement.

While the structure of the courts system changed, the common law was retained, and this, in the words of Mark Coen, 'severely diluted the symbolic potential of the new courts as manifestations of self-determination.' By and large (and with some exceptions), the new system subsumed the jurisprudence which had gone before it, but the Courts of Justice Act refined several procedural aspects of the common law system. While the principle of trial by jury was retained in the Act, jury trial was 'no longer as of right in actions of contract either in the High Court or the Circuit Court, while in all civil cases tried with a jury the majority of nine will determine the verdict.'[37] The jury's limitations in civil actions can be seen as part of a slow demise over the past century.[38] Grand juries would no longer play a part in the criminal process, determining whether defendants should be sent forward for trial.

Another 'most striking'[39] feature of the 1924 Act was its positioning of the Supreme Court at the apex of the judicial system, with no mention of the controversial appeal to the Judicial Committee of the Privy Council. The Judiciary Committee had referred to the court as the 'Supreme Court of Appeal', and this remained the position in the final legislation. Commenting on the Act, Horan explained that '[t]he decision of this court is final and conclusive in all cases, and although the right to petition his majesty in council is specially reserved by the Constitution, as in the case of other Dominions, the judicial committee has already given evidence that it will interpret this provision very strictly.'[40]

Although the 1924 Act had quite a difficult passage through the houses of the Oireachtas, as Robert Marshall points out, this was 'only half the task'. The most delicate aspect of the legislation was the appointment of a new judiciary to administer justice. A common theme running through many chapters in this

37 Ibid., p. vi. See Courts of Justice Act 1924, ss 94 and 95.
38 Bryan McMahon, *Judge or jury? The jury trial for personal injury cases in Ireland* (Cork, 1985); Rory O'Hanlon, 'The sacred cow of trial by jury', *Ir. Jur.*, 25:1 (1990), 57. The Courts Act 1971 abolished civil jury trials in the Circuit Court, despite the recommendations of the Committee on Court Practice and Procedure, *Jury trial in civil actions. Jury challenges: third and fourth interim reports of the Committee on Court Practice and Procedure* (Dublin, 1966). The Courts Act 1988 abolished civil juries in all personal injuries actions except trespass to the person and false imprisonment. As Barton points out, '[n]otwithstanding the continuing subsistence of the right in all other common-law causes of action for wrongs, the exercise thereof gradually fell into abeyance, except for those causes of action in trespass, malicious prosecution, false imprisonment, and defamation'. Bernard Barton, 'Runaway jury', *Law Society Gazette*, 117:4 (2023), 38–41, at 40. The Defamation (Amendment) bill 2023 includes a proposal to abolish the legal right to trial by jury in High Court defamation proceedings.
39 Horan, *Courts of Justice Act*, p. v.
40 Ibid. See further Thomas Mohr, *Guardian of the Treaty: the Privy Council appeal and Irish sovereignty* (Dublin, 2016).

book is the need to ensure that the new legal order was accepted as legitimate by the public. The professionalisation of the judiciary was one of the aims of the legislation, and as Mohr points out, legal training was now to be 'an essential requirement for judicial office within the Irish Free State.'[41]

Those involved in the design and development of the new courts system were acutely aware of the importance of re-establishing the primacy of the rule of law. Mark Coen observes that '[t]he structural features of a courts system, its underlying culture and the way in which it is perceived by the public combine to create narratives about the rule of law, state legitimacy and national identity'.[42] As Laura Cahillane points out, 'the Irish state-builders aimed to create a modern, liberal, democratic, polity based on these ideals including aspects such as popular sovereignty, democracy, and a separation of powers'.[43] Thomas Mohr argues that this was particularly evident in the context of the popular success of the Dáil courts, while Daire Hogan, Laura Cahillane, Robert Marshall and Bláthna Ruane each examine how these concerns played out when it came to appointing new judiciary. As Bláthna Ruane observes, the legitimacy of the new courts 'enabled the shattered legal system to stabilise quickly, and to respond to the other challenges facing the state.'[44]

There was also evidently a concern for efficiency and economy in the administration of justice, particularly following what Robert Marshall describes as 'the dark winter of 1922–3.' As Diarmaid Ferriter describes, '[f]inancial probity and centralisation were deemed to be of the utmost importance.'[45] Laura Cahillane indicates that judicial salaries in Ireland were generally lower than those in England and Wales. Judicial retirement also brought savings, and Daire Hogan explores why and how the Courts Act 1924 provided that judges should retire in their early seventies. Mark Coen demonstrates that around the country, the visual symbols of the outgoing regime were sometimes retained, simply to avoid the expense of removal. Lynsey Black and Danielle Jefferis also demonstrate this concern for keeping control of the Free State's finances, examining the impact of cross-Border smuggling on Revenue.

Alongside this pragmatism were flickers of idealism. This was evident in relation to, for example, the position of the Irish language under the new legislation, which is considered by Úna Ní Raifeartaigh and Róisín Costello.[46] Although the Act sought to provide some sort of status for the language, it was 'limited in scope and fell far short of providing a detailed, practical

---

41 Mohr, 'The Dáil courts'.
42 Mark Coen, '"A new order in this country": symbolism and the new courts'.
43 Laura Cahillane, 'Remuneration of judges under the 1924 Act'.
44 Ruane, 'Establishing judicial independence'.
45 Ferriter, 'Ireland in 1924'.
46 Úna Ní Raifeartaigh and Róisín Á. Costello, 'The Courts of Justice Act 1924 and the Irish language in the courtroom'.

framework' for allowing the Irish language to 'take its place within the courtrooms of the nation.' The continuation of republican ideals of access to justice[47] can be contrasted with the sidelining of women despite their roles in the Revolution. They were more likely to appear in court as litigants, criminal defendants, witnesses and social workers, than as barristers or solicitors.

The 1924 legislation is also considered in this book from comparative perspectives: Donal Coffey evaluates the Act against similar schemes in other common law jurisdictions,[48] while Brice Dickson identifies parallels between developments in appeal routes north and south from the 1920s onward.[49] The 'leapfrog' appeal procedures he describes are similar to procedures set out in the 1924 Act and discussed by Hilary Biehler.[50] These chapters illustrate some of the parallels and divergences in legal systems North and South after the 1920s.

Although this is a book with a historical focus, the 1924 Act has continuing relevance. Several innovations introduced by the Act have been retained, such as the concept of compulsory judicial retirement. As Daire Hogan notes, Ireland was one of the first common law jurisdictions to introduce a judicial retirement age,[51] but this is now common in such other jurisdictions as the United Kingdom, Canada and Australia, though notably not in the Federal Courts of the United States,[52] where octogenarian judges sometimes develop cult followings.

The ideal of decentralised justice was core to the 1924 Act; as one contemporaneous commentator noted, '[t]he vital principle of the scheme is decentralisation – the devolution of a considerable amount of jurisdiction from the Supreme to the local courts.'[53] Litigants no longer had to travel to Dublin for such a wide range of civil actions. Although the decentralisation of justice proved somewhat controversial when it came to the Circuit Court, the principle remained. The expansion of the jurisdiction of the District and Circuit Courts, discussed by Paul Kelly and Patricia Ryan, is evidence of this continuing emphasis on localised justice.

New appellate structures and procedures were another innovation of the 1924 Act. A Court of Criminal Appeal was established, comprising two High

---

47 See, e.g., Mohr, 'The Dáil courts' and Costello, '"Twenty-six high courts"'.
48 Donal K. Coffey, 'The Courts of Justice Act in comparative perspective'.
49 Brice Dickson, 'Appeal routes in Northern Ireland'.
50 Hilary Biehler, 'Section 29 of the Courts of Justice Act 1924 and the certification process: a long-lasting legacy'.
51 Daire Hogan, 'The introduction of a retirement age for judges'.
52 Stephen J. Choi, Mitu Gulati and Eric A. Power, 'The law and policy of judicial retirement: an empirical study', *The Journal of Legal Sutdies*; 42:1 (2013), 111–50, and Phillip D. Oliver, 'Assessing and addressing the problems caused by life tenure on the Supreme Court', *Journal of Appellate Practice and Process*, 13:1 (2012), 11–32.
53 Horan, *Courts of Justice Act*, p. v.

Court judges and one Supreme Court judge.⁵⁴ The proposal from the Judiciary Committee found expression in section 8 of the Act and was a relatively uncontroversial proposal, receiving very little debate in the Oireachtas. Appeals from the Circuit Court in civil cases were to be grounded for the first time on stenographers' notes. Section 29 of the Courts of Justice Act 1924 regulated the circumstances in which an appeal might be taken from the Court of Criminal Appeal to the Supreme Court. ⁵⁵ Hilary Biehler points out that although section 29 has since been repealed,⁵⁶ and the Court of Criminal Appeal replaced by the Court of Appeal, the legacy of the certification process is of continued relevance.

While several characters loom large on the pages of this book, two in particular merit special mention. First, James Campbell, Lord Glenavy. A former Conservative MP and Irish lord chancellor, he was appointed to chair the Judiciary Committee in 1923. Kevin Costello characterises this appointment as 'a gesture of assurance to the Southern Unionist community',⁵⁷ while Mark Coen suggests that it indicated prioritising inclusivity over radical reform.⁵⁸ Glenavy played an important role in chairing the committee and preparing its report in 1923. However, his influence on the development of the new courts system did not end there. As Cathaoirleach of the Seanad, he played a surprisingly disruptive role when introducing the 1923 bill. As Costello describes, although Glenavy had 'expressly endorsed the committee's unanimous proposal for a Circuit Court with a £300 jurisdiction', he then attempted to subvert this proposed reform. He was also instrumental in delaying, for seven years, the introduction of rules to govern the operation of the Circuit Court.

The other individual whose contribution to the development of the modern Irish legal system cannot be overlooked is Hugh Kennedy.⁵⁹ As a

---

54 Section 8. See Desmond Greer, 'A security against illegality? The reservation of Crown cases in nineteenth-century Ireland' in Norma Dawson (ed.), *Reflections on law and history* (Dublin, 2006) for a discussion of what preceded this.
55 Biehler, 'Section 29'.
56 Court of Appeal Act 2014, s. 1(2), s. 73 and sch. 1.
57 Costello, 'Twenty-six high courts'.
58 Coen, 'A new order'.
59 Several scholars have reflected on Kennedy's contribution. See e.g. Hugh Geoghegan, 'Three judges of the Supreme Court of the Irish Free State: their backgrounds, personalities and mindsets' in Larkin and Dawson (eds), *Lawyers, the law and history* (Dublin, 2013); Ronan Keane, 'The voice of the Gael: Chief Justice Kennedy and the emergence of the new Irish court system, 1921–1936', *Ir. Jur.*, 31:1 (1996), 205–25; Thomas Mohr, 'The influence of Chief Justice Hugh Kennedy on Irish legal scholarship and publishing', *Ir. Jur.*, 64 (2020), 97–137; Ailsa C. Holland, 'The papers of Hugh Kennedy: a research legacy for the foundation of the state', *Ir. Jur.*, 24:2 (1989), 279–304; Ronan Keane, 'Kennedy, Hugh', *DIB*; Patrick C. Kennedy, *Hugh Kennedy: the great but neglected chief justice* (Limerick, 2005) and Tom Daly, 'Hugh Kennedy: Ireland's (quietly) towering nation-maker' in Rehan Abeyratne and Iddo Porat (eds), *Towering judges: a comparative study of constitutional judges* (Cambridge, 2021).

drafter of the 1922 Constitution, a member of the Judiciary Committee, a TD, attorney general and chief justice, he was pivotal to the development of both legal structures and legal doctrine. As Donal O'Donnell observes, 'Hugh Kennedy played a significant role in the establishment, not just of the courts system, but of the State itself … He was determined not only to establish a truly independent courts system, but also to demonstrate that while it represented a decisive shift from the pre-existing system, it would hold itself to the highest standards.'[60] Kennedy was keen to ensure that the Free State courts had a distinctly Irish character, including by promoting Irish-language competency for members of the legal professions.[61] Behind the scenes, he worked on changing legal culture by seeking to introduce new modes of address and new judicial attire. He persevered in the face of opposition to his proposals. For example, he brought forward not one but two sets of alternative judicial robe designs,[62] though these failed to attract sufficient support among members of the new judicial establishment. Although the use of 'my lord' was ubiquitous even after 1924, towards the end of his life he sought to change to Irish modes of address.[63] Describing his sudden death in 1936, Gerard Hogan makes the observation that 'Kennedy had been such a dominant force in the momentous changes in the legal system from the days of the Civil War through the very establishment of the court system that it must have been almost hard at the time to visualise the Supreme Court without his forceful presence.'[64]

While several chapters are devoted to explaining the new legal structures and the shape of the new judiciary, this book is more than a description of a new courts system. Certainly, the procedural aspects of the Courts of Justice Act were the essential scaffolding around which litigation was pursued and justice was administered. However, the authors of the chapters which follow have gone further than mere description. They have woven compelling narratives shedding light on the forgotten stories, dramas, innovations and concerns of the 1920s. They have brought individual legal actors to life and they have vividly described what it was like to be a judge, a lawyer or a litigant in the new courts. They have, in short, illuminated an aspect of twentieth-century Irish legal history that hitherto received little attention. They have done so by making use of a wide range of archival and manuscript sources, as well as contemporary newspaper reports and published scholarship. Collectively, the chapters in this book invite the reader to reconsider what we think we know and to reflect on a century of change.

60 O'Donnell, 'Who would be a chief justice?'
61 Niamh Howlin, *Barristers in Ireland: an evolving profession since 1921* (Dublin, 2023), pp 28 and 100–3. He raised this issue as early as 1925, and in 1929 the Legal Practitioners (Qualification) Act 1929 was passed.
62 As detailed in the *Judicial attire in the 1920s* exhibition; see examples in the plates section.
63 Memo. to Exec. Council from Dept. Justice, 1 Feb. 1936, NAI TSCH/3/S8613.
64 Hogan, 'Winter of 1936–7'.

CHAPTER TWO

Ireland in 1924: the historical context

DIARMAID FERRITER*

Some of the Irish Republican poachers had turned gamekeepers by 1924, including Kevin O'Higgins, the minister for home affairs (subsequently justice) in the new Free State. The private papers of O'Higgins, held in the UCD Archives, do much to illuminate this transition. As a defiant Sinn Féin TD and minister during the War of Independence, in 1920 O'Higgins wrote to his fiancé Brigid Cole to tell her he was 'grinning to himself at the futility of force against spirit'. The following year, he was equally resolute: 'whether we win, lose or draw eventually, the moral value of the struggle is unquestionable – probably not since the persecutions of the early Christians has human nature risen to finer heights in endurance for an ideal than in Ireland today'.[1]

Where did such declarations lie with the creation of the new state? The tone of the O'Higgins correspondence notably shifted after the signing of the Anglo-Irish Treaty in December 1921, and during the Civil War his letters were imbued with the perspective of the responsible governor in the midst of state building and Republican resistance. He now asserted that 'politics is the science of the second best ... the best is rarely attained in this world, and even idealists have a duty to keep their feet on the ground and take stock of facts, particularly if the destinies of a country happen to be in their charge'.[2]

O'Higgins and his colleagues continued to occupy that space and employ such logic in 1924. In parallel, O'Higgins sought to frame a Civil War narrative that depicted his once fellow idealists as renegades and wreckers. Such contentions found powerful expression in October 1924 in an address O'Higgins delivered to the Irish Society at Oxford University entitled 'Ireland today' (subsequently published under the title 'Three years hard labour'). This speech included a provocative defence of the pro-Treaty side and underlined the scale of their challenges during the Civil War:

---

* Full professor of modern Irish history at the School of History, University College Dublin.
1 O'Higgins to Brigid Cole, 29 Sept. 1920, Kevin O'Higgins papers, UCDA P197/26, and O'Higgins to Cole, Mar. 1921, UCDA P197/66.
2 O'Higgins to Tom O'Higgins, 30 Dec. 1922, UCDA P197/108.

to form a just appreciation of developments in Ireland in 1922 it is necessary to remember that the country had come through a revolution and to remember what a weird composite of idealism, neurosis, megalomania and criminality is apt to be thrown to the surface in even the best regulated revolution.

He and his governmental colleagues, he recalled, were 'eight young men in City Hall standing amidst the ruins of one administration with the foundations of another not yet built and with wild men screaming through the keyholes'.[3]

The 'wild men' were fairly flattened by 1924, their plight not helped by the assertion of the IRA chief-of-staff Frank Aiken that year that 'even if our men have to live on potatoes and water for a year it is their duty to stay' in Ireland and continue the fight, a thoroughly unrealistic demand given their social and political abjectness. Up to 600 IRA men had left the country by mid 1924.[4] On his release from prison in July 1924, Ernie O'Malley, who had been captured and incarcerated in November 1922 as assistant chief-of-staff of the anti-Treaty IRA, received some money from the Irish White Cross to travel to Spain: 'I still have 8 pieces of lead in me and my funds are rather limited.'[5] Éamon de Valera, president of Sinn Féin, remained one of the most despised 'wild men', though he was no such thing. He was imprisoned from August 1923 to July 1924, and after his release remained publicly defiant – 'we have not changed … no new policy' were the messages he enunciated in his 1924 speeches – though privately, he was keen to find a way of 'getting out of the Straightjacket [sic] of the Republic.'[6]

The women on the anti-Treaty side, including Sighle Humphreys of Cumann na mBan, were also facing an arduous transition period; the private papers of Humphreys, also held in the UCD Archives, underline 'the negotiation of class and gendered political identities within a nationalist context.'[7] Her diary entries from 1924 include a draft circular for Cumann na mBan in which she refers to the 'old activities' of the organisation (including drilling and first aid) and the need for their activism to be updated; a preoccupation with the 'Object of present struggle and the right of women to participate'.[8]

3   Kevin O'Higgins, 'Ireland Today', 31 Oct. 1924, UCDA P197/141.
4   Gavin Foster, *The Irish Civil War and society: politics, class and conflict* (London, 2015), p. 212.
5   Ernie O'Malley to Madge Clifford, 28 July 1924, in Cormac K.H. O'Malley and Nicholas Allen (eds), *Broken landscapes: selected letters of Ernie O'Malley, 1924–1957* (Dublin, 2011), pp 9–10.
6   Papers of Éamon de Valera, UCDA P150/1885–1889, Aug. 1924 and P150/1584, n.d. but c.1924.
7   Elizabeth Kyte, 'Sighle Humphreys: a case study in Irish socialist feminism, 1920s–1930s', *Saothar*, 36 (2011), 27–36.
8   Ibid.

Labour activists faced similar dilemmas given the extent to which they had been politically squeezed by the polarisation of the Civil War. As both playwright and committed socialist, Seán O'Casey questioned what had changed for those he termed 'the inanimate patsies' of the tenements during an era when an estimated 800,000 Irish people were living in overcrowded conditions. His play *Juno and the Paycock*, set during the Civil War and written in his ill-lit tenement on the North Circular Road in Dublin, was first staged at the Abbey Theatre in March 1924, audiences hearing Juno declare, after the death of her son, 'Sacred heart o' Jesus take away our hearts o' stone and give us hearts o' flesh!'[9] That prayer, however, 'was not to be answered.'[10]

Nor were the pleas of those concerned with hidden suffering, including Jesuit priest Fr Edward Boyd Barrett, who wrote in 1924 of the plights of the patients, numbering over 3,000, in the Richmond and Portrane mental asylums. These institutions were, he lamented,

> in a bad way. They are overcrowded. They are both understaffed and inefficiently staffed. Curable and incurable cases are herded together. There is practically no treatment ... the asylums are unsuitable for their purpose in almost every respect ... It is lamentable that public interest is cold and public co-operation non-existent in the fight against mental diseases.[11]

The public was more concerned with shortage of housing; this was certainly a priority for the Cumann na nGaedheal government, and it made additional funding available for social housing. By 1924 its 'million pound scheme' for urban local authority house building had resulted in the construction of 959 new dwellings. But overall, 'the focus of government attention moved from social to private housing'; the Housing (Building Facilities) Act 1924 offered significant subsidies for private house building, 'which covered approximately one sixth of the usual building costs at the time'. This resulted in a 'dramatic increase' in private house building; 'in contrast, local authorities' social house building programme was reined in as central government proved unwilling to continue the programme of long-term subsidisation' of local authority house building initiated in the pre-Independence era, notably with the Labourers (Ireland) Act 1906 and the Housing Act 1908.[12]

In relation to welfare provision, and an overall figure for public expenditure in 1923–4 of £28.7 million, the government faced a storm of

---

9   Seán O'Casey, *Juno and the Paycock and The plough and the stars* (Dublin, 1969), p. 72.
10 David Krause, *Seán O'Casey and his world* (New York, 1976), p. 26.
11 Cited in Brendan Kelly, *Asylum: inside Grangegorman* (Dublin, 2020), p. 118.
12 Michelle Norris, 'Social housing' in Declan Redmond and Michelle Norris (eds), *Housing contemporary Ireland: policy, society and shelter* (Dublin, 2005), pp 164–5.

controversy over the decision by the minister for finance Ernest Blthye to cut a shilling from the 10-shilling old age pension in the 1924 budget (those aged 80 and over were spared). It caused lasting political damage to Cumann na nGaedheal. As with housing, pre-Independence initiatives loomed large in relation to the pension debate. The old age pension had been introduced by a British Liberal government in 1908 and, as underlined by the economic historian Cormac Ó Gráda, was embraced so enthusiastically in Ireland that its cost caused consternation in London. The *Irish Times* had noted wryly in 1909 that

> with fewer inhabitants than Scotland by a quarter of a million, Ireland has established claims to nearly 74,000 more pensions. This surely is a major tribute to the longevity of our race and to the healthy character of our much-abused climate.[13]

This was partly about welfare fraud on a grand scale due to lying about age in order for those supposedly at or over the qualifying age of 70 to receive what was then a five-shilling payment. Compulsory registration of births had not been introduced in Ireland until 1864, hence the scope for skulduggery. There was surely much satisfaction on the part of a colonised people that they could raid the imperial exchequer for more than their share, though it was no laughing matter when the new Free State discovered that the pension – doubled to a maximum of ten shillings after the First World War – absorbed the bulk of welfare spending.

The pension was a crucial safety net and released thousands from the indignity of poor relief or the workhouse and allowed elderly farmers to 'retire gracefully and pass their land on'.[14] But in the early 1920s, the pension proved to be 'a fiscal nightmare' for the government, accounting for £3.2 million of the overall £20 million budget for public spending in 1922–3. The ideological bent of ministers was also relevant, including Seamus Burke, the minister for local government, who suggested the day when the pension was 'fair game' was gone. Burke also contended in 1924 that 'one of the most serious defects of the Irish character is this tendency to dependence of one kind or another ... the number of people who lead a parasitic existence ... [is] increasing relative to the number of people who are striving to make an honest living'.[15] In tandem with welfare spending cuts, income taxes were lowered from 25% to 15% between 1924 and 1926.[16]

Members of the National Army also faced the new stringency and 1924 was clouded by tension as a result. The army had become bloated due to the

---

13 Cited in Cormac Ó Gráda, '"The greatest blessing of all": the old age pension in Ireland', *Past and Present*, 75:1 (2002), 124–61.
14 Ibid.
15 *Dáil Éireann deb.*, vol. 17, col. 3054 (25 June 1924).
16 Ó Gráda, '"The greatest blessing"', at 148.

Civil War and 37,000 soldiers were deemed 'surplus to requirements' and demobilised, of whom only about 9,000 found alternative employment. The reduction in the army financial estimates was dramatic – from £10.5 million in 1923–4 to £4 million for 1924–5.[17] Army reorganisation was discussed by the government in February 1924, and it became an urgent crisis soon after. In March, two army officers, Major-General Liam Tobin and Colonel Charles Dalton, gave an ultimatum to the government demanding that it do more to achieve an Irish republic or face mutiny: 'we can no longer be party to the treachery that threatens to destroy the aspirations of a nation.'[18] It was a remarkably audacious move by those in the army who considered themselves keepers of the flame of Michael Collins who had been their commander-in-chief before his killing during the Civil War. They had formed the Irish Republican Army Organisation (IRAO), regarded ex British Army officers and post-Truce (after July 1921) recruits as being given preferential treatment in the army, and further maintained that Irish Republican Brotherhood (IRB) members within the army had undue sway over promotion and retention of army personnel.

The ultimatum was quickly depicted as an assault on the democratic foundations of the state. The minister for defence, Richard Mulcahy, responded: 'two army officers have attempted to involve the army in a challenge to the authority of the government. This is an outrageous departure from the spirit of the army. It will not be tolerated.'[19] Kevin O'Higgins declared that never again would the institutions of the state 'take their stride from a soldier's boot'.[20] That was a clever sound bite, but it deflected attention away from his own agenda and determination to sideline Mulcahy who resigned in protest at being told the army council (of which he was a member) would have to resign.

Mulcahy had presided over the difficult scheme of demobilisation and as historian Ronan Fanning saw it, 'Mulcahy's selfless and dignified response to his own humiliation averted the prospect of a mutiny, and copper-fastened the primacy of civilian over military authority as well as the democratic legitimacy of the infant state'.[21] That too is what is claimed by the champions of O'Higgins, Mulcahy's nemesis in cabinet. The subsequent report of the Army Inquiry Committee to investigate the crisis, chaired by High Court judge James Creed Meredith, found that the mutiny had been engineered by Collins loyalists resentful of the demobilisation process; it was critical of the

17 Ronan Fanning, *Independent Ireland* (Dublin, 1983), p. 49.
18 Maryann Gialanella Valiulis, *Almost a rebellion: the Irish Army mutiny of 1924* (Cork, 1985), p. 51.
19 Ibid., p. 53.
20 John M. Regan, *The Irish counter-revolution 1921–1936: Treatyite politics and settlement in independent Ireland* (Dublin, 2001), p. 197.
21 Ronan Fanning, 'Mulcahy, Richard', *DIB*.

army for allowing the IRB to be reorganised but did not accept membership of it influenced appointments. It asserted the Army Council had not been guilty of 'muddling, mismanagement and incompetence'. But Meredith's own conclusions, private and unpublished, were that Mulcahy had failed to deal with the problem of the IRAO officers 'in a direct and straightforward way' and 'gave the impression he would go behind the back of the cabinet and join hands and assist the organisation in getting control of the army for a particular purpose' and therefore was not guiltless of mismanagement.[22]

The despair of the demobilised soldiers, stood down through no fault of their own and who faced a bleak vista, is captured in their appeal testimonies from 1924. Patrick Beirne from Castlerea declared, 'I have 8 years of the best of my life spent in the country's causes and have no means of living whatsoever to fall back on'; Mulcahy dismissed him as 'surplus to requirements and below average ability'.[23] Joseph Rooney averred 'my case is typical of that of many officers – old IRA men dismissed summarily, although ... there were no grounds for complaints against me.'[24] Martin Nolan, who had joined the Irish Volunteers in 1914 and the National Army in February 1922, had taken charge of the Four Courts after its surrender in June 1922:

> I know certain men who have been kept on in the army who did not take half the interest or have half the results to their credit that I have ... now I am in the ranks of the unemployed. No work available and no chance of any in the future makes me wonder how I am going to support my wife and child. The nation thanks me for my good work, but that is not enough to keep my family.[25]

None of them were reinstated. In May 1924, the Association of Ex-Officers and Men of the National Army decried the president of the Executive Council W.T. Cosgrave and other TDs 'who have waded through the blood of 2,000 men into their present positions' without providing those soldiers with decent pensions.[26]

As to the unfinished business of an all-Ireland republic, some held out hope that the Boundary Commission, allowed for under article 12 of the Anglo-Irish Treaty, would interpret the wording contained in this article – that the Commission would determine the border 'in accordance with the

22 James Meredith to W.T. Cosgrave, detailing Meredith's reservation to the Committee's report, 10 June 1924. Irish Military Archives (IMA), Papers of the Army Inquiry Committee (AIC), IE-MA-AMTY 04-003.
23 Claims for reinstatement by demobilised soldiers, Statement of Patrick Beirne, and Richard Mulcahy to Department of Defence, 3 Mar. 1924, AIC, IE-MA-AMTY 01-60.
24 Statement of Joseph Rooney, 13 May 1924, AIC, IE-MA-AMTY 03-070.
25 Statement of Martin Nolan, 19 Apr. 1924, ibid.
26 Circular letters from the Association of Ex-Officers and Men of the National Army, May 1924, UCDA P4/1599.

wishes of the inhabitants, so far as may be compatible with economic and geographic conditions' – in a way that would favour nationalists, recommending such changes and transfers of territory as to render Northern Ireland inoperable.

The British Labour government that year, the first of its kind, had no desire to contemplate such radicalism or reopen the Irish question; prime minister Ramsay MacDonald agreed with the colonial secretary J.H. Thomas that the Treaty had to be 'relied upon as the sheet anchor in all dealings with the Irish Free State'.[27] One of the cabinet secretaries, Tom Jones, was wary of a scenario that would see 'Ireland ... back again in our politics.'[28] As historian D.G. Boyce saw it, the Labour Party had 'no Irish past to live down or to live up to.'[29] But it did have to grapple with the refusal of Ulster Unionists to have anything to do with the Boundary Commission by declining to nominate a representative. In 1924, James Craig, as prime minister of Northern Ireland, was prepared to tolerate a Boundary Commission that would only contemplate minor modifications to the border and was willing to support the involvement of former Unionist leader Edward Carson with the Commission, but his Unionist backbenchers were having none of that and instead, a formal policy of non-cooperation was adopted.[30]

Omagh-born Kevin O'Shiel, the head of the Free State's North-Eastern Boundary Bureau, which was preparing information for the Commission, had, from 1922–3, attempted to spread optimism about the Commission's potential by stressing the value of 'the organised force of public opinion'. O'Shiel believed some form of unity was 'within the grasp' of the Cumann na nGaedheal government.[31] But his more pessimistic assessment in 1924 was that 'we are entirely in the dark as to how the Commission will result and its finding may prove much less favourable than most of us imagine.'[32] It was that sense of uncertainty and frustration that prompted W.T. Cosgrave to tell the British government in August 1924 that if there was no progress with the Commission 'the Dáil would become a revolutionary parliament and the issue of an Irish republic would come to a head in the imperial parliament.'[33] This was wishful thinking. Kevin O'Higgins displayed more acuity and awareness of the deficiencies of the ambiguous wording of article 12 of the Treaty in recording privately in September 1924 that he was still hoping for 'a straight deal on the proviso to article 12', but if such was not achieved, he would

27 Ivan Gibbons, 'The first British Labour government and the Irish Boundary Commission 1924', *Studies*, 98:391 (2009), 321–33.
28 Ibid., at 328.
29 D.G. Boyce, *The Irish question and British politics, 1868–1996* (2nd edn, London, 1996), p. 78.
30 Alvin Jackson, 'Craig, James', *DIB*.
31 Memoranda, Kevin O'Shiel to the cabinet, 14 Oct. 1922, and 30 May 1923, NAI DT S4743 and S2027.
32 Memo., O'Shiel to cabinet, 25 Sept. 1924, NAI DT S4084.
33 Gibbons, 'The first British Labour government', p. 328.

consider the British to have been 'foolish but not nearly as foolish as ourselves.'[34]

The British government decided to appoint a representative for the Northern Ireland government, choosing journalist and Unionist Joseph Robert Fisher, a close associate of James Craig and firm advocate of partition, while the chairman appointed in June 1924 was Richard Feetham, a British-born judge of the South African Supreme Court, and very knitted into the British establishment. W.T. Cosgrave appointed, not O'Shiel, who might have been a better fit, but the Free State's minister for education, Eoin MacNeill. He was Ulster born and a Catholic, but he was hardly wily enough to vindicate nationalist claims; historian Joe Lee concluded he combined 'integrity with incompetence'.[35] The commissioners first met in November 1924, agreeing 'no commissioner would consult any of the governments as to the work of the Commission or make any statement as to such work to any government or individual without first consulting his colleagues'. In the event, 'Feetham and MacNeill scrupulously adhered to this. Fisher did not'.[36] The real drama and consequences of that, however, belonged to 1925.

There were other public and private musings in 1924 on the possibility of Irish unity, poet W.B. Yeats, as a senator, declaring 'I have no hope of seeing Ireland united in my time, or of seeing Ulster won in my time; but I believe it will be won in the end, and not because we fight it, but because we govern this country well'.[37] The attorney general, Hugh Kennedy, a close confidante of W.T. Cosgrave and strongly nationalist – he referred to Northern Ireland as 'the pseudo-province' – complained of the treatment of northern nationalists who were 'gerrymandered into disenfranchised silence'. But, as revealed in correspondence in his private papers held in the UCD Archives, he was more nuanced and cautious about any assumption of the inevitability of unity and wary of promotion of the idea of an all-island parliament that might dilute the status of the Oireachtas:

> the general line – ultimately unity is good. It can come in many ways. It may come eventually if we have good government down here, but good government is a lot to ask for from a relatively poor country and a people so long detached from any respect for order.[38]

Judging by their pronouncements, Irish Catholic Church leaders were also preoccupied with that perceived lack of respect and operated alongside the government as parallel moral arbiters, moving quickly into the vacuum

34 Kevin O'Higgins to Patrick McCartan, 12 Sept. 1924, UCDA P197/110.
35 J.J. Lee, *Ireland, 1912–1985: politics and society* (Cambridge, 1989), p. 147.
36 Ted Hallett, 'Eoin MacNeill and the Irish Boundary Commission' in Conor Mulvagh and Emer Purcell (eds), *Eoin MacNeill: the pen and the sword* (Dublin, 2022), pp 247–75.
37 Donald R. Pearce, *The Senate speeches of W.B. Yeats* (London, 1961), p. 87.
38 Kennedy to W.T. Cosgrave, 30 Sept. 1924, UCDA P4/419.

generated by the Civil War in a state where 93% of the citizens were Catholic. It is worth considering the assessment of historian Deirdre McMahon about the impact the Civil War had on the Catholic Church; the depth of Republican hostility

> with its potential for anti-clericalism shocked many in the clergy and the Hierarchy. In the years after the Civil War the bishops' pastorals were full of gloomy, doom-laden pronouncements about the inherent sinfulness of the people and the need for constant vigilance against threatening influences which might corrupt them.[39]

There was much evidence of those mindsets in 1924 as underlined by historian Margaret O'Callaghan's analysis of the rhetoric of the bishops. The new Catholic archibshop of Dublin Edward Byrne lamented that the guidance of bishops 'had fallen on many unheeding ears. Acts which were declared to be grave sins are still being committed with appalling frequency.'[40] The same year, Cardinal Michael Logue, archbishop of Armagh and primate of all Ireland, lauded efforts to 'restore peace and tranquillity' but added caveats:

> there is another reparation which is less thought of but infinitely more important, to bring back our people to a sense of peace, charity, honesty and obedience in all things to God's law ... There are some abuses to which I must reluctantly refer. The dress, or rather the want of dress of women at the present day is a crying scandal.[41]

A 'regular mania' for dancing was also denounced and regarded as 'mostly objectionable on the score of morality. They seem to be the outcrop of the corruption of the age'.[42]

Keeping the tides of foreign filth away from Ireland was a dominant theme, but others, including some Protestants, saw in the rhetorical excesses a misplaced and, given the renowned religiosity of the Irish, ironic characterisation of a fallen people. Consider, for example, the assertion in the *Church of Ireland Gazette* in March 1924 in response to the Catholic bishops' Lenten pastorals:

> when one reads through all pastorals one begins to wonder whether, after all, Ireland is not the worst country in the world. We may say at once that in our humble opinion at any rate, any foreign reader who peruses the jeremiads of the bishops surely must believe that this is a terrible place.[43]

39 Deirdre McMahon, 'The politician: a reassessment', *Studies*, 87:348 (1998), 344–52.
40 Margaret O'Callaghan, 'Religion and identity: the Church and Irish independence', *The Crane Bag*, 7:2 (1983), 69–76.
41 Ibid., at 71.
42 Ibid., at 68.
43 Ibid., at 73.

Cardinal Logue addressed students at Maynooth seminary in June 1924 and told the young priests they would have to 'meet a divided people who had lost much of their reverence for religion and the church and endeavour to bring men back to a sense of their religious duties – they should keep out of politics until they had more experience.'[44]

In the meantime, the business of governance and new legislative initiatives, including the new courts system, as covered in detail in this book, continued apace. The papers of Hugh Kennedy offer a broad overview of the multitude of practical and administrative issues that preoccupied legislators and civil servants in 1924, a year when 62 pieces of legislation were passed. Financial probity and centralisation were deemed to be of the utmost importance; the secretary of the Department of Finance, J.J. McElligott, was adamant in 1924 that payment be made for meals provided for government officials holed up in government buildings at the start of the Civil War in the summer of 1922.[45]

Other preoccupations included the Ministers and Secretaries bill, the Land Commission, electricity, local government and Dublin reconstruction. Reform of the licensing laws was also a major priority; indeed, it was asserted by the Department of Justice in 1923 that this issue and related alcohol abuse was 'practically the biggest and most urgent social problem that there is before the government'.[46] Contemporary statistics revealed that in England and Wales there were 86,722 licensed premises (a ratio of 1 for every 415 of the population), in Scotland 56,841 (1:695) and in Ireland 16,396 (1:263). An important factor in the promotion of new legislation was the determination of Kevin O'Higgins, who stated in 1923 that 'we need a genuine licensing code, not a bewildering maze of statutes and decisions, which, while creating offences also provided ingenious means of escape for unscrupulous people, and for people otherwise honest but who were driven to lie and worse in the struggle for existence'.[47] According to historian Madeleine Humphreys, the Licensing Act 1924, particularly the sections dealing with a reduction in trading hours, compulsory endorsement of licenses after conviction for an offence, and the position of district justices in their application of this law (they had been far too lenient) 'clearly symbolizes O'Higgins' acute anxiety that the judiciary should understand its subservience to the state while the publicans would know their privileged monopoly demanded exceptional responsibility'.[48]

There were many indications in the various assertions in 1924 about morality, recreation and drinking as to the shaping of the social climate and

44 Ibid., at 74.
45 J.J. McElligott to Kennedy, 7 Mar. 1924, UCDA P4/737.
46 'Licensing law reform', 19 Mar. 1923, NAI Department of Justice, H47A.
47 Diarmaid Ferriter, *A nation of extremes: the Pioneers in twentieth-century Ireland* (Dublin, 1999), p. 93.
48 Cited in Ferriter, *A nation of extremes*, p. 93.

very expansive definitions of transgression, sentiments that were to have lasting consequences, especially for women. Jesuit priest Fr Richard Devane observed in 1924 that prostitution had been 'impossible to deal with ... effectively' under British rule, but '[n]ow a new order has opened up and things can be done with comparative ease.'[49] 1924 also saw the establishment of an interdepartmental committee of inquiry on venereal disease and a growing preoccupation with unmarried mothers. The ethos that was solidifying was very much about 'imposing, particularly on women, standards of idealized conduct that would return the nation to purity'.[50]

The attempts to create a new Irish courts system took up much of Hugh Kennedy's time in 1924 and there was high praise from some of his colleagues on the back of those efforts. In April, district justice Louis Walsh, a regular correspondent and fellow Judiciary Committee member, referred to the new Courts of Justice bill as 'by far the biggest legislative reform attempted in our history ... to substitute for British institutions one worthy of the special genius of our race'. Its progress, suggested Walsh, was due to Kennedy's 'Irish instincts, breadth of view, freshness of outlook and courage.'[51] The same instincts, however, were not satisfied in relation to Kennedy's desire to see Irish judges don distinctive Irish garb for their professional robes, or what he referred to as 'an ocular demonstration to the man in the street that our courts are really Irish ones.'[52] In this, he found himself at odds with the pre-Independence attorney general and Lord Chancellor Lord Glenavy (James Campbell), a devout Unionist.

Amid his busyness, Kennedy also found time to socialise, imbibe and satisfy his considerable appetites; he told Cosgrave in August 1924 he was 'run down ... tonsillitis ... too many parties'.[53] There was also authorisation that year from the secretary of the Commissioners of Public Works for the bailiff of the Phoenix Park 'to kill one fat doe and deliver it to the attorney general.'[54] Judging by appearances, Kennedy, 'a small portly man whose high-pitched voice and rosy cheeks made him an easy target for press cartoonists', enjoyed every morsel of it.[55]

---

49 Maria Luddy, 'Sex and the single girl in 1920s and 1930s Ireland', *The Irish Review*, 35 (2007), 79–91.
50 Ibid.
51 Louis Walsh to Kennedy, 4 Apr. 1924, UCDA P4/1129.
52 Nov. 1923–Dec. 1924, UCDA P4/1164–1165, and James I. Dougherty, '"Ocular demonstration"' or "tremendous treasure"', *History Ireland*, 18:3 (2010), 34–7.
53 Kennedy to W.T. Cosgrave, 20 Aug. 1924, UCDA P4/417.
54 Printed authorisation from J.J. Healy, Sec. Commissioners of Public Works, 1924, UCDA P4/1674.
55 Ruadhán Mac Cormaic, *The Supreme Court* (Dublin, 2016), pp 14–19.

CHAPTER THREE

The Dáil courts and opposition to the Courts of Justice Act 1924

THOMAS MOHR*

INTRODUCTION

This chapter examines the relationship between the Courts of Justice Act 1924 and the Dáil courts. The Dáil courts were not completely ignored by the 1924 Act but were relegated to the margins of this important statute. Just two years earlier, the Dáil courts had been widely celebrated as one of the most successful fruits of the Irish revolutionary period and had become symbols of national pride and regeneration. Yet, these courts were abolished in the latter half of 1922 and little effort was made to revive them in the years that followed. Consequently, only passing reference was made to them in the provisions of the 1924 Act.

Abolition did not mean that memories of the Dáil courts ceased to have influence over the law and politics of the new Irish State. This chapter examines the continued influence of these courts in the context of the enactment of the Courts of Justice Act 1924. In particular, it examines the influence of the Dáil courts as part of anti-Treaty opposition to the 1924 Act and the new system of courts that it created.

THE DÁIL COURTS

The aftermath of the 1916 Easter Rising witnessed the emergence of voluntary arbitration courts as alternatives to the 'Crown courts', the official courts of the United Kingdom. In 1920 the first Dáil Éireann replaced these voluntary tribunals with a new system of courts that asserted coercive jurisdiction. The new system would be popularly known as the 'Dáil courts'.

The Dáil courts included local courts known as 'Parish Courts' and 'District Courts' that were staffed by persons without formal legal qualifications. They included a small number of women judges, a feature that

---

* Associate professor at the Sutherland School of Law, University College Dublin.

would not reappear in Ireland until the 1960s.[1] There were also provisions for District Courts to have circuit sittings over which a separate body of judges presided. At the apex was a Supreme Court that acted as a court of final appeal.[2] The circuit judges and the Supreme Court judges were all qualified barristers and included Cahir Davitt, Diarmuid Crowley, Arthur Clery and James Creed Meredith. There were also special tribunals intended to deal with disputes over land known varyingly as the 'Land Settlement Commission', the 'Land Commission' and the 'National Land Commission'.[3] These were popularly known as 'Dáil Land Courts'.[4]

The Dáil courts experienced rapid expansion after a truce with British forces was declared in July 1921. They provided an alternative to local Crown courts that had declined during the period of conflict. The Dáil courts continued to sit after the Articles of Agreement for a Treaty between Great Britain and Ireland (henceforth 'the Treaty') were signed on 6 December 1921 and survived the outbreak of civil war on 28 June 1922. Yet, their days were numbered and the process of abolishing the Dáil courts was made public in July 1922.

THE ABOLITION OF THE DÁIL COURTS

The Dáil courts were abolished in three separate stages. The first stage occurred on 25 July 1922 when all Dáil courts based in Dublin were abolished, but not Parish Courts and District Courts outside of Dublin.[5] The second stage involved the abolition of the Dáil Land Courts on 17 September 1922.[6] The third and final stage occurred on 30 October 1922 when all remaining Dáil courts were abolished.[7]

1 See the chapter by Niamh Howlin and Mark Coen.
2 Department of Home Affairs, 'Judiciary – rules and forms, Parish and District Courts', 1921 NAI DE 2/8/18.
3 This institution should not be confused with the 'Land Commission' created by the Crown in 1843 and based in Dublin Castle.
4 According to a pamphlet issued by the Dáil Ministry of Home Affairs in 1921, a special system of land courts was established in 1920. These courts were intended to be provisional and were replaced in the autumn of 1920 with a 'land settlement commission'. *The constructive work of Dáil Éireann No. 1 – the national police and courts of justice* (Dublin, 1921), p. 18. This was put into effect by a Dáil decree passed on 17 September 1920 that used the terms 'Land Commission' and 'National Land Commission'. *Dáil Éireann deb.*, vol. F, no. 17, col. 232 (17 Sept. 1920) and Decree No. 32, National Land Commission, NAI DE 2/8/32. However, it was still common practise to refer to 'Dáil Land Courts'. E.g., the term 'Dáil Land Court' was used and defined in s. 1(1) Dáil Éireann Courts (Winding-Up) Act 1923 Amendment Act 1924.
5 Dáil Éireann Courts (Winding-Up) Act 1923, s. 1(2).
6 Dáil Éireann Courts (Winding-Up) Act 1923 Amendment Act 1924, s. 1(2). On the actions of these land courts after this date of abolition and the attitude of the State courts towards them, see *The King (Kelly) v. Maguire and O'Shiel* [1923] 2 IR 58 and [1923] 57 ILTR 57.
7 Dáil Éireann Courts (Winding-Up) Act 1923, s. 1(2).

The first of these three stages attracted particular controversy because it fell in the middle of *habeas corpus* proceedings for an anti-Treaty prisoner being heard by a Dáil court based in Dublin. This has resulted in accusations that the Provisional Government initiated abolition of the Dáil courts based on fears that they would make an undesirable decision in one particular case.[8] Other commentators blame the outbreak of the Irish Civil War in June 1922 for the abolition of the Dáil courts.[9] It is now evident that the fate of the Dáil courts had been sealed before the initiation of any controversial legal proceedings involving anti-Treaty prisoners and also predated the outbreak of the Civil War.[10] By the middle of 1922 the Provisional Government had come to favour temporary retention of the former Crown courts combined with the creation of a provisional system of 'district justices' at the expense of the Dáil courts.

The Provisional Government made the mistake of delaying public announcement of the decision to abolish the Dáil courts until late July 1922. A controversial application for an order of *habeas corpus* heard by Diarmuid Crowley, sitting as a judge of the Dáil Supreme Court, finally pushed the Provisional Government to publicise their decision and begin the process of abolishing the Dáil courts. The Provisional Government's procrastination facilitated claims that the entire process was a kneejerk reaction to a pending court decision that was anticipated to be unfavourable to its interests. George Gavan Duffy called it a 'panic decision'.[11] This unfortunate history also allowed anti-Treaty newspapers to argue that abolition had occurred on the orders of the British government and, in particular, under the sinister influence of Winston Churchill.[12] The process of abolition continued throughout 1922 despite occasional acts of defiance led by Crowley.

As mentioned earlier, the Provisional Government abolished the Dáil courts and proclaimed a temporary retention of former Crown courts alongside the creation of a new system of temporary district justices. The temporary district justices were intended to replace former Crown courts of summary jurisdiction and local Dáil courts. The local Crown courts, known

8   E.g., see Dorothy Macardle, *The Irish republic* (Dublin, 1951), p. 768. For a general analysis of the legal issues raised by this application see Gerard Hogan, 'The Count Plunkett *habeas corpus* application and the end of the Dáil Supreme Court', *Irish Jurist*, 68 (2022), 25–49.
9   E.g., see Mary Kotsonouris, *Retreat from revolution: the Dáil courts, 1920–1924* (Dublin, 1994), p. 13 and (Dublin, 2020), p. 3. See also *Poblacht na hÉireann (Southern Edition)*, 30 Aug. 1922.
10 See Thomas Mohr, 'British involvement in the creation of the Consititution of the Irish Free State', *Dublin University Law Journal*, 30 (2008), 166–86, at 181–2 and Thomas Mohr, 'The "provisional period" – law and the birth of the Irish Free State 1921–1922', *Irish Jurist*, 70 (2023), 345–74 at 368–70.
11 *Dáil Éireann deb.*, vol. 4, col. 1310 (24 July 1923).
12 E.g., *Republic of Ireland (Scottish)*, 14 Oct. 1922, p. 3; *Republic of Ireland (Southern)*, 18 July 1922, p. 1 and *Republic of Ireland (War News)*, 15 July 1922, p. 1; 15 Aug. 1922, p. 1 and 3 Oct. 1922, p. 1.

as 'petty sessions', had either collapsed during the period of conflict or were no longer considered politically acceptable.[13]

The former Crown courts, together with the temporary system of district justices, may have been preferred over the Dáil courts as a consequence of their greater professionalism, resources and organisation. All of the former Crown courts rested on well-developed foundations of institutional support while the district justices took over many of the supports enjoyed by the petty sessions.[14] In addition, the Provisional Government had reason to doubt the loyalty of those Dáil court judges who opposed the Treaty, a consideration that did not apply with the same force to the former Crown courts. Issues of loyalty ensured that the temporary district justices would all be required to swear an oath to the state.[15] The former Crown courts and the new system of temporary district justices, now collectively called the 'state courts' by members of the Irish government, would continue to function until an entirely new judicial system was brought into existence by the Courts of Justice Act 1924.[16]

THE DÁIL COURTS AND THE COURTS OF JUSTICE ACT 1924

The work of the Judiciary Committee included accepting proposals from members of the public. It received proposals to either revive or in some way replicate the structure of the Dáil court system by recreating the Parish Courts and District Courts at local level.[17] There were also proposals to bring former judges of the Dáil Parish Courts and District Courts into the new system by having them sit alongside a person with legal training when hearing cases of the type heard by the old Petty Sessions.[18] Some proposals recommended that the new court system be associated with the Dáil courts as a means of winning popular acceptance, or at least avoiding popular rejection, for the former.[19] There were also submissions recommending that the new courts adopt the simpler and more expeditious procedures of the Dáil Parish and District Courts.[20] Yet, there were also submissions that emphasised

13 See Niamh Howlin's chapter on the District Court.
14 District Justices (Temporary Provisions) Act 1923, ss 4, 5 and 10 and sch. 2.
15 Ibid., sch. 1.
16 E.g., see the speeches of Kevin O'Higgins, *Dáil Éireann deb.*, vol. 4, cols 1307–10 (24 July 1923). O'Higgins also referred to the Dáil courts as 'state courts' on at least one occasion but immediately clarified his meaning. E.g., *Dáil Éireann deb.*, vol. 4, col. 1326 (24 July 1923).
17 'Reorganisation of courts', unsigned and undated, NAI AGO/1/201.
18 Louis Walsh to Hugh Kennedy, 25 July 1922, Kennedy papers, UCDA P4/1067.
19 'Reorganisation of courts – copy of memo. by B.J. Goff, Solicitor', 26 Aug. 1922, UCDA P4/1067 and Paul Vignoles, Dáil court organiser, to acting min. home affairs, 26 Aug. 1922, UCDA P4/1067.
20 Walsh to Kennedy, 25 July 1922, UCDA P4/1067; Reddin & Reddin Solicitors to Hugh

the shortcomings of the Dáil local courts, in particular the Parish Courts, and recommended that any retained judges from these tribunals be assisted or eventually replaced by persons with legal training.[21]

Some of the most notable submissions came from James Creed Meredith, a former president of the Dáil Supreme Court who would later join the Judiciary Committee and assist in drafting the 1924 Act. Meredith's submissions to the Judiciary Committee drew on his experience with the Dáil courts to support arguments on how the new system of courts might operate. It is worth noting that he did not include suggestions of any kind of revival of the system that had operated under the Dáil courts.[22]

The text of the 1924 Act did not completely ignore the prior existence of the Dáil courts. The 1924 Act allowed persons who had been sent forward for trial by any Dáil court to be tried by the new courts.[23] Experience as a judge of the Dáil Supreme Court was recognised as a valid qualification for judicial office under the 1924 Act. This applied to appointments to the new Supreme Court, High Court and District Court but not, strangely, to the new Circuit Court. It is worth noting that judicial office in the Dáil Parish Courts or in the Dáil District Courts were not recognised as valid qualifications under the 1924 Act.[24] This reflected wider policy that legal training be an essential requirement for judicial office within the Irish Free State.

The Irish government made limited attempts to link the new court system created by the 1924 Act with the glow of nostalgia associated with the Dáil courts. For example, both systems used the term 'District Court'. In addition, W.T. Cosgrave claimed that aspects of the Circuit Courts created by the 1924 Act had been 'borrowed to a large extent from the Dáil system' and downplayed connections with the system of assize circuits used by the Irish courts as part of the United Kingdom.[25] The accuracy of such claims is open to debate.

George Gavan Duffy, a signatory of the Treaty who served as minister for foreign affairs for the first half of 1922, proved to be one of the strongest parliamentary supporters of the Dáil courts. He deplored the abolition of

Kennedy, 5 Aug. 1922, UCDA P4/1067 and 'Judiciary – preliminary memo. of Judge Meredith', 28 Aug. 1922, UCDA P4/1067.
21 Walsh to Kennedy 25 July 1922, UCDA P4/1067; Muiris Ó Lochlainn, Dáil court organiser, to assistant minister for home affairs, 27 July 1922 UCDA P4/1067 and Vignoles, to acting minister for home affairs, 26 Aug. 1922, UCDA P4/1067.
22 Meredith memo., 28 Aug. 1922, P4/1067 and 'Memo. by Judge Meredith on reconstruction of judiciary', received Feb. 1923, P4/1091 and Kotsonouris, *Retreat from revolution*, p. 113 and 2020 edn, p. 102.
23 Courts of Justice Act 1924, s. 104.
24 Ibid., ss 16 and 69. See also s. 43, concerning qualification for appointment as a judge of the Circuit Court. Experience as a judicial commissioner appointed under the Dáil Éireann Courts (Winding-Up) Act 1923 was deemed practice at the Bar for the purposes of the Courts of Justice Act 1924, ss 16 and 69.
25 *Dáil Éireann deb.*, vol. 5, cols 84–5 (25 Sept. 1923).

these courts and hoped that aspects of them might be retained under the new judicial system. Gavan Duffy believed that it might be possible to amalgamate aspects of the Dáil courts into the new system. He argued that it might have been possible to retain some local Dáil courts to hear 'matters of ordinary commercial disputes and any agricultural disputes which do not require a great deal of law, and which require mainly common-sense'.[26] Gavan Duffy lost the ears of his ministerial colleagues after he resigned his ministerial post and began to clash with them with increased bitterness in parliamentary debates. He lost his seat in the 1923 election and had very little political influence when the Courts of Justice Act 1924 was finally enacted.

It is worth remembering that the consequences of the Dáil courts' proceedings had not been entirely consigned to history in 1924. There remained a formidable task of reviewing cases decided by the Dáil courts and of dealing with cases that were pending before them at the time of abolition. The task was initially undertaken by judicial commissioners and assistant commissioners in what would become known as the 'Dáil Courts (Winding Up) Commission'.[27] This function was transferred to the High Court soon after the new system of courts was put in place by the 1924 Act.[28] The process of reviewing the decisions of the Dáil courts was necessary, notwithstanding its length and expense, although it is questionable whether this should be presented as some form of revival or reinstatement of the Dáil courts.[29] Contemporary newspapers often confused this commission with the Dáil courts which ensured that references to these courts were still appearing in the press during and after the enactment of the Courts of Justice Act 1924.[30]

The most significant aspect of the Dáil courts that continued after 1924 was reflected in the new judiciary. Judges appointed under the 1924 Act included members of the judiciary of the Dáil courts, for example James Creed Meredith and Cahir Davitt.[31] The new judiciary also included judges of the former Crown courts, for example Charles O'Connor and William Johnston, together with new judges that had not served under either system, for example Hugh Kennedy and James FitzGibbon. Many of the temporary district justices appointed between 1922 and 1924 became permanent members of the new District Court.[32] The mixed origins of the new judiciary established under the Courts of Justice Act 1924 reflected the mixed origins of the Irish State itself that drew on a combination of revolutionary history,

26 Ibid., vol. 4, col. 1312 (24 July 1923).
27 Dáil Éireann Courts (Winding-Up) Act 1923, Dáil Éireann Courts (Winding-Up) Act 1923 Amendment Act 1924 and Dáil Éireann Courts (Winding-Up) Act 1925.
28 Dáil Éireann Courts (Winding-Up) Act 1925, s. 3.
29 Kotsonouris, *Retreat from revolution*, pp 134–5 and 2020 edn, p. 123 and Mary Kotsonouris, *The winding up of the Dáil courts, 1922–1925: an obvious duty* (Dublin, 2004), p. 27.
30 E.g., see *Freeman's Journal*, 17 Apr. 1924, and *Limerick Leader*, 28 Apr. 1924.
31 See Robert Marshall's chapter.
32 See Niamh Howlin's chapter on the District Court.

heritage derived from the United Kingdom and features that were entirely new.

ANTI-TREATY OPPOSITION TO THE COURTS OF JUSTICE ACT 1924

The abolition of the Dáil courts provided an obvious source of ammunition for opponents of the Treaty to attack the Courts of Justice Act 1924. Yet, arguments relating to the Dáil courts did not appear as frequently in this context as might be expected. Instead, the abolition of the Dáil courts tended to be used to support wider arguments challenging the legal foundations of the Irish Free State.[33] Other reasons were found to oppose the 1924 Act and the system of courts it created.

On 25 October 1922 a group of opponents of the Treaty, led by Éamon de Valera, attempted to create their own parliament and government in opposition to the Provisional Government and the third Dáil Éireann. The new anti-Treaty authorities made a proclamation on 18 November 1922 demanding the suppression of the former Crown courts together with the new system of temporary district justices. Their proclamation also declared that anyone who worked for or cooperated with these courts was 'an enemy of the republic'.[34] De Valera and his colleagues had little hope of enforcing this proclamation as military reverses in the Civil War undermined their position. Despite some calls to preserve the Dáil courts, the self-proclaimed anti-Treaty authorities made little effort to do so.[35] By late 1922 it had become all too clear which side was going to win the Irish Civil War and the attempt to create new parallel institutions, as had been done in 1919 and 1920, could not hope to succeed.

The Civil War came to an end in 1923 and the last anti-Treaty internees were released in 1924. De Valera and his colleagues continued to assert the existence of an alternative government and legislature to those established by the 1922 Constitution of the Irish Free State. These were based on anti-

33 E.g., see the proclamation of 18 Nov. 1922 reproduced in *The Nationalist and Leinster Times*, 16 Sept. 1922; *Poblacht na hÉireann (Scottish Edition)*, 21 Oct. 1922, 2 Dec. 1922, and 6 Jan. 1923; *Poblacht na hÉireann (War News)*, 29 June, 26 Oct., 29 and 30 Dec. 1922; *Éire – The Irish Nation*, 3 Mar., 25 Aug. 1923.
34 The only exception provided was for those who had a 'licence from the minister for home affairs of the republic'. *Poblacht na hÉireann (Scottish Edition)*, 2 Dec. 1922.
35 See *Correspondence of Mr de Valera and others* (Dublin, 1922), p. 22. It is worth noting that the unsigned author of this letter dated 29 Aug. 1922 wrote 'Except for the Supreme Court, the repub. courts should be maintained'. The rejection of the Dáil Supreme Court was never explained. It may have been prompted by knowledge that several of its judges supported the Treaty. Alternatively, it may be that Diarmuid Crowley was not held in high esteem by all opponents of the Treaty at this time. Crowley would later alienate former supporters by accepting a government offer of becoming a judicial commissioner in winding up the Dáil courts.

Treaty membership of the second Dáil Éireann which, it was insisted, had not been properly dissolved. These claims were not replicated in the judicial sphere and opponents of the Treaty accepted the reality of the abolition of the Dáil courts.[36] A prominent source of resistance was neutralised in 1923 when Diarmuid Crowley accepted a position under the Dáil Courts (Winding Up) Commission and later received a pension from the Irish Free State.[37] No real effort was made to revive the Dáil courts after the Civil War concluded.

Recognition of the *de facto* abolition of the Dáil courts did not mean that prominent opponents of the Treaty were prepared to recognise the 'state courts' between 1922 and 1924. The authorities of the Irish Free State may have hoped that this would change with the enactment of the Courts of Justice Act 1924 and the creation of an entirely new system of Irish courts. If so, they would soon be disappointed.

Declarations refusing to recognise the courts continued long after the 1924 Act came into force.[38] The anti-Treaty media greeted the official opening of the new courts created by the 1924 Act with renewed condemnation of the Irish Free State and a declaration that 'its new legal system is based on deliberate deception and organised hypocrisy'.[39] The new Irish courts were soon labelled as 'camouflaged British courts'.[40] In 1925 *An Phoblacht* claimed that 'everybody' regarded the new Irish courts with the 'fullness of contempt'.[41]

The anti-Treaty media attacked the courts created by the 1924 Act on several different grounds. They argued that only a minority of TDs had voted in favour of this legislation when the total number of those who voted against the legislation was combined with those who boycotted the Oireachtas.[42] Anti-Treaty newspapers also alleged corruption in the appointment of the new judiciary in 1924.[43] There were also objections to the substantial number of Protestants appointed to the new bench. This context allowed *Éire – The Irish Nation*, a prominent anti-Treaty newspaper, to endorse claims that 'under the new dispensation the orangemen and the freemasons rule Ireland'.[44] The same newspaper insisted that a secret agreement concluded in London

36 E.g., see *An Phoblacht*, 17 July 1925, in which correspondence from Countess Markievicz speaks of the 'suppressed Republican courts' while Crowley described himself as a 'barrister of law' by 1925. See Diarmuid Ó Cruadhlaoich, *The oath of allegiance* (Dublin, 1925), p. iii.
37 Crowley endured bitter criticism from other opponents of the Treaty for accepting this position. E.g., see *An Phoblacht*, 3 July 1925, p. 4. His stance was defended by Countess Markievicz in *An Phoblacht*, 17 July 1925, p. 2. Crowley was the sole beneficiary of the Dáil Supreme Court (Pensions) Act 1925.
38 E.g., see *An Phoblacht*, 26 June, 11, 25 Sept., 6, 13, 20 Nov. 1925.
39 *Éire – The Irish Nation*, 28 June 1924.
40 *An Phoblacht*, 24 July 1925.
41 Ibid., 7 Aug. 1925.
42 *Éire – The Irish Nation*, 17 May 1924.
43 Ibid., 21, 28 June 1924.
44 Ibid., 3 May 1924.

alongside the Treaty demanded 'the complete control of the judicial bench, which it is proposed to hand over to the Unionist minority'.[45] On another occasion *Éire – The Irish Nation* went even further by condemning 'the firm grip which the Protestant section of the community have got upon all the branches of government'.[46] This newspaper concluded, '[i]t is an insult to the Catholic majority, and it is absolute proof that in the Free State only the servile tools of England will get place and preferment'.[47] The appointment of Protestants to the bench was also associated with conspiracy theories centred on the freemasons who were alleged to have used their influence in securing appointments to the judiciary in addition to the Seanad, the Garda Síochána and the army.[48] Attempts to associate the new judiciary with Unionism were also evident in the use of phrases such as the 'royal Irish Free State judicial bench'.[49]

The anti-Treaty media traced the origins of their charges of corruption and sectarian preference to the work of the Judiciary Committee and the subsequent drafting of the Courts of Justice Act 1924. *Éire – The Irish Nation* concluded:

> It would really seem that the new Act, which owed its inspiration and origin to Lord Glenavey, [sic] was passed for this very purpose. The gullible public were informed that its aim was to bring some desirable changes in legal procedure. What it has done is ... to give an insignificant minority a grip on the throttle valve of the law.[50]

Opponents of the Treaty also challenged the 1924 Act through its association with the 1922 Constitution, which they opposed on many grounds.[51] By the mid-1920s opposition to the courts often focused on the constitutional provisions recognising the king. *Éire – The Irish Nation* argued that the constitutional position of the king was no 'exercise of ornamental functions' but, instead, constituted the source of all executive power.[52] It concluded that the king 'runs through the Free State Constitution from the first line to the last' which ensured that 'its courts are his courts'.[53] These

---

45 Ibid. See 21 June 1924.
46 Ibid., 21 June 1924.
47 Ibid., 3 May 1924.
48 Ibid., 28 June, 3 May 1924. On the alleged influence of Protestant finance see ibid., 1 Dec. 1923.
49 Ibid., 16 Oct. 1925.
50 Ibid., 3 May 1924.
51 See Thomas Mohr, 'Opposition to the 1922 Constitution of the Irish Free State', UCD Working Papers in Law, Criminology & Socio-Legal Studies, Research Paper No. 8/2023 SSRN: https://papers.ssrn.com/sol3/papers.cfm?abstract_id=4487179.
52 *Éire – The Irish Nation*, 26 Apr. 1924.
53 Ibid. On the use of the king in the wording of writs see ibid., 16 Feb., 26 Apr. 1924.

sentiments were echoed by *An Phoblacht* in 1925 when it asked, '[a]re not the courts his majesty's courts still?'[54]

Opponents of the Treaty also argued that the new judiciary created by the 1924 Act was tainted by the requirement that judges make a declaration to uphold the 1922 Constitution.[55] This requirement had not been included in the original draft of the Courts of Justice bill, which had required short and entirely secular declarations from judges about to take office.[56] A more elaborate declaration, which included the reference to the Constitution, was added in response to calls by Professor William Magennis of University College Dublin. Magennis wanted a wording that would 'mark the solemnity of the appointment of a judge' and include a reference to God.[57] Opponents of the Treaty soon labelled this declaration an 'oath' notwithstanding denials by the Irish government.[58] It provided yet another means of attacking the 1924 Act and the new judiciary.

The anti-Treaty media also raised the existence of the appeal from the Irish Supreme Court to the Judicial Committee of the Privy Council under article 66 of the Constitution to attack the new system of courts. The existence of the Privy Council appeal allowed *An Phoblacht* to argue that the Irish Free State failed a key test of sovereignty as its courts did not enjoy supreme jurisdiction. It concluded that the Irish Supreme Court, created by the 1924 Act, was really a 'sub-Supreme Court'.[59]

Rejection of the state courts that sat between 1922 and 1924 and the new system of Irish courts that emerged under the 1924 Act saw some opponents of the Treaty indulge in nostalgia for the Dáil courts. Yet, there were surprisingly few calls for their revival. Instead, as mentioned earlier, memories of the Dáil courts tended to be used in wider arguments attacking the legitimacy of the Irish Free State.[60] The calls for revival of the Dáil courts that were made in the mid-1920s were often rendered uncertain by possible confusion with the preceding system of arbitration courts.[61]

54 *An Phoblacht*, 30 Oct. 1925 (capitalisation removed), and Ó Cruadhlaoich, *The oath*, p. 60.
55 Courts of Justice Act 1924, s. 99. *An Phoblacht*, 17 July 1925, and Ó Cruadhlaoich, *The oath*, pp 59–62.
56 *Dáil Éireann deb.*, vol. 5, col. 236 (10 Oct. 1923).
57 Ibid., cols 236–8 and cols 1344–6 (4 Dec. 1923).
58 Crowley referred to it as an 'Oath or Declaration': Ó Cruadhlaoich, *The oath*, p. 61. However, Countess Markievicz had no qualms in referring to it as an oath: *An Phoblacht*, 17 July 1925. For denials that this requirement constituted an oath see *Dáil Éireann deb.*, vol. 5, cols 1345–6 (4 Dec. 1923).
59 *An Phoblacht*, 26 June 1925. See also *Poblacht na hÉireann (Scottish Edition)*, 16 Sept. 1922, and Ó Cruadhlaoich, *The oath*, p. 60. For more on the Privy Council appeal in the Irish Free State see Mohr, *Guardian of the Treaty*.
60 See n. 29.
61 E.g., see a 1925 speech of Daniel Mannix, archbishop of Melbourne, who praised the 'rough and ready justice' that had been dispensed by courts five years earlier when 'Ireland was Ireland'. This might refer to either of these two systems of courts. *An Phoblacht*,

CONCLUSION

By 1924 abolition of the Dáil courts had been accepted in practice by most opponents of the Treaty. Many continued to challenge the legality of abolition but used these arguments to attack the new Irish state rather than attempt to restore the Dáil courts or any other form of alternative tribunals. The legacy of the Dáil courts was strong enough to ensure that they could not be entirely ignored by the Courts of Justice Act 1924. Yet, they were relegated to the margins of this historic legislation. The new courts took over the facilities, supports and system of law enjoyed by the state courts that sat between 1922 and 1924 and not those of the Dáil courts. Even those who opposed the new system of courts created in 1924 recognised that the Dáil courts were now out of the running.

Yet, memories of the Dáil courts never faded. The decades that followed witnessed accounts of the Dáil courts that celebrated their informal nature, their celerity in decision-making and their economy in terms of legal costs. In the mid-1930s Ernie O'Malley, an eloquent veteran of two conflicts and staunch opponent of the Treaty, composed a requiem to a lost system of dispute resolution rooted in basic essentials:

> Parish and District Courts settled cases quickly on their merits; there was no forensic eloquence; common sense and good will replaced involuted legal formulas. Justice was elemental, strict, but impartial and human; costs were low.[62]

This eulogy was a thinly-veiled attack on the judicial systems that preceded and followed the brief span of life allotted to the Dáil courts. The example of the Dáil courts was raised during the enactment of the 1924 Act to support calls for more informal court proceedings and the removal of wigs and gowns from Irish courtrooms.[63] The Dáil courts were also raised in calls for the new system of courts to provide an expeditious and less costly means of resolving legal disputes.[64] Reducing the longevity and cost of litigation remain elusive goals in twenty-first century Ireland. Such consideration may help explain the enduring fascination with the brief career of the Dáil courts.

---

21 Aug. 1925. A letter to another anti-Treaty newspaper in 1924 specifically called for the revival of the 'arbitration courts'. *Éire – The Irish Nation*, 23 Aug. 1924.
62 Ernie O'Malley, *On another man's wound* (Dublin, 2002), p. 185.
63 *Dáil Éireann deb.*, vol. 5, cols 289–92 (11 Oct. 1923).
64 E.g., see Walsh to Kennedy, 25 July 1922, UCDA P4/1067 and Meredith memo., 28 Aug. 1922, UCDA P4/1067. See also *Freeman's Journal*, 20 Sept. 1922, and *Dáil Éireann deb.*, vol. 5, col. 385 (12 Oct. 1923).

CHAPTER FOUR

The 'judicial interregnum', 1922–4: the new Constitution in the old courts

MAURICE G. COLLINS*

The enactment on 12 April 1924 of the Courts of Justice Act 1924, establishing a new court system in the state, undoubtedly constituted a landmark in Irish legal history. However, the Constitution that mandated the establishment of that new system, that prescribed the jurisdiction of the courts to be so established, and that set out what was intended to be the fundamental law of the newly constituted Irish Free State had come into operation on 6 December 1922. What of the period between December 1922 and April 1924 (the 'interregnum' of the title)?

As of 6 December 1922, justice continued to be administered in the (former) Crown courts. These were the courts constituted by the Supreme Court of Judicature Act (Ireland) 1877 and subsequently significantly reconfigured by the Government of Ireland Act 1920 (which only came into effect on 3 May 1921), which partitioned the court system (and the country) and established a new Supreme Court of Judicature for Southern Ireland, comprising his majesty's High Court of Justice in Southern Ireland and his majesty's Court of Appeal in Southern Ireland.[1]

Partition was by no means the only challenge that the Crown courts had faced in this period. From 1920 onwards a rival court system – the Dáil courts – had functioned in parallel to them and effectively in competition with them. A great deal has been written about the Dáil courts and their legacy continues to be the subject of discussion and dispute.[2] They had been a very visible, and

---

* Judge of the Supreme Court.
1 Government of Ireland Act 1920, ss 38 and 39. The Act also established a High Court of Appeal for Ireland but that was abolished by the (UK) Irish Free State (Consequential Provisions) Act 1922 enacted on 5 Dec. 1922, the day before the adoption of the Free State Constitution.
2 See Thomas Mohr's chapter, as well as Cahir Davitt, 'The civil jurisdiction of the courts of justice of the Irish Republic, 1920–1922', *Ir. Jur.*, 3:1 (1968), 112–30 and Mary Kotsonouris, *Retreat from revolution: the Dáil courts, 1920–1924* (Dublin, 1994). It seems difficult to quarrel with the assessment of Nial Osborough that the legacy of the Dáil courts has been more significant in the sphere of political history than in the sphere of legal history: W.N. Osborough, *Studies in Irish legal history* (Dublin, 1999) at p. 271 (cited in Thomas Mohr, 'The "provisional period" – law and the birth of the Irish Free State', *Ir. Jur.*, 70 (2023), 345–74.

at least *politically* significant, manifestation of the Republican counter state. But whatever the hopes of some in the Republican movement that the Dáil courts would supplant the Crown courts once independence was attained, those hopes had been disappointed. However controversially, the Dáil courts had been abolished as of 6 December 1922.[3]

As early as 16 January 1922 – the very day of the 'handover' of Dublin Castle – the new Provisional Government issued a proclamation directing that 'all law courts ... [and] judges ... hitherto acting under the authority of the British government shall continue to carry out their functions unless and until pending the Constitution of the Parliament and government of Saorstát na hÉireann'.[4] The two regimes continued to operate in parallel for a while but, as Mohr puts it, the 'Provisional Government finally chose the former Crown courts at the expense of the Dáil courts.'[5] In its decree suspending the sitting of the Dáil Supreme Court, the government explained that the 'former British courts are now in Irish hands under the terms of the Treaty. They are now Irish courts ...'.[6] In the context of justifying the suspension of the Dáil Supreme Court (in very fraught political circumstances) that characterisation of the former Crown courts as Irish courts may readily be understood but, as we shall see, it is rather at odds with subsequent government rhetoric in this context.

In any event, while these courts were permitted to continue, they did so under the shadow of the guillotine. Article 10 of the Treaty – which bound the Free State government to pay 'fair compensation' to (inter alia) judges discharged by it or who retired in consequence of the 'change of government' effected pursuant to the Treaty – reflected the clear understanding that the services of the serving judges might be dispensed with by the new government (or withdrawn from the government through retirement). The precariousness of the judges' position was graphically expressed by Lord Chief Justice Molony to a senior British official in May 1922: the judges were, he said, 'simply waiting to see will the tide turn or engulf us.'[7] While the tide did not engulf them in 1922, neither did it turn.

3 Subsequently, the Oireachtas enacted the Dáil Éireann Courts (Winding-up) Act 1923 for the purposes of winding-up the Dáil courts and disposing of the proceedings pending before them 'at the date when the authority of such Court was withdrawn': s. 4. The King's Bench Division had by then held that the Land Court (a branch of the Dáil courts) had no lawful authority because they had not been established by an act of a competent legislature: *R (Kelly) v. Maguire & O'Sheil* [1923] 2 IR 58. That conclusion is hardly reconcilable with Irish constitutional theory and, in any event, the 1923 Act clearly recognised the Dáil courts (as did the provisions of the Courts of Justice Act 1924 recognising service as a judge of the Dáil Supreme Court as qualifying service for the purposes of appointment – see the discussion in Thomas Mohr's chapter).
4 Transfer of services hitherto administered by the British government in Ireland, dated 16 Jan. 1922.
5 Mohr, 'The "provisional period"', at 369.
6 *I.L.T.&S.J.* 56 (1922), 172: set out in full in Osborough, *Studies*, p. 272.
7 Cited in Bláthna Ruane, 'Régime change: the fate of the senior Crown judiciary following the Anglo-Irish Treaty', *Ir. Jur.*, 54:2 (2015), 96–114, at 103.

Following the eruption of Civil War, the courts were once again confronted with *habeas corpus* applications raising difficult and fateful issues as to whether the conditions for martial law existed and as to the authority of military tribunals to try and punish those accused of taking up arms against the government – now, of course, the Provisional Government rather than the Crown. These issues were significantly complicated by the status and limited functions of the Provisional Government and the limited legislative capacity of the Dáil during the 'provisional period.'

Even so, in the period between the outbreak of the Civil War and coming into operation of the Constitution (on 6 December 1922), the Provisional Government prevailed in two significant cases, namely *R (Childers) v. Adjutant General of the Provisional Forces*[8] and *R (Johnstone) v. O'Sullivan*.[9] Any detailed discussion of these decisions is beyond the scope of this chapter.[10] But their significance to the Provisional Government is reflected in the fact that the attorney general, Hugh Kennedy KC, appeared personally in both. The judgment of the master of the rolls in *Childers* – said to have been delivered by candle-light in the dining hall of the King's Inns[11] – powerfully conveys the traumatic impact of the Civil War on the judges. Dismissing the suggestion that there was no state of war in the country, O'Connor MR first referred to the affidavit evidence that had been filed on behalf of the Provisional Government (which, he said, presented so appalling a picture that it 'might well describe the seat of the great war between France and Germany') and then uttered this *cri de coeur*:

> But if there was no affidavit at all, I would be bound to take judicial notice of the fact that, for months this country has been enduring a state of war. I am sitting here in this temporary makeshift for a court of justice. Why? Because one of the noblest buildings in this country, which was erected for the accommodation of the king's courts and was the home of justice for more than a hundred years, is now a mass of crumbling ruins, the work of revolutionaries, who proclaim themselves the soldiers of an Irish Republic.

And so to the Free State Constitution. The Constitution of the Irish Free State (Saorstát Éireann) Act 1922 was enacted by Dáil Éireann, sitting as 'a constituent assembly in this provisional parliament'. As a matter of Irish

---

8 [1923] 1 IR 5. This was a decision of O'Connor MR, who had of course given the celebrated (if legally questionable) decision in *Egan v. Macready* [1921] 1 IR 265.
9 [1923] 2 IR 13.
10 See Ronan Keane, '"The will of the general": martial law in Ireland 1535–1924', *Ir. Jur.*, 25:1 (1990), 150–80 and Gerard Hogan, 'Hugh Kennedy, the *Childers habeas corpus* application and the return to the Four Courts' in Caroline Costello (ed.), *The Four Courts: 200 years* (Dublin, 1996), pp 177–219.
11 Hogan, 'Hugh Kennedy', at 192.

constitutional theory, that Act was the Constitution's root of title.¹² Article 64 of the Constitution provided that the 'judicial power of the Irish Free State (Saorstát Éireann) shall be exercised and justice administered in the public courts established by the Oireachtas by judges appointed in [the] manner hereinafter provided.' Those courts were to include a court of first instance – the High Court – whose power would extend to 'the question of the validity of any law having regard to the provisions of the Constitution.' Only the High Court would have original jurisdiction to entertain such a question but its decisions were subject to appeal to a new court of final appeal – the Supreme Court – whose constitutional jurisdiction was also entrenched.¹³

Of course, no such courts were established as of 6 December 1922. Speaking in the Dáil during the committee stage of the Constitution bill, the minister for home affairs, Kevin O'Higgins, explained that it was intended to call together a judicial committee to revise the entire justice system and it was hoped:

> to evolve an entirely new judicial system, which will supersede both the British courts and the Dáil courts, as formerly known. The committee will, of course, aim at absorbing whatever is best in both of these systems. The new system will be set up in relation to Irish requirements, and it will be the aim of the committee to set up a system of justice which the people can really regard as their own, and as suited to their needs and their genius.¹⁴

Meanwhile, article 75 of the Constitution provided for the continuing jurisdiction of the existing courts on a transitional basis, in the following terms:

> Until courts have been established for the Irish Free State (Saorstát Éireann) in accordance with this Constitution, the Supreme Court of Judicature, County Courts, Courts of Quarter Sessions and courts of summary jurisdiction, as at present existing, shall for the time being continue to exercise the same jurisdiction as heretofore, and any judge

12 That was the view stated by Kennedy CJ in *State (Ryan) v. Lennon* [1935] IR 170 and, on that point at least, FitzGibbon J agreed with him. A contrary view was subsequently expressed by the Judicial Committee in *Moore v. Attorney General of the Irish Free State* [1935] IR 472. However, the decision of the Supreme Court in *The Criminal Law (Jurisdiction) Bill, 1975* [1977] IR 129 leaves no room for doubt as to what the position is as a matter of Irish constitutional theory.
13 Art. 65 and art. 66. The finality of decisions of the Supreme Court was controversially qualified by the possibility of a further appeal by way of petition to the Judicial Committee of the Privy Council. Thomas Mohr, *Guardian of the Treaty: the Privy Council appeal and Irish sovereignty* (Dublin, 2016) gives an illuminating account of the operation of the Privy Council appeal until its abolition by the Constitution (Removal of Oath) Act 1933.
14 *Dáil Éireann deb.*, vol. 1, col. 20 (10 Oct. 1922).

or justice, being a member of any such court, holding office at the time when this Constitution comes into operation, shall for the time being continue to be a member thereof and hold office by the like tenure and upon the like terms as heretofore, unless, in the case of a judge of the said Supreme Court or of a County Court, he signifies to the representative of the Crown his desire to resign. Any vacancies in any of the said courts so continued may be filled by appointment made in like manner as appointments to judgeships in the courts established under this Constitution: Provided that the provisions of article 66 of this Constitution as to the decisions of the Supreme Court established under this Constitution shall apply to decisions of the Court of Appeal continued by this article.

That this was a transitional and merely temporary provision was emphasised by article 75, which provided that any Supreme Court of Judicature or County Court judge who was not, with his consent, appointed as a judge of a court established under the Constitution, he (and the judges were, of course, all male) would, for the purposes of article 10 of the Treaty, be treated as if he had retired on consequence of the change of government effected in pursuance of the Treaty.

A Judiciary Committee was then appointed under the chairmanship of Lord Glenavy. Writing to each of the committee's members (in terms apparently drafted by Hugh Kennedy, who was also a member of the committee), the president of the Executive Council, William T. Cosgrave, again emphasised the alien character of the existing justice system and stressed the need for the creation of an Irish justice system.[15]

The former Crown courts might not have had the confidence or affection of the people, or even of the government but they persevered with their task nonetheless.[16] The coming into force of the new Constitution did not significantly alter the nature of their work. The Civil War continued to rage (on 8 December 1922 – a mere two days after the formal establishment of the new Free State – Rory O'Connor, Liam Mellows, Dick Barrett and Joe McKelvey had been summarily executed, without legal process of any kind, in Mountjoy Prison) and, in the circumstances, it is unsurprising that the

---

15 See Niamh Howlin, 'Reflecting on a century of Irish courts', where the text of the letter is reproduced on p. 2.
16 Ruane, 'Régime change', gives an account of some of the tensions and suspicions between the judges and the government. Many decisions of the Crown courts during the War of Independence had upheld the interests of the Crown and cleared the way for the summary execution of Republican prisoners – including most notoriously *R v. Allen* [1921] 2 IR 241 in which the lord chief justice gave the judgment of a unanimous five judge divisional court. *Egan v. Macready* [1921] 1 IR 265 was a rare and celebrated exception to that pattern of rejection. Ruane and other commentators suggest that Hugh Kennedy was hostile to many of the Crown judges, particularly Molony CJ.

courts continued to be confronted by a constant stream of *habeas corpus* applications. Now, however, the provisions of the new Constitution could – and immediately were – prayed in aid of such applications.[17] There was, of course, other litigation also but, in my view, the *habeas corpus* jurisdiction gives the best insight into the operation of the courts in the interregnum and in particular how those courts approached the new Constitution.

I will focus here on two decisions. The first – *R (O'Brien) v. Military Governor of North Dublin Union Internment Camp*[18] – is significant for a number of reasons, not least because it involved a judicial determination that the 'state of war' arising from the Civil War had come to an end but also because it appeared – though briefly and misleadingly - to herald a new era of constitutional activism. The significance of the second – *R (Cooney) v. Clinton (Note)*[19] – is that, at the end of the interregnum period, the old Court of Appeal effectively pulled a thread in the Free State Constitution that in due course helped contribute to its ultimate unravelling.

In *O'Brien*, Nora Connolly O'Brien – who was the daughter of James Connolly and who was subsequently appointed to the Seanad by both Éamon de Valera and Sean Lemass[20] – had been detained (without trial) by the military authorities in January 1923. In late May 1923 Frank Aiken, chief-of-staff of the IRA, instructed the anti-Treaty forces to 'dump arms' which was widely interpreted as a ceasefire order. At the same time, Éamon de Valera issued a statement suggesting that 'the continuance of the struggle in arms would be unwise in the national interest'. Ms Connolly O'Brien's sister then applied for her release, on the basis that, in light of these developments, a 'state of war' no longer existed.[21]

The indefatigable attorney general once again appeared in person for the respondents. O'Connor MR rejected the application, on the basis that the evidence established that hostilities had not in fact ceased. However, on appeal the Court of Appeal took a different view. Molony CJ (with whom Ronan LJ agreed) framed the essential issue as

17 Art. 6 of the Constitution provided that the 'liberty of the person is inviolable, and no person shall be deprived of his liberty except in accordance with law' and also entrenched the *habeas corpus* jurisdiction of the High Court in terms similar to art. 40.4.2 of Bunreacht na hÉireann. It also provided, however, that 'nothing in this art. contained shall be invoked to prohibit, control or interfere with any act of the military forces of the Irish Free State (Saorstát Éireann) during the existence of a state of war or armed rebellion.' That proviso was subsequently said to have been merely declaratory of the pre-existing law: *R (O'Brien) v. Military Governor of North Dublin Union Internment Camp* [1924] 1 IR 32, Molony CJ at 38.
18 [1924] 1 IR 32.
19 [1935] IR 245.
20 See Lawrence William White, 'O'Brien, Nora Connolly', *DIB*, from which it is evident that Ms Connolly O'Brien never lost her Republican zeal.
21 That the civil courts had jurisdiction to inquire into and determine that question was clear from *R v. Allen* and *R (Garde) v. Strickland* [1921] 2 IR 317.

whether there is or is not that deliberate, organised resistance by force and arms to the laws and operations of the lawful Government, amounting to war or armed rebellion, which justifies what is sometimes called martial law, but which is in fact no law at all, but summary justice administered under the supervision of a military commander.[22]

Placing significant reliance on various public statements made by Éamon de Valera to the effect that the cessation of hostilities was permanent rather than temporary, Molony CJ held that the 'great success of the army' had made the application possible

and just as it was their duty to defeat the rebellion, which they have done, so it is our duty, when the rebellion has been defeated, to restore to the applicant her 'inviolable right of personal liberty,' which we now do by ordering, pursuant to article 6 of the Constitution, a writ of habeas corpus to issue directed to the general Richard Mulcahy, commander-in-chief of the Forces.[23]

The Court of Appeal's judgment was given on 31 July 1923. The attorney general then persuaded the court to direct a formal return to the writ rather than directing the immediate release of the prisoner (as Ronan LJ was inclined to do). Two days later, on 2 August 1923, the governor certified that Ms Connolly O'Brien was detained in military custody in accordance with the provisions of the Public Safety (Emergency Powers) Act 1923. That Act had been enacted the previous day, 1 August 1923 and provided for the continued detention in custody of persons then in military custody. Ms Connolly O'Brien's counsel, Alex Lynn BL – who later unsuccessfully sued General Mulcahy for the loss of his wig and gown and brief bag after they were seized in a military raid[24] – was admirably undaunted by this dramatic development.

Noting that the bill had passed the houses of the Oireachtas only the previous night, Mr Lynn relied on article 47 of the Constitution to contend that the bill was not yet in force, arguing that, in the absence of a declaration that the bill was 'necessary for the immediate preservation of the public peace, health or safety', a period of seven days had to elapse before the governor-general could validly give assent to it.[25] In response, the attorney general

22 *R (O'Brien) v. Military Governor of NDU Internment Camp* [1924] 1 IR 32, at 38–9.
23 Ibid., at 42.
24 *Evening Herald*, 7 Mar. 1924 (accessible on Ruth Cannon BL's excellent website www.ruthcannon.com).
25 Art. 47 provided that any bill passed or deemed to have passed by both Houses might be suspended for a period of 90 days on the written demand of two-fifths of the members of Dáil Éireann or a majority of the members of Seanad Éireann presented to the president of the Executive Council not later than seven days from the day on which the bill was passed or deemed to have been passed. Such a bill might then be submitted by referendum

argued that the assent of the governor general could not be questioned and, the bill having received that assent, the court was bound to assume that it had been properly converted from the bill stage to the Act stage. This was a version of the 'enrolled bill rule', a well-established common law orthodoxy precluding any form of procedural challenge to the validity of an act of parliament once passed by both Houses and given royal assent.

That the attorney should deploy such an argument is rather surprising. In any event, it was robustly rejected by the Court of Appeal. Molony CJ considered that the approach advocated by the government would render article 47 'nugatory'. The application presented 'a grave question – an important question' that the court had to decide 'to the best of our ability, and in this case in favour of the liberty of the subject'.[26] Ronan LJ was even more trenchant. Article 47 was, in his view, 'a very important article of the Constitution', 'the essence and substance' of which was the creation of a referendum. 'A referendum is a most important element in a democratic constitution, and the substance of a referendum is that in certain cases and in certain circumstances the people themselves are to have a vote to determine whether a law shall be passed or not – that the law shall be finally submitted, in the words of this article "to the decision of the people."' The arguments made by the government – in essence, that whether or not there should be a referendum was a matter for the president of the Executive Council – made 'a farce of the entire thing'. The giving of royal assent to a bill within a few hours of its passing the two Houses 'would be an absolute fraud on the Constitution' and accepting the construction of article 47 contended for by the government 'would sweep the referendum out of the Constitution'.[27] If that soaring rhetoric seems familiar, it may be because it seems to anticipate the language later used by the Supreme Court in *McKenna v. An Taoiseach (No. 2)*[28] in relation to article 47 of the 1937 Constitution and the place of the People in the 1937 constitutional settlement.

Accordingly, Ms Connolly O'Brien was released. But there was a further twist. Many other prisoners were in military custody at that point and in order to prevent their release the Oireachtas immediately passed the Public Safety (Emergency Powers) (No. 2) Act 1923, section 1 of which provided that the Public Safety (Emergency Powers) Act 1923 (which was set out in full in a schedule) should immediately come into operation and have the force of law.

---

to the people. Art. 47 did not apply to money bills or to bills declared by both Houses to be '*necessary for the immediate preservation of the public peace, health or safety.*' Art. 47 was deleted from the Constitution by the Constitution (Amendment No. 10) Act 1928, which also deleted art. 48, which provided for the initiation by the people of proposals for laws or constitutional amendments.

26 *R (O'Brien) v. Military Governor of NDU Internment Camp* [1924] 1 IR 32, at 48–9.
27 Ibid., at 50–1.
28 [1995] 2 IR 10.

Section 2 contained the necessary declaration to disapply article 47 and the bill received the immediate assent of the governor general. [29]

In *Attorney General v. McBride*,[30] the High Court (Hanna J) suggested that *R (O'Brien) v. Military Governor* had declared the Public Safety (Emergency Powers) Act 1923 null and void. That does not appear to be correct. The only order made by the Court of Appeal was an order quashing the return to the writ and directing the release of the prisoner and, as we have seen, the Act was subsequently re-enacted. Even so, it is a remarkable decision, not least because the judges who gave it had been stalwarts of the pre-1922 legal regime.

But not everyone was impressed. The anonymous author of an unsigned column in the *Freeman's Journal* observed that the 'authors of the *John Allen* judgment' (a reference to the controversial decision in *R v. Allen*[31] in which Lord Chief Justice Molony had presided) had decided that the war was over and 'as far as the Court [of Appeal] could decree it, the camps were to be thrown open and the ten thousand fighters set free for the dumps.'[32] Fortunately, the author went on, the Oireachtas had intervened by passing the Public Safety bill through its remaining stages. But again 'the judiciary came to the help of the Irregulars' and once again the Oireachtas had had to 'come to the rescue of the citizens of the Irish Free State'. But, the author allowed, there were some compensatory aspects of the situation, one of which was that it was:

> gratifying that even at the twelfth hour the British judiciary in Ireland should have shown a zealous determination to vindicate the rights of the citizen, even though he be a Republican in opposition to the Constitution.[33]

But, whether as a result of such criticism or otherwise, any such 'zealous determination' seems to have rapidly receded. In November 1923, the master of the rolls had little difficulty in rejecting a *habeas corpus* application founded

29 During the debate on the bill in the Dáil, Darrell Figgis – one of the architects of the Constitution – suggested that it would be sufficient compliance with art. 47 to make an *ex post facto* declaration. Responding, Professor William Magennis – a professor of metaphysics in UCD – observed that this suggestion showed that Deputy Figgis was 'not acquainted with the ways of the law courts'. A judge might well 'without going to any great length to discover or invent difficulties' hold that art. 47 required the declaration to accompany and be an integral part of the legislation. What the president proposed (i.e. the inclusion of the declaration in the text of the bill itself) 'puts it out of the power of any logic chopping gentleman, on or off the Bench, to utilise that argument.' *Dáil Éireann deb.*, vol. 4, col. 23 (2 Aug. 1923).
30 [1928] IR 451.
31 [1921] 2 IR 241.
32 *Freeman's Journal*, 3 Aug. 1924, p. 4.
33 Ibid.

on a contention that the Public Safety (Emergency Powers) Act 1923 did not have the force of law because the legislative assembly that had enacted it had not been summoned in accordance with article 24 of the Constitution and, in particular (it was said), the Seanad had not been summoned in the name of the king as it ought to have been. There was no such irregularity in O'Connor MR's view and, even if there had been, the 'three estates in the parliament' – king, Dáil and Seanad – had waived it: *R (Murphy) v. Military Governor, Mountjoy Prison*.[34]

We next come to *R (Cooney) v. Clinton*. It involved a number of *habeas corpus* applications which were heard together, all challenging the legality of detention in military custody pursuant to statutes enacted by the Oireachtas.[35] The only recorded High Court decision relates to O'Connell, who was detained pursuant to the Public Safety (Powers of Arrest and Detention) Temporary Act 1924 (which had been enacted to replace the Public Safety (Emergency Powers) Act 1923 on its expiry): *R (O'Connell) v. Military Governor of Hare Park Camp*.[36] It was argued on his behalf[37] that the Act was contrary to the Constitution, and in particular article 64 (which vests the judicial power in the courts), article 70 (guaranteeing trial in due course of law and prohibiting the establishment of 'extraordinary courts' other than for dealing with military offenders against military law) and article 72 (guaranteeing trial by jury other than in respect of minor offences or offences against military law).

A divisional court (Molony CJ, Dodd and Pim JJ) rejected these arguments, with all of its members emphasising the broad scope of the legislative powers of the Oireachtas. According to Molony CJ, 'within the whole area of the Irish Free State it is a free and unfettered legislature and … there is nothing in the Treaty or the Constitution, or the statutes confirming same, which, limits the power of the Oireachtas to make such a provision as is here impugned.'[38] According to Dodd J, the policy of the Act was a matter for the Oireachtas and not any concern of the court, and the court had to be careful not to overstep the powers conferred on it.[39] A notably formalistic approach was taken to article 6's prescription that 'no person shall be deprived of his liberty except in accordance with law' and to article 70's requirement that 'no one shall be tried save in due course of law'. But that was a feature of the subsequent jurisprudence also, including the majority judgments in *State*

34 (1924) 58 ILTR 1.
35 *R (Cooney) v. Clinton, R (Corcoran) v. Clinton* and *R (O'Connell) v. Military Governor of Hare Park Camp* [1935] IR 245.
36 [1924] 2 IR 104.
37 By, inter alia, George Gavan Duffy BL, who had resigned as a minister in the Provisional Government in protest at the abolition of the Dáil courts and who would go on to become an ordinary judge, and subsequently, president of the High Court.
38 [1924] 2 IR 104, at 111.
39 Ibid., at 117.

(Ryan) v. Lennon.⁴⁰ It should be said, however, that Pim J allowed that a permanent law giving the executive power to deprive any citizen of his liberty without trial would be 'contrary to the spirit of article 6, and therefore a violation of the Constitution' but that, in his view, was 'a very different thing from a temporary law made in abnormal times and for a temporary purpose.'⁴¹

The decision was appealed to the Court of Appeal. The appeal was heard and decided along with *R (Cooney) v. Clinton* and *R (Corcoran) v. Clinton*.⁴² The appeals were heard on 9 April 1923 (just before the enactment of the Courts of Justice Act 1924) and, once again, the state respondents were represented by the attorney general.⁴³ It appears from the newspaper report that the Court of Appeal actually dismissed the appeals at the conclusion of the hearing but indicated that they would give a considered judgment later. It is also evident from the newspaper report that the members of the court all appeared to have considerable difficulty with the attorney general's submission that the impugned legislation did not amend the Constitution but was nonetheless consistent with it.

In *R (Cooney) v. Clinton* the government relied on section 3 of the Indemnity Act 1923 (enacted in August 1923) as having the effect of validating a sentence of imprisonment that had been imposed on the prisoner by a special military tribunal in April 1923. In turn, the prisoner argued that the section violated articles 6, 70 and 72 of the Constitution. O'Connor MR (with whom Ronan and O'Connor LJJ agreed) acknowledged that the argument raised 'a grave constitutional question' though he was 'far from saying that under the Constitution as it stood at the date of the passing of the Indemnity Act there was not power in the Oireachtas to pass such an act without any amendment of the Constitution.' However, it was in his view 'quite unnecessary' to consider that question further, having regard to the terms in which the power of amendment conferred by article 50 of the Constitution was framed. In his opinion:

> It is difficult to see how, during the period of eight years, any Act passed by the Oireachtas can be impeached as *ultra vires* so long as it is within the terms of the scheduled Treaty.

As for the argument that 'any Act of Parliament purporting to amend the Constitution should declare that it was so intended', the master of the rolls was unpersuaded:

40 [1935] IR 170. Bunreacht na hÉireann contains equivalent guarantees in art. 40.4.1 and art. 38.1. After some uncertainty, it is now well-established the references to '*in accordance with law*' and '*in due course of law*' import something more than simply a law enacted by the Oireachtas (see Hogan et al., *Kelly: The Irish Constitution* (5th edn., Dublin, 2018), ch. 7.4 (art. 40.4.1) and ch. 6.5 (art. 38.1).
41 [1924] 2 IR 104, at 118.
42 [1935] IR 245.
43 See the report of the hearing in the *Irish Independent*, 10 Apr. 1924.

I cannot accede to that argument in view of the express provision that any amendment made within the period may be made by ordinary legislation.[44]

The appeal in *R (O'Connell) v. Military Governor*[45] failed on the same basis. The Public Safety (Powers of Arrest and Detention) Temporary Act 1924 was 'no doubt drastic legislation' but was clear in its meaning and had to be observed if it came within the powers of the Oireachtas which in the court's view it did, for the same reasons as in *R (Cooney) v. Clinton*. No separate reasons were given for rejecting the appeal in *R (Corcoran) v. Clinton*.

Article 50 of the Constitution provided that amendments to it could, for a period of eight years, be made by way of ordinary legislation enacted by the Oireachtas and, thereafter, any such amendment had to be submitted to a referendum. At the time that *R (Cooney) v. Clinton* was decided (23 May 1924), the Oireachtas was clearly competent to enact amendments to the Constitution. But it had never exercised its power of amendment (the first amendment Act – the Constitution (Amendment No. 1) Act 1925 – was not passed until 1925) and neither the Indemnity Act 1923 nor the Public Safety (Powers of Arrest and Detention) Temporary Act 1924 purported to amend the Constitution in any respect. But if *R (Cooney) v. Clinton* was correct, the Constitution was largely defunct, certainly as a basis for judicial review of legislation enacted by the Oireachtas. On the Court of Appeal's analysis, if the Oireachtas enacted legislation conflicting with the Constitution, it was the Constitution, rather than the legislation, that would have to yield.

The doctrine of implied amendment did not come entirely out of the blue. During the committee stages of the Public Safety (Emergency Powers) bill 1923, George Gavan Duffy himself had sought to move an amendment to the bill which would have provided that anything in the bill which was found to contravene the rights provisions of the Constitution should be void. He justified the amendment by reference to the possibility that a judge could decide that 'any Act which we pass, not intending to amend the Constitution, does in fact amend it.' However, the amendment had been ruled out of order.[46]

Notwithstanding the master of the rolls' careful statement that he was 'far from saying' that the statutory provisions relied on by the government to justify the detentions were beyond the competence of the Oireachtas, it is difficult to escape the inference that such was his position and that of his colleagues on the court. Were it otherwise, the court would surely have rejected the applications on the same basis as the divisional court, instead of

---

44 [1935] IR 245, at 247.
45 Ibid.
46 *Dáil Éireann deb.*, vol. 4, col. 6 (10 July 1923).

effectively taking a wrecking ball to the Constitution (that had been in operation for less than eighteen months). The court appears to have made an unspoken calculation that that was a better outcome than declaring the state's regime of military detention unconstitutional. If so, that calculation was very questionable. A holding that the detention of the applicants was unlawful because the legislative basis for such detention violated the Constitution would have upheld the integrity of the Constitution and the Oireachtas could, if it considered it appropriate, have passed an Act amending the Constitution to expressly permit the continuance of military detention.

In any event, at the time of these decisions, the Courts of Justice Act 1924 had been enacted but had not yet commenced. On 5 June 1924, Hugh Kennedy resigned as attorney general, preparatory to becoming the new state's first chief justice. In the Dáil on the following day, 6 June 1924, the president of the Executive Council was asked by an opposition TD, Tomás MacEoin, whether he was aware of the decisions and whether he proposed to introduce legislation to amend article 50 'so as ensure its interpretation in accordance with the intention of the Constituent Assembly.'[47] After confirming that he was indeed aware of the decisions, Cosgrave stated that:

> the late Court of Appeal was not competent to define the interpretation of the Constitution. The late attorney general on behalf of the Government refused to submit the question as to whether the Public Safety Act was constitutional or otherwise, and though pressed by the Court, refused to adopt this view that the Public Safety Act amended the Constitution though not purporting to do so expressly. The late attorney-general had advised the Government that the Constitution could not be amended incidentally, but that any amendment by legislation must be by legislation directed expressly to that purpose.
>
> Certain of the judges in the late Court of Appeal, according to my information, were reluctant to recognise the position of Dáil Éireann as a constituent assembly, and pressed upon the late attorney general to argue that the Constitution was itself an ordinary statute and was subject to amendment like an ordinary statute. The late attorney-general in open court unequivocally declined to argue this point of view or submit any contention founded upon it.[48]

The 'late Court of Appeal' referred to here was the Court of Appeal established by the Government of Ireland Act 1920, which was about to pass into history. The 'late attorney general' was, of course, Hugh Kennedy.

---

47 Ibid., vol. 7, col. 21 (6 June 1924).
48 Ibid.

The president's response prompted a follow-up question from Tom Johnson, the leader of the Labour Party and opposition leader. He asked whether there was not at least a possibility – perhaps even a probability – that judges might take the same approach in the future and suggested that it was necessary to deal either with the Constitution or 'with every bill that comes forward' by including in them a statement to the effect that it did not abrogate or affect the Constitution and must be read subject to it.[49] Again, the president was dismissive:

> I fear that that would be implying that there was some foundation for the contention that it would be possible to amend the Constitution by legislation, not expressly directed to that purpose. As regards the first part of the question, I have only got to reiterate that it was not competent for the late Court of Appeal to pronounce upon the Constitution, and that within the Constitution itself there is a provision stating the court which would have the right to interpret it.[50]

The emphatic assertion that the Court of Appeal was not 'competent' to 'pronounce upon the Constitution' is a little surprising. Even if it could perhaps be said to find some plausible basis in the text of the Constitution, the Court of Appeal (and the High Court) had in fact pronounced on the Constitution more than once during the interregnum, without any apparent jurisdictional objection on the part of the government. Furthermore, if the existing courts lacked competence to interpret the Constitution, how were disputes about its meaning and effect to be resolved prior to the establishment of the new court system and how might the rights it conferred on citizens be rendered effective in that period?

In any event, in *R (Cooney) v. Clinton*, the Court of Appeal had indeed 'pronounced' on the effect of article 50 and, unfortunately, the government's dismissal of its pronouncement turned out to be a significant misjudgment.[51] *R (Cooney) v. Clinton* was cited with approval by Murnaghan J in his judgment in *State (Ryan) v. Lennon*. FitzGibbon J, the other judge in the majority, had, in *Lynham v. Butler (No. 2)*,[52] stated a provisional view that 'upon the principle *leges posteriores priores abrogant*, any enactment of the Oireachtas, clearly inconsistent with the Constitution, passed within the

49 As George Gavan Duffy had suggested in respect of the Public Safety (Emergency Provisions) bill 1923.
50 *Dáil Éireann deb.*, vol. 7, col. 21 (6 June 1924).
51 See the discussion in Maurice Collins, 'A new constitution; a new language? How the new courts talked about the Free State Constitution 1922' in Laura Cahillane and Donal Coffey (eds), *The centenary of the Irish Free State Constitution: constituting a polity?* (London, 2024), pp 135–52 as well as J.M. Kelly, *Fundamental rights in the Irish law and Constitution* (Dublin, 1961), pp 4–6.
52 [1933] IR 74.

period during which amendment of the Constitution by ordinary legislation is permitted, should be construed as an amendment *pro tanto.*'[53] His judgment in *State (Ryan) v. Lennon* was consistent with that approach.

I do not mean to suggest that the doctrine of 'implied amendment' was, in itself, the entire undoing of the Free State Constitution. The position was much more complex. The Constitution's fatal flaw was more fundamental, namely that article 50 provided for its amendment by ordinary legislation (for a very period of eight years), without immunising itself from amendment in that manner (a lesson learned by the framers of the 1937 Constitution). But a very significant part of the problem was that courts – both the existing courts and those established by the Courts of Justice Act 1924 – accepted, without much or any resistance, the proposition that article 50 did not require the Oireachtas to make clear its intention to amend or frame amendments in clear and express textual terms (exemplified by the Public Safety Act 1927, challenged unsuccessfully in *Attorney General v. McBride*,[54] as well as article 2A, at issue in *State (Ryan) v. Lennon*).[55]

Although decided on 23 May 1924, *R (Cooney) v. Clinton* was not reported until 1935.[56] It was not referred to in *Attorney General v. McBride* and, it seems, may have been overlooked for a period.[57] In any event, the new High Court of Justice and the Supreme Court of Justice (as well as the Court of Criminal Appeal) were established as and from 5 June 1924, with the new judges being 'sworn in' in Dublin Castle on 11 June 1924.[58] Only two of the serving senior court judges were asked to serve in the new courts, including the former master of the rolls, now to be a judge of the new Supreme Court.[59]

At last, the new state had 'a system of judiciary and an administration of law and justice [constructed] according to the dictates of our own needs and after a pattern of our own designing.' In the ringing words of the new chief justice, the moment had arrived 'when, after a week of centuries, Irish courts, fashioned in freedom by an Oireachtas again assembled, are thrown open to administer justice according to laws made in Ireland by free Irish citizens for the well-being of our dearly-loved land and its people.'[60]

53 Ibid., at 112.
54 [1928] IR 451.
55 See the discussion in Kelly, *Fundamental rights*, pp 4–6.
56 When it was reported as a note to *State (Ryan) v. Lennon* [1935] IR 170.
57 Leo Kohn, *The Constitution of the Irish Free State* (London, 1932) contains a discussion, pp 245–6, of the implied amendment doctrine from which it is apparent that the author had not seen the decision of the Court of Appeal. Given the involvement of Hugh Kennedy in the work (he wrote the foreword, from which it is clear that he had read the work in manuscript several times as it was being revised and rewritten), that is somewhat curious.
58 See Ronan Keane, 'The voice of the Gael: Chief Justice Kennedy and the emergence of the new Irish court system 1921–1936', *Ir. Jur.*, 31 (1996), 205–25.
59 Ruane, 'Régime change', at 108.
60 Remarks in Dublin Castle on 11 June 1924: see 'The Irish Free State judiciary – new courts opened', 58 *I.L.T.&S.J.* (1924), 151, at 152.

Regrettably, the reality was rather different. The 'laws made in Ireland' subsequent to June 1924 were often draconian in nature and the Constitution that all the judges of the new courts swore to uphold proved wholly inadequate to protect citizens against such laws. The seeds of self-destruction within the Constitution first identified in *R (Cooney) v. Clinton* led ultimately to *State (Ryan) v. Lennon* and the final implosion of the Constitution, and the constitutional democracy it had sought to establish.

As Bláthna Ruane has observed, the judges of the former Crown courts:

> made a valuable contribution in enabling the official courts system to continue in operation in enormously difficult circumstances, at real risk to themselves. This helped to provide some degree of stability and affirmation of the importance of the rule of law at a critical and turbulent moment. But in the end, this did not save them.[61]

It is important to assess their legacy fairly. Undoubtedly – and unsurprisingly – their limited constitutional jurisprudence exhibits a positivist approach (exemplified by the divisional court's decision in *O'Connell*). The notion of a fundamental law imposing significant constraints on the legislative competence of parliament was no doubt alien and unfamiliar to judges and practitioners alike. But it must be acknowledged that such was a feature of both post-1924 jurisprudence and early post-1937 constitutional jurisprudence also.[62] The doctrine of implied amendment reflected common law principle, expressed in the Latin phrase *leges posteriors priores contrarias abrogant*. But, far from repudiating the relevance of such a principle to a Constitution enshrining fundamental rights, the new courts endorsed and applied it – with varying degrees of enthusiasm – in *Attorney General v. McBride* and *State (Ryan) v. Lennon*.

The reality is that Irish lawyers – and, in consequence, the judges drawn from their ranks – were generally conversative in their legal philosophy.[63] In 1932 – well after the establishment of the new courts – Hugh Kennedy was still hoping for 'the emancipation of our schools of law and political studies from the thraldom which has made them negligible wraiths'.[64] That hope was not fulfilled in his lifetime. In truth, the establishment of the new courts, while hugely significant in terms of creating a court system that had political legitimacy and enjoyed the confidence and trust of government and citizen

---

61 Ruane, 'Régime change', at 14.
62 Not least in the first reference under art. 26 of the 1937 Constitution, *Re Article 26 and the Offences Against the State (Amendment) Bill 1940* [1940] IR 470.
63 See in this context the discussion in Donal Coffey, 'The judiciary of the Irish Free State', *Dublin University Law Journal*, 33:1 (2011), 61–74 and in Laura Cahillane, *Drafting the Irish Free State Constitution* (Manchester, 2016), pp 174–6.
64 Foreword to Kohn, *The Constitution*, p. xiii.

alike, did not result in any significant shift in constitutional jurisprudence in the Free State. The decision in *O'Brien* remained an outlier and the Constitution continued to be largely ineffective. It was to be many decades before the state saw any real signs of a 'constitutional spring' and then only after the adoption of a new Constitution in 1937.

CHAPTER FIVE

Comfortably housed? The law courts at Dublin Castle, 1923–31

EVAN McGUIGAN*

On 27 May 1931, an official from the Office of Public Works (OPW) – the body charged with maintaining government buildings – arrived at the state apartments of Dublin Castle to carry out an inspection. For the preceding eight years, the apartments and other portions of the complex had been used by the Irish Free State to temporarily house the newly established Supreme, High and Circuit Courts. The arrival of the OPW official, however, signalled the beginning of the end of the courts' run at the Castle.

The reconstruction and reopening of the Four Courts, the state's primary judicial complex, was now nearing actualisation. The official had been seemingly delegated to consult with the chief justice, Hugh Kennedy, on what furniture he wanted transferred to the courts' soon-to-be permanent home. But there was an immediate problem upon their meeting; the chief justice had not been notified regarding the official's arrival at the Castle, nor of the impending nature of the courts' relocation across the river. Kennedy was shocked that he was out of the loop and issued a letter directly to the minister for justice, James FitzGerald-Kenney, venting his frustration over the lack of communication 'from anybody whatsoever' regarding the Four Courts' re-opening and demanding further information 'as soon as possible'.[1] For the chief justice, this episode represented a reversal of roles compared to the run up to the law courts' move to the Castle in 1923, when he had been firmly involved in most of the key decisions undertaken throughout.

The rationale for the presence of the courts in Dublin Castle during this period is well known. The opening salvos of the Irish Civil War in June 1922 saw the near-total destruction of the Four Courts. Artillery fire and a massive explosion had reduced most of the complex to a smoking ruin and left thousands of legal documents, both live and archival, with the consistency of

---
* Historian and former guide and information officer for the Office of Public Works at Dublin Castle. I would like to thank Niamh Howlin for the opportunity to contribute to this publication, and my family, Laura Fitzachary, Jack Penders and James Treanor for their help during the researching, writing and editing process.
1 Hugh Kennedy to James FitzGerald-Kenney, 29 May 1931, NAI OPW/5/13930/31.

'the finest powder'.[2] The legal profession in the city found themselves immediately on the hunt for new accommodation, and a decision was reached by the Provisional Government – with Kennedy attending in his capacity as the government law officer – in September to relocate them to the Castle grounds.

While events up until this point have been well-documented,[3] the story behind the facilitation of the judicial system at Dublin Castle has been relatively under-examined – although recent work from William Derham and Niamh Howlin has touched upon elements of the transfer.[4] This chapter builds upon this research and dedicates itself fully to showcasing how the temporary arrangement came into practice. It will also investigate how the likes of Kennedy and other judges, as well as state officials, politicians and OPW architects, grappled with hosting the judicial arm of the newly independent regime in a building with the historical 'associations'[5] of Dublin Castle, which had functioned for centuries as the nerve centre of British rule in Ireland.

The Four Courts is naturally viewed as the principal residence of the Irish judiciary today, but it is also arguable that Dublin Castle carries a weighty claim as the courts' ancestral home. Commissioned to be built in August 1204 by King John of England following the Anglo-Norman invasion, the original medieval fortress was indeed crafted with the 'administration of justice' specifically in mind.[6] In November of that year King John introduced several English judicial writs and mandated that they run throughout Ireland.[7] The lord deputy, in his role as the representative of the monarch in Ireland, was later installed to act as the head of the Dublin Castle administration and have his authority exercised by the lords justices during his absence from the island. The construction of the fortress was not completed until 1230,[8] but the intention had already been made clear; administrative, financial and judicial matters concerning Dublin and the Pale were to be centralised within its stone walls. Symbolically, these functions cemented the Castle's reputation as the centre point of English influence in Ireland.

Alterations to the Castle continued throughout the Middle Ages, with records from the period referencing a great hall located against the west

2 Constantine P. Curran to Hugh Kennedy, 3 July 1922, NAI AGE/2002/16/475.
3 Michael Fewer, *The battle of the Four Courts* (London, 2018) encompasses the opening days of the Civil War with a focus on the events at Inns Quays and its immediate aftermath.
4 William Derham, '(Re)making majesty: the throne room at Dublin Castle, 1911–2011' in Myles Campbell and William Derham (eds), *Making majesty: the throne room at Dublin Castle, a cultural history* (Kildare, 2017), pp 281–5; Niamh Howlin, *Barristers in Ireland: an evolving profession since 1921* (Dublin, 2023), pp 31–3 and 213–18.
5 Memo. to min. finance, 31 Aug. 1922, NAI TSCH/S1669A.
6 Conleth Manning, '"But you are first to build a tower" – the Bermingham Tower, Dublin Castle', *Ulster Journal of Archaeology*, 74 (2017), 145–54.
7 Colin Veach and Tadhg O'Keeffe, 'King John and the origins of colonial rule in Ireland', *History Ireland*, 24:4 (2016), 24.
8 Seán Duffy, John Montague, Kevin Mulligan & Michael O'Neill, *Dublin Castle: from fortress to palace, vol. 1* (Dublin, 2022), p. 28.

curtain wall from which the courts operated. A plan of Dublin Castle drawn up by Thomas Watson in 1606 vividly demonstrates this layout, showcasing a hall with the four superior courts – Exchequer, Chancery, King's Bench and Common Pleas – located at each of its corners.[9] But by the time the island came under English rule to a fuller degree, the courts had largely vacated the premises. They were moved on to grounds next to Christ Church Cathedral in the early 1600s and then eventually to their purpose-built home on Inns Quay by 1796.[10]

The medieval stronghold of Dublin Castle, meanwhile, was largely destroyed by a fire in April 1684 before being gradually rebuilt throughout the eighteenth century into its current iteration; a Georgian palace with spacious ceremonial rooms.[11] The state apartments – the site's new focal point – acted as the centre of the viceregal court in Ireland as well as an official residence of the Irish lord lieutenant, the British king's representative and head of the executive in Ireland, while the surrounding myriad of office blocks accommodated business associated with governance, taxation, police, intelligence and the military. Louis Paul-Dubois, the French writer, summed the complex up in 1908 as 'the centre and symbol of government ... that veiled, anonymous, and all-powerful institution, housed in the old fortress, which stands solidly on high ground in the heart of the capital, half-screened by a curtain of business houses'.[12]

It is highly possible that Dublin Castle's historical gravity crossed the minds of those who attended the Provisional Government meetings in mid-1922 as they discussed where to house the law courts in the aftermath of the Four Courts' shelling. Hugh Kennedy was undoubtedly aware of its significance, especially having been previously critical of judicial operations under the rule of the Dublin Castle administration during the revolutionary period. Ties between the Irish executive and the Irish bench had been close pre-Independence; judges were frequently members of the Privy Council, who participated in the making of executive orders to implement British rule in Ireland.[13] Kennedy had once remarked that 'a judge might drop into the Castle in the morning on his way to court and as part of the executive make an order in council and then go to the bench and try an issue between the executive and the people'.[14] Now, Kennedy had the Castle in his sights once more.

9 Thomas Watson, 'Plan of the Castle of Dublin', 1606, NLI MS 2656 (18). See also J.B. Maguire, 'Seventeenth-century plans of Dublin Castle', *The Journal of the Royal Society of Antiquaries of Ireland*, 104 (1974), 5–14.
10 Colum Kenny, 'The Four Courts in Dublin before 1796', *Ir. Jur.*, 21:1 (1986), 107–24.
11 Duffy et al., *Dublin Castle: from fortress to palace*, pp 124–6.
12 Louis Paul-Dubois, *Contemporary Ireland* (Dublin, 1908), p. 187.
13 David Foxton, *Revolutionary lawyers: Sinn Féin and Crown courts in Ireland and Britain, 1916–1923* (Dublin, 2008), p. 18.
14 Thomas Towey, 'Hugh Kennedy and the constitutional development of the Irish Free State, 1922–1923', *Ir. Jur.*, 12:2 (1977), 355–70, at 366.

But as influential as Kennedy was, it was perhaps Michael Collins, the minister for finance and chairperson of the Provisional Government, who played the most significant role regarding the transfer. Both men had developed a close working relationship by this point – Collins once remarked to W.T. Cosgrave after the Anglo-Irish Treaty negotiations that he wished Kennedy had been part of the Irish delegation.[15] Collins had long held the Castle in his sights too, as typified by the guerrilla campaign he led against the administration's intelligence apparatus during the War of Independence,[16] and revelled in the handover ceremony of January 1922: 'I am as happy a man as there is in Ireland today ... Have just taken over Dublin Castle'.[17]

In May, the Provisional Government requested a detailed report from the OPW regarding the accommodation available at the Castle as the scramble for office space from various state departments intensified.[18] Dublin Castle was highly coveted, both due to its central location and the fact that it was one of the few large-scale complexes to survive significant bombardment in the preceding decade of turbulence. The report produced a month later recommended that the most 'economical and satisfactory' use for the Castle was in fact as a house for the future Free State parliament.[19] Correspondence from the Ministry of Finance to the OPW shortly afterwards, however, accentuated Collins's influence in the matter;

> Mr Collins is taking a personal interest in the disposition of the accommodation available in the Castle and the recent Office of Works' report to the secretary to the Provisional Government is being brought up for his personal decision. He has, however, told O'Brien that under no circumstances whatever is any department to be placed into the Castle until he has given his decision and O'Brien wishes me to communicate this to you.[20]

Some of those departments in the running – Labour, Inland Revenue and the Post Office – were granted the green light by Collins to move in by June.[21] But the destruction at Inns Quay altered the situation further. Kennedy pressed forward the urgency of the legal profession's case at a Provisional Government meeting on 31 July, where it was arranged that he would inspect the remaining space available at the Castle. Another report was furnished to

15 Margery Forrester, *Michael Collins: the lost leader* (Dublin, 2006), p. 282.
16 Michael T. Foy, *Michael Collins's intelligence war* (Gloucestershire, 2008), pp 292–9.
17 Meda Ryan, *Michael Collins and the women who spied for Ireland* (Cork, 1996), p. 145.
18 Diarmuid O'Hegarty, sec. Provisional Govt., to the OPW, 23 May 1922, NAI OPW [5]25374/25.
19 Report on the utilization of Dublin Castle for govt. offices, 18 June 1922, NAI OPW [5]25374/25.
20 Sec. min. finance to Sir Phillip Hanson, 16 June 1922, NAI OPW [5]25374/25.
21 Report on accommodation for head quarters Post Office work, 26 June 1922, NAI TSCH/S1669A.

the Ministry of Finance at the end of August, mere days after Collins's assassination in Cork, acknowledging that an arrangement of a 'quasi permanent nature' was needed for the courts and that the state apartments of Dublin Castle were 'admirably suited for the purpose'.[22] Curiously, the report also felt the need to reference the potential historical constraints involved in this transfer, adding that:

> The only argument that can be made against the proposal – and it is an argument of doubtful validity – is the objection on sentimental grounds to providing for the administration of justice in buildings with the peculiar associations of Dublin Castle.[23]

These sentimental grounds ended up holding no sway. The report was immediately submitted to the Provisional Government, now chaired by Cosgrave, another of Kennedy's allies. On 13 September it was formally agreed that the law courts would be granted a temporary home at the Castle, with the move announced publicly in the Dáil by the minister of home affairs, Kevin O'Higgins, the following day.[24]

The news was favourably received, with the *Irish Independent* declaring the Castle as the 'ideal place' for the law courts and forecasting 'cordial approval' for the decision.[25] While the *Irish Independent* may have captured the mood in legal circles, its prediction that the transfer would be effected by November that year proved wide of the mark. The lord chief justice of Ireland, Sir Thomas Francis Molony (who was directly involved in the planning for the courts' relocation), had also been hopeful of a swift execution of the planned proposals and was evidently keen to return the day-to-day business of the courts to some semblance of normality.

Since the seizure of the Four Courts by anti-Treaty forces in April, the courts had been provided with improvised lodgings in the King's Inns and rented offices in Westmoreland and Molesworth Street.[26] This arrangement had proved to be deeply unsatisfactory. Space at the respective venues was limited to such an extent that Molony ended up facilitating staff of the Minors' Office at his own house for six months, writing wearily to the OPW in October: 'I think the time has come to resume the privacy of my own home'.[27] Although Molony's original hope of a 26 October start date at the Castle was never realised, he did successfully petition for a section of office space on the

22 Memo. to min. finance, 31 Aug. 1922, NAI TSCH/S1669A.
23 Ibid.
24 Notes from meeting of Provisional Govt., 14 Sept. 1922, NAI TSCH/S1669A.
25 *Irish Independent*, 18 Sept. 1922.
26 Ronan Keane, 'A mass of crumbling ruins: the destruction of the Four Courts in June 1922' in Caroline Costello (ed.), *The Four Courts: 200 years* (Dublin, 1996), p. 161.
27 Lord chief justice to Sir Phillip Hanson, 11 Oct. 1922, NAI OPW/5 20375/23.

ground level of the state apartments to be granted that same month to some of his personnel ahead of a formal opening the following year.[28]

Amid Molony's requests, the OPW were preparing a skeletal layout for the law courts in the dormant apartment rooms. Its chairman, Sir Phillip Hanson, was centrally involved in both preparing Dublin Castle for the arrival of the courts and for overseeing the entirety of the judges' stay there. Hanson was already acutely familiar with the Castle grounds; he had worked there between 1898 and 1903 as the private secretary to George Wyndham, who had served as the under-secretary of state for war and then chief secretary for Ireland.[29] He commissioned Harry Allberry, a deputy principal architect within the OPW, to draw up the initial plan for the transfer. Allberry had two decades of experience in the OPW behind him[30] and, like Hanson, had been seconded from the board to the Ministry of Munitions[31] during the First World War, a stint that resulted in Hanson's knighthood in 1920.[32]

The first draft that Allberry provided to Hanson on 5 October proved to be a close match to the layout that was eventually agreed upon. The Privy Council chamber, where Lord FitzAllan Howard had formally installed the Provisional Government during the handover ceremony with Collins less than ten months prior, was to be fitted out as court no. 1. The drawing room would be partitioned to accommodate court no. 2 and court no. 3. The throne room, graced previously by King George IV and Queen Victoria during royal visits to the country, was to be repurposed as court no. 4. Allberry also earmarked the round supper room, which lay directly above the old base of the Bermingham tower, for court no. 5, although plans for a sixth court in an adjoining room seemingly fell by the wayside soon after his report.[33]

Some of Allberry's other suggestions were explicitly rejected. He had mooted the chapel royal – the Anglican chapel of the lord lieutenant affixed to the record tower in the Castle's lower courtyard – as a potential venue for the law library. The gothic revival-styled place of worship was originally constructed at the start of the nineteenth century under the direction of Francis Johnston for a then-colossal sum of £50,000.[34] But now the building was left empty and purposeless following the lord lieutenant's departure. Kennedy, with the apparent backing of 'various members of the Bar', viewed Allberry's idea as unsuitable given the chapel's 'remoteness' from the state apartments in the upper courtyard.[35] He expanded on his reasoning several

28 Hanson to lord chief justice, 20 Oct. 1922, NAI OPW/5 20375/23.
29 *Irish Times*, 25 Oct. 1955.
30 Linde Lunney, 'Allberry, Harry', *DIB*.
31 *Irish Builder*, 28 Apr. 1917.
32 *London Gazette*, 30 Dec. 1919.
33 Report on the proposed transfer of law courts to the Castle by Harry Allberry, 5 Oct. 1922, NAI OPW/5 20375/23.
34 William Derham, 'Chapel royal, Dublin Castle', *History Ireland*, 25:1 (2017), 35.
35 Note on the courts at the Castle from Sir Phillip Hanson, 18 Oct. 1922, NAI OPW/5 20375/23.

months later, writing that he had 'objected to it being turned to secular uses while the possibility of its being consecrated remained a question, as it still is'.[36] This would not be the last time where Kennedy would adopt a delicate approach with regard to Dublin Castle's nuanced background. The law library itself would end up being fitted in St Patrick's hall, contrary to the original suggestion from Allberry that the prestigious former ballroom be used merely as a foyer.

Deliberations on the proposed layout continued into January 1923. A plan made by the OPW architects and Molony was presented to Kennedy that same month for some final amendments[37] before being finally approved on 5 February.[38] Some of Kennedy's last-minute revisions included securing a more spacious office for the chief justice's secretary[39] and ensuring that the courtroom doors were marked by their allocated numbers, as opposed to the specific court held within.[40] The work to prepare the state apartments for the law courts was now ramped up; but while these renovations were not structurally invasive, many practical obstacles remained. Boilers and lighting were found to be in poor condition and many of the staircases and walls were remarked upon as being dirty and worn-looking,[41] most likely as a result of the Red Cross military hospital held in them during the First World War[42] and the turmoil experienced on site throughout the War of Independence.[43] The months leading up to the courts' opening also saw Kennedy and Hanson exchange numerous letters regarding furniture. Kennedy regularly went into detail on what he viewed as the type of desks, benches and chairs most appropriate for judicial business, lamenting how previous library seating had resulted in a 'disastrous effect on the Bar robes'.[44]

The courts finally opened their doors to the public at Dublin Castle in time for the Easter sittings on Wednesday 11 April 1923.[45] Once inside, attendees were greeted with courtrooms that consisted largely of oak benches, desks and an array of seating, some with temporary spatial partitions inserted. The *Irish Law Times and Solicitors' Journal* noted that the architecture of the rooms had been left largely unaltered and described the spaces as 'attractive and artistic in appearance'.[46]

36 Hugh Kennedy to min. local govt., 21 July 1923, UCDA P4/795.
37 Kennedy to Hanson, 2 Feb. 1923, NAI OPW/5 20375/23.
38 Extract from minutes of meeting of committee on accommodation for govt. departments, 5 Feb. 1923, NAI OPW/5 20375/23.
39 Kennedy to Hanson, 24 Jan. 1923, NAI OPW/5 20375/23.
40 Kennedy to Hanson, 2 Feb. 1923, NAI OPW/5 20375/23.
41 H.G. Leask to chairman of the OPW, 13 Jan. 1923, NAI OPW/5 20375/23.
42 Sylvie Kleinman and Aodhán Ó'Raghailligh, 'Scenes of gaiety now filled with beds', *History Ireland*, 24:4 (2016), 6–7.
43 David Neligan, *The spy in the Castle* (London, 1999), pp 121–4. See also Michael Hopkinson (ed.), *The last days of Dublin Castle: the Mark Sturgis diaries* (Kildare, 1999).
44 Kennedy to Hanson, 12 Mar. 1923, NAI OPW/5/21612/23.
45 *I.L.T.&S.J.*, 57 (1923), 93.
46 Ibid.

Some telling changes had been enacted on certain aspects of the apartment rooms – not least the throne room, which had the royal symbols on the top of the throne canopy, as well as the throne itself, removed and placed into storage.[47] These symbolic pieces, which included the crown and the English lion and Scottish unicorn holding respective shields bearing the Irish harp, were conveyed to the Office of Arms for safe-keeping and eventually returned to the room by 1963 upon its renovation.[48] The numerous paintings of lord lieutenants that had adorned the portrait gallery were similarly extracted[49] as it was divided into three separate rooms for clerks and associates.[50] These amendments clearly mirrored the political climate of the time, as well as the impending arrival of a new judicial order. The shadow of the Castle's history was difficult to evade however, and indeed was referenced at the first jury case held on site on 17 April 1923. When summing up evidence to the jury for *Moult v. Mangan*, Arthur Samuels, a High Court justice and former Unionist MP, 'recalled the fact that this was the first trial that had taken place in the Castle for the last 270 years, or, perhaps, a little more'.[51]

Certain reminders of the Castle's past were not as easy to censor, with the most noticeable example being the three large ceiling paintings in St Patrick's hall. Commissioned by George Grenville, the marquis of Buckingham, in 1787 and painted by Italian artist Vincenzo Wáldre, its central piece is an allegorical representation of King George III flanked by the figures of Britannia and Hibernia in a baroque style. The two other neoclassical paintings depict the paying of homage to King Henry II upon his arrival to Ireland in 1171 and the lighting of the paschal fire by St Patrick at Slane. Grenville had supervised the design and subject matter of these works closely, which were clearly conceived to extoll the virtues and benefits of the links between Great Britain and Ireland.[52] The hall continued to display several ornaments associated with the Castle's previous role as the viceregal court in Ireland, including the banners hung from the top of the walls on either side of the hall bearing family crests of members of the Order of St Patrick[53] – an exclusive Irish knighthood instituted in 1783.[54] The symbol of this chivalric

47 Leask to chairman of the OPW, 2 Feb. 1923, NAI OPW/5 20375/23. The theme of symbolism in the courts during this period is explored further in Mark Coen's chapter.
48 Derham, '(Re)making majesty', pp 294–8.
49 Report on the decoration of the law courts, 17 July 1923, NAI OPW/5/11880/25. See also Róisín Kennedy, *Dublin Castle art* (Dublin, 2010), p. 49.
50 *Freeman's Journal*, 10 Apr. 1923.
51 *I.L.T.&S.J.*, 57 (1923), 95.
52 Kennedy, *Dublin Castle art*, pp 19–23.
53 *Irish Independent*, 14 Jan. 1931.
54 Michael Casey, 'The most illustrious Order of Saint Patrick', *Dublin Historical Record*, 44:2 (1991), 4–8. See also Peter Galloway, *The most illustrious order: the Order of St Patrick and its knights* (London, 1999), pp 11–25.

order, the eight-pointed star, also remained in place at the edges of the ceiling. It was underneath these paintings and emblems that the law library would be based and where its numerous visitors would conduct their work throughout the courts' eight-year stay at the Castle.[55]

Kennedy's determination to present a reformed and independent legal system to the wider public may have jarred with certain aspects of the venue in which the courts were operating, but he appears to have adopted a considerate approach to all shades of the Castle's heritage. He lobbied for jury trials to not be held in the throne room, claiming that it was 'likely to suffer'[56] from such use. Hanson, however, largely brushed aside these protestations.[57] In 1924, upon hearing of an alleged attempt to sell off relics and records based in the complex to foreign buyers, Kennedy immediately voiced his concerns directly to Cosgrave: 'I consider the preservation of our national antiquities of whatever kind a matter of national and historical importance'.[58] His fondness of the building was also evident in a Christmas card issued by his office in 1924, portraying a monk writing a manuscript backdropped by the Castle's tricolour-bearing record tower and chapel royal.[59]

While the opening of the courts for business in April 1923 had been a low-key event, Kennedy ensured that this was not the case the following year when the passing of the Courts of Justice Act 1924 established a new judicial system for the Irish Free State. The inauguration of the new judiciary, devised largely by Kennedy himself,[60] took place on 11 June 1924 in Dublin Castle. The *Irish Times* recounted how crowds gathered in the Castle yards and watched from windows and balconies as Kennedy, the new chief justice, led the incoming judges, all dressed in morning suits and silk hats, past a guard of honour from the south-east corner of the upper yard and up to the throne room.[61] The chief justice's speech, which was delivered in Irish and English, declared that 'this is surely a precious moment – the moment when the silence of the Gael in the courts of law is broken'. Now, it was the 'voice of the Gael' that would be heard in the courts of Ireland.[62] The ceremony was a crowning moment for both Kennedy and Cosgrave and represented 'an important symbolic step' for the state,[63] as well as another milestone in Dublin Castle's transformation under the new regime.

55   *Irish Times*, 24 Oct. 1923.
56   Kennedy to min. finance, 4 Jan. 1924, UCDA P4/1052.
57   Hanson to min. finance, 8 Jan. 1924, NAI OPW/5/11880/25.
58   Kennedy to Cosgrave, 15 Oct. 1924, UCDA P4/1341.
59   Christmas card, 1924, UCDA P4/69.
60   Ronan Keane, 'The voice of the Gael: Chief Justice Kennedy and the emergence of the new Irish court system 1921–1936', *Ir. Jur.*, 31 (1996), 205–25, at 221.
61   *Irish Times*, 21 June 1924. Footage of this procession can also be viewed courtesy of British Pathé, 'New Irish Courts (1924)'.
62   *Freeman's Journal*, 12 June 1924.
63   Ruadhán Mac Cormaic, *The Supreme Court* (Dublin, 2016), p. 32.

However, even in the moment of the judiciary's triumph, debate regarding the long-term use of Dublin Castle continued to rumble on. The Dáil debated a report from the Joint Committee on Temporary Accommodation for the Oireachtas on 10 July, a month after the ceremony. A permanent settlement for the housing of government business at Leinster House had not yet been reached and the report had recommended that Dublin Castle would represent the only 'suitable alternative' should the first choice fall through.[64] Many deputies were wary of disturbing the current arrangement for the courts and of a potential backlash from the legal profession.[65] For some, such as the Labour Party's William Davin, the Castle's 'historical associations' rendered it as a problematic option.[66] The Farmers' Party leader Denis Gorey, on the other hand, was not at all concerned about such qualms: 'Dublin Castle stands for the present. It stands for victory; it stands for triumph'.[67] Gorey's thinking was perhaps predictive of future attitudes in political circles to the Castle – particularly from the time of the first Fianna Fáil government onwards – but despite his enthusiasm, Leinster House was confirmed as the permanent home for the Oireachtas later that year.

By the time of these debates, it had already been largely acknowledged that the courts' relocation to the Castle had been a successful enterprise. Molony wrote in May 1923 to Hanson to commend the OPW on its efforts and declare the judges as 'very comfortable' with the arrangement.[68] But the transition was not without teething problems. Of particular concern was the round room; stamping machinery associated with the Inland Revenue Department was situated directly underneath this room and generating aural disturbance[69] to such an extent that Molony floated the idea of abandoning it as a court room altogether.[70] Although business would continue in court no. 5, it did expedite the need for a sixth court room. George's hall, located in the western portion of the upper yard buildings and built as a supper hall for the July 1911 visit of King George V, was earmarked for this very purpose. Kennedy pushed in early 1924 for the hall to be swiftly furnished but was again blocked by Hanson who declared the work 'not urgent'.[71] By September, the need for the hall was deemed urgent enough for £1,700 to be signed off for the associated works.[72] This amount was on top of the £20,000 originally allocated by the Ministry of Finance for the courts' transfer.[73]

64 *Dáil Éireann deb.*, vol. 8, col. 9 (10 July 1924).
65 *Freeman's Journal*, 3 May 1924.
66 *Dáil Éireann deb.*, vol. 8, col. 9 (10 July 1924).
67 Ibid.
68 Molony to Hanson, 4 May 1923, NAI OPW/5/11880/25.
69 Commissioners of public works to min. finance, 20 Oct. 1923, NAI OPW/5/11880/25.
70 Molony to Hanson, 4 May 1923, NAI OPW/5/11880/25.
71 Hanson to min. finance, 8 Jan. 1924, NAI OPW/5/11880/25.
72 Commissioners of Public Works to min. finance, 13 Sept. 1924, NAI OPW/5/11880/25.
73 Commissioners of Public Works to min. finance, 20 Oct. 1923, NAI OPW/5/11880/25.

The law courts' footprint extended to further portions of the complex. The Bedford tower, situated directly opposite the state apartments and formerly utilised as the Castle's main guard building, facilitated the winding-up of the Dáil courts; its remaining civil cases were partially concluded at the Castle before being allocated to the High Court in 1925.[74] The chapel royal was also eventually utilised – against Kennedy's wishes – for Circuit Court sittings in April 1927.[75] Although initially a temporary measure, its use as a court was renewed in 1928 and continued until September 1931.[76] The OPW again endeavoured to make sure their work did not interfere with the building's structural or historical integrity, as well as 'the rich beauty of the ornamentation'.[77]

Structural issues did, however, become an issue in the state apartments. Hanson and Allberry identified 'considerable' damage to the roof in August 1928 and commissioned urgent repairs to be carried out,[78] but work was postponed until 1930 due to the disappointing response to tenders.[79] The restoration was insufficient to prevent stormwater bursting through the ceiling during a High Court sitting held by James Creed Meredith on 15 July 1931 – Meredith ensured the safety of court documents first before evacuating the attendees.[80] By this stage though, work on the new Four Courts complex was almost complete and the government and OPW were already preparing for the Castle's future once the judges were relocated. The idea of using the apartment rooms for state receptions and entertainment had been raised in 1930[81] by various state departments, with External Affairs keen to end the practice of hosting such events at 'inconvenient' venues such as hotels and restaurants.[82]

The transfer of the law courts from the Castle back to the Four Courts was again largely organised by the OPW, although the Department of Justice was also given significant latitude on this occasion. With various targeted dates having fallen by the wayside, a planned reopening in time for the Michaelmas sittings came into view in early 1931.[83] A strike within the building trade briefly threatened to derail this plan and, along with the OPW's intent to

---

74 Mary Kotsonouris, *The winding up of the Dáil courts, 1922–1925: an obvious duty* (Dublin, 2004), pp 71–2 and 75. The history of the Dáil courts is addressed in Thomas Mohr's chapter.
75 *Irish Times*, 26 Apr. 1927.
76 Memo. on the chapel royal's use as a court, 10 May 1932, NAI TSCH/S5410.
77 *Irish Times*, 14 Apr. 1927.
78 Hanson to Harry Allberry, 1 Aug. 1928, NAI OPW/5/11819/30.
79 Note from Sir Phillip Hanson, 18 Apr. 1930, NAI OPW/5/11819/30.
80 *Irish Times*, 16 July 1931.
81 OPW to Dept. of the President, 17 May 1930, NAI TSCH/S1669A.
82 Dept. External Affairs to committee of allocation of premises in Upper Castle, 1 May 1931, NAI TSCH/S1669A.
83 Report on the Four Courts occupation, 28 Apr. 1931, NAI OPW/5 13930/31.

seemingly keep its cards close to its chest on the issue, appears to have led to the misunderstanding between Kennedy and the OPW official on 27 May regarding progress on the move.[84] A high workload with court business meant that Kennedy was not heavily involved in the transfer, and he was also frustrated in his efforts to secure an elaborate ceremonial opening of the Four Courts. The Department of Justice felt unable to sanction such an event owing to financial constraints as well as security concerns over anti-Treaty elements.[85] Work commenced in July to transport roughly 10,000 books of law and associated documents from St Patrick's hall to the rebuilt Four Courts library,[86] and a First World War memorial that had been erected in the state apartments in 1924 to commemorate members of the Bar who perished in the fighting was later relocated in September.[87] The reopening of the Four Courts took place on 12 October with a modest religious service and some low-key speeches, during which Hanson received the chief justice's congratulations for the restoration work.[88]

The business of the law courts resumed apace, while Dublin Castle – which had broadly succeeded in its mission, as described by the *Irish Independent*, to 'comfortably' accommodate the judges[89] – continued its transition under successive Irish governments. The Castle was utilised for the Eucharistic Congress a year after the law courts' exit[90] and hosted numerous foreign dignitaries and state events over the course of the succeeding decades.[91] Simultaneously, the legal profession would maintain a footprint on site; the Children's Court was located at the upper yard until the early 1980s and the work of tribunals of inquiry are still regularly conducted in George's hall. Perhaps the most important symbolic function currently carried out, however, remains the administration by the chief justice of the declaration of office to the Irish president-elect on inauguration day in St Patrick's hall – ensuring that, as decreed in 1204, justice continues to play a role at Dublin Castle to this day.

---

84   OPW to Dept. Justice, 5 June 1931, NAI OPW/5 13930/31.
85   James FitzGerald-Kenney to Kennedy, 16 Sept. 1931, UCDA P4/1058.
86   *Irish Times*, 12 Aug. 1931.
87   Memo. on the Bar Council war memorial, 3 Feb. 1932, NAI OPW/5 9455/24.
88   Mary Kotsonouris, *Retreat from revolution: the Dáil courts, 1920–25* (Kildare, 1994), p. 119.
89   *Irish Independent*, 2 Oct. 1922.
90   *Irish Times*, 2 July 1932.
91   John Gibney and Kate O'Malley, *The handover: Dublin Castle and the British withdrawal from Ireland, 1922* (Dublin, 2022), pp 147–50. See also Derham, '(Re)making majesty', pp 286–7 and 303–4.

CHAPTER SIX

Establishing judicial independence

BLÁTHNA RUANE*

The establishment of the new courts in 1924 was a critically important but under-appreciated success of the Irish Free State. It was crucial to the restoration of the rule of law and order, on which the survival of the new state depended. The new courts' legitimacy enabled the shattered legal system to stabilise quickly, and to respond to the other challenges facing the state.

The establishment process actually began with the drafting of the Constitution in early 1922. Its broad policies were translated into the Courts of Justice Act 1924 and largely dictated the critical characteristics of the new judiciary. Establishing a new judicial system was not just about determining the numbers of courts or judges, or what new constitutional or statutory powers they should have. By far the most important challenge was whether they would achieve legitimacy and public confidence in exercising their powers.[1] That was not inevitable and the bitter upheaval and legal partisanship from which they sprang did not augur well. Unusually, but very significantly, it was an era in which perceived judicial bias was a major political issue for Treatyite leaders. This chapter gives a brief overview of the legally fraught formative background to the establishment of judicial independence achieved under the Courts of Justice Act 1924. It considers the extent to which the Treatyites were prepared to create independent courts in light of the difficulties they experienced from conflicts with courts acting against their political interests. Subsequent chapters explore particular facets of those new arrangements in greater detail.

The Treatyite leaders had very strained relations with both the official courts and the rival, unofficial Dáil courts established by Dáil Éireann in 1920 to supplant the Crown courts. Both courts had experienced considerable upheaval during the War of Independence. The British forces had suppressed the Dáil courts and their judges were harassed and faced imprisonment. Later, during the Civil War, the Dáil courts became a focus for pro- and anti-Treaty hostilities.[2] The Crown courts were attacked by militant radical

---

* Senior counsel, and adjunct professor of law at the Sutherland School of Law at University College Dublin.
1 See further Robert Marshall's chapter.
2 See further the account in Thomas Mohr's chapter. For an overview of the Dáil courts, see Mary Kotsonouris, *Retreat from revolution: the Dáil courts, 1920–24* (Dublin, 1994).

nationalists. The Four Courts and other court buildings were destroyed, and judges were subjected to violence and threats.[3] Both courts had been turned into institutional symbols of conflicting regimes and became military targets.

Impartial decision-making and judicial independence had a special resonance for the Treatyite leaders, many of whom themselves had suffered imprisonment. By 1922 they had deep animosity towards many Crown judges, who were perceived as being pro-British, and hostile to radical nationalists. Under the British system in Ireland, although judges were supposed to be independent, in reality, senior judges could be politically involved in the British administration. The role of Irish lord chancellor (which was abolished in 1922)[4] had been a hybrid political/judicial role at the pinnacle of the system, but in addition, other senior judges were members of the Irish Privy Council and could also be given temporary authority as lords justices to act in the place of the viceroy when he was away. They might sign orders in council or issue proclamations.[5]

Judicial appointments were made largely on political and/or religious grounds[6] and overall their political and social composition did not reflect the Irish population. Political considerations affected not only appointment but could also affect retirement. The senior judges (other than the lord chancellor) held their offices for life subject to good behaviour, unless removed by the Crown on an address from both houses of parliament, and their salaries were protected.[7] There was a ban on judges being elected to or sitting in the House of Commons, but notably not the House of Lords.[8] Political pressure was sometimes brought to bear on a judge to retire,[9] which could in addition facilitate other appointments for political purposes. A judge

3 David Foxton, *Revolutionary lawyers: Sinn Féin and Crown courts in Ireland and Britain 1916–1923* (Dublin, 2008), pp 181–4; León Ó Broin, *W.E. Wylie and the Irish Revolution, 1916–1921* (Dublin, 1989), pp 130–1; Bláthna Ruane, 'Régime change: the fate of the senior Crown judiciary following the Anglo-Irish Treaty 1921', *Ir. Jur.*, 54 (2015), 96–104, at 103.
4 Irish Free State (Consequential Provisions) Act 1922, sch. 2, pt. ii.
5 See, e.g., the order in council of 10 Dec. 1917 under the Universities Act 1908 by the lords justices and Privy Council of Ireland signed by James Campbell (lord chief justice of Ireland), J.O. Wylie (a justice of the High Court (Irish Land Commission)), Jonathan Pim (a justice of the King's Bench division) and Bryan Mahon, an Irish general in the British Army. See *I.L.T.&S.J.*, 52 (1918), 10 and Proclamation of martial law in Ireland 26 May 1916 signed by Richard R. Cherry, then lord chief justice and J.O. Wylie, then a justice of the High Court (Irish Land Commission), UK Parliamentary Archives, Lloyd George papers LG/D/15/15.
6 V.T.H. Delany, *The administration of justice in Ireland* (Dublin, 1962), p. 66; Maurice Healy, *The old Munster circuit* (London, 2001), pp 133–4; Laurence W. McBride, *The greening of Dublin Castle* (Washington DC, 1991), pp 246–51.
7 An Act for Securing the Independency of Judges, and the Impartial Administration of Justice 1782 (21 & 22 Geo. III, c. 50), ss 1–3 and the Supreme Court of Judicature (Ireland) Act 1877 (40 & 41 Vict., c. 57), ss 6, 13, 15, 17, 18.
8 The Supreme Court of Judicature (Ireland) Act 1877 (40 & 41 Vict., c. 57), s. 13.
9 See Daire Hogan's analysis in his chapter.

might be encouraged to retire with the allurement of a title. British Liberal prime minister Herbert Asquith adopted this technique to smooth political difficulties associated with appointments. Thus in 1915, Richard Cherry, then the Irish lord chief justice, who was in poor health, was pressurised by Asquith to resign, and offered the carrot of a title. This was to allow prominent Unionist James Campbell, later Lord Glenavy, a former solicitor general and attorney general, who lobbied shamelessly for high judicial office, to fill Cherry's position. Asquith also surveyed other judges for similar purpose. Eventually in late 1916 Cherry acquiesced, and Campbell duly succeeded him.[10]

Judges also sometimes engaged in unofficial political activities. Most notably, James O'Connor, then a lord justice of appeal, was publicly involved in peace talks with prime minister Lloyd George in Downing Street and in 1921 in private discussions with northern Unionists Sir James Craig, Sir Edward Carson and Sinn Féin leader Éamon de Valera.[11]

Although in 1920 the senior Crown judiciary had significantly, but privately, displayed independence in successfully resisting the proposed establishment of a three-judge tribunal, to try cases without a jury,[12] their public standing had been badly eroded by some controversial judgments refusing reliefs on various claims brought by imprisoned radical nationalists, particularly the notorious *R v. Allen*[13] in February 1921, challenging charges or sentences in military courts carrying a death sentence. Later Sir Charles O'Connor, master of the rolls, in *Egan v. Macready*,[14] refused to follow the reasoning relied upon in the *Allen* case and made absolute a conditional order of *habeas corpus* in favour of a prisoner. The difference suggested to many Republicans that the *Allen* decision was influenced by the political outlook of the judges. In addition, the county courts' handling of many compensation claims for malicious injuries and damage caused by Crown forces and militant Republicans created resentment. This was because they awarded compensation to policemen and soldiers but in other cases refused to compensate Irish citizens for the destruction of their property by the British military. Such compensation was recouped from the rates paid by the local population.

The bitterness towards the Crown judges emerged in August 1921 when the Dáil met in secret session, to make contingent arrangements for the resumption of war, if the proposed peace talks failed. The minister for home

---

10 R.F.V. Heuston, *Lives of the lord chancellors, 1885–1940* (Oxford, 1964), pp 270–3.
11 See, for example, *Documents on Irish foreign policy*, vol. 1 (Dublin, 1998), pp 224–6, and 229–31; de Valera papers, UCDA P150/1902. Sir James O'Connor, *History of Ireland, 1798–1924* (London, 1925), vol ii, p. 336.
12 Thomas Jones, *Whitehall diary, vol. iii: Ireland, 1918–1925*, ed. Keith Middlemas (Oxford, 1971), pp 19, 33.
13 [1921] 2 IR 241. See Maurice Collins's chapter.
14 [1921] 1 IR 265.

affairs, Austin Stack, sought extreme powers, 'to give the Ministry power to deal with [county and superior courts judges] in any way they thought fit by regulation by "fine, imprisonment or otherwise" which would include the death penalty if same was found necessary'. This, he argued, was on account inter alia of their handling of compensation claims and 'the execution of men like Allen'. It says much for the febrile atmosphere that Republican Sinn Féin leaders Éamon de Valera, Michael Collins and Arthur Griffith did not dismiss the chilling proposal. All reflected unease about aspects of the proposal, but equally, they considered generally that if the truce broke down, further serious steps would then have to be considered. The result was that Stack's motion was withdrawn.[15] The Treaty was signed and so the point was not re-visited.

Dealing with the Dáil courts also produced major problems. The Treatyites had wanted the Dáil courts to continue[16] but the British wanted the Crown courts to function until the new courts were established. On 16 January 1922, the Provisional Government announced that the Crown courts would continue, unless otherwise ordered, pending the constitution of the new government and parliament.[17] However the Treatyites hoped, unrealistically, that the Constitution would be adopted quickly and the new courts established soon thereafter, so that the transition phase would be short. In the meantime, while the difficult constitutional drafting process was underway, various problems with maintaining the Dáil courts were emerging. There were practical difficulties from having the two competing courts in operation.[18] The Dáil courts had significant jurisdictional deficits, owing to their hurried establishment.[19] In addition, some of those involved in the Dáil courts were perceived by the Treatyites to be anti-Treaty.[20] British approval of the draft Constitution was required to ensure that it complied with the

15 *Dáil Éireann deb.*, vol. S, col. 7 (26 Aug. 1921), Decree as to purported exercise of public functions. The motion itself did not refer to the death penalty but did refer to 'or otherwise'. Stack's speech on 26 Aug. 1921 however signalled that he envisaged 'or otherwise' as including the death penalty. For the wording of the motion, see *Dáil Éireann deb.*, vol. T, col. 17 (10 Jan. 1922), app. 4.
16 Provisional Govt. cabinet minutes, 20 Jan. 1922, NAI TSCH/S1449. See also Thomas Mohr's chapter.
17 Notice of transfer of services hitherto administered by the British government in Ireland, 16 Jan. 1922, NAI TSCH/S1. See also Heads of working arrangements for implementing the Treaty agreed between British and Irish ministers, 24 Jan. 1922, NAI TSCH/S1; The Provisional Government (Transfer of Functions) Order 1922 (315/1922).
18 Dáil Cabinet minutes 24 and 27 Feb. 1922, NAI TSCH/S1449; Memo. of Éamonn Duggan, 14 Mar. 1922, NAI DE 4/11/62.
19 Irish government official statement re suspension of sittings of Dáil courts, UCDA P4/1067.
20 Handwritten memo. of Seóirse MacNiocaill (undated); memo. to P. O'Siocháin, 21 Apr. 1922; Dómhnall de Brún to E.J. Duggan, min. home affairs, 22 Mar. 1922; report of Pádraig Crump, 29 Aug. 1922 NAI JUS/H140/5–30; Notes of minutes of the Provisional Government meetings, 11 July 1922 (P.G. 56); 13 July 1922 (P.G. 59); 15 July 1922 (P.G. 61); 17 July 1922 (P.G. 63); 21 July 1922 (P.G. 67), NAI TSCH/S1315.

Treaty and in early June in negotiations on the draft Constitution, the British insisted that the Crown courts, rather than the Dáil courts, should continue until the new courts were established under the Constitution,[21] which arrangement was ultimately provided for in article 75.

Confrontation with the Dáil courts came quickly. By 14 July 1922 the Provisional Government had controversially suspended most of the Dáil courts.[22] Shortly afterwards on 19 July an order of *habeas corpus* from the Dáil Supreme Court was sought for the release of a prominent anti-Treatyite, George Plunkett, from prison. The basis for the application was inter alia an attack on the validity of the Treaty and the actions of the Provisional Government established under it.[23] A conditional order was granted by Crowley J, who was well known for his Republican sympathies. The defendant Treatyites ignored the order, consistent with their view that the Dáil courts by then had no jurisdiction. The powers of most of the Dáil courts were then rescinded by order signed by the minister for home affairs, Éamonn Duggan, on 25 July.[24] Republicans regarded the Treatyites' actions as *ultra vires*, as flouting the authority and independence of the Dáil courts and infringing the rule of law. This confrontation was followed by another politically sensitive application on 5 August 1922 by another prominent Republican, Kathleen Clarke, for a conditional order of *mandamus* directed to the speaker of the second Dáil to summon it. With no appearance from the speaker, Crowley J later made absolute an order of *mandamus* but that too was ignored by the Treatyites. Further steps were taken in October completing the abolition of the Dáil courts.[25] So the judicial independence of the Dáil courts themselves had also become controversial, but so too was the Provisional Government's treatment of them and their attitude to judicial independence.

A further complication bearing upon judicial independence arose during the process of adopting the new Constitution. The draft Constitution was prepared by a Constitution Committee, established in January 1922 by the Provisional Government. It provided for the separation of powers of the three arms of government but that still left many issues regarding how judicial independence would be addressed. As part of their approval of the draft Constitution in June 1922, the British insisted that, in accordance with Dominion status, there should be a right to petition the king for an appeal to the Judicial Committee of the Privy Council from the intended Supreme

21 Draft conclusions of meeting of British signatories to the Treaty with Ireland, 12 noon, 9 June 22, TNA CAB 43/1, pp 84–5.
22 On 13 July 1922 a notice was sent to the court registrars indicating that the Dáil Éireann cabinet had ordered the cessation of all Circuit Courts: Seóirse MacNiocaill, assistant minister for home affairs, to each registrar, 13 July 1922, NAI TSCH/S1449. MacNiocaill also wrote to judge Davitt suspending the Supreme Court.
23 Kotsonouris, *Retreat*, p. 20.
24 Ibid., p. 83.
25 James Casey, 'Republican courts in Ireland 1919–1922', *Ir. Jur.*, 5:2 (1970), 321–42, at 339–40.

Court's decisions. The appeal was deeply resented by both the pro- and anti-Treaty sides, as an affront to national sovereignty and the independence of the new Irish judiciary. An additional dimension to Irish opposition to the appeal was that the Privy Council judges could include some senior British judges of Unionist sympathy, such as Lord Carson, who had recently made very hostile speeches in the House of Lords[26] during debates relating to the Treaty, even questioning its legal validity as a Treaty. In negotiations on the draft, the Treatyites demanded and received assurances from the British that those judges who had spoken out on a controversy would not sit in cases pertaining to that controversy.[27]

The potential for the political outlooks of the new Irish judges to affect their decisions had also caused concerns among the drafters of the constitution. When the important innovation in the draft Constitution of allowing the superior courts to determine the validity of laws relative to the Constitution was being considered, there were fears that the judges would be too conservative in exercising such powers, as had occurred in the United States.[28] However, the possibility of amending the Constitution through the initiative was influential in allaying fears over the impact of such potential judicial conservatism.[29]

Various important facets of judicial independence were expressly regulated in articles 68 and 69 of the Constitution. Judges were to be independent in the exercise of their functions, subject only to the Constitution and the law. Judges were specifically prohibited from sitting in the Oireachtas or holding any other paid position. Gone therefore was the possibility that an Irish judge would sit in the Oireachtas pronouncing on legal issues, such as Lord Carson had done in the House of Lords. Various other aspects affecting judicial independence were addressed. The tenure of the superior court judges was explicitly protected by prohibiting their removal from office except for stated misbehaviour or incapacity and then only by resolutions passed by the Dáil and Senate. So incapacitated judges could now be removed in a transparent process. A specific retirement age was to be established in implementing legislation.[30] The drafters notably did not follow the English system or indeed the American system, under which the senior or Supreme Court judges held office for life. The other important questions of remuneration, pensions and declarations on appointment were also to be

26 See, e.g., Lord Carson in *Hansard 5 (Lords)*, vol. 48, cols 36–53 (14 Dec. 1921), Lord Sumner: ibid., vol. 48, cols 165–72 (16 Dec. 1921), Viscount Cave; ibid., vol. 49, cols 606–11 (16 Mar. 1922).
27 Conclusions of cabinet meetings, 11 a.m. and 8.15 p.m., 2 June 1922, TNA CAB 23/30 pp 164–5 and 187–8.
28 Explanatory statement of draft B of Constitution submitted by James G. Douglas, C.J. France and Hugh Kennedy. Constitution Committee 1922, NAI TSCH/S8954, E2 p. 14.
29 Memo. of Kevin O'Shiel, 'about 15 Mar. 1922', NAI TSCH/S8953.
30 See further Daire Hogan's account in his chapter.

prescribed by law. Reduction of the judges' remuneration during their continuance in office was specifically constitutionally prohibited.[31]

An important insight into the mindset of the Provisional Government emerges from the fact that on 23 May 1922 its approval of the general provision requiring judges to be independent was subject to there being a clause preventing judges from becoming involved in politics.[32] The drafting committee responded that such involvement could be addressed within the context of removal for stated misbehaviour, and so no insert was required.[33] That scenario would doubtless have been in Griffith's and Collins's minds weeks later when, during negotiations in London with the British on the draft Constitution, law officer Hugh Kennedy found himself negotiating with Lord Hewart, by then lord chief justice. Previously, as attorney general, Hewart had been one of the British negotiators of the Treaty. Hewart was quietly brought back by Lloyd George to help them again to negotiate over the Constitution. The drafting committee would apparently have regarded involvement akin to Hewart's as grounds for removal for stated misbehaviour. Equally, the earlier involvement of Sir James O'Connor in peace negotiations would have been unacceptable.

There were two specific but minor exceptions to the heightened segregation of judges' activities into the purely judicial sphere. Under article 35, a senior judge might act as chairman of a committee of privileges, to determine whether a bill was a money bill or not. This had been expressly sought by the southern Unionists.[34] Pursuant to article 60, which provided for the office of the Crown's representative, letters patent constituting the office of governor general were later adopted.[35] Under those letters patent, the chief justice or the senior judge of the Supreme Court might act in place of the governor general in the event of his death, incapacity, removal or absence. Both powers were evidently seen as likely to arise infrequently and as uncontroversial.

The one major exception to the policy of maximising judicial independence relates to the method of appointment of judges under article 68. The Executive Council was clearly determined to keep complete control over who became a judge. Appointments were to be made by the Crown's representative in Ireland, on the advice of the Executive Council. That, in reality, meant selection by the Executive Council, which was not unusual for that era. That power could be used apolitically but was also open to potential political misuse. However, from the other provisions it was at least clear that

---

31 See also the account of Laura Cahillane in her chapter.
32 Extract from Provisional Govt. minutes, 23 May 1922, NAI TSCH/S8954A.
33 Darrell Figgis to Michael Collins, 24 May 1922, NAI TSCH/S8954A.
34 MacNeill papers, UCDA LAI/G/233, pp 23–4.
35 Letters patent passed under the great seal of the United Kingdom, constituting the Office of Governor General of the Irish Free State, 6 Dec. 1922, NAI TSCH/S2119.

it was expected that once appointed, judges would behave independently. There had been a suggestion at the drafting committee stage that the selection of judges for the Supreme Court by the executive should be approved by the proposed Senate but that was rejected.[36]

Overall, by October 1922, the trajectory for the judiciary was towards a much higher level of judicial independence. The broadly representative Judiciary Committee appointed by the Provisional Government in January 1923 to advise on the new courts put forward pragmatic proposals,[37] many of which were embodied in the Courts of Justice Act. The Act required the new judges to take a declaration (section 99) that they would perform their duties 'without fear or favour', and that they would uphold the Constitution. The latter requirement was unremarkable and justifiable in committing the judge to uphold a Dominion constitution, embodying the Crown, albeit that it would constitute a conscientious barrier for many Republicans.

Several other requirements such as the size and exact method of payment of salaries,[38] legal qualifications,[39] tenure[40] and retirement[41] were addressed. They were frequently finessed during the debates on the bill with drafting amendments enhancing judicial independence. Unlike the resident magistrates of old, all judges now had to be legally well qualified for their respective positions, which emphasised that all cases were expected to be determined in accordance with law and not on an *ad hoc* basis. Salaries were significantly reduced but intentionally pitched at a level to attract good candidates and enough to remove financial insecurity as a threat to independence. There were now specified retirement ages, with limited exceptions. Circuit Court judges, who were not covered by the constitutional protection regarding removal, received the same protection from removal under section 39. District justices were somewhat less protected from removal but this was likely due to an expectation of teething problems of inexperienced appointees to this new court.

There was one statutory area where Kennedy and Cosgrave sought to keep some control in judicial affairs, through the arrangements for the adoption of the rules of court by the rules committee. For the superior courts they wanted to get rid of the Crown robes and the wigs worn in court by the judiciary and the Bar and to change them to a Gaelicized style, and to replace 'my lord' with

---

36 Notes on Draft C of the Constitution for the members of the Provisional Government from Alfred O'Rahilly, 12 Apr. 1922, Constitution Committee 1922, NAI TSCH/S8954, C1, p. 7. Criticism by George O'Brien, 24 Mar. 1922, Constitution Committee 1922, NAI TSCH/S8954, K5, p. 12.
37 Report of Judiciary Committee, NAI TSCH/S1739.
38 Ss 13, 14, 15, 41, 42, 74, 75.
39 Ss 16, 43, 69.
40 Ss 39, 73.
41 Ss 12, 40, 72, 100.

'a bhreithimh', 'judge' or 'sir'.[42] They knew that the conservative elements wanted no change.[43] While ostensibly a somewhat superficial issue, the dispute actually raised niche but significant questions about the power of the courts to make their own rules of procedure, independently of the executive, and it affected the symbolic tone of the new judiciary. By giving the minister substantial control over the operation of the Superior Courts Rules Committee that was to be established, they hoped to control that process and the robes and mode of address provisions. That power was not however an attempt to control judicial decision-making. In any event, ultimately the conservative elements won when the rules were finally adopted in 1926 and little change was effected.[44]

Apart from the legislation, the selection of the senior judges was inevitably going to be crucial. The senior Crown judges had already made sure that the British compensation system did not compel them to take new positions, if offered.[45] Some were too old. Some felt alienated from the new regime or would have been unacceptable to the Executive Council for reappointment. On the approach to judicial selection, Cosgrave and Kennedy had privately expressed strong views against appointment for political reasons.[46] Cosgrave believed judges should be appointed on merit and should be independent and there should be no automatic entitlement for the attorney general to have first refusal over vacancies.[47] In the event a relatively mixed group of appointees was chosen for the most important positions. Kennedy became chief justice, as expected, reflecting Cosgrave's confidence in him. Sir Charles O'Connor, who had given the judgment in *Egan v. Macready* and later the important *Childers* case,[48] was appointed to the Supreme Court. The remainder of the superior courts appointments further reflected an attitude of inclusiveness, particularly in regard to religion and the southern Unionists.[49] Unlike for appointments to the Senate, the Executive Council was under no obligation to the British to be inclusive.

This approach was particularly notable because the Executive Council included a pro-Treaty ex-Dáil court judge (James Creed Meredith), and other former Crown court judges (William Wylie, William Johnston, Thomas O'Shaughnessy). No Supreme Court anti-Treatyite Dáil court judges were appointed to senior positions. Even if personally acceptable, the oath of judicial office would likely have caused a barrier for Republicans at that

42 Kennedy to An Breithimh Cathal Paor, 18 Aug. 1926, UCDA P4/1168 (24). See also the analysis of Úna Ní Raifeartaigh and Róisín Costello in their chapter.
43 *Seanad Éireann deb.*, vol. 2, col. 646 (30 Jan. 1924).
44 See Kevin Costello's chapter.
45 Ruane, 'Régime', at 105.
46 UCDA P4/1390 (8–9).
47 *Dáil Éireann deb.*, vol. 5, cols 1559–60 (6 Dec. 1923).
48 *R (Childers) v. Adjutant General of the Provisional Forces* [1923] 1 IR 5.
49 See the analysis of Robert Marshall in his chapter.

critical stage. A highly regarded king's counsel, Patrick Lynch, who had some links to the anti-Treatyites, and was later a Fianna Fáil attorney general, was offered the High Court but declined it.[50]

What emerges from this overview is that, notwithstanding the chilling start in 1921 of a Dáil debate about power to execute Crown judges, and notwithstanding the political controversies with the Dáil courts and apprehensions regarding Privy Council judges, the Treatyite leadership nonetheless genuinely embraced the concept of judicial independence and established new courts with a much greater degree of judicial independence than theretofore. They did not reserve untoward powers to allow them to interfere with the courts, other than in regard to the robes controversy. They gave enhanced protections to the judges from interference but also, importantly, imposed greater restrictions on the judges to act independently. However they deliberately kept control over the appointments process, which gave them a limited influence on the likely general direction of the courts. In their first appointments of the most senior judges, they were notably inclusive towards the southern Unionist community, even though they had no commitment to the British to do so.

Overall their policy was generally successful and enabled the courts to achieve a high degree of legitimacy quickly, which paid dividends in re-establishing the rule of law. It helped to garner significant public acceptance of the new powerful role given to the judiciary for the constitutional review of legislation. The promise of that power of review was never realised but the far more fundamental task of establishing judicial legitimacy was successfully achieved. That legitimacy proved to be critical to the transformation of the rule of law in Ireland, underpinning the separation of powers and the establishment of a stable democracy.

---

50 Minutes of the Exec. Council, 4 June 1924, NAI TSCH/S10921.

CHAPTER SEVEN

A balanced judiciary: the early appointments to the superior and Circuit Courts

ROBERT D. MARSHALL*

This chapter reviews early appointments to the new court system established by the Irish Free State in 1924. It considers the circumstances then prevailing and examines the backgrounds of 21 men to whom appointments were offered.[1] This includes their age, social and educational backgrounds, religion and politics, as well as their achievements prior to appointment. Extrapolating the criteria from the circumstances is necessary, given that the lengthy discussions are not recorded in the minutes of the Executive Council. The circumstantial evidence is confined to what could have been available to the Executive Council and their individual personal knowledge. It is not the purpose of this chapter to assess the judges' success or otherwise thereafter, and there is no critique of their judicial careers.

The Courts of Justice Act 1924,[2] like the Land Act 1923[3] and the Ministers and Secretaries Act 1924,[4] was a constitutional statute enacted in the early years of the Irish Free State. The expression 'constitutional statute' distinguishes those statutes that fleshed out the institutions of the new state from regulatory statutes intended to govern everyday life. The structure established by a constitutional statute was as important as the personnel chosen to staff it, for they would bring to the institution their own life

---

* Retired solicitor and a former president of the Irish Legal History Society (2012–15).
1 This includes Patrick Lynch KC, who declined appointment to the High Court: cabinet minute, 4 June 1924, NAI C2/102. Over the previous ten years Lynch had a varied career. Appointed Crown prosecutor for Kerry he resigned to stand against Éamon de Valera in the 1917 by-election. Subsequently he represented the family in the 1920 inquest into the death of Thomas MacCurtain when Wylie KC appeared for the 'authorities'. Lynch appeared before O'Connor MR against Kennedy in the Childers *habeas corpus* application. Lynch may have been disturbed by the circumstances in which the case concluded. Appendices 2–4 provide information on the individual applicants and appointments in tabular form.
2 Commenced 5 June 1924 (SI 5/1924) as to ss 1, 2, 3 and pts i and iv except as related to the District and Circuit Courts.
3 Commenced 9 Aug. 1923 (SI 42/1923).
4 Commenced 2 June 1924 (SI 4/1924).

experiences, personal backgrounds and culture. Such attributes would determine the character of the institution on the one hand and its legitimacy in the face of public opinion on the other. Consequently, for the cabinet that had broadly accepted the report of the Judiciary Committee, enacting the Courts of Justice Act in 1924 was only half the task. Whether the legislation was the least difficult part of the task may be moot, but the appointment of the new judiciary would be the most delicate.

The delicacy arose from the need to ensure that those appointed would inspire public confidence and strengthen the legitimacy of the new state.[5] W.T. Cosgrave had articulated this sentiment at the first convention of Cumann na nGaedheal in April 1923 when he said that the party 'ought to bring home to everyone the vital need for a sound national organisation, knowing neither creed nor class but working for the best interest of the whole of the people and the whole of the nation.'[6] Attorney General Kennedy expressed a similar view, in March 1924, concerning judges for the Court of Appeal. Such men needed 'a theoretical and practical understanding of the law'. They would be

> men of judicial mind and temperament which implies patience, steadiness and sound judgement excluding impulsiveness, intolerance of argument, domineering interference with the rights of advocacy and over rapidity born of self-sufficiency. They would not permit the constitutional liberties of the country to be whittled down in any degree and will regard the national status as in a special manner entrusted to them to preserve intact and to fight against every attempted encroachment.

They would 'be servient to the Irish people and the living nation but independent of all else besides'. He continued: 'this must be the general fundamental test of fitness for our court of appeal by the light of which the Executive Council must examine all possible candidates for that great responsibility.'[7] Political culture in Ireland was evolving from one in which all power devolved from the sovereign to one in which the legislative, executive and judicial powers were separated. That was only one part of the picture: there was the polarising division between what Prager has called the Irish Enlightenment norms with their roots in the late eighteenth century, and the Gaelic Romantic norms harking back to Fenianism and the 'ideal of a republic now virtually established'.[8] Both traditions were represented on either side of the Treaty split. Three further cultural groups can be identified: the former

5   See Donal K. Coffey's chapter.
6   *Irish Times*, 28 Apr. 1923; cited by Jeffrey Prager, *Building democracy in Ireland* (Cambridge, 1986), p. 133.
7   Memo. from attorney general to president of the Executive Council in reply to note by (Patrick?) Hogan, Mar. 1924 UCDA P4/568.
8   Prager, *Building democracy*, pp 16 and 38–50. Virtually in this context bears a meaning akin to meetings being held electronically in current times as opposed to 'almost' established.

Irish Parliamentary Party elite, and the Southern Unionists, both shrinking, and the Labour Party.

The legal elite had been partitioned in 1921 with the establishment of the Royal Courts of Justice in Northern Ireland, a process completed by the establishment of the inn of court of Northern Ireland.[9] At partition, save Moore J, the judges elected to remain in Southern Ireland but a significant number of barristers, whose practices drew predominantly on instructions from the portions of the North Eastern and North Western circuits lying within Northern Ireland, chose to base themselves in Belfast. A further fissure opened up with the Civil War as those opposed to the Treaty, if willing to practice in the new court system, as they had done in the courts of Southern Ireland prior to June 1924, could not expect appointment by the Free State government to the new judiciary.

In consequence, the pool of talent available for appointment was reduced to those who supported the Treaty or acquiesced in changing times, who groped towards a collective understanding but had to learn toleration of difference. In the administration of the law, the judges would be a part of the process of welding 'contending ideological constructs heretofore immune to debate and discourse into a single integrated national set of convictions',[10] not all of which would be represented on the bench.

Political culture aside, the appointments did not take place in a vacuum. The Judiciary Committee, appointed to make recommendations for a new court system, had deliberated during the closing stages of the Civil War, which ended with the Suspension of Offensive Order published by the Anti-Treaty Irish Republican Army on 30 April 1923. That war had resulted in the destruction of the imposing 'footpace and precincts of judicature',[11] so that justice was bereft of the symbolism of Gandon's building and administered in courtrooms set up in Dublin Castle, for centuries the seat of the former British administration.

Gradually the new state attained financial security. With some commercial hesitation, it had been supported in the dark winter of 1922–3 by the Bank of Ireland with ways and means facilities and a loan of £3 million:[12] its governor, Henry Seymour Guinness, was a member of the Senate along with fellow director Andrew Jameson. The financial success of December 1923 in floating a national loan of £10 million, oversubscribed by £200,000,[13] was confirmed in January 1924 when the stock rose four points to commence trading at £99 per £100 of stock.[14] That success was a market proxy for the reliable payment

9   See further A. Hart, *A history of the inn of court of Northern Ireland* (Belfast, 2013), ch. 4.
10 Praeger, *Building democracy*, p. 17.
11 *Application of Sir James O'Connor* [1930] IR 623, at 631.
12 Ronan Fanning, *A history of the Department of Finance* (Dublin, 1978), pp 80–98.
13 *Prospectus*, 24 Nov. 1923; 'Buy national loan today', advertisement, *Freeman's Journal*, 5 Dec. 1923.
14 'The Saorstát loan soars four points above issue price', *Freeman's Journal*, 8 Jan. 1924.

of judicial salaries. This growing confidence was overshadowed by dissension known as the army mutiny of March 1924 and the difficulties which surrounded the establishment of the Boundary Commission. There remained also the final financial settlement with the British which was under negotiation until 1926.[15] Not always easy, these negotiations included liability for compensation for the destruction of property and the funding of land purchase under the Land Purchase Acts 1881–1923. Careful control of expenditure was therefore essential. The new state did not have the resources of the British Empire and like the old age pension, judicial remuneration would not be immune from a cold wind. Total judicial remuneration was projected to reduce from £53,700 to £37,000, and the details of this are explored in Laura Cahillane's chapter.[16]

The common factor laid down in the legislation both directly and by implication was that all appointees would have qualified as barristers.[17] The outgoing judiciary had been drawn from the Irish Bar, which was identified with the former establishment.[18] The path to judicial office until 1921 had been a ladder commencing with assistant revising barrister of the electoral lists, progressing to revising barrister, Crown prosecutor and perhaps serjeant at law before appointment as solicitor general and attorney general. William Wylie saw that he had no chance of either office as he was not a member of parliament and so would not obtain a judgeship. He avoided that fence by becoming law officer to the Irish government.[19]

With the exception of Hynes in the West Riding of Cork, the hostility to whom 'was undoubtedly well founded', Kennedy was not inclined to agree there was much opposition to the County Court judges. From what he heard 'the present session … had been remarkably successful'.[20] That admitted fourteen possibilities.

15 See John Fitzgerald and John Kenny: '"Till debt do us part": financial implications of the divorce of the Irish Free State from the United Kingdom, 1922–1926', *European Review of Economic History*, 24:4 (2020), 818–42.
16 Cahillane and Hogan also recognise the need for frugality in the new regime. The question of savings as a result of the establishment of the new system is beyond the scope of this paper but regard must be had to vacancies, the previous judicial retinues, the costs associated with assizes which were being abolished, the re-assignment of jurisdiction both as between courts and the transfer of functions from County Court judges to officials. An additional complication is treatment of the allowance for abolition of office payable to those re-employed under the new system.
17 Courts of Justice Act 1924, s. 16.
18 The Bar had resolved on 23 June 1920 that it was unprofessional for barristers to appear before the Dáil courts. Kenneth Ferguson, 'A portrait of the Irish Bar 1868–1968' in Kenneth Ferguson, *King's Inns barristers 1868–2004* (Dublin, 2005), p. 89.
19 Wylie memoir, the British National Archives (TNA) PRO 30/89/1 and 2. Wylie's career is recounted in Robert D. Marshall, 'Lieutenant W.E. Wylie KC: the soldiering lawyer of 1916' in Felix M. Larkin and N.M. Dawson (eds), *Lawyers, the law and history* (Dublin, 2013).
20 Kennedy to Cosgrave, 22 Jan. 1923, NAI S1739.

With respect to the superior courts, Daire Hogan outlines in his chapter why and how the Courts Act 1924 provided that judges should retire at the age of 72 or, in the case of a judge reappointed from the previous courts, 75.[21] The Supreme Court appointees were older, on average, at 57 years, while the High Court appointees were younger, at 52 years. In the High Court, Wylie and Murnaghan, both aged 42, balanced O'Shaughnessy, aged 73 (for whom section 100 of the 1924 Act appears to have been inserted). In the Circuit Court the average age was 54 where Charles Wyse Power at 32 was by ten years the youngest of the twenty appointments in this study. His colleagues Conner, Doyle, Wakely and Kenny were all in their sixties.

With the exception of Murnaghan, who was born in St Louis, Missouri, the nominees were all born in Ireland. Seven of the superior court nominees including Wylie and O'Connor were born in Dublin and two in Belfast. Only O'Byrne (Wicklow) and Lynch (Clare) were born outside a large city. Wylie was brought up in Coleraine and Murnaghan in Omagh, both Ulster towns. The Circuit Court appointees were more broadly based. Two came from Dublin, one from Offaly, one from each of Ulster and Connaught, and four from Munster. Of the twenty-one, Conner (Cork) and Wakely (Offaly) were both Justices of the Peace with small estates.[22] Otherwise none of the appointees had a farming background.

None of those offered appointments were late vocations to the Bar. The eldest upon being called was Charles Drumgoole at 29; the youngest O'Connor, Sullivan and Power at 21. Murnaghan, Devitt and Power had not taken silk at the time of their appointments. In the superior courts the average age of the appointees on taking silk was 40: Wylie the youngest at 33 and Johnston and Sullivan the eldest at 43. In the Circuit Court the average age was almost 43, McElligott the youngest at 37 and Kenny the eldest at 53.[23]

George O'Brien, called to the Bar in 1913,

> found the library a very congenial place. In spite of a good many personal animosities and jealousies the atmosphere was friendly. Professional *espirits de corps* was very high. Political and religious differences did not prevent amicable relations in the library. In the smoking room and the dressing room much good conversation and many amusing stories were to be heard.[24]

Would that stand following the subsequent changes in the political landscape?

The judges appointed had all attended King's Inns as they were required to be members of the Irish Bar but only Sullivan, O'Shaughnessy, Kenny and

---

21 Courts of Justice Act 1924, ss 12 and 100.
22 Wakely, whose Ballyburly house had been burned (*Freeman's Journal*, 28 Feb. 1923), had sold his to the Land Commission before his appointment.
23 Kenny had taken silk in 1915.
24 James Meenan, *George O'Brien: a biographical memoir* (Dublin, 1986), p. 44.

MacElligott did not hold university degrees.[25] Of those who did, the chief justice,[26] four High Court and two Circuit Court judges had attended University College Dublin. Two Supreme Court judges, one High Court judge and three Circuit Court judges attended Trinity College Dublin. Two High Court judges graduated from Queen's University Belfast. Three judges had been called to the English Bar: Kenny (1886), Doyle (1902) and Hanna (1913). Hanna also held an LLB from London University. Murnaghan held an LLD. Meredith who held an MA and DLitt. (1912) from Dublin University (TCD) also graduated BA (1895) and MA (1898) from the Royal University of Ireland (UCD). Of those who graduated from Dublin University, two (O'Connor and Doyle) were Catholics.[27]

Five appointees had been involved in writing legal textbooks. Johnston, the most prolific, had written on local government,[28] the Land Purchase Acts[29] and the Labourers Acts.[30] Kennedy had co-authored a work on the Town Tenants (Ireland) Act 1906.[31] Conner wrote on the fishery laws of Ireland[32] and had been joint editor for Ireland of the *English and Empire Digest*. Wakely had assisted Richard Cherry in the first edition of *The Land Purchase Acts*,[33] and Hanna had written on workmen's compensation.[34] Meredith wrote on philosophy,[35] while Johnston[36] and Murnaghan[37] both wrote on medieval Irish legal history.[38] Wylie confined himself to writing rules for show-jumping at the RDS.[39]

25 O'Shaughnessy was educated at Queen's College Galway. This is confirmed by directories published during his lifetime but none state that he graduated.
26 He was auditor of the Literary and Historical Society at UCD 1900–1.
27 They graduated in 1876 and 1882 respectively. Both had been auditors of the College Historical Society at TCD.
28 H.M. FitzGibbon and William J. Johnston, *The law of local government in Ireland: including the Local Government Act, 1898, the orders in council* (Dublin, 1899).
29 William J. Johnston, *Handbook of land purchase in Ireland* (2nd edn, Dublin, 1903).
30 William J. Johnston, *Handbook on the Labourers Act* (Dublin, 1907).
31 Arthur Clery, Hugh Kennedy and Michael Dawson: *Town Tenants (Ireland) Act, 1906* (Dublin, 1907).
32 H.D. Conner, *The Fisheries (Ir.) Acts, 1842 to 1901* (Dublin, 1892; 2nd ed. 1907).
33 Richard R. Cherry and John Wakely, *The Irish land law and land purchase acts, 1881, 1885, and 1887* (Dublin, 1888).
34 Henry Hanna, *The law of workmen's compensation* (Dublin, 1907).
35 James Creed Meredith, *Kant's critique of aesthetic judgement* (Oxford, 1911).
36 William Johnston, 'The parliament of the Pale', *Law Quarterly Review*, 34 (1918), 291–303; 'The first adventure of the common law', *Law Quarterly Review*, 36 (1920), 9–30; 'Ireland in the medieval law courts', *Studies*, 12:48 (1923), 553–70.
37 James A. Murnaghan, 'The development of supreme judicature in Ireland', *Studies*, 1:1 (1912), 130–45 and 'The lordship of Ireland and the counties palatine', *Studies*, 2:5 (1913), 846–59.
38 Osborough comments that Murnaghan's pieces 'compare very well with the better known offerings' of Johnston. W.N. Osborough, *The law school of University College Dublin* (Dublin, 2014), p. 53.
39 Terence de Vere White, *The story of the Royal Dublin Society* (Tralee, 1955), pp 185–8.

Along with Lieutenant William Wylie KC, Gerald FitzGibbon KC had served as a sergeant in the Trinity College OTC in the defence of the college during Easter Week 1916. He 'felt very bloodthirsty about [the] rebels since [he] saw men they shot down in St Stephen's Green and Haddington Road and saw all Sackville street in flames'.[40] Gradually he became disenchanted with the British government and by May 1922 he wrote that the British Empire was 'a stinking mass of prudity' and he put no faith in 'a syndicate of international Jews, Welsh attorneys and Canadian shysters'. He despaired that although he was 'quite prepared to stand in for an Irish republic and to hell with king George, my religion disqualifies me for Ireland.' The king's advocate in admiralty continued:

> I see no reason why I should profess loyalty to a king and an empire which has betrayed me to my enemies and theirs but I am not allowed to join the Irish Republic because I do not worship the Pope.[41]

This was FitzGibbon at his lowest, depressed that no money was coming in, that he could not start over abroad, and seeing so many 'loyalists' selling up and departing. Circumstances changed, he was elected one of the four TDs for Dublin University, then elected *pro tem* as deputy speaker and became thick as thieves with W.T. Cosgrave while professing to hate political life.[42] Along with Gavan Duffy he protested at the executions of December 1922 but on the slightly different basis that the government should have obtained Dáil approval for the summary executions.[43]

Cosgrave's pledge that creed would be unknown in making appointments was honoured.[44] Breaking the appointments down by religious profession we find a difference between the superior courts and the Circuit Court. In the nominees to the superior courts there were six Roman Catholics of whom Lynch declined appointment, three Presbyterians (all from Ulster), two Church of Ireland, and Meredith who with his wife returned himself in the 1911 Census as 'Christian (no sect)'.[45] In the Circuit Court there were no Presbyterians, seven Roman Catholics and two members of the Church of Ireland. FitzGibbon, Conner and Wakely, each held the senior office of chancellor in one or more of the united dioceses of that Church.[46]

40   FitzGibbon to William Hume Blake, 10 May 1916. FitzGibbon papers, TCD MS 11107/1. I am grateful to Dr Rory Sweetman for drawing this correspondence to my attention.
41   FitzGibbon to Blake, 6 May 1922. TCD MS 11107/34, pp 4–5.
42   FitzGibbon to Blake, 2 June 1923. TCD MS 11107/41, p. 3.
43   *Dáil Éireann deb.*, vol. 2, col. 3 (8 Dec. 1922).
44   It may not now be possible to recover the reasons why the popular Rosnethal, the first Jewish KC and a deputy County Court judge (1923–4), was not appointed.
45   The outgoing complement of the superior courts following partition had comprised six Catholics and two Protestants. Lawrence W. McBride, *The greening of Dublin Castle* (Washington, 1991).
46   *Church of Ireland Directory 1923*, RCB Library, Dublin. For a discussion on the role of

All of these factors went to collegiality and competence. They had been factors in the appointment of judges prior to the establishment of the Irish Free State. Their reach across the fissures thrown up by the turmoil since the introduction of the third Home Rule bill would be crucial in the healing process. That reach had coloured membership of the committee to draft the Constitution, the Judiciary Committee and the appointments in April 1924 to enquire into the army mutiny.[47]

The government of the new state could have been excused for discounting from eligible members of the Bar those who had held appointments under the former regime. This did not happen. Involvement with the former regime was not a bar to appointment and that was not because there were no nationalists available for appointment. Lynch KC declined an invitation. T.J. Campbell KC of Belfast,[48] Dudley White KC and James McLoone KC applied but were not appointed. Jeremiah (Diarmaid) Crowley (formerly of the Dáil Courts Winding Up Commission), Arthur Clery BL (a former judge of the Dáil courts), Michael Comyn KC, Thomas S. McCann KC,[49] William Carrigan KC were amongst those who, although eligible, neither applied nor were appointed. John Muldoon KC,[50] the registrar in lunacy, was not a practising barrister.

Involvement in the former regime covered more than judicial office in the legal establishment. Charles O'Connor had a routine career from revising barrister to attorney general for Ireland before being appointed master of the rolls in 1912. FitzGibbon had been king's advocate in the Admiralty Court. Wylie had prosecuted Cosgrave at the military trials in 1916 and had been appointed law officer in 1919. In that capacity Wylie represented the Crown at the MacCurtain inquest and was appointed judicial commissioner of the Land Commission in the autumn of 1920.

From the County Court, William J. Johnston KC had elected to move south at partition and T.L. O'Shaughnessy KC, a privy councillor for Ireland and a lord justice, had been recorder of Dublin since 1905, having previously been a Crown prosecutor. Both were appointed to the High Court. Charles Francis Doyle KC (1910), Charles Drumgoole KC (1913) and John Wakely KC (1904), (the king's deputy lieutenant for Co. Offaly and a justice of the peace), were all outgoing County Court judges appointed to the new Circuit Court.[51]

chancellors in the legal structure of the Church of Ireland see Robert D. Marshall, 'The constitution of the Church of Ireland in action' in Kevin Costello and Niamh Howlin (eds), *Law and religion in Ireland, 1700–1970* (London, 2021).
47 Cabinet minute, 2 Apr. 1924, NAI C2/78.
48 A former editor of the *Irish News*.
49 McCann was to be offered the Circuit Court should Henry Conner KC decline. Cabinet minute, 2 June 1924, NAI C2/100.
50 John Muldoon was a nationalist MP for various constituencies from 1905 to 1918 when he was defeated in Cork East. In 1926 he was appointed registrar in the Office of the Chief Justice. See Ferguson, *King's Inns barristers*.
51 To them should be added County Court Judges Daniel J. O'Brien and John Henry Pigot,

Henry Hanna KC, appointed in consequence of O'Connor's retirement in 1925, was third serjeant-at-law. Matthew Kenny, whom Frank Callanan has described as 'one of Parnell's most foul-mouthed opponents in the split' and would replace Conner in 1926, had been a nationalist MP between 1882 and 1895, and was appointed Crown prosecutor for Kerry in 1917.[52] Henry Daniel Conner (1910) and Henry Hanna (1918) had both contested the Dublin St Stephen's Green constituency in the Unionist interest while William Johnston, a revising barrister, had stood as a liberal in Londonderry South (1910) against John Gordon KC.[53]

Equally, some of those appointed had been involved on the Nationalist side. The athletic Meredith, president of the Supreme Court of Dáil Éireann and chief judicial commissioner of the Dáil Courts Winding Up Commission, had been a member of the crew of *Chotah*, which landed arms at Kilcoole on 1 August 1914. Charles Wyse Power was a youthful circuit judge of the Dáil courts and assistant commissioner of the Winding Up Commission. Kennedy, the sole Gaelic romantic appointed, had been a legal advisor to the Provisional Government, attorney general to the Executive Council of the Free State, and was elected to the vacancy in the fourth Dáil consequent upon Michael Hayes choosing to sit for the National University of Ireland.

Appendices 2, 3 and 4 highlight that most of those who were appointed were not recorded as having applied formally. Some lobbying took place but from surviving papers it appears to have been limited. William Johnston contributed £10 privately in August 1923 to Kennedy's election fund,[54] and on enquiring in April 1924 as to procedure was advised by Kennedy to write also to the Executive Council, which Johnston did.[55] Some days later, Kennedy replied to Eugene Sheehy's representation that Sheehy's name would be included 'in the list to be considered by the Executive Council'.[56] Blythe[57] and

both approved on 2 June 1924 (NAI C2/100), but not appointed on 6 Aug. 1924: cabinet minute 29 July 1924, NAI C2/101 and cabinet minute 10 Aug. 1924, NAI C2/121. Pigot was subsequently appointed a temporary assistant County Court judge for Dublin serving from 1925–8: Cabinet minute NAI C1/196 and NAI S 8497.

52 Frank Callanan, *T.M. Healy* (Cambridge, 1996), p. 243. B.M. Walker (ed.), *Parliamentary election results in Ireland, 1801–1922* (Dublin, 1978). Kenny was appointed in June 1917 by attorney general James O'Connor following the resignation of Patrick Lynch to contest the East Clare by-election.
53 Johnston secured 3,513 votes against 3,845 votes: John Gordon KC. Walker, *Parliamentary election results*. Gordon was appointed attorney general for Ireland in 1915 and to the Court of King's Bench in 1916. He died in Dublin in Sept. 1922.
54 Johnston to Kennedy, 13–22 Aug. 1923, UCDA P4/1407.
55 Correspondence between Johnston and Kennedy, 13–22 Aug. 1923 and 19–23 Apr. 1924, UCDA P4/1606 and P4/1407. Correspondence Johnston and Cosgrave 17–20 Apr. 1924 and to Kevin O'Higgins, 17 Apr. 1924, NAI S9875. Johnston is not listed in the paper circulated to the Executive Council reproduced in Appendix 1.
56 Correspondence between Sheehy and Kennedy, UCDA P4/1607.
57 Ernest Blythe aka Ernán de Blaidgh, a Lisburn-born member of the Church of Ireland, was minister for finance in 1924.

Campbell KC, both Ulstermen, corresponded concerning the possible appointment of Campbell to which Blythe was giving 'friendly consideration'.[58]

The new legal elite of the Irish Free State formed gradually between January 1922 and June 1924. Here, the earlier endorsements of Michael Collins should not be overlooked. Kennedy, Murnaghan and O'Byrne had all been members appointed before Collins's death to prepare a draft Constitution for the Irish Free State. Similarly, Wylie was invited by Collins to act as chairman of the Irish Civil Service Compensation Committee and appointed shortly after Collins' death.[59] Wylie had met Collins in John Anderson's office at Dublin Castle preparatory to the handover.[60] He was present when his friend James McMahon introduced the departmental heads to their new political masters following the departure of Viscount FitzAlan, the last lord lieutenant, from Dublin Castle on 16 January 1922.[61]

The Judiciary Committee included Meredith KC (president of the Dáil Supreme Court), Cahir Davitt (a judge of the Dáil Circuit Court), Charles Andrew O'Connor (the master of the rolls), County Court Judge Johnston, Sullivan KC and John O'Byrne. In April 1924, FitzGibbon and Meredith were appointed to enquire into the army mutiny.[62]

There are other personal relationships to be remembered. Here we are looking for footprints in the sand. The governor general and the attorney general were both longstanding members of the Irish Bar and so were acquainted with all those eligible. Healy, the governor general, had only a formal role in the appointments and neither his papers at UCD nor *Letters and leaders*[63] make reference to those appointments. He was not as close to Cosgrave as Kennedy but the minister for justice was a cousin and family visitor to 'the Lodge'. Kevin O'Higgins played no role in the passing of the Courts of Justice Act,[64] yet it would be quite out of character for Healy to have withheld his counsel. Healy considered Wylie had 'behaved pluckily over the new Coercion Act'[65] and resigned as legal adviser in August 1920. Wylie in

---

58 Correspondence between Campbell and Blythe. Blythe papers, UCDA P24/415 (5–8).
59 Letter of invitation, Collins to Wylie, 6 June 1922, TNA PRO 30/89.3/9. Provisional Government minute, 25 Sept. 1922, NAI PG14 and S 1716; and draft appointment, undated, UCDA P4/459(i).
60 John Wheeler-Bennett, *John Anderson Viscount Waverly* (London, 1962), p. 80. John Anderson, later Viscount Waverly, was appointed under-secretary for Ireland following the 1920 review of the Dublin bureaucracy by Warren Fisher. See Lloyd George papers, House of Lords Record Office, LG/F/31/1/32 and Marshall, 'Lieutenant W.E. Wylie', pp 141–5.
61 *Freeman's Journal*, 17 Jan. 1922, p. 5. Henry A. Robinson, *Memories wise and otherwise* (London, 1923), ch. 40.
62 Cabinet minute, 2 Apr. 1924, NAI C1/36.
63 Timothy Michael Healy, *Letters and leaders of my day* (London, 1928), vol. ii, ch. 46.
64 John P. McCarthy, *Kevin O'Higgins, builder of the Irish state* (Dublin, 2006), p. 124.
65 Restoration of Order in Ireland Act 1920 (10 & 11 Geo. V, c. 31).

turn took good care not to cross Healy.[66] Healy gave to O'Shaughnessy a full-length portrait of Isaac Butt and on 16 April 1916 a copy of his book, *Stolen waters*.[67] On 1 August 1910, Healy thanked Johnston for a copy of a book and regretted the bitterness over his appointment to the Belfast County Court.[68] Timothy Sullivan was Healy's double first cousin and son-in-law. Sullivan's acceptance of the presidency of the High Court was written on notepaper headed 'Vice Regal Lodge'.[69] Matthew Kenny and Healy were against Parnell in committee room 15. At Kenny's request, Healy had gone to Omagh for the 1895 Convention at which Dillon ousted Kenny, although the convention 'adopted a decent man instead of Kenny ... named Murnaghan'.[70]

Of the eleven appointed to the superior courts, only Serjeant Hanna had neither prior involvement with the formation of the state nor a Healyite connection.

CONCLUSION

It is easy now to overlook how each individual took considerable personal risk in accepting appointment to the judiciary of a new state in difficult and uncertain times. Never before had Irish judges been appointed on the recommendation of an Irish government responsible to a democratically elected Irish parliament. Otherwise, there was nothing radical about the 1924–6 appointments.

Circumstances required that the judges appointed should be safe pairs of hands who would reassure the general public but also agricultural and business interests. All came from the sub-culture of the Irish Bar to supervise litigation in a continuing common law tradition. There was no legal revolution but appointments were clearly intended to reassure both those who sought radical change and those who feared it.

Deciding the appointments took time in a discussion involving the entire ministry and to the credit of those involved it was neither recorded nor disclosed.[71] Partition and the Civil War reduced the pool of talent available

66 Healy; *Letters and leaders*, vol. ii, p. 624, and Wylie: 'He trusted me and I took damn good care not to betray that trust'. Wylie memoir, TNA PRO 30/89/1 and 2.
67 Copy of letter from Healy to O'Shaughnessy in author's possession. See also Healy to O'Shaughnessy, 26 Nov. 1925, NAI S1011.
68 Healy to Johnston, 1 Aug. 1910, Johnston papers, TCD MS 10066/289. Healy was presumably commiserating as the appointment in May 1910 went to Robert McIlroy KC.
69 Sullivan to sec. Exec. Council, 4 June 1924, NAI S 9871A.
70 Healy, *Letters and leaders*, p. 422, Murnaghan was James A. Murnaghan's father who held the seat until 1910.
71 Cabinet Committee minutes, 27 May 1924, NAI C2/97 ('discussed at some length'); 2 June 1924, NAI C2/100 ('appointments approved subject to acceptance'. This meeting lasted from 11.30 a.m. to 5.40 p.m.); and 4 June 1924, NAI C2/102.

and the unavoidable absence of anti-Treaty lawyers resulted in a culture of broadly party political appointments until the 1970s. Otherwise, the twenty appointments made in 1924–6 were balanced, facilitated by the number of appointments to be made. Those appointed included two outgoing judges of the King's Bench, five outgoing judges of the County Court of whom two were promoted to the High Court. There were two representatives of established legal dynasties of different traditions and two from the Dáil Courts Winding Up Commission. None of the outgoing judiciary associated with the Irish Parliamentary Party was reappointed. Matthew Kenny was the sole survivor of the nationalist parliamentary tradition that had so dominated Irish polictics for almost forty years.

The challenge for those appointed was to fuse their different cultural backgrounds into a new identity.

CHAPTER EIGHT

The introduction of a retirement age for judges

DAIRE HOGAN*

That judges would henceforward retire at a fixed age was an integral element of the reconstruction of the judicial system in 1924. A new approach was envisaged to the process for appointing judges, or more precisely to the considerations to be borne in mind by the government of the day in making appointments. For centuries judicial appointments had owed more to political services and connections than to professional standing at the Bar and had not been 'as they should be, the reward for learning and talent.'[1] Hugh Kennedy privately and publicly commented on this,[2] as did Sir John Ross,[3] who noted in 1918 that a member of the Bar 'has no chance of rising, who relies on learning, ability and professional propriety'.[4] In tandem with a vision of giving proper recognition to such qualities in the selection of judges and thus the commencement of judicial careers the Courts of Justice Act 1924 introduced the principle of such careers ending at a set age.

The Judiciary Committee had recommended this for judges of the District Court and Circuit Court, but had been silent on that aspect of the tenure of judges of the superior courts. Such a proposal as applicable to them first appeared at the end of June 1923 in the initial draft of the bill to give effect to the committee's report. This draft was prepared on the instructions of Kennedy, then the attorney general, by Arthur Carew Meredith KC, a brother of the late master of the rolls (1906–12), Richard E. Meredith, and a cousin of James Creed Meredith KC, a member of the committee, who had been president of the Dáil Supreme Court and was soon to be a member of the new

---

* Former president of the Irish Legal History Society.
1 9 *Irish Jurist*, 15 Feb. 1857, p. 31; see also *I.L.T.&S.J.*, 43 (1909), 271.
2 Hugh Kennedy to W.T. Cosgrave, 13 Aug. 1923, UCDA P4/1390; Kennedy, 'Judicial reorganisation in the Irish Free State', *Law Journal*, 59 (1924), 70–2; see also Laura Cahillane's chapter.
3 Judge of the High Court, 1896–1921, lord chancellor of Ireland, 1921–2, previously Unionist MP for Londonderry, 1892–5.
4 Ross to Edward Shortt, chief secretary for Ireland, undated, autumn 1918, as forwarded by Ross to Austen Chamberlain, 21 Jan. 1919, Cadbury Research Library (CRL): special collections, University of Birmingham, Austen Chamberlain papers AC 24/1/39.

High Court and thereafter of the Supreme Court. The report of the committee had been submitted to the government on 25 May 1923 and was published on 12 June. Kennedy lost no time in putting the legislative drafting in hand and by the first week of July he was acknowledging to Meredith that 'the time is now ripe for our reading and considering [the draft bill] together'.[5]

The committee stated at the end of their report that 'as we have been able to concur in a unanimous report we have not thought it necessary to set out the reasons upon which our recommendations are based.'[6] Kennedy emphasised this unanimity in explanatory articles which he contributed to a London legal journal in February 1924.[7] Lord Glenavy[8] had been chairman of the committee and was then chairman of the Senate. When speaking in the Senate debates on other aspects of the reforms he said (to Kennedy's mind, entirely wrongly – 'such a tissue of falsehood'[9]) that the committee

> with the exception of one were unanimous in favour of the wig and gown, but they declined to make any recommendation upon it because the dissenting member said that he would bring in a minority report if we did, and we did not want to break up the unanimity of the committee on a small matter of that kind.[10]

Presenting a united front to the world was thus important to the committee. Since it had considered and recommended an age limit for the lower courts, its silence on whether this should also apply to the superior courts suggests that its members were not of one mind on the subject, if they discussed it at all. It cannot be taken as indicating that it had considered the subject in an indirect way, as W.T. Cosgrave, perhaps somewhat disingenuously, was to suggest in saying that since a retirement age of 70 had been recommended by the committee for the Circuit Court 'we took that to apply to the other cases'.[11] Members of the committee who had judicial experience in the old court system, Glenavy (born in 1851), Charles A. O'Connor (born in 1854), who had been appointed master of the rolls in 1912, and William Johnston[12] (born in 1868) may have been hesitant about such an innovation. The conventional view, as expressed by James O'Connor, a lord justice of appeal, in his submission to the committee, was that the

5 Kennedy to Meredith, 7 July 1923, UCDA P4/1097(1).
6 *Report of the Judiciary Committee* (Dublin, 1923), p. 26.
7 *Law Journal*, 59 (1924), 70–2, and 87–9.
8 James H.M. Campbell had held office as lord chief justice of Ireland (1917–18) and as lord chancellor of Ireland (1918–21). He was made a peer as Lord Glenavy following his retirement from that office.
9 Kennedy to Louis Walsh, 7 Feb. 1924, UCDA P4/1125(1).
10 *Seanad Éireann deb.*, vol. 2, col. 15 (30 Jan. 1924).
11 Ibid.
12 Johnston was appointed a judge of the County Court in 1911, to the High Court in 1924 and to the Supreme Court in 1939.

independence of the judges required that they would hold office for life,[13] or 'during their good behaviour' in the phrase used in the statute of 1782 that had provided for this security of tenure.[14]

Ireland was among the first of the common law jurisdictions to introduce a retirement age. There was no such limit for judges of the superior courts in the United Kingdom until 1959, when a retirement age of 75 was brought in.[15] Lord Justice A.T. Lawrence (1843–1936) was promoted to be lord chief justice of England at the age of 77 in April 1921, to keep the place warm for Gordon Hewart, the attorney general (and reportedly learned eleven months later of his resignation and replacement by Hewart when reading his daily newspaper).[16] Samuel Clarke Porter QC (1875–1956) was aged 71 when he was appointed from the Bar to the bench as a lord justice of appeal in Northern Ireland in 1946. New Zealand had set a retirement age of 72 in 1903,[17] although no reference was made to this in a summary of the country's judicial system that was made available to the Judiciary Committee.[18] Retirement ages were introduced later in Canada[19] and in Australia.[20]

That judges of advanced years might have a diminished capacity for the discharge of their functions had been a commonplace observation for centuries. Lord Mansfield (1705–93), chief justice of King's Bench in England between 1756 and 1788, had acknowledged this when writing to his friend the duke of Rutland, then the lord lieutenant of Ireland, in 1785: 'I go downhill with gentle decay ... The load of business grows too great.'[21] Ripeness of years and length of judicial service are of course in themselves not correlated with a diminution of physical or mental capacity but, as Ronan Keane has remarked, 'mental infirmity, deafness, remoteness from ordinary life and increasing rigidity of views marred some lengthy judicial careers.'[22]

13 Lord Justice O'Connor, memo. (undated) on suggested changes in Ireland's judicial system, UCDA P4/1092 (84).
14 An Act for Securing the Independency of the Judges and the Impartial Administration of Justice, 21 & 22 Geo. III, c. 50 (Ir.) (1782).
15 Judicial Pensions Act 1959.
16 Entry on Lawrence (later Lord Trevethin) in *Oxford DNB* (revised by Robert Stevens).
17 The Supreme Court Judges Act 1903.
18 A.F. Blood, 'memo. on courts and judiciary of Australia and New Zealand', prepared for the Bar Council, 7 Dec. 1922, UCDA P4/1089(10). The most striking point in the memorandum, in the context of later concerns of the Bar that the new system would introduce a decentralisation of the courts and hence of the Bar, may have been that the four puisne judges of the High Court of New Zealand were stated to be assigned to and resident in Auckland, Wellington, Canterbury and Otago respectively. The land mass of New Zealand is broadly equivalent to (slightly larger than) that of Great Britain.
19 An Act to amend the Supreme Court Act 1927.
20 The Constitution Amendment (Retirement of Judges) bill 1977 was approved by referendum that year.
21 Mansfield to Rutland, 11 Dec. 1785, cited in Norman S. Poser, *Lord Mansfield: justice in the age of reason* (Montreal, 2013), p. 383.
22 Entry on Palles in the *Oxford DNB*, although Palles himself was specifically stated not to be within the scope of that observation.

There was moreover, fairly or unfairly, a general sense of judges having a propensity to retain office beyond a time when there might be grounds for concern about their capacity or competence and fitness, and as being able only to make a lesser contribution to judicial efficiency. When Lord Aberdeen, the lord lieutenant, was informed in September 1906 by Porter, the master of the rolls, of his intention to stand down, he remarked to James Bryce, the chief secretary, that 'for a judicial dignitary to retire *before* he becomes defective in his powers seems to be in itself a commendable thing.'[23] A decade later Asquith, the prime minister (who was himself a QC), noted in frustration to Buckmaster, the lord chancellor, that 'the occupants of the Irish bench – especially the antiquated and infirm – stick to their places like wax',[24] as he sought early in 1916 to bring about a vacancy on the Irish bench that might be filled by James H.M. Campbell.[25]

The course of judicial careers and of retirements in the superior courts in the decades before 1923 illustrates some potential difficulties in the conduct of judicial business which the adoption of a retirement age would have been intended to address. The period for which Christopher Palles held judicial office, between 1874 and 1916, was exceptional, but there were many other lengthy judicial careers in this era, as indicated in Table 8.1:

Table 8.1: Lengthy judicial careers, ending 1897–1923

Judge	Length of judicial career	Judge	Length of judicial career
Christopher Palles	42 years	R.R. Warren	29 years
Hedges Eyre Chatterton	36 years	Charles Barry	27 years
Lord Morris	34 years	William Drennan Andrews	27 years
John George Gibson	33 years	William Johnson	27 years
Gerald FitzGibbon	31 years	Dodgson Hamilton Madden	26 years
Walter Boyd	30 years	Peter O'Brien	24 years

In the County Court there were some very extended judicial careers. Thomas Rice Henn (1814–1901), first appointed to the bench in 1859, retired as recorder of Galway at the age of 84 in December 1898, 'to the surprise and to the regret of the public and his friends he has felt his duty to retire though still in perfect health and in the full possession of all his facilities.'[26] He had

23   Aberdeen to Bryce, 11 Sept. 1906, Bryce papers NLI, MS 11,014 (1).
24   Asquith to Buckmaster, 11 Jan. 1916 (Buckmaster papers), cited in R.F.V. Heuston, *Lives of the lord chancellors, 1885–1940* (Oxford, 1964), p. 272.
25   See more generally Daire Hogan, 'James Henry Mussen Campbell QC, MP: a life in law and Unionist politics' in Niamh Howlin and Felix Larkin (eds), *Confluences of law and history: Irish Legal History Society discourses and other papers, 2011–2021* (Dublin, forthcoming).
26   *Irish Times*, 7 Jan. 1899.

been unable to sit for some time in 1897.[27] Sir Francis Brady bt., who died in office as County Court judge of Co. Tyrone in 1909, aged 85, had first been appointed in 1861.[28]

In the quarter of a century ending in 1923, 27 judges of the High Court or the Court of Appeal[29] had ceased to hold office, either through retirement or, in the case of eleven men, by virtue of having died in office:

Table 8.2: Judges who died in office, 1897–1923

Judge	Year of death in office	Age at death	Judge	Year of death in office	Age at death
Charles Barry	1897	74	George Wright	1913	66
R.R. Warren	1897	80	John Francis Moriarty	1915	60
William O'Brien	1899	70	William Kenny	1921	75
James Murphy	1901	76			
Gerald FitzGibbon	1909	72	John Gordon	1922	72
Samuel Walker	1911	81	John Blake Powell	1923	62

Some of these deaths were sudden, others followed a period of illness or poor health. To these judges in Ireland might be added Lord Morris who died at the age of 74 in 1901. He had retired as a lord of appeal in ordinary in May 1900 (then receiving the hereditary title of Morris and Killanin) but he continued to be eligible to sit on appeals in the House of Lords, and did so at the request of the lord chancellor in the summer of 1901.[30]

Four judges retired in that period while over the age of 80, and four between the ages of 75 and 80:

Table 8.3: Judges retiring aged 75 or older, 1897–1923

Judge	Age at retirement	Year of retirement
Hedges Eyre Chatterton	84	1904
Christopher Palles	84	1916
William Johnson	83	1909
Walter Boyd	82	1916
Dodgson Hamilton Madden	78	1919
William Drennan Andrews	77	1909
James O. Wylie	75	1920
John George Gibson	75	1921

27 I.L.T.&S.J., 31 (1897), 146.
28 I.L.T.&S.J., 43 (1909), 217 and 231.
29 For completeness the termination of office of Sir John Ross (aged 69) in Dec. 1922, when the office of lord chancellor of Ireland was abolished and after he held judicial office for 26 years (from 1896), might also be noted.
30 I.L.T.&S.J. 35 (1901), 253 and 320.

In total, taking into account also those who died in office, six judges ceased to hold office at or over the age of 80 and six at or over the age of 75. Two of the judges in the existing courts in 1923 were aged 79 and 75 respectively, namely W.H. Dodd, born in March 1844, and Stephen Ronan, born in April 1848. All of the sitting judges were entitled to receive compensation from the British government upon the abolition of those courts.[31] The claims filed in 1924 generally included actuarial reports indicating the life expectancy (and hence, by extension, the anticipated period of future service as a judge) of each claimant. These extended well into (and in one case beyond) the eighth decade (70s) of their lives.

Andrew Marshall Porter was 69 in 1906 when he stepped down, Peter O'Brien (raised to the peerage as Lord O'Brien of Kilfenora in 1900) was 71 in 1913, Hugh Holmes was 74 in 1915 and Dunbar Plunket Barton 64 in 1918. Four men stepped down at ages much younger than for any conventional retirement and in each case this was specifically attributed at the time to ill health. These were Edmund Bewley, the judicial commissioner of the Land Commission (aged 60, in 1898); Richard E. Meredith (aged 57, in 1912); Redmond Barry (aged 46, in 1913, who died very shortly afterwards) and R.R. Cherry (aged 57, in 1916). However, retirements on health grounds would not have been confined to these instances. Although discretion and a sense of decorum inhibited contemporary references being made to a judge being absent from court through illness or infirmity, or to having decided to retire on such grounds, the basis of such absences and such retirements will naturally have been no secret among the legal community.

Taking the last decade before Independence, two of the judges with the highest profiles, Peter O'Brien and Christopher Palles, who retired in 1913 and 1916 respectively, had both in effect been unable to discharge their judicial functions for about twelve months prior to their retirements being announced.[32] The *Law Times* speculated in January 1916 that if Palles was unable to go on circuit at the start of March he would tender his resignation 'though after his long and brilliant services he might well rest for a year before taking such a step'.[33] In the event his resignation took effect in June.[34] Walter Boyd, who retired shortly before Palles, was reportedly 'well over 80 and stone deaf,'[35] a condition elsewhere described more generously as 'the advance of years [having] added a considerable degree of deafness' to his other traits and

31 Irish Free State (Consequential Provisions) Act 1922, s. 2 and sch. 2.
32 Between Nov. 1912 and Nov. 1913 there were four references in the *Irish Law Times and Solicitors' Journal*, and twelve in the *Law Times* to the state of O'Brien's health. Between Nov. 1915 and Apr. 1916 the *Law Times* made five references to Palles in that context.
33 *Law Times*, 140 (22 Jan. 1916) 250.
34 *Law Times*, 141 (24 June 1916) 135.
35 Asquith to Buckmaster, 17 Jan. 1916 (Buckmaster papers), cited in Heuston, *Lives of the lord chancellors*, p. 273.

idiosyncracies.[36] W.E. Wylie attributed the willingness of his uncle, the judicial commissioner of the Land Commission, to retire in his favour in 1920 not only to family goodwill but to underlying illness: 'I knew that uncle James Wylie was in very bad health and was meditating retirement'.[37] William Kenny had not been in good health before his death in February 1921,[38] and John Blake Powell did not sit in court for some time in 1923, and was not present when the courts opened in Dublin Castle in April on their transfer from the King's Inns.[39]

The judicial system had had some slack, as evidenced by a decision at the time not to fill the place vacated by Palles,[40] and seventeen months elapsed before William Moore KC, MP (subsequently lord chief justice of Northern Ireland, 1925–37) was appointed in November 1917. Excess judicial capacity had been acknowledged by a legislative provision in 1907 that the next two vacancies that arose in the High Court would not be filled, which took effect in December 1909 when Andrews and Johnson retired.[41] A decade later Ross believed that further reductions in the judicial establishment were called for: 'the next two vacancies in the King's Bench should not be filled up. There is no work to justify the retention of eight [King's Bench Division] judges, there is hardly work for six.'[42] James O'Connor's view in 1923 was that there were too many judges, and that even in the pre-war days only the Chancery judges had been regularly engaged for much more than half of their time.[43] In the turmoil of 1921 and in light of the impending judicial reorganisation on foot of the Government of Ireland Act 1920, no steps were taken to fill the vacancies in the High Court arising on the death of Kenny and the retirement of Gibson in the spring of that year. The Act had envisaged the establishment of separate court systems north and south, to be connected only by a High Court of Appeal for Ireland (which was abolished in 1922).[44] This court reorganisation did take effect in Northern Ireland in 1921 but in the south was superseded by political developments and eventually by the 1924 legislation.

A concern for efficiency and economy in the administration of justice was an element in the reconstruction of the judiciary, bearing in mind the major financial challenges that the new state faced. The Committee had recommended a smaller complement of High Court judges than before, so the new system was

36 Maurice Healy, *The old Munster circuit* (Dublin, 1939), p. 33.
37 W.E. Wylie, 'memoir' in Léon Ó Broin, *W.E. Wylie and the Irish Revolution* (Dublin, 1989), p. 123.
38 *I.L.T.&S.J.*, 55 (1921), 44.
39 *Irish Times*, 12 Apr. 1923.
40 Asquith to James O'Connor, 22 June 1916: Asquith papers, Bodleian Library (Oxford) and 45:9; *Law Times* 141 (1 July 1916) 159.
41 Supreme Court of Judicature (Ireland) Act 1907, s. 1.
42 Ross to Chamberlain, 21 Jan. 1919, CRL AC 24/1/38.
43 Lord Justice O'Connor memo., UCDA P4/1092 (95).
44 Government of Ireland Act 1920, ss 38–53 and sch. 7; Irish Free State (Consequential Provisions) Act 1922, s. 6(1).

to have less capacity to accommodate or bear with any of their number no longer being able or willing[45] to pull their weight. It was in that context, in the light of experience in recent decades, that a retirement age for the superior courts was put forward.

The initial working draft of the 1923 bill had provided, in section 12, that

> the age of retirement of all judges of the High Court and the Supreme Court shall be [70] years but the Executive Council [i.e., the government] may on the advice of the attorney general extend the age of retirement in the case of any judge to [75] years.[46]

This reflected the Judiciary Committee's recommendation of such an extension being available for the lower courts. The draft's square brackets around particular ages were removed before the bill was published and introduced in the Dáil at the end of July.[47] When it came before the Oireachtas in the autumn of 1923 no objection was raised to the principle of a retirement age. The debate focussed on whether, for the superior courts, this should be 70 or 75 or, as ultimately adopted, 72. The provision for the government to have power to extend the age of retirement in the case of any judge to 75 years was refined in October to say that any extension would be made 'after consultation with the chief justice and attorney general.'[48] Senators expressed unease about the implications of any such governmental power for (perceptions of) the independence and indeed the reputation of the judiciary, and in April 1924 the government abandoned that proposal, for all courts.[49]

The 1924 Act provided for a retirement age of 72 for the Supreme and High Courts. The appointment of Thomas Lopdell O'Shaughnessy (1850–1933) to the new High Court[50] at the age of 73 was possible because he already held judicial office, as recorder of Dublin (since 1905), and hence an extended retirement age of 75 was applicable to him.[51] The age limit was set at 70 for the Circuit Court and 65 for the District Court,[52] subject initially to an extension of that age to 70 in the case of justices in the cities of Dublin and Cork.[53] The age for future appointments in the superior courts was reduced in 1995 to 70.[54]

---

45 Such was thought of W.E. Wylie. According to Robert D. Marshall in the *DIB*, 'His decision to limit himself to the role of land judge irked his brethren on the bench, who faced an increased workload'.
46 Initial draft of the Public Courts of the Irish Free State bill, UCDA P4/1097(8).
47 Courts of Justice bill 1923, as introduced (31 July 1923), NAI 2002/14/1396.
48 Minutes of meeting of the government, 6 Oct. 1923, NAI C.2/8, 2002/14/1396; Courts of Justice bill as passed by Dáil Éireann (11 Dec. 1923), NAI TSCH/3/S3195.
49 *Seanad Éireann deb.*, vol. 2, col. 13 (24 Jan. 1924); *Dáil Éireann deb.*, vol. 6, col. 35 (2 Apr. 1924).
50 See Robert Marshall's chapter.
51 Courts of Justice Act 1924, s. 100.
52 Ibid., s. 12 (High and Supreme Courts), s. 40 (Circuit Court) and s. 72 (District Court).
53 This was repealed by the Courts of Justice (District Court) Act 1946, s. 15(1).
54 Courts and Court Officers Act 1995, s. 47.

CHAPTER NINE

Remuneration of judges under the 1924 Act

LAURA CAHILLANE*

The ideas of fairness and trust were important concepts underlying the creation of the Irish Free State in 1922. Many ordinary Irish people had a mistrust of public institutions due to their experience under the British regime.[1] Thus, the Irish state-builders aimed to create a modern, liberal, democratic, polity based on these ideals including aspects such as popular sovereignty, democracy, and a separation of powers.[2] It was felt there was a need to demonstrate to the people that the new institutions of state would be trustworthy and drawn up in accordance with those same ideals so the people would have confidence in them and the stability of the new state would be assured.

The establishment of the new judicial system would be one of the key tenets of this. In the same way as the new Constitution embraced the concepts of popular sovereignty and the separation of powers, the new judicial system also needed to be re-drawn in a way that would inspire the trust of the people. In a break with British tradition, the new judiciary would be completely independent of the other two branches of government and would be linked with the concept of popular sovereignty – such a crucial concept in the 1922 Constitution – since the judges would be the people's judges rather than judges of the Crown.

There were many problems with the existing judicial system, particularly with the judges, who were objects of contempt in the eyes of many Irish people. Ruane has explained this as follows:

> The political reality was that by 1922 many of them were heavily compromised in the eyes of the new radical nationalist leaders, such as Kennedy and Gavan Duffy, who were themselves later to become highly

---

* Associate professor in law at the University of Limerick.
1 See Wilfred Ewart, *A journey in Ireland* (London, 1922); Tom Garvin, *The evolution of Irish nationalist politics* (Dublin, 1981), and Tom Garvin, *1922: the birth of Irish democracy* (Dublin, 2005).
2 See Laura Cahillane, 'Constituting a polity' in Laura Cahillane and Donal Coffey (eds), *The centenary of the Irish Free State Constitution: constituting a polity?* (London, 2024).

influential senior judges in the new régime. It is clear, however, that this antipathy was not based on religious grounds but rather on political grounds, and a belief that many of them had not been impartial as judges. The gulf also reflects a deeper clash of judicial cultures, one long established in Ireland and the other newly emerging. The judicial climate had shifted and the new leaders were now attempting to create a new judicial system under which there would be much greater structural judicial independence from the executive and legislature than that which had applied to the senior Crown judiciary.[3]

Hugh Kennedy was one of the principal drafters of the 1922 Constitution,[4] and was also the first attorney general and first chief justice of the Irish Free State. Importantly, he also sat on the Judiciary Committee and thus is described by Towey as 'deeply involved in shaping the future of the judiciary'[5] and he was one of the primary critics of the *ancien régime*. In a letter to W.T. Cosgrave discussing the judiciary, Kennedy referred to the 'bad repute of the Anglo-Irish bench and its position as an enemy institution in the eyes of the people'.[6] In a *Law Journal* publication, he openly criticised the fact that many of these judges had been appointed for political reasons:

> It was well recognised amongst those who sought promotion to the bench that the only safe avenue of promotion was the whip's office of one or other of the political parties in England. Mere pre-eminence in the legal profession in Ireland ... led nowhere, certainly not to the pre-eminent positions on the bench.[7]

In the letter to Cosgrave, he even went on to mention particular judges who, he felt, had been appointed or promoted solely for political reasons.[8] As Towey notes, Kennedy felt that in order to restore confidence in the administration of justice in the new state, it would be crucial to create a judicial system completely independent of politics: '[t]here can no longer be any mixing up of judicial and executive functions. This should be impressed on the people'.[9]

3 Bláthna Ruane, 'Régime change: the fate of the senior Crown judiciary following the Anglo-Irish Treaty 1921', *Ir. Jur.*, 54:2 (2015), 96–114, at 114. See also Ruane's chapter in this volume.
4 For information on the drafting of the Irish Free State Constitution, see Laura Cahillane, *Drafting the Irish Free State Constitution* (Manchester, 2016).
5 Thomas Towey, 'Hugh Kennedy and the constitutional development of the Irish Free State, 1922–1923', *Ir. Jur.*, 12:2 (1977), 355–70.
6 Hugh Kennedy to W.T. Cosgrave, 13 Aug. 1923, Kennedy papers, UCDA P4/B/30.
7 Hugh Kennedy, 'Judicial reorganisation in the Irish Free State', *Law Journal*, 59 (1924), 70–2.
8 Kennedy to Cosgrave, 13 Aug. 1923, UCDA P4/B/30. For more on judicial appointments see Robert Marshall's chapter.
9 Ibid. As quoted in Towey, 'Hugh Kennedy', at 364.

Kennedy made a vital point about the lack of separation between extant executive and judicial functions involved in some judicial roles, for example that of the lord chancellor. Furthermore, judges could be sworn to act as lords justices and governors of Ireland and have executive functions. Many judges were also privy counsellors, a role which carried functions such as signing orders in council and issuing proclamations.[10] Kennedy pointed to the fact of judges signing the proclamation supressing Sinn Féin, as evidence of this problem: 'A judge might drop in to the Castle of a morning on his way to court and as part of the Executive make an order in council, and then go on to the bench and try an issue between the executive and the people.'[11]

Kennedy was far from the only figure concerned about the status of the judiciary.[12] Another notable critic of the existing system – George Gavan Duffy, who would go on to become president of the High Court – alleged that the Crown judges were corrupt.[13] All of this meant that there would need to be a new process which would align more strictly with the separation of powers as set out in the new Constitution, which would avoid the frequent dalliances with politics and would ensure judicial independence. Judicial remuneration was an important part of this process and many of the debates in the Oireachtas, during the promulgation of the Courts of Justice Act 1924, regarding judicial remuneration were infused with concerns around judicial independence.

DISCUSSIONS ON REMUNERATION IN THE OIREACHTAS DEBATES

Salaries

The first question which arose in relation to remunerating the new judges of the Irish Free State was how much they should be paid. Under the British regime, judges were highly paid. For example, the judges of the superior courts in Ireland received the following salaries in 1923:

Table 9.1: Judicial remuneration in 1923[14]

Office	Salary
Lord chief justice	£5,000
Lords justices of the Court of Appeal and master of the rolls	£4,000
Puisne judge of the High Court of Justice	£3,500

10   This is also discussed by Ruane, 'Régime change', at 98.
11   Kennedy to Cosgrave, 13 Aug. 1923, UCDA P4/B/30.
12   For more detail on concerns in relation to the status of the judiciary and the need to ensure legitimacy, see the chapters by Donal Coffey, Robert Marshall, and Thomas Mohr.
13   Gavan Duffy to Richard Mulcahy, 28 July 1922, Gavan Duffy papers, UCDA P152/272(2).
14   See 'Memo. by the judges of the Supreme and High Courts in support of their claims for improvement in their salaries and pensions' in *Report of the select committee on judicial salaries, expense allowances and pensions* (Dublin, 1953).

Judicial salaries in England at the time were slightly more generous; most judges in England received salaries of £5,000, with certain roles such as the lord chief justice, master of the roles, and lords of appeal receiving more. The lord chancellor's salary was particularly lucrative at £10,000.[15]

The report of the Judiciary Committee had recommended that the president of the Supreme Court should receive £4,000, with each judge receiving £3,000 per year, with the president of the High Court receiving £3,000, and other members of the High Court receiving £2,500.[16] When these figures were proposed to be included in the Courts of Justice bill, questions were raised in the Dáil as to the disparity between the proposed and the older salaries. Cosgrave responded to the queries by acknowledging that the British salaries were higher but he pointed out that the State could not compete. He also noted that in many other countries, judicial salaries did not match those in England and he stressed the need for frugality:

> It is a time for economy. We have very, very large sums to meet under article 10 of the Treaty, and even if the sums were inadequate – and our advice is that they are not; that they are fair – we are certainly approaching a period in the history of our country when economy must be practised ... Generally speaking, these salaries compare favourably with the salaries that were paid before, and having regard to all the circumstances, I do not know that there would be any justification for the Government to recommend to the Dáil higher salaries than the committee recommended'.[17]

Figures based on those recommended by the Judiciary Committee were eventually agreed upon.[18]

Financial hierarchy

A further issue arose then as to the suitability of having a salary hierarchy for judges. A number of deputies argued that there should be equal pay for equal work and also claimed that a higher salary in higher courts could affect the independence of judges in that it could be an incentive to curry favour with those holding the power of promotion. This particular issue arose in response to a point initially raised by Professor William Magennis, who called attention

15 *Hansard 5* (Commons), vol. 514, cols 27–31 (17 Apr. 1953). There was some disparity with judges in Northern Ireland, who were not as well paid as their English counterparts, most judges receiving a salary of £3,000 rather than £5,000 as in England. See Lord Carswell, 'Founding a legal system: the early judiciary of Northern Ireland' in Felix Larkin and Norma Dawson (eds), *Lawyers, the law and history* (Dublin, 2013), p. 17.
16 *Report of the Judiciary Committee* (Dublin, 1923).
17 *Dáil Éireann deb.*, vol. 5, col. 5 (10 Oct. 1923).
18 See below.

to the contradiction in the bill as to status since it was contemplated that judges of the High and Supreme Courts 'may discharge the same duties under the same responsibilities' and yet 'a distinction is made between them in regard to salary and also to precedence.'[19] Although his argument on this point was actually that Supreme Court judges should be treated as distinct 'and their duties reserved to the judges of that special class', he felt that 'interchangeability of the two seems to me to be somewhat of a blot on the bill.' It was Captain William Redmond who later argued that all judges, apart from the chief justice and the president of the High Court, should be put on an equal footing: 'I think that it would be advantageous to the State if it could be possible to have all judges placed upon an equal footing, with the exceptions that I have mentioned, and I would ask the government to take this suggestion into their consideration.'[20]

Redmond also pointed out that the practice of having most of the judges on an equal financial footing was in operation in England and that it worked 'very well there'. Many deputies echoed the sentiment that putting all judges on an equal footing as regards pay would be more suitable than a hierarchy and would not risk their independence:

> We think that they should get equal pay for equal work. Certainly I do not wish to increase the salaries of the judges of the High Court, and I would rather reduce the salaries of the judges of the Supreme Court, but as long as there is the possibility of promotion for a judge that judge to a certain extent loses his independence, and for an extra £500 a year a man might be inclined to become what people might think to be unduly subservient to the people who have it in their power to promote him to an extra £500 a year. That is why I should like to see all the judges placed on the same level. I think the principle of giving Judges employed on similar work a similar rate of pay is a sound one on the whole.[21]

In order to do this, the suggestion was that the salaries should be lowered to £2,000 for all judges apart from the chief justice and president of the High Court. However, the 'brain drain' point was then made in relation to the likelihood of the finest minds from the Bar being incentivised to seek appointment to the bench across the water.[22] Indeed this was something that was clearly of concern in legal circles. In a letter published by the *Irish Times* two days before this debate, Lord Justice James O'Connor criticised certain provisions of the bill and he railed against the 'brain drain' and warned against the reduction of judicial salaries:

19 *Dáil Éireann deb.*, vol. 5, col. 5 (10 Oct. 1923), Professor Magennis.
20 Ibid., Captain Redmond.
21 Ibid., Major Cooper.
22 Ibid., Professor Magennis.

The tendency to export intellect is the result of a natural law. Canada makes bitter complaint that New York – and to some extent London – sucks her best and freshest brains. It is not altogether the quest of material gain, though, that, to be sure, has a great deal to do with it. It is the hunger for the intellectual quality to be found in a great capital ... While protesting against the decentralisation of the profession, I likewise protest against the cutting down of the salaries of the High Court bench. The argument that the Bench is too highly paid is a fallacy. The emoluments ought to be such as to attract the best brains in Ireland; if you want to keep a young, brilliant and ambitious lawyer from trying his chances in London, you must give to the plums of the profession a flavour comparable with that on the other side of the Channel. That is not all: a supreme judge must have prestige. His prestige will, of course, partly depend upon himself; upon his legal acumen, his general erudition, and, above all, on his character. But it will partly depend upon something else, to wit his general station. This ought to be of the best; he should have the little elegancies which refine the mind and lift him up in the estimation of his neighbours; he is, necessarily, more or less aloof from the community; that aloofness should not be that of a hermit in a cottage, but of a personage, who lives a life of repose, contemplation and dignity. And it is because Great Britain has furnished its judges with these things that its judges have a prestige and a reputation which is found nowhere else.[23]

An editorial published in the *Irish Times* the same day referred to O'Connor's letter, observing that lawyers had not generally commented in public about the provisions of the bill but noting that this should not necessarily be taken as approval:

[T]he persons who were best qualified to analyse the merits and defects of this bill – namely the members of the legal profession in the Free State – have maintained a strict silence. It is broken today for the first time by Lord Justice O'Connor ... their silence, however, has created the impression that, as a body, they approve of the essential provisions of the Courts of Justice bill. It is, we think, an erroneous impression. We believe that the views of a majority in both branches of the law are stated today, fairly, reasonably and forcibly by Lord Justice O'Connor.[24]

Some of these comments may have had an impact as it was eventually agreed that this section would stand as originally proposed; the idea of financial

23 See 'The real danger: an export of intellect: letter from the lord justice', *Irish Times*, 8 Oct. 1923. I am grateful to Daire Hogan, who drew my attention to this letter.
24 Editorial, *Irish Times*, 8 Oct. 1923.

parity was dropped and so there was no need to further reduce the proposed salaries.

The status of judges

However, the issue of equal pay for equal work related to a bigger discussion about the status of the judges more generally and whether they were all to be regarded as equal – particularly the district judges, who were referred to in the Act as district justices.[25] A discussion on this point was sparked by a remark from Ernest Blythe, minister for finance, when discussing the issue of salaries for the district justices in the Dáil:

> It is to be remembered, of course, that in other respects the status of the district justices is not made equal to the status of the judges, who are appointed by the governor-general on the advice of the Executive Council, and who can be removed only in a particular way. These particular justices can be removed in another way. However, it is not a matter of very much importance.[26]

In the midst of a discussion which followed about travelling expenses which initially ignored the statement on the status of district judges, Captain Redmond brought attention back to this point and requested clarity on whether the district justices were to be actual judges or not. Eventually the attorney general, John O'Byrne, accusing Redmond of a 'thoroughly mischievous suggestion', clarified that:

> It is perfectly clear that the district justices are judges, and that view of their office has been acted on by the government, which has in every instance had them appointed by the process presented for the appointment of judges in the constitution. Further, article 69 provided that all judges, which includes district justices, shall be independent in the exercise of their functions.

Later, following on from this clarification, Deputy Johnson called for the amendment of the title 'district justice' to 'district judge'.[27] However, this was refused, more for practical reasons than anything else in that this office had already been created and it would be too troublesome to change it at this stage:

> The great objection to this alteration of the designation of these judges is that they have now been established for a considerable time and

---

25 For more on the District Court, see Niamh Howlin's chapter.
26 *Dáil Éireann deb.*, vol. 5, col. 17 (4 Dec. 1923).
27 Ibid., col. 21 (11 Dec. 1923), Johnson.

operating through the country under this particular title, and we do not want to shake our own institutions. Moreover, there is nothing derogatory in the word 'justice'.[28]

And so, the title district justice remained until the Courts Act 1991 altered this to bring it into line with the other judicial titles.[29]

The whole debate about the status of the district justices was also bound up in the discussion about the appropriate source for these salaries, which is discussed below, but also in the related discussions of issues such as travel expenses and bonuses.

Bonuses

Originally there had been a proposal in the bill that: 'Every circuit judge shall receive a salary of £1,500 per annum, together with an addition or bonus thereon calculated at the rate for the time being applicable to the case of a civil servant in receipt of the like salary with the right to bonus thereon ...'.[30] It is not clear where this originated from as the issue of a bonus was not mentioned in the report of the Judiciary Committee, which instead referred to allowances: 'The salary of each circuit judge to be £1,500 a year, with such allowances as are at present made to the County Court judges, and with the like rights as to pensions.'[31] This proposal was the only example of a bonus being attached to a judicial salary and the appropriateness of this was questioned. The minister for finance, Blythe, then agreed to remove the bonus and raise the salary to £1,700 instead. He seemed happy to do so since, he noted, this would have the consequence of costing the state less in the long run.[32]

A further interesting discussion followed this on the need to pay higher salaries for certain district justices; the senior justice in Dublin was to receive a sum of £1,200 per annum, the other of the justices in Dublin and also the justice assigned to Cork city was to receive £1,100 per annum, with all other justices receiving £1,000.[33] Curiously, these distinctions were proposed, not

28 Ibid., attorney general.
29 S. 4 of the Act referred to 'judges of the District Court', although s. 20 still made reference to 'justices of the District Court.' Subsequent legislation has made use of both titles.
30 *Dáil Éireann deb.*, vol. 5, col. 17 (4 Dec. 1923).
31 *Report of the Judiciary Committee* (Dublin, 1923), p. 18.
32 'It will cost the state something less than £1,500 with bonus'. See ibid.
33 'The senior of the justices of the District Court for the time being assigned to the police district of Dublin metropolis shall receive a salary of £1,200 per annum, and every other of the justices aforesaid and also the Justice for the time being assigned to a district comprising or including the City of Cork shall receive a salary of £1,100 per annum. Every other justice of the District Court shall receive a salary of £1,000 per annum.' Suggestions were also made during the debates to extend this higher salary to the judges presiding over the cities of Waterford, Limerick and Galway also but this was not accepted. The *Report of*

due to the cost of living in these cities but rather due to the 'very important business coming before them,'[34] and despite the earlier discussions about equality and the status of judges, no question was raised in relation to variance here. Instead, the debates moved on to a different question regarding differentiation.

The central fund

The final matter that had to be settled in relation to remuneration during the debates on the bill was in relation to the source of the salaries. The salaries of the Supreme, High and Circuit Court judges were all to come from the central fund of the Irish Free State but it was proposed not to take the salaries of district justices from this fund but instead that these would be voted on by the Oireachtas every year:

> The reason for that is largely that the number of district justices will not be fixed, as the number of judges will be fixed. It will give the Oireachtas annually an opportunity of saying that there are far too many district justice and that there is no work for them. It will also give them the opportunity of saying that the courts are congested, that there should be more district justice, and that sufficient appointments are not being made.[35]

This led to a rather lengthy discussion on the appropriateness of such a vote but also on the fact that such an arrangement could affect the independence of the justices, and as noted earlier, would set them apart, thus questioning their status as judges. Deputy Thomas Johnson pointed out that a discussion in the Oireachtas could potentially lead to deputies raising questions as to judicial decisions, whereas this would not be possible in the case of other judges.[36] After the clarification from the attorney general that the district justices were indeed judges, as envisaged by the Constitution, it was argued by Johnson that this strengthened the case for the financial arrangements to be kept the same for all judges and indeed that the Oireachtas should not be

---

the *Judiciary Committee* had recommended the following: 'The salaries of the Dublin metropolitan justices should be maintained at their present figures, with the addition hereinafter provided in the case of the two junior justices. The district justices should be paid a salary of £1,000 yearly, increasing by annual increments to £1,200, and the assistant district justice when appointed should be paid a salary commencing at £700 yearly, increasing by annual increments to £900, with the payment to district and assistant justices of their travelling expenses, subject to strict vouching.' See *Report of the Judiciary Committee*, p. 13.

34   Dáil Éireann deb., vol. 5, col. 17 (4 Dec. 1923), Blythe.
35   Ibid.
36   Ibid.

involved: 'it would be competent for a deputy to discuss the fitness of a district justice to fill his position and the temptation will always be there.'[37] Given the discussion on the status of the judges and the assurance from the attorney general that all judges were to be viewed and treated equally, some deputies were perplexed by this proposed differentiation:

> If these judges are to be treated as independent judges why should they not receive their pay in a manner similar to the other judges? No answer has been given to that question. No case has been put forward for differentiation beyond saying that there may be too many of them appointed.[38]

Deputy Patrick McGilligan further probed the minister's reasoning for the differentiation:

> The minister for finance has stated as his reason for the change that he is not sure of the number of district justices to be appointed. But in the case of the Circuit Court judges, in connection with which it is stated that the number shall not exceed eight, he charges their salaries to the central fund. In the case of the district justices a similar statement appears in the bill – that the number shall not exceed thirty-three – yet it is proposed to pay them with money voted by the Oireachtas. I am still unconvinced that any case for payment out of supply has been made.[39]

The main concern raised here related to judicial independence and the possibility of individual judges being discussed in the Oireachtas as part of a debate on salaries. In the end, the ceann comhairle was asked to give some reassurance on this point but his conclusion did not provide much confidence:

> I think that if the salaries of the district justices were on the estimates it would be made clear, either by standing order or a ruling from the chair, that the decision of a district justice could not be discussed or reviewed in the Dáil, but I fear that the problem that would be presented to the chair would not be solved by such a ruling, because, undoubtedly, when an estimate would be presented, to pay the salaries of thirty-three or any number of district justices it would be open to discuss the fitness of such persons for the position. I think that could not be prevented. While their decision could not be discussed, I have great faith in the ingenuity of deputies.[40]

37 Ibid.
38 Ibid., Redmond.
39 Ibid.
40 Ibid.

Following a long debate that sometimes meandered into other areas, eventually transitory arrangements were agreed to which would allow some control over numbers in the District Courts for the first three years by allowing a vote on salaries during that period and that after 1927 the salaries would come from the central fund in the same way as all other judicial salaries.

PROVISIONS ON REMUNERATION IN THE 1924 ACT

The arrangements which were finally agreed and inserted into the Act were as follows. Section 13 dealt with judges of the High and Supreme Courts and provided that '[t]he president of the High Court shall receive £3,000 per annum, and each ordinary judge thereof £2,500 per annum, and the chief justice shall receive £4,000 per annum, and each judge of the Supreme Court £3,000 per annum.' Section 14 detailed pension arrangements for the superior court judges providing that those retiring after at least 15 years' service would receive a pension for life of two-thirds of his salary at the time he ceases to act as judge and any judge vacating his office owing to age or permanent infirmity, after having completed five or more years' service (but less than fifteen years' service), would receive a pension of one-sixth of his salary with the addition of one-twentieth of said salary for every completed year of service in excess of the five years. Section 15 stated that the remuneration and pensions of the superior court judges would be 'charged upon and be payable out of the central fund of Saorstát Éireann or the growing produce thereof.'

Circuit Court judges were dealt with in section 41, which allocated a salary of £1,700 per annum and provided for the same pension arrangements as the superior court judges. Section 42 also contains a similar provision to that contained in Section 15 making the same arrangements that salaries and pensions of Circuit Court judges would be payable out of the central fund.

A salary of £1,000 per annum is allocated to ordinary district justices under section 74. As outlined earlier in the Oireachtas debates, further arrangements were then made in that £1,200 per annum is allocated to 'the senior of the justices of the District Court for the time being assigned to the police district of Dublin metropolis'. All other ordinary justices in that district, as well as 'the justice for the time being assigned to a district comprising or including the City of Cork', were allocated a salary of £1,100 per annum. All other district justices were to receive £1,000 per annum. Again, following the arrangements which had been agreed during the debates on the Act, the source of the salaries was split between two periods and set out as follows:

The several salaries aforesaid shall until the end of the financial year ending on the 31st day of March, 1927, be paid out of moneys to be annually provided by the Oireachtas, and shall thereafter be charged on and be payable out of the central fund or the growing produce thereof.

A different arrangement is made for the pensions of District Court justices in section 75, which states that the office of a District Court justice

> shall be a pensionable office within the Superannuation Acts, 1834 to 1919, and the pension, gratuity or allowance granted to or in respect of a Justice of the District Court on his retirement or death shall be ascertained in the manner and subject to the conditions prescribed by those Acts.

An interesting provision is contained in sections 45 and 70 which deal with vacancy in office in the cases of Circuit and District Court judges respectively. It specifies that in case of the illness of any such judges, a deputy may be appointed to act in their place, on the recommendation of the attorney general, but the remuneration paid to such deputy would be 'as may be sanctioned by the minister for finance'. Such provision is not included in section 11 on vacancy in office of superior court judges, which simply provides that 'whenever the office of any judge of the High Court or of the Supreme Court shall become vacant a new judge may be appointed in his place.'

CONCLUSION

It is not surprising that issues relating to independence and status would arise in the debates on the financial arrangements in the bill, considering the desire to establish a new, completely independent judiciary that would be set apart from the previous system. However, it is interesting that in many of the debates on the remuneration arrangements, the issues that dominated were those of independence and equality of judges. It is also noteworthy that the government resisted attempts at establishing financial parity between judges and that they persisted in treating the District Court judges differently despite insisting that they were equal. Some rather worrying comments were also evident, like those of the minister for finance, quoted above, where he misunderstands the position of the justices. Given the importance of securing confidence in the administration of this new system of justice, perhaps more consideration should have been given to some of the proposals on equality, status, and independence of judges – particularly in the case of the district justices, whose status remained somewhat obscure, despite the assurances given by the attorney general during these debates. However, like many other things during the period of the Irish Free State, it seems that arguments based on principles were defeated by the demands of practicality and alacrity.

CHAPTER TEN

'On the fly and on the sly': a District Court in action

NIAMH HOWLIN*

INTRODUCTION

Part III of the Courts of Justice Act 1924 dealt with the District Court, or An Chúirt Bhreithiúnais Dúithche.[1] There were to be thirty-three districts, presided over by District Court justices.[2] However, as Kotsonouris points out, the District Court had effectively been 'in operation for almost two years before it was formally established.'[3] She uses the memorable phrase 'on the fly and on the sly'[4] to describe the Court's creation. Twenty-seven men had been appointed as temporary resident magistrates under the Provisional Government (Transfer of Functions) Order 1922.[5] The title 'resident magistrate', with its negative connotations, was dropped, and the new appointees were styled 'district justices', adopting the terminology of the popular Dáil courts.[6] There had been 150 applications for these posts, and Kevin O'Higgins declared in December 1922 that the men appointed had been well-received: '[a]s in the case of the Civic Guard, a great mass of the people welcomed them and gave unmistakable signs of their satisfaction at their advent.'[7] He described their role in the following terms: 'As to the work, it is hard; the areas are very large, and no justice has less than twenty days' work in the month. Some of them have more.'[8] Kotsonouris described them as 'men who set out in the midst of a Civil War, without experience, preparation or guidelines, to establish the rule of law in communities who could have no certainty that the new order would survive the conflict.'[9]

---

* Associate professor at the Sutherland School of Law, University College Dublin.
1 Courts of Justice Act 1924, s. 67.
2 Ibid., s. 69. This part of the legislation was commenced on 16 Aug. 1924 by the Courts of Justice Act 1924 (Commencement) (No. 4) Order 1924 (SI 10/1924).
3 Mary Kotsonouris, *'Tis all lies, your worship': tales from the District Court* (Dublin, 2011), p. 1.
4 Ibid., p. 5.
5 *Iris Oifigiúil*, 28 Oct. 1922.
6 See Thomas Mohr's chapter. This terminology changed in the 1990s: see Laura Cahillane's chapter.
7 *Dáil Éireann deb.*, vol. 2, col. 5 (13 Dec. 1922).
8 Ibid.
9 Kotsonouris, *'Tis all lies'*, p. ix.

The appointments made in 1922 were confirmed by the District Justices (Temporary Provisions) Act 1923.[10] In the words of the minister for justice, Kevin O'Higgins, the measure was 'a temporary bill to meet the necessities of the situation existing at present'.[11] He was at pains to ensure that these justices had a popular mandate, and were appointed by the minister on the advice of the Executive Council and 'not patronage appointments',[12] like the old resident magistrates. The appointment, remuneration and retirement age of district justices are considered in the chapters by Laura Cahillane and Daire Hogan.[13]

This chapter examines how the District Court operated during the twilight period of 1923, focusing on an individual district as a case study. Kevin Costello points out that the District Court was 'the true workhouse' of the new courts system. It was a local court of limited jurisdiction, replacing the Petty Sessions Courts,[14] and as Kotsonouris points out,

> For a year and half, the justices had to carry out the administration of the law throughout the country without a framework of higher courts for the purpose of appeal or to send serious crimes forward for trial; neither were there rules of court. Anti-Treaty forces frequently tried to kill the justices or disrupt their courts.[15]

One member of the Dáil described it as 'the poor man's court. Very many cases that will crop up in ordinary everyday life will be decided there.'[16] This snapshot of a single District Court in its first year of operation demonstrates the nature of such cases.

BALLYBAY DISTRICT COURT IN 1923

Ballybay was a small town near Castleblayney, Co. Monaghan, with a population of less than 2,000.[17] Former solicitor Bartholomew Goff[18] was

---

10 This was commenced on 27 Mar. 1923.
11 *Seanad Éireann deb.*, vol. 1, col. 13 (14 Mar. 1923).
12 Ibid.
13 Alongside district justices were peace commissioners. District Justices (Temporary Provisions) Act 1923, s. 4. They were described by Kevin O'Higgins as 'honorary justices, not to exercise judicial functions, but to administer what I call ministerial functions, a certain number of the small duties of the Petty Sessions justices in the past.' *Dáil Éireann deb.*, vol. 2, col. 5 (13 Dec. 1922).
14 The Courts of Justice Act 1924, s. 77, provided that the jurisdiction of the District Court included 'all powers, jurisdictions, and authorities which ... were vested by statute or otherwise in justices or a justice of the peace sitting at Petty Sessions'.
15 Kotsonouris, *'Tis all lies'*, p. 2.
16 *Dáil Éireann deb.*, vol. 2, col. 5 (13 Dec. 1922), O'Connell.
17 According to the 1911 census, its urban and rural districts had a combined population of 1,890. The majority (1,102 or 58 per cent) were Roman Catholics.
18 An active member of the Gaelic League in the early part of the century, his name appears

appointed as district justice under the District Justices (Temporary Provisions) Act 1923, and was supported by two peace commissioners. At his first sittings in Ballybay on 13 February 1923, Goff expressed his sympathy for the minister for justice, Kevin O'Higgins, whose father had recently been 'most cruelly murdered'.[19] He condemned such acts of violence as 'unmanly, un-Irish and unchristian.' Goff hastened to add that this 'was not a matter of politics, as the court knew no politics in any sense', but it is difficult not to discern a whiff of political statement here. Goff had just five cases before him at his first sittings;[20] three related to drunkenness and two concerned motor vehicles that were driven without lights. He made his views on drunkenness very clear, asking one defendant if he were not ashamed of his drunkenness, and said that such cases were 'a disgrace to any Irishman'.[21] He also commented on the 'grave danger' of unlighted vehicles, and described having encountered several on a recent night-time drive.

Table 10.1: Listed cases in Ballybay District Court 1923

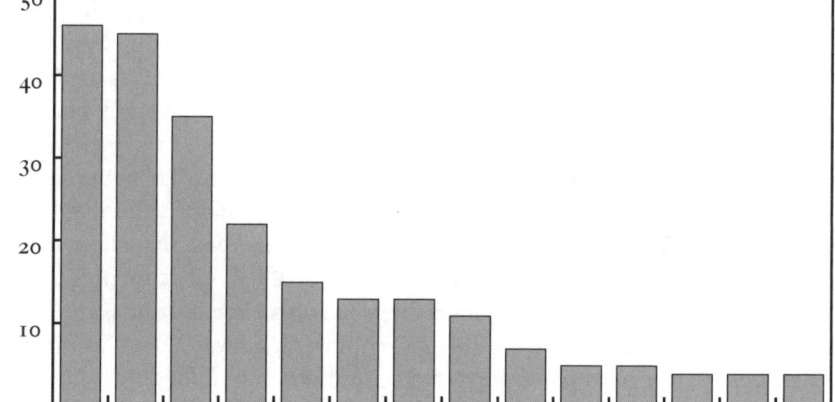

as 'P.S. Mac Eachach' in the order book, and he was listed as 'Partholan S. Mac Eachach' in the official *Calendar of District Courts* (Dublin, 1924). Goff was also the district justice for Carrickmacross and Castleblayney. See Lynsey Black and Danielle Jefferis's chapter.
19 *Northern Standard*, 16 Feb. 1923.
20 13 Feb. 1923, Ballybay District Court Order Book 1922–1925, NAI DC/BBY/1 (hereafter Ballybay DCOB)
21 *Northern Standard*, 16 Feb. 1923. Later statements about drunkeness, dancing and gambling, as well as commentary on political issues, led to complaints being made about Goff: NAI TSCH 5/6642.

Altogether, there were 233 cases listed in the Ballybay District Court in 1923, covering a range of matters such as malicious injury, trespass to property and assault. An overview of the nature of the cases can be seen in Table 10.1. The most common cases heard related to the non-payment of local rates and the use of threats, which included threatening language and the more serious offence of threatening to kill. As will be seen, the Civil War impacted upon the kinds of cases being dealt with at this level.

While it is impossible to consider all of these categories of cases in a short chapter, the following sections highlight some of the issues which came before the District Court in 1923, and reflect upon what this tells us about life in a small Irish town.

CONTRACT DISPUTES

One category of case that came before the court was contract disputes of relatively low value. Examples from 1923 generally relate to contracts entered into by individuals hiring themselves out as labourers or servants, generally for six months at a time. Often this was done at hiring fairs, which were common in Ballybay and other towns in the region.[22] Conditions were hard and payment was poor, and sometimes labourers found themselves unable to remain until the end of their contracted period. These were generally pursued as breach of contract cases.[23] In one case from October 1923, a girl aged sixteen was hired at £10 for a period of six months. She returned to her family after four months, saying she 'would drown herself before she would go back'.[24] She claimed that the work was hard and dangerous, that she was not adequately fed, and that her employer, Mr Steward, had made inappropriate remarks to and about her.[25] The proceedings in court were unruly, as the girl's mother, both cross-examined the former employer, and was herself examined as a witness.[26] The local paper reported both mother and daughter shouting at the judge and the complainant. At one stage in the proceedings, Goff commented that the defendant was 'a good-looking girl', in response to which her mother shouted 'and she's not 17 'til March!', to the apparent hilarity of those in court. Goff held that there was sufficient cause for the girl leaving, and no breach of contract. Despite his own comment about the defendant's appearance, he added, 'A man like Stewart having a young girl like the defendant ought to be very careful about what he would say to her.'[27]

22 The *Northern Standard* reported on a hiring fair in Ballybay in June 1922 where 'hiring was dull' and 'labour was plentiful.' *Northern Standard*, 2 June 1922. See also the National Folklore Schools Collection, including vol. 946, p. 136; vol. 951, p. 74 and vol. 948, p. 202. Available at www.duchas.ie.
23 E.g., 19 May, 12 June, 13 Nov. 1923, Ballybay DCOB.
24 *Northern Standard*, 12 Oct. 1923.
25 9 Oct. 1923, Ballybay DCOB.
26 *Northern Standard*, 12 Oct. 1923.
27 Ibid.

THE STREETS OF A COUNTRY TOWN

The court regularly heard cases of trespass in relation to livestock which roamed on other people's crops and grazing land.[28] In March 1923, for example, David Miller complained about 'three cows and one goat' on his meadowland. The case was adjourned until the next court day, and in the meantime the defendant was ordered to repair the broken fence.[29] Goats were also the cause of several actions for nuisance on the road.[30] There were some repeat offenders whose goats frequently wandered on the streets of the town.[31]

Another aspect of life in a small rural town is evidenced by the number of nuisance actions for 'lack of closet accommodation'.[32] These cases were taken by the local Rural District Council against owners and occupiers of premises that did not have adequate sanitation facilities. This was essentially a public health issue, and medical doctors frequently testified in court. At one hearing, a Dr Hunter swore that there was 'a large amount of unsanitariness in the town.'[33] In one set of proceedings against a landlord, heard in December 1923, the defendant was prepared to 'put up dry closets', but the solicitor for the Council said that 'earth closets' were unacceptable.[34] The district justice actually went to view the premises in question on Hall Street, following which he fined the landlord. These problems continued into the new year, with a number of cases in February 1924 concerning a 'want of water closet or other privy accommodation', or 'wooden privies', which were 'filthy and dilapidated'.[35]

VULNERABLE PERSONS

In December 1923 a case of serious child neglect was brought by ISPCC inspector Bernard Mallon. Mary Catherine Connolly was convicted of having wilfully neglected her two children, 'in a manner likely to cause them unnecessary suffering or injury to their health.'[36] Neither Connolly nor the children's father, John White, appeared in court. Both parents were married to other people, but had lived together for a few years. They were a 'mixed' couple of different denominations. Connolly's mother described White as 'a genteel beggar', often drunk. She said that her oldest grandchild was staying 'in the convent' and the other was at home. When the ISPCC inspector visited the house on Meetinghouse Lane, he found it to be dirty, with bedding of loose hay and a torn quilt on the floor. Goff was highly critical of the parents,

28 E.g. 13 Mar. 1923, Ballybay DCOB.
29 13 Mar. 1923, ibid.
30 E.g., there were three such cases on 13 Nov. 1923, ibid.
31 E.g., Elizabeth McCaffrey: 13 Nov. and 11 Dec. 1923, ibid.
32 E.g., 13 Nov. 1923, ibid.
33 *Northern Standard*, 21 Dec. 1923.
34 Ibid.
35 12 Feb. 1924, Ballybay DCOB.
36 8 Dec. 1923, ibid.

sentencing the father to a month in Mountjoy Prison, and the mother to a month in Dundalk Gaol,[37] 'and the children to be committed to some institution'.[38]

This was not the only instance when the district justice ordered that a child be institutionalised. In one case brought by the Society of St Vincent de Paul, two children, aged ten and six years, were committed to St Martha's industrial school until they had each reached the age of sixteen.[39] They had been 'found begging on the public street'.[40]

The District Court also had the authority to commit individuals to asylums if they were deemed to be 'dangerous lunatics'. Although this arose infrequently in 1923, there were seven committals to the Monaghan lunatic asylum by the peace commissioners in 1924.[41]

DISPUTES BETWEEN NEIGHBOURS

Most of the violence that came to the attention of the District Court involved neighbours beating one another during a dispute. Examples of the kinds of tort actions brought in 1923 included threatening language and assault. The hostility and ill-feeling could lead to a tangle of litigation between multiple parties, arising from a long-held feud or grudge that bubbled over into an altercation. For example, August 1923 saw 'a series of summonses' between Agnes Courtney, James Loughran, and James and Bernard Kavenagh for 'assault and abusive language.'[42] All five cases were adjourned for two months.[43] When the cases came up again in October, they also included actions by Jane Kavenagh and John Kennedy. In total, fourteen actions, which included assault, threatening language and trespass, were adjourned by consent.[44] Eventually, the various cases were dismissed on the merits in November.[45]

THEFT AND DAMAGE TO PROPERTY

Theft in Ballybay tended to be of small items of jewellery, or of eggs and fowl. For example, domestic servant Mary Ellen McEntee was accused of stealing eggs and a gold watch from two separate individuals in May 1923.[46] Patrick

37 18 Dec. 1923, ibid.
38 *Northern Standard*, 21 Dec. 1923.
39 Under the Elementary Education Act 1876, s. 12. In a similar case the following year, a two-year-old boy was committed to High Park industrial school in Drogheda, also until he reached the age of sixteen years: 9 Sept. 1924, Ballybay DCOB.
40 12 June 1923, Ballybay DCOB.
41 Under the Lunacy Regulation (Ireland) Act 1871 (30 & 31 Vic., c. 118).
42 *Northern Standard*, 17 Aug. 1923, p. 2.
43 14 Aug 1923, Ballybay DCOB.
44 9 Oct. 1923, ibid.
45 13 Nov. 1923, ibid.
46 8 May 1923 Ballybay DCOB; *Freeman's Journal*, 11 May 1923.

Lavelle, described in one newspaper report as 'a returned Yankee',[47] came before the District Court on charge of stealing 'six head of fowl'.[48] The *Northern Standard* described this as 'a sequel ... to the many complaints of alleged fowl stealing in the outlying districts'.[49] Lavelle, who apparently had no fixed abode, had returned from the United States about a year before with a bad reputation, according to prosecution witness Rose Curley. His brother told the court that he 'believed he had fought with the British army during the European war.' When he was discovered by a member of the Civic Guard sitting at the side of the road with a bag of birds, Lavelle was also found to be in possession of items of women's jewellery that had been reported stolen. He was separately charged with illegal possession,[50] and, being unable to afford bail, was committed to Dundalk Gaol to await trial in October.

Jurisdiction over malicious damage[51] cases worth less than £20 was codified in the 1924 Act, and there are several examples of such cases in Ballybay, where turf or trees were damaged or livestock was injured.[52] Many of these cases were listed multiple times and ultimately dismissed. A case taken by Margaret McGovern against James, Anne and Mary McGovern for destroying doors and a house appeared to be a family dispute, and was dismissed on the merits.[53] John McGovern brought a similar action against Margaret, and against John and Patrick Hanratty three months later, which was similarly dismissed.[54] Similarly, actions for malicious injury taken by John McConville against Elizabeth McConville for damage to fences and injury to cattle in June were postponed for a month, and then dismissed without prejudice.[55]

HOMICIDE AND FIREARMS

Occasionally cases of murder or manslaughter came before the District Court. In one case in 1923, a man named Charles Webster was accused of the manslaughter of a four-year-old child, Betty Dunleavy.[56] She had been hit by his motor vehicle, but a coroner's inquest had ruled that it was accidental. The district justice held that there had been no criminal negligence, and Webster

47 *Weekly Freeman's Journal*, 21 July 1923.
48 *Northern Standard*, 2, 13 July 1923. 10 July 1923, Ballybay DCOB.
49 *Northern Standard*, 13 July 1923.
50 10 July 1923, Ballybay DCOB.
51 See N. Howlin, 'Compensation for malicious injuries' in Oonagh Breen and Noel McGrath (eds), *Palles: the legal legacy of the last Lord Chief Baron* (Dublin, 2022).
52 E.g., 12 June 1923, Ballybay DCOB.
53 13 Mar. 1923, ibid.
54 12 June 1923, ibid.
55 12 June, 10 July, ibid.
56 29 Sept, 9 Oct. 1923, ibid.

was discharged.⁵⁷ The child's mother, Catherine Dunleavy, later brought an action against another woman for abusive language.⁵⁸ She claimed that the defendant, with whose child her daughter had been playing when she was killed, 'was always slandering the dead child and her'.⁵⁹ Goff adjourned the proceedings for three months, warning McGuirk to behave herself in the meantime. When the case came on again in March 1924, the complainant did not appear, and the case went no further.⁶⁰

Other violent deaths arose from the continued state of disturbance around the country. For example, in April 1923, a young girl named Bridget Markey was accused of murdering her aunt, Bridget Geoghegan.⁶¹ A group of armed and unknown men had entered her house demanding tea, and she lifted one of their revolvers and discharged it, killing her aunt.⁶² She was cleared of responsibility at the coroner's inquest, and Goff said she left the District Court 'without a stain on her character'.⁶³ The real responsibility, he said, lay with the armed men:

> The men who came to Markey's house that day carrying lethal weapons, instead of being engaged in peaceful and useful labour, were going about the country as part of a wicked conspiracy ... What pain these armed men had caused in that family! They had sent a poor woman to an untimely grave. Imagine the ordeal they put the young lady through, that he had now discharged from the dock!⁶⁴

Sherry and James Laurence Reilly were brought before the peace commissioner following the killing of a man named J.H. Conlon following the general election result in Monaghan in August 1923.⁶⁵ They were remanded on bail⁶⁶ and came before the District Court at the next sittings in September. The district justice received informations from seven prosecution witnesses and five defence witnesses.

On several occasions, individuals were charged either with threatening to shoot or with unlawful possession of firearms. In November 1923, farmers James Mulligan and James McGinety were brought before the peace

57 *Northern Standard*, 12 Oct. 1923.
58 18 Dec. 1923, Ballybay DCOB.
59 *Northern Standard*, 21 Dec. 1923. The newspaper reported that Mrs McGuirk had apparently called her 'a crooked-eyed poor house b——'.
60 11 Mar. 1924, Ballybay DCOB.
61 10 Apr. 1923, ibid.
62 *Northern Standard*, 12 Apr. 1923.
63 *Freeman's Journal*, 12 Apr. 1923.
64 Ibid.
65 *Frontier Sentinel*, 8 Sept. 1923, p. 3. The three elected representatives for Monaghan in the fourth Dáil were Patrick McCarvill from the Republican Party, and Ernest Blythe and Patrick Duffy from Cumann na nGaedheal.
66 29 Aug. 1923, Ballybay DCOB.

commissioners on charges of assault and illegal possession of firearms.[67] When they appeared before the district justice, they were accused of threatening to shoot soldier Michael Goodman 'in furtherance of an armed revolt against the government.'[68] As Goodman, who was stationed in Clones, had since taken ill,[69] the case was adjourned to the Castleblayney district sessions on 4 December, to be tried under the Public Safety (Emergency Powers) Act 1923.[70]

Another case under the Public Safety Act arose the following month. A Colt revolver was found in a baby's cradle.[71] The owner of the house, Thomas McQuillan, had allegedly threatened to shoot a neighbour who was tending to his potato crop. McQuillan had previously served in the British Army, and was said to have also served in, and possibly deserted, the Free State Army. A charge of threatening to shoot was dropped, but McQuillan was convicted of illegal possession under the Public Safety (Emergency Powers) Act 1923. Goff commented that it was 'serious' to have 'disbanded soldiers going about committing outrages',[72] and said that he would like to give a twelve-month custodial sentence. Solicitor McWilliam pointed out that the maximum under the legislation was six months[73] however, so McQuillan was sentenced to six months in Dundalk Gaol.[74]

ALCOHOL

Alcohol featured regularly in the Ballybay District Court. Prosecutions for drunkenness were common, and Goff took a firm stance against public inebriation. These included individuals who were both 'drunk and incapable' and those who were 'drunk and disorderly', and were brought under the Licensing Act 1872[75] by members of the Civic Guard. The District Court dealt with applications relating to licences to sell alcohol. The 1924 Act provided that all licensing jurisdiction previously exercised by justices of the peace were conferred on the District Court, with the exception of the power to grant new licences, which was reserved for the Circuit Court.[76] Temporary licence transfers were usually granted as a matter of routine.

67   7 Nov. 1923, ibid.
68   13 Nov. 1923, ibid.
69   *Freeman's Journal*, 16 Nov. 1923.
70   *Northern Standard*, 23 Nov. 1923.
71   Ibid., 21 Dec. 1923.
72   *Northern Standard*, 21 Dec. 1923. See Diarmaid Ferriter's chapter.
73   In fact, s. 5(2) of the Act allowed for sentences of up to twelve months; it is probable that there were no copies of such recent legislation readily available for consultation.
74   18 Dec. 1923, Ballybay DCOB.
75   35 & 36 Vic., c. 94, s. 12.
76   Courts of Justice Act 1924, s. 50.

DISPOSAL OF CASES

Table 10.2 indicates how listed cases were disposed of at Ballybay District Court. Over a quarter of cases (64) were adjourned, either for a specified period (such as two months), or until the next sitting of the District Court, either in Ballybay or in nearby Castleblayney.[77] One-fifth of cases were dismissed, either on the merits, without prejudice, or with costs. In 33 cases, defendants were ordered to pay either a fine or damages, and in a further 30 cases they were ordered to pay their rates, plus costs. In criminal cases, defendants were rarely kept in custody, and were more commonly allowed out on bail and/or recognizances. Four people were sentenced to periods of imprisonment in Dundalk Gaol following conviction, while one child was committed to an industrial school.

Table 10.2: Disposal of cases, Ballybay District Court, 1923

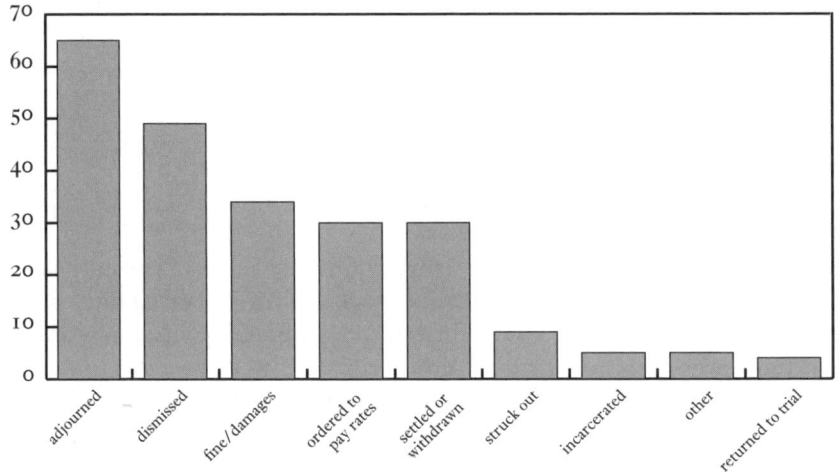

Almost everything that arose in the court in 1923, and which was not adjourned or dismissed, was disposed of by way of a fine or an order for compensation. Custodial sentences were rarely imposed, and those which were tended to be of fairly short duration, and without hard labour. The 1924 Act subsequently allowed for sentences of six months' imprisonment with or without hard labour.

---

77 Interestingly, on three instances in May and July 1923, a case was adjourned 'until the next quarter sessions'.

CONCLUSIONS

The records of the District Court are valuable sources, not only for legal historians, but also for social, economic and local historians. Local newspaper accounts of the sessions, while not exhaustive, generally add colour and detail, and convey a greater sense of the atmosphere in the District Court. Ó Tuathaigh described the District Court as

> The first point of reference beyond that threshold where social disapproval encounters the law and its administration, where actions of which society disapproves are translated into legal categories of 'crime and misdemeanour' and those accused face the due process of law. It is the crowded (sometimes literally) foyer of the formidable edifice of the law and its administration.[78]

A close examination of the cases coming before the District Court tells us what drove people to litigation, and what kinds of minor offences were being pursued by the police. Interpersonal rows, which sometimes escalated from threats to violence, were played out in local courtrooms. District Court proceedings also tell us about living standards in different parts of the country. For example, we can see how much rent was paid for modest dwellings, and whether it was paid weekly or monthly. Nuisance actions which arose out of 'a want of closet accommodation' and trespass actions for wandering goats shed light on the material reality of life in a small town in the twentieth century. Elements of Ireland's system of carceral control are evident in the District Court's committal of children to industrial schools and of individuals with mental health problems to local asylums.

The District Court was where most members of Irish society interacted with the machinery of justice. As Paul Kelly points out in the next chapter, this continues to be the case, with demographic changes presenting new challenges for the District Court and its officers.[79]

---

78 Gearóid Ó Tuathaigh, 'Foreword' in Kotsonouris, *'Tis all lies'*, p. xii.
79 See Kate Waterhouse, *Ireland's District Court: language, immigration and consequences for justice* (Manchester, 2014) and Caroline O'Nolan, *The Irish District Court: a social portrait* (Cork, 2013). Waterhouse, at p. 1, describes the contemporary District Court as 'fundamentally a world of incomprehensible, organised chaos.'

CHAPTER ELEVEN

The District Court, 1924–2024: 'big bang' 100 years on

PAUL KELLY[*]

The enactment of the Courts of Justice Act 1924 could be regarded as the 'big bang' of the Irish legal universe, creating as it did an entirely new legal architecture with the intention of making a clean break with the system imposed by the historic colonialists. Wisely, however, the Provisional Government resisted the temptation to throw the baby out with the bathwater, and many elements and structures of the previous system were retained. I suspect we would like to think that they captured much of what was good and had proven effective over the centuries, but also established a structure that enabled the new Irish courts to evolve and develop a system reflective of the new nation and its people. The District Court's role and structure have changed greatly over the past 100 years, which have seen it embrace a wide variety of new business. At the same time, Irish society and the legal system have evolved enormously. Matching this change, the District Court too has evolved, having to grapple with new legal areas such as family law and regulatory matters, and dealing with language barriers and the rise in social media usage. Without doubt, the District Court has borne witness to a century of change and has seen its role and workload expand throughout the years.

    This chapter aims to chart the development of the District Court over the past century, illustrating how it has evolved into its current form reflecting the changing nature of Ireland's socio-legal landscape. It will analyse the various reforms that have shaped the District Court, highlighting how its jurisdiction has expanded and describing its current structure and work. Finally, it will conclude by exploring how socio-legal trends have impacted the District Court, the challenges these changes have brought and how this court has transformed from its origins in 1924 to the workhorse of the modern Irish justice system.

---

[*] President of the District Court.

PETTY SESSIONS AND REPUBLICAN COURTS: THE BIRTH OF THE DISTRICT COURT

The District Court replaced the antiquated system of Courts of Petty Sessions.[1] Originally, Courts of Petty Sessions were presided over by justices of the peace. These were lay judges, without formal legal training. Howlin points out that '[b]ecause of the poor reputation of some amateur JPs, in 1814 salaried stipendiary or 'Resident' Magistrates, better known as 'RM's, were introduced, and these were extended to every county by the Constabulary (Ireland) Act 1836.'[2] McMahon notes that the Petty and Quarter sessions were 'the preferred venue for "small claims" litigation',[3] while McCabe observes that '[f]or most purposes the common law was represented to the small litigant and offender by the authority of the local magisterial bench.'[4] By the early twentieth century, as Kotsonouris points out, the Courts of 'Petty Sessions were manned by resident magistrates appointed by the lord lieutenant and by honorary justices of the peace; neither group was composed of professional lawyers'.[5]

Thomas Mohr outlines in his chapter how the Dáil courts were established in 1920. The four-tiered structure began with Parish Courts, followed by District Courts, Circuit Courts and the Supreme Court. Initially, the Dáil District Courts sat on a monthly basis and dealt with cases of greater severity than those which came before the Parish Courts.[6] Long before the term was coined, these courts focused on restorative justice and were extremely popular among the Irish people.[7]

While the District Court itself came into being as part of the Courts of Justice Act 1924, Niamh Howlin demonstrates in her chapter that its judges were first provided for in the District Court (Temporary Provisions) Act 1923. Section 1(1) of the 1923 Act stated:

> It shall be lawful for the governor-general of the Irish Free State on the advice of the Executive Council from time to time to appoint fit and

---

1 Law Reform Commission, *Consolidation and reform of the Courts Acts* (LRC CP 46-2007).
2 N. Howlin, 'The Irish courts system and the court houses' in Colum O'Riordan, Paul Burns and Ciaran O'Connor (eds), *Ireland's court houses* (Dublin, 2019), p. 2.
3 Richard McMahon, 'The Court of Petty Sessions and society in pre-Famine Galway' in Raymond Gillespie (ed.), *The remaking of modern Ireland, 1750–1950: Beckett prize essays in Irish history* (Dublin, 2004), p. 101.
4 Desmond McCabe, 'Open court: law and the expansion of magisterial jurisdiction at Petty Sessions in nineteenth-century Ireland' in N.M. Dawson (ed.), *Reflections on law and history* (Dublin, 2006), p. 127.
5 Mary Kotsonouris, *'Tis all lies, your worship': tales from the District Court* (Dublin, 2011), p. 5.
6 Ronan Keane, 'The Irish courts system in the 21st century: planning for the future', *Bar Review*, 6:6 (2001), 321–8, at 322–3.
7 Kotsonouris, *'Tis all lies'*, p. 5.

proper persons being barristers-at-law in Saorstát Eireann of at least two years' standing or solicitors of the Supreme Court in Saorstát Eireann to be magistrates with the title of 'district justices' and to perform the duties and have the powers prescribed by this Act.

As a result, solicitors and barristers with sufficient experience were eligible to be appointed as judges of the District Court. They were given the power to conduct all matters that originally vested in justices of the peace. Non-judicial functions that previously vested in justices of peace were passed on to what were now known to be 'peace commissioners'.[8] In effect, this was the professionalisation of the judiciary and the end of lay administration of justice.[9]

Section 68 of the Courts of Justice Act 1924 enabled the minister for home affairs to appoint District Court judges, provided that the number of appointments did not exceed thirty-three. Temporary assistant justices were an interesting feature of the 1924 Act. They were tasked with dealing with cases that had generated additional business for the District Court in addition to covering any absenteeism. Under the Courts of Justice Act 1936, these temporary assistant justices could be granted the same powers as a fully appointed judge for a period of time, allowing them to ensure that no arrears built up in the case load.[10]

A key aspect of the constitution of the District Court was its nature as a court of local jurisdiction, meaning that judges only exercised their powers in their relevant areas. In civil matters, the court's jurisdiction was exercised 'wherein the defendant or one of the defendants ordinarily resides or carries on any profession, business or occupation'.[11] In criminal cases, the court's jurisdiction was exercised 'wherein the crime has been committed or the accused has been arrested or resides.'[12] The 1924 Act also provided that where a district comprised a Gaeltacht area, a judge with sufficient knowledge of the Irish language would be appointed to that district to dispense with the need for an interpreter.[13]

In the early days of the District Court, its jurisdiction mainly comprised of general civil administration and criminal matters carrying prison sentences of six months or less. The Oireachtas, in following recommendations made by the Judiciary Committee, solidified the jurisdiction of the District Court in the Courts of Justice Act 1924.[14] These were as follows:

8   District Justices (Temporary Provisions) Act 1923, s. 4.
9   Keane 'The Irish courts system', at 323.
10 Courts of Justice Act 1936, s. 51.
11 Courts of Justice Act 1924, s. 79.
12 Ibid.
13 Ibid., s. 71. See the chapter by Úna Ní Raifeartaigh and Róisín Costello.
14 Courts of Justice Act 1924, s. 77.

CIVIL JURISDICTION

The District Court was given the power to hear contractual matters up to a value of £25 and claims in tort not exceeding £10, excluding those outside the remit of the District Court as set out in the 1924 Act.[15] Additionally, the following matters also vested in the jurisdiction of the District Court: ejectment for non-payment of rent or overholding in any class of tenancy where the rent does not exceed £26; and the recovery of monies not exceeding £25 by or on behalf of the state or any minister or government department or any officer thereof.

CRIMINAL JURISDICTION

The District Court's criminal jurisdiction was initially exercised in the following circumstances:

i. larceny, receiving, embezzlement or false pretences – where the money or property involved did not exceed £20 in value;[16]
ii. assault – involving actual bodily harm;
iii. indecent assault;
iv. burglary or housebreaking or attempts at either;
v. riot or unlawful assembly;
vi. malicious damage to property – where the cost of the damage does not exceed £20.
vii. The maximum sentencing power of the District Court pursuant to the 1924 Act was a term of imprisonment not exceeding six months. As a prerequisite to cases being heard in the District Court, the District Court justice must have been satisfied that the facts proved against the accused constituted an offence which was minor in nature. Where the District Court justice was not satisfied that the offence was not minor in nature they could send it forward to the Circuit Court, as is still the case today.

The 1924 Act also provided for the licensing jurisdiction of the District Court. Section 50 provided that the Circuit Court had jurisdiction to grant a new licence entitling an applicant to sell intoxicating liquor for consumption on a specified premises. As such, the District Court's licensing jurisdiction largely was of a limited and local nature, focusing on common but very important issues that affected towns across Ireland, such as late bar extensions, occasional and festival licences, and most important of all in the 'Ballroom of Romance' era, the licensing of public dancing!

15 Ibid., s. 77(A)(ii).
16 Ibid., s. 77 (B)(i).

Overall, the nature of the District Court's jurisdiction in 1924 reflects its history as a successor to the Petty Sessions as well as its creation in the aftermath of the War of Independence and the Civil War. In a sense, this court brought together the traditional structure of the old legal system yet with a distinctive influence from the Republican courts which had so effectively supplanted the colonial system during the revolutionary period. Keane notes that this reflected the Irish experience under a foreign system and that while the new system certainly maintained continuity, it was a different system nonetheless.[17]

CENTURY OF CHANGE: THE EVOLUTION AND REFORM OF THE DISTRICT COURT'S ROLE

It is clear that the modern functioning and appearance of the District Court has changed greatly from its origins in 1924, matching the increasing depth and complexity of the law. As the twentieth century progressed, so also did the role of the District Court. One of the first major changes to Ireland's legal order was the death of the Free State with the enactment of the 1937 Constitution. Article 38.4.5 provided for the summary hearing of minor offences, but the District and Circuit Courts, both creatures of statute, were relatively unaffected.[18] A key moment for the modern District Court came in 1961 with the passage of the Courts (Establishment and Constitution) Act 1961. This Act ushered in the birth of the new District Court,[19] and created the position of the president of the District Court.[20]

There were twenty-seven district justices under the Courts of Justice Act 1924. The Courts (Supplemental Provisions) Act 1961 provided for the appointment of thirty-four District judges,[21] and the Court and Court Officers Act 1995 provided for fifty District judges.[22] In 1926, there was one judge for every 110,073 persons in the Free State.[23] Today, there is approximately one judge for every 71,515 people.[24] The greatest legislative increase of judicial staffing in the history of the state was provided for in section 6 of the Courts Act 2023, which brought the total number of District Court judges, in addition to the president, up to seventy-one. In spite of that

17 Keane, 'The Irish courts'.
18 See further Gerry Whyte, Gerard Hogan, David Kenny and Rachael Walsh, *Kelly: The Irish Constitution* (Dublin, 2018), para 6.247–6.250.
19 Courts (Establishment and Constitution Act) 1961, s. 5.
20 Ibid., s. 5(2). See Appendix 5.
21 Courts (Supplemental Provisions) Act 1961, s. 28.
22 Courts and Court Officers Act 1995, s. 11.
23 The population stood at 2,971,992: Department of Industry and Commerce, *Census of population Saorstát Éireann* (Dublin, 1926).
24 There are 72 judges and a population of 5,149,139: Central Statistics Office, *Census 2022 summary of results* (Dublin, 2023).

growth, case loads have also increased dramatically, with it becoming Ireland's busiest court, eight times busier than the Circuit Court.[25] In 2022 the Court received 466,114 cases. These cases spanned areas from licensing and liquidated debt claims to domestic violence, guardianship, custody and access orders, child care orders, and assault, road traffic and public order offences.[26] The physical nature of the court has altered too, reflecting a changing approach to the administration of justice. Under the old system of Petty Sessions, there were around 600 buildings in use as active courthouses, which compares with around 120 in use today.[27]

This rapid growth reflects the expansion of the District Court's jurisdiction over the twentieth century, which saw its workload grow to reflect the increasing complexity of Irish law. Indeed, the major impact of EU regulation alone has dramatically altered the considerations of which the court must be cognisant.[28] As mentioned, the court's jurisdiction began with low-level civil matters to the amount of £25 and minor criminal matters with no equitable jurisdiction. Now, the Court deals with civil cases up to the amount of €15,000,[29] although parties of course can consent to unlimited jurisdiction.[30] Dowling and Mullalley note the following areas as compromising the main civil business of the District Court:

- hire-purchase and credit sales agreements;
- actions arising out of claims in tort;
- actions on behalf of the State or a local authority to recover a debt;
- ejectment proceedings for non-payment of rent or overholding, where the annual rent does not exceed €15,000;
- wrongful detention of goods;
- claims arising out of contract;
- malicious damage cases;
- various family law matters;
- small claims;[31]
- liquor and dance hall licences; and
- applications in relation to party structures pursuant to the Land and Conveyancing Law Reform Act 2009.[32]

25 Mary Carolan, 'Claims of assault, parental abuse and fraud – a day in one of Ireland's busiest District Courts', *Irish Times*, 8 Dec. 2023.
26 Courts Service, *Courts annual report 2022* (Dublin, 2023).
27 See Burns, O'Connor and O'Riordan, *Ireland's court houses*.
28 Kotsonouris, *'Tis all lies'*, p. 32.
29 Courts and Civil Law (Miscellaneous Provisions) Act 2013, s. 15.
30 Courts of Justice Act 1924 (as amended), s. 77A.
31 See Mary Donnelly and Fidelma White, *Consumer law: rights and regulation* (Dublin, 2014), ch. 10.7.
32 See Karl Dowling and Suzanne Mullalley, *Civil procedure in the District Court* (Dublin, 2014), ch. 1A.

In the criminal domain, the District Court is empowered to deal with summary offences that include assault (including sexual assault), drugs, criminal damage, theft, burglary, road traffic offences, and public order offences.[33] It can impose custodial sentences not exceeding two years. There are now also a host of regulatory jurisdictions and offences in the domains of planning enforcement, fisheries,[34] waste management[35] and many more.[36]

One particular area that has seen major growth is road traffic prosecutions. Kotsonouris has noted that the advent of section 49 of the Road Traffic Act 1961 and scientific testing for drink driving gave rise to a wave of litigation across a vast array of procedural issues.[37] This matched the growing importance of the car in Irish society; as the proliferation of vehicles increased, so too did litigation arising from them.[38] This remains the case with road traffic offences making up 54% of District Court criminal business.[39] Another important area where the Court's jurisdiction has expanded is in the area of family law. While jurisdiction existed under the Children Act 1908, this was criticised as outdated and concerned crimes done to or by children.[40] The current framework is far more focused on child welfare, with the District Court playing a key role in safeguarding children.[41] The process for seeking protection from domestic violence has changed too. Until 1976, women in Dublin seeking protection or financial assistance from the fathers of their children had to attend the District Court office set up in the courtyard of the Bridewell Garda station, often being required to discuss details of domestic abuse at the public counter.[42] The Family Law (Protection of Spouses and Children) Act 1976 brought radical change that helped to make the process more appropriate and strengthen the rights of vulnerable spouses and children in abusive situations.[43] Proceedings became more focused on children's welfare, and there was an obligation to have proceedings heard *in camera*, making the process fairer and less traumatic for parties. The District Court now plays a vital role in the making of orders for maintenance, custody, guardianship and access, as well as in the making of care orders under the Child Care Act 1991.[44] As will be discussed below, this area is to become even

33 See generally Genevieve Coonan, Kate O'Toole and Mary O'Toole, *Criminal procedure in the District Court* (2nd edn, Dublin, 2022).
34 See generally Sea Fisheries Acts 1959–2005.
35 For low level offences, see the Waste Management Act 1996, s. 58.
36 See generally Dowling and Mullalley, *Civil procedure*, ch. 22.
37 Kotsonouris, *'Tis all lies'*, p. 29.
38 Ibid., p. 30. This point is also made by Kevin Costello in his chapter.
39 Courts Service, *Courts annual report 2022* (Dublin, 2023).
40 H. Buckley, C. Skehill and E. O'Sullivan, 'Protecting children under the Child Care Act 1991 – getting the balance right', *Irish Journal of Family Law*, 2:1 (1999), 7–11, at 10.
41 Child Care Act 1991.
42 Kotsonouris, *'Tis all lies'*, p. 58.
43 Ibid.
44 S. 24.

busier as there are plans to grant further jurisdiction to the court in dealing with family matters as well as ensuring the process is more user-friendly and reflects the values of modern Irish family law.

It is clear that the District Court's jurisdiction has increased not just in raw monetary terms but also in respect to what kind of matters now come before it. While areas like civil and criminal summary proceedings have evolved naturally from the traditional jurisdiction the Court enjoyed upon its establishment, areas like family law and regulatory matters represented a new challenge that the Court grappled with and now form key parts of daily business for District Court judges across the country. Having examined the changes that have come to the Court over the past 100 years, the following section now seeks to examine how the Court has dealt with societal changes and what reforms lie immediately ahead.

CHALLENGES AND CONTINUING GROWTH: THE COURT'S IMMEDIATE FUTURE

As we have seen, the District Court operates within a variety of areas of law and oversees hundreds of thousands of cases[45] every year. The Court has had to adapt and modernise in order to deal with the rising caseload. As noted above, there has been continuous reform of the court structure with the creation of new fields in which the court operates. There has been a general increase in the volume of cases before the court in recent years with a particular rise in civil and family cases. The introduction of the Family Courts bill 2022 is set to expand the District Court's jurisdiction in respect of family law matters, which would further increase cases; it would, however, also implement a more cohesive family law structure within the court system.

Currently, family law proceedings in Ireland operate within the general courts system resulting in highly sensitive cases involving children taking place within buildings where non-family law cases are also heard.[46] It can be extremely challenging to deal with the very high caseload before each district. Furthermore, family law judges are not required to be specialised in family/child law and are not appointed to family law judicial roles based on any specific experience. There are longstanding concerns in respect of vulnerable individuals and children attending court and being involved in sensitive cases where there are inadequate facilities or support services.[47] The Joint Oireachtas Committee on Justice and Equality commented in 2019 on

---

45 In 2022 there were 547,519 incoming cases to the District Court: Courts Service, *Courts Annual Report 2022*.
46 Joint Oireachtas Committee on Justice and Equality, *Report on the reform of family law* (Dublin, 2019), p. 18
47 Ibid., p. 22.

the lack of security and growing safety concerns for court attendees and court staff alike.[48]

The Family Courts bill 2022[49] has been a long-awaited reform to the current system of family justice with a number of major changes proposed in order to implement a more efficient and cohesive system that will better safeguard vulnerable individuals in court proceedings. The bill sets out the guiding principles on which it is based, namely: the welfare of children being the primary concern in all family law cases; the strong encouragement to find resolution in cases through mediation or alternative dispute resolution; and proper case management to ensure no undue delay in respect of hearings. One of the key proposals contained within the Family Courts bill 2022 is the establishment of a new Family Courts system which will be assigned jurisdiction for family and child cases from the current general courts.[50] Furthermore, the bill proposes the introduction of a principal judge of the Family District Court to oversee the case management of the court. The judges who are to be appointed to the Family Courts will be selected based on relevant background, experience and knowledge of family law enabling the area of family law to become increasingly specialised.[51]

Further developments in terms of implementing technology in the courtrooms has proven to be extremely beneficial; this was especially seen throughout the Covid pandemic. The utilisation of modern technology such as video calling to allow for greater levels of remote hearings allows for shorter waiting times for cases to be heard before the court. The availability of remote hearings in the District Court varies greatly between the counties. The number of courtrooms with the ability to hold remote hearings increased due to the impact of the pandemic, however some courtrooms in rural areas do not yet have access to the technology available in other parts of the country.

There has been some pushback against using remote hearings in place of in-person hearings. In the Joint Oireachtas Committee's *Report on courts and courthouses*, it was noted that the Council of the Bar of Ireland stated that the use of remote hearings can be detrimental to a person's right to the access of justice.[52] This is especially true in respect of the District Court, which often sees people from various socio-economic backgrounds and who may not own a computer or have access to internet or an appropriate space to be a part of the hearing. These aspects are easily taken for granted and it is important that there is provision made for persons who may struggle to attend a virtual hearing.

---

48 Ibid.
49 Family Courts bill 2022.
50 Ibid., s. 10.
51 Ibid., s. 15.
52 Joint Oireachtas Committee on Justice, *Report on courts and courthouses* (Dublin, 2022), p. 59.

The most significant changes however have been in the thinking and mindset of judges and other court actors. Over the past 30 years or so, there has for example been greater focus on human rights and civil liberties, as well as a paradigm shift in the attitude to victims. The Victims Rights Directive[53] and the legislation that followed it has moved the victim from being simply a witness to having a central role in the process, and supports for victims have improved dramatically. Victim impact statements are now sought, and provided in many cases. In the criminal justice sector, greater emphasis is now placed on diversion from criminal behaviour, and alternatives to custody, such as community service, restorative justice, driver re-education, and solution-focussed courts (e.g., the Drug Treatment Court) now play a much more prominent part in dealing with offenders. Juvenile justice saw a change in approach and emphasis with the Children Act 2001 introducing a welfare based approach, focussing on diversion, education, welfare and inter agency cooperation (Tusla, HSE, the Gardaí etc.), with detention as a last resort.[54]

In family law and child care matters, there has been increasing complexity, and greater use of and reliance upon experts such as psychologists, attachment and parental capacity experts, guardians ad litem and social workers. For example, the insertion of the new article 42A into the Constitution following the referendum on the 31st amendment to the Constitution gave constitutional recognition to enhanced rights of children, including, significantly, a specific obligation on courts to ascertain and 'give due weight to' the views of children in court cases affecting them. While admirable and long-overdue, this has greatly lengthened the time taken to deal with guardianship, child custody, access and child care cases in the District Court. Most such cases now require additional adjournments to facilitate this, and increase the complexity of the cases and the decisions to be made by the judges.

Other societal changes have had significant impacts on the District Court. As the court that deals with over 85% of all court cases annually,[55] it is the one in which most people who have business in court find themselves, voluntarily or not. Twenty-first century phenomena such as immigration, urbanisation, language and interpretation issues, equality and access to services issues, and the use of social media are daily challenges for District Court judges all over the country.

In 1924 and the following years of that decade, the court would have been notable for the absence of women in any role other than that of defendant, witness, or family member of one.[56] The first women solicitors, Dorothea Heron and Helena Early, were admitted to the roll of solicitors in 1923, and

53 Directive 2012/29/EU.
54 Children Act 2001, s. 96.
55 Courts Service, *Annual report 2022*.
56 See further the chapter by Niamh Howlin and Mark Coen, 'Where were the women?'.

few women solicitors appeared in District Courts in the early years. Female barristers were an equally rare sight – the first women barristers, Frances Kyle and Averil Deverell, were called to the Bar in 1921. Court clerks and registrars were more likely to be men, while female Gardaí would not appear until 1959. A female judge was unheard of for the first four decades of the Irish court system, until in 1964, Eileen Kennedy, a solicitor from Carrickmacross, Co. Monaghan, made history becoming the first woman judge in Ireland when she was appointed by President de Valera to the District Court. She presided over the Dublin Metropolitan Children Court (i.e. the District Court dealing with juvenile offenders) until her death in 1983, less than a year before she was due to retire. Her ground-breaking report on the reformatory and industrial school system published in 1970[57] led to the closure of several such unsuitable institutions, and paved the way for the enactment in 2001 of the Children Act, which transformed juvenile justice and established the Children Court in its present form. The District Court was therefore somewhat ahead of the curve, as it took many more years for women to be appointed to the higher courts

Some societal phenomena have however taken longer to evolve: the urban/rural divide is still evident in certain respects – someone's name appearing in local newspapers or online media, where reports of proceedings in the local District Court are given prominence almost on a par with reports of GAA matches, still cause great embarrassment in the locality! The basis for the creation of districts (in 1924 the distance a man could travel on a horse in a day!) is perhaps also anachronistic in an age of cars, motorways and extensive public transport.

An example of how things have changed can be gleaned from a newspaper report cited by Kotsonouris. The report outlined a case where a young boy appeared before a court for stealing a watch that he then sold to a shopkeeper for a shilling, having told him that he found the watch on the road. He wanted to use the shilling to pay for a night's lodging. The judge was told by the solicitor that he came from a family of eight and pleaded with the judge not to send him to an industrial school. However, the judge made the decision to send the boy, who was due to turn fourteen the following week, to an industrial school as it would be better for his mother seeing as she wouldn't have to take care of him.[58] Today, he would probably have been taken into care on foot of an application under section 18 of the Child Care Act 1991, while section 96 of the Children Act 2001 would in all likelihood have prevented the judge from imposing a sentence of detention. Or perhaps his mother might have obtained an order for maintenance enabling her to better look after the child.

57   Eileen Kennedy, *Reformatory and industrial schools systems* (Dublin, 1970) (the 'Kennedy report').
58   Case reported in *Wicklow People*, 9 Feb. 1924 and cited Kotsonouris, *'Tis all lies'* pp 53–4.

CONCLUSION

The District Court has changed immensely since the foundation of the Free State's courts in 1924. It began life dealing with a limited range of low-level claims across the multiple districts throughout the country. Over the course of the twentieth century, the court's role expanded and evolved, reflecting the increasingly complex legal system which developed in Ireland. Spanning areas like road traffic, family law and regulatory practice, the District Court's jurisdiction has grown. Its judges have also had to adapt, being required to deal with broad areas of law and grapple with the changes brought by technology and societal developments. Challenges still remain, particularly with regard to technology, the impact of Covid-19 on our legal system as well as the need to enhance and improve the family law system. Without doubt, upcoming reforms will bring both difficulties and opportunities for the court to play its vital role as the point-of-contact court for most court users throughout the country. To conclude, the District Court, from humble and archaic beginnings, has been the workhorse of the Irish justice system and continues to play this role at the ever-changing coalface of the administration of justice.

CHAPTER TWELVE

'Illegal, immoral and unpatriotic': cross-border smuggling and the courts

LYNSEY BLACK* AND DANIELLE C. JEFFERIS**

INTRODUCTION

The partition of Ireland was first legislatively achieved by the Government of Ireland Act 1920 that provided for a 'Northern Ireland' and a 'Southern Ireland'. The 1920 Act had been an attempt to realise Irish demands for some form of self-governance while also accommodating the Protestant and Unionist majority in the north-east of the island. In those fevered years, however, events soon overtook this initial statutory framework and at its enactment it was already too little, too late. In 1919 the War of Independence erupted, culminating in the 1921 Anglo-Irish Treaty, under which the mooted partition of Ireland as two co-equal parts of a whole was undone. The Treaty instead created the newly independent Irish Free State, and accorded to 'Northern Ireland' the right to 'opt out' of independence, a right it immediately exercised.[1] Instead of two self-governing entities within the overall structure of the UK, which the 1920 Act had envisaged, there was now an independent Irish Free State with 'Dominion' status within the Commonwealth, and the partially self-governing, but not independent, entity of Northern Ireland. The boundary that had been set in the 1920 legislation, a boundary that traced the pre-existing county borders, became the new international frontier between these two jurisdictions. The Boundary Commission, which in 1924 and 1925 was tasked with exploring and proposing amendments to the border, seemed to suggest a degree of

---

* Assistant professor in the School of Law and Criminology, Maynooth University and principal investigator on the Irish Research Council Laureate Award CONSPACE (Contested Space: Penal Nationalism and the Northern Ireland Border).
** PhD researcher in the School of Law and Criminology, Maynooth University, researching on the IRC-funded project CONSPACE.
1 Recent publications which examine the birth of Northern Ireland include: Brendan O'Leary, *A treatise on Northern Ireland: volume II, control* (Oxford, 2019); Diarmaid Ferriter, *The Border: the legacy of a century of Anglo-Irish politics* (London, 2019); Cormac Moore, *Birth of the Border: the impact of partition in Ireland* (Dublin, 2019); Donnacha Ó Beacháin, *From partition to Brexit: the Irish government and Northern Ireland* (Manchester, 2019).

impermanence to this frontier but in 1925, at the abandonment of this exercise, the *status quo ante* prevailed.[2] The land boundary of the six northeastern counties formed the outer limits of the new entity of Northern Ireland, as well as forming the outer limits of the newly downsized United Kingdom.

For those who lived along this approximately 300-mile boundary, illustrated in Figure 12.1 below, the division of Northern Ireland from the Irish Free State was achieved in a much more tangible fashion by the introduction of a customs barrier in 1923. The sundering of the island of Ireland was cemented, with all its new mundane bureaucracy, by Ireland's assertion of its fiscal independence.

Figure 12.1: Map of Northern Ireland Border[3]

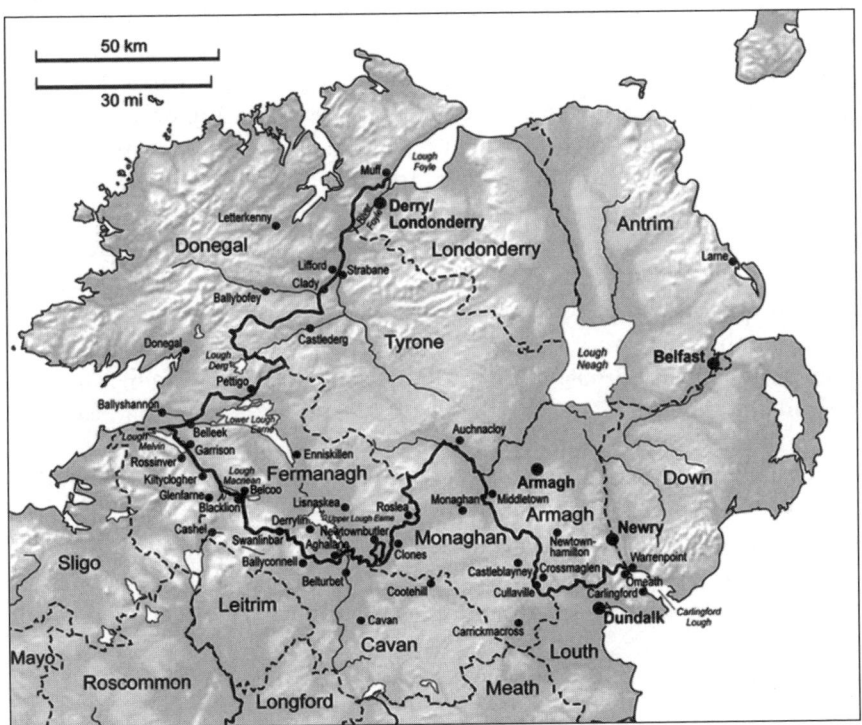

2 Paul Murray, *The Irish Boundary Commission and its origins, 1886–1925* (Dublin, 2011).
3 Map courtesy of Catherine Nash, Bryonie Reid, Brian Graham, 'Borderlands' website (www.irishborderlands.com/irishborder/index.html) and Catherine Nash, Bryonie Reid, Brian Graham, *Partitioned lives: the Irish borderlands* (Abingdon, 2013), p. 18.

On 1 April 1923, control of customs and excise was transferred from London to Dublin, and the land boundary on the island became a customs barrier. Immediately, tariffs were placed on various goods.[4] New procedures and infrastructure sprang up to facilitate this. The Customs (Land Frontier) Regulations 1923 stipulated that 'no person shall import or export any ordinary merchandise into or from the Irish Free State except by one of the approved routes specified'.[5] Approved routes in and out of Northern Ireland were duly designated. Border roads were categorised under a tripartite classification system: approved routes, unapproved routes and concession roads. Approved routes were the official routes by which dutiable goods could cross the border. All motor vehicles travelling across the border could do so only by these approved routes. These roads were therefore the border crossings at which customs facilities were constructed. Non-dutiable goods could be taken by the unapproved routes and individuals could use these roads if they travelled on foot, by bicycle, or by horse-drawn conveyance (motor cars were dutiable from the inception of the customs barrier). A small number of exceptions were granted for persons travelling on unapproved routes by motor car, such as for local doctors or vets. Concession routes generally linked two places in Northern Ireland or two places in the Irish Free State by roads that had to transit the other jurisdiction by necessity. From the point at which the customs barrier was created, those travelling across the boundary, whether it be on foot, bicycle, car, or train, could be inspected by customs officials.[6] Initially, there were fifteen approved routes and Leary has suggested that there were as many as 150 unapproved routes.[7] Rail presented a different logistical problem. Five railway companies served both Northern Ireland and the Free State, and the Great Northern Railway Company had routes that crossed the border at eleven places.[8] Goods travelling across the border by railway benefitted in the early years from light-touch inspection and Murray and Wincott outlined the mutual agreement of customs north and south to accept the official goods manifests for each train.[9]

While there *was* debate over the introduction of a tariff barrier, the haste with which arrangements were put in place and the lack of detail on how it

---

4 In a parliamentary debate six months prior, the president of the Executive Council, W.T. Cosgrave, had stated: '[o]f course it would be a very dangerous thing to alter the taxes right away'. *Dáil Éireann deb.*, vol. 1, col. 129 (16 Nov. 1922).
5 The Customs (Land Frontier) Regulations 1923, s. 2(1).
6 Catherine Nash and Bryonie Reid, 'Border crossings: new approaches to the Irish Border', *Irish Studies Review*, 18:3 (2010), 265–84.
7 Peter Leary, *Unapproved routes: histories of the Irish Border, 1922–1972* (Oxford, 2016).
8 M.H.C. Baker, *Irish railways since 1916* (London, 1972), cited in Moore, *Birth of the Border*, pp 195–6.
9 C.R.G. Murray and Daniel Wincott, 'Partition by degrees: routine exceptions in border and immigration practice between the UK and Ireland, 1921–1972', *Journal of Law and Society*, 47:1 (2020), 145–63.

would operate somewhat stifled discussion. Just two weeks prior to the introduction of the new tariffs, it seemed less than certain it would proceed as scheduled. The minutes of an Executive Council meeting of 16 March detail discussions between government and business representatives with a view to postponing the customs barrier. It is noted that: 'After *prolonged* discussion it was decided to adhere to the decision already made in the matter, viz, that the new customs regulations should come into force as from 1st April next.'[10] When details of dutiable goods were finally announced, most debate concerned the position of specific Irish industries affected (such as the Ford motor plant in Cork[11]). As noted by a commentator in the *Economist* (reproduced in the *Freeman's Journal*), there was a sense that a customs barrier with Northern Ireland was inevitable.[12] However inevitable the system seemed though, there were many unknowns regarding how it would operate and details remained vague until the eleventh hour.

When it came, the consequences of Ireland's fiscal independence were contested. Some argued that it could lead to the achievement of Irish unity while others warned that it heralded only the further alienation of the six north-eastern counties. The *Irish Times*' view was that such administrative division would inevitably push the two jurisdictions further apart: '[t]he Free State government's new protective duties must strengthen the solidity of the customs barrier. A new gap, social and moral, between North and South will be created by the mere smuggling of boots and soap from Belfast to Dublin'.[13]

James Craig, prime minister of Northern Ireland, appeared to agree with the view that a customs barrier would enshrine partition. In a meeting in Belfast in March 1923 he suggested that the barrier be postponed 'for all time' claiming that: '[t]he proposal to set up a Customs barrier on the Southern border would make the South, and not the North, responsible for partition.'[14] Meanwhile, others considered that the customs barrier was one weapon in the arsenal of diplomacy that could be used lure Northern Ireland back into the fold of the Irish Free State. In a March 1923 memorandum of the North East Boundary Bureau,[15] Joseph Johnston wrote that, 'the fiscal

10 *Documents on Irish foreign policy (DIFP)*, 'Extract from minutes of a meeting of the Executive Council (C.1/65)', doc. no. 49, 16 Mar. 1923. Emphasis added.
11 See, e.g., *Dáil Éireann deb.*, vol. 2, col. 44 (23 Mar. 1923). See also, D.S. Jacobson, 'The political economy of industrial location: the Ford Motor Company at Cork, 1912–26', *Irish Economic and Social History*, 4 (1977), 36–55.
12 'Nothing is clearer than that Ireland will set up her own customs houses, and it almost equally clear that North-East Ulster will, by "contracting out," insist on remaining under the immediate jurisdiction of the British Parliament and within the customs and excise system and boundaries of Great Britain.' *Freeman's Journal*, 6 Nov. 1922.
13 *Irish Times*, 28 Apr. 1924.
14 Ibid., 3 Mar. 1923.
15 The North East Boundary Bureau came into being in October 1922 under the direction of Kevin O'Shiel, an Omagh barrister, former advisor to Michael Collins on Northern Ireland and assistant legal advisor to the Provisional/Free State government. The Bureau was

policy pursued by the Free State, if it is of the right kind, will be the deciding factor in inducing [the Northerner] to return'.[16]

At its commencement, the customs barrier was inseparable from the fundamental questions of Irish independence and Irish unity. Something else was clear also; the introduction of tariffs on a range of goods, from tobacco to sugar to clothing, created the conditions for smuggling. The new courts system, consolidated in the Courts of Justice Act 1924, no less than the introduction of customs, signalled the changes wrought by independence: '[i]f there were no other evidences of the changes that have been so rapidly coming into operation in the Irish Free State they would be obvious in the administration of the law.'[17] In these newly constituted courts, a new class of criminal would be dealt with in the person of the smuggler. This chapter offers a snapshot of the profile of smuggling cases appearing before the District Court in the early years of the Free State, exploring some of the debate such cases provoked.

CROSS-BORDER SMUGGLING

While in theory, control of customs and excise had transferred from London to Dublin on 6 December 1922, HM Customs and Excise continued in their capacity, acting as 'agents' for the Irish Free State, until the end of the fiscal year on 31 March 1923. At this juncture, trade between Ireland and the United Kingdom became foreign, rather than domestic.[18] The *Sunday Independent*, on 1 April 1923 (April Fools' Day *and* Easter Sunday), reported that '[t]he Free State customs tariff operated from 12 o'clock last night', and noted that many Free State households had been stockpiling supplies in anticipation of higher prices. Remarking on the intensity of such activity in the part of Co. Donegal that abutted the Northern Ireland town of Strabane, the newspaper stated that: 'A civic guard has been posted on the Lifford bridge to end the hoarding'.[19] The *Dundalk Democrat*, well placed to observe the effects of the customs barrier, found that, '[t]he new customs barrier is giving the newspapers a lot of miscellaneous copy'.[20] The piece continued

tasked with research and fact-finding on the border, and particularly with putting forward the Irish position and the perspective of northern nationalists for consideration by the Boundary Commission. See Final Report of the North-Eastern Boundary Bureau, NAI DT S4743. Stephens to Kevin O'Higgins (Dublin), 26 Feb. 1926, cited in *DIFP*, vol. ii, 1922–6, doc. no. 380, 'Work of the North Eastern Boundary Bureau'.
16 North Eastern Boundary Bureau, 'Suggested fiscal changes', Mar. 1923, NAI NEBB/1/3/4.
17 *Weekly Irish Times*, 23 Aug. 1924.
18 Gilbert Denton and Tony Fahy, *The Northern Ireland land boundary, 1923–1992* (Belfast, 1993).
19 *Sunday Independent*, 1 Apr. 1923.
20 *Dundalk Democrat*, 7 Apr. 1923.

with praise for the manner in which customs officers conducted themselves and an assurance that these officers would soon be able to distinguish the guilty from the innocent cross-border traveller:

> It is the least bit inconvenient; but people will soon get used to that, and meantime the officers are courteous and not too fussily officious. They are also new to this work, for nothing of the sort has ever come their way before. In a little while they will learn to look for the furtive eye that tells a traveller has a full quart of whiskey concealed under the soiled collars in his suit case; and will be able to sort out the innocent people and send them promptly about their business.[21]

Leary reports the first case of smuggling in the Free State courts as that of Lawrence Hoey, aged 31, of Dundalk, Co. Louth, who appeared before B.J. Goff at Dundalk District Court on Friday 15 June 1923, two weeks after he had been apprehended smuggling cigarettes and 'hard confectionary'.[22] As reported by state solicitor J.B. Hamill, 'this was the first case brought under the customs regulation', and he accordingly asked the judge, 'to impose the fullest penalty he could in order to warn the public that they must observe the regulation'.[23] At its inception, the lower courts found themselves tasked with the symbolic function of communicating the significance of Ireland's fiscal independence and the necessity of observing the legal reality of the new border. Newspapers north and south ran notices publicising the newly released details of how the system would work (such as the *Freeman's Journal* article, 'System explained')[24] but the magnitude of such changes fell heavily on border communities. There is some indication that judges handed down more lenient penalties initially, as citizens familiarised themselves with the new requirements. District Justice Goff, passing sentence on Dougles Hughes on 4 November 1924, said that he would impose a nominal fine of ten shillings only for what he considered a mere technical infringement of the regulations, but warned that 'it was necessary for the public to know' the various regulations with regard to routes and crossings.[25]

The meandering path of the new border was a demarcation that 'held little social or economic significance and frequently violated the micro-boundaries of everyday life'.[26] Towns such as Newry and Strabane lost significant swathes of their natural catchment area and suffered the economic consequences. For

21 Ibid.
22 See Niamh Howlin's chapter on Ballybay District Court.
23 *Fermanagh Herald*, 16 June 1923.
24 *Freeman's Journal*, 30 Mar. 1923.
25 *Dundalk Democrat*, 4 Nov. 1924.
26 Peter Leary, 'Bicycles, 'barrows, and donkeys: pinning a tale on the Irish Border', *Folklore*, 129 (2018), 111–28, at 111.

some observers, these towns represented the 'Achilles heel' of Northern stubbornness and a point at which pressure for reunification could be applied.[27] Derry, in particular, became isolated in its precarious geographic position. As noted by the North Eastern Boundary Bureau: 'the Derry trade was the most vulnerable point in the economic structure of the six counties'.[28] 'Drastic measures' were deemed necessary to prevent smuggling in these areas, where the motivations to commit such offences were often compelling, including suggestions that Free State troops should be stationed at the Derry–Donegal boundary, that unapproved routes should be closed, and that female searchers should be recruited.[29]

CASES BEFORE THE COURTS

Although smuggling emerged as 'a small-scale and relatively marginal pursuit' through the 1920s,[30] it had the effect of bringing many 'ordinary' citizens within the reach of the new courts system where offences were prosecuted in the District Court.[31] In the Revenue Commissioners' first annual report it was recorded that, to year end 31 March 1924, there had been 425 seizures of goods and that: '93 persons were convicted of smuggling and penalties amounting to £570 13s. 0d. were recovered.'[32] As Johnson wrote, smuggling was 'a phenomenon recognized by and probably indulged in to a greater or lesser degree by the majority of the population in the border counties'.[33] In the Revenue Commissioners' second annual report, it was stated that a total of 1,528 smuggled goods were seized, resulting in the conviction of 138 persons and penalties amounting to £282 13s. 9d.[34] These figures remained relatively steady through the remainder of the 1920s before they exploded during the economic war of the 1930s.[35]

To give a snapshot of the smuggling prosecutions appearing before the District Court, Table 12.1 offers an overview of the cases appearing before the

---

27 Boundary Commission, 'Customs – imperial preferences and the North-East', 23 Mar. 1923, NAI NEBB/1/6/3.
28 E.M. Stephens to Kevin O'Shiel, 19 Jan. 1923, NAI NEBB/1/8/30.
29 *Irish Times*, 18 Oct. 1924.
30 Leary, 'Bicycles, 'barrows, and donkeys', at 112.
31 See chapters by Niamh Howlin and Kevin Costello for more on the establishment of the District and Circuit Courts respectively.
32 Revenue Commissioners of Saorstát Éireann, *First annual report – Year ended 31 March 1924* (Dublin, 1926), p. 41.
33 D.S. Johnson, 'Cattle smuggling on the Irish Border, 1932–38', *Irish Economic and Social History*, 6 (1979), 41–63, at 42.
34 Revenue Commissioners of Saorstát Éireann, *Second annual report – Year ended 31 March 1925* (Dublin, 1927), p. 46.
35 See the annual reports of the Revenue Commissioners.

Monaghan District Courts from April 1923 until the end of 1926.[36] The Order Books for the District Courts of Ballybay, Castleblayney, Carrickmacross, Clones and Monaghan town were consulted.[37]

Table 12.1: Overview of smuggling cases before Monaghan County District Courts, April 1923–December 192

District Court	Number of Defendants (Male/Female)	Outcomes	Penalties (and details of items)
Ballybay	1 (M)	Convicted (1)	1 conviction £100 or Dundalk Prison 1 month (tobacco)
Carrickmacross	None		
Castleblayney	15 (M)	Convicted (11) Withdrawn (4)	11 convictions £169 4s. or Dundalk 6 months (tobacco and cigarettes) 5s. and costs 3s. 6d., or Dundalk 7 days (motor cycle) £1 and costs £2 1s. 6d. or Dundalk 7 days (motor cycle) 10s. (motor car) £1 (fowl) £1 (fowl) £10 or Dundalk 3 months (tobacco, soap and pomade) £100 (mitigated to £25) or Dundalk 6 months (sugar) £9 4s. 4d. or Dundalk 6 months (clothing) £13 18s. 6d. or Dundalk six months (clothing) Two charges of 4s. each or Dundalk 7 days (fowl and merchandise)
Clones[38]	12 (9M/3F)	Convicted (9) Withdrawn (1) Charge Proved (2)	9 convictions £70 or Mountjoy Prison 3 months (motor car) £5 or Mountjoy 1 month (watches and alarm clocks) £11 3s. 10d. or Mountjoy 1 month (cigarettes and tobacco) £11 3s. 10d. or Mountjoy 1 month (cigarettes and tobacco)

36 Order Books, Monaghan District Court, NAI CS/DC/MN/1.
37 Similar materials for the other border counties were not available in the National Archives.
38 There is a gap of 18 months in the Order Books available for Clones District Court, from early 1924 until Sept. 1925.

District Court	Number of Defendants (Male/Female)	Outcomes	Penalties (and details of items)
Clones[38] (*continued*)	12 (9M/3F)	Convicted (9) Withdrawn (1) Charge Proved (2)	9 convictions (*continued*) £30 or Mountjoy 1 month (parts of a motor car) £50 or Mountjoy 1 month (gold watches and watch parts) £20 or Dundalk 1 month (gold watch) 4s. 7d. or Mountjoy 21 days (shoes and handkerchiefs) £20 or Mountjoy 1 month (personal clothing and tobacco) Charges were dismissed in two cases in which the judge held the charge to be proved.
Monaghan	25 (23M/2F)	Convicted (14) Withdrawn (5) Dismissed Without Prejudice (2) No Appearance (4)	14 convictions £5 or Dundalk 1 month (motor car) £3 or Prison 1 month (tobacco, tea and sugar) £13 or Dundalk 1 month (watches) 18s. 8d. (clocks, hardware, motor car) £10 or Dundalk 3 months (sugar) £100 (sugar and tea) £3 6s. 6d. (pastry) £2 (horse and cart, cases of eggs, boot polish and soap) £4 (horse and cart, cases of eggs) £7 (men's leather boots) 15s. or Dundalk 14 days (sweetened bread or sugar confectionary) £100 (mitigated to £20) or Mountjoy 6 months (blouse and ladies clothes) £7 (wireless component parts) £7 (wireless component parts)

Across these five districts, a total of 53 persons appeared on smuggling charges. Of these, 35 persons were ultimately convicted, and cases were withdrawn or dismissed in the remaining 18 cases. Defendants were convicted for offences that involved the smuggling of clothing, watches and clocks, pastry/confectionary, tea, tobacco/cigarettes, motor cars and motorbikes, fowl, and various other goods. Under the Customs Consolidation Act 1876,[39]

39 39 & 40 Vic., c. 36.

penalties were set at a maximum of £100 or treble the value of the goods. Penalties across the Monaghan District Courts ranged from 4s. 7d. for a case of smuggling one pair of shoes and some handkerchiefs, to cases in which the judge imposed the maximum statutory penalty of £100. In one case in which a penalty of £169 4s. was imposed this represented treble the value of the goods. Annie Magwood, at Monaghan District Court before Justice M.J. Hannan, was charged with smuggling twelve pounds of sugar across the border. It was noted that everything possible had been done under the Customs Offences Act, and the small penalties being imposed on persons were having no appreciable effect on the rates of smuggling in the area. As a result, the Revenue Commissioners had insisted upon the £100 penalty.[40] Following Annie's conviction on 25 January, Justice Hannan declared that he had no discretion but to impose the full penalty of £100, or else to hand down an alternative of six months' imprisonment. He stated that Revenue could reduce the sentence if they so wished in the circumstances, but that he had not the power to do so as they had decided to proceed under a certain section of the Act that required the mandatory fine. Hannan assured the court that in light of the poverty of the defendant, he would recommend that the fine be reduced.[41] This was one of a number of cases in which the maximum fine was handed down, to be subsequently mitigated by Revenue. Judges could also attach a period of imprisonment for non-payment of the financial penalty and in several cases, defendants ultimately ended up in prison. Across all of the Monaghan districts, at least three men were imprisoned for failure to pay: Francis Rock (convicted 1 September 1923), Samuel Martin (convicted 7 April 1925), and Frank Hanratty (convicted 11 May 1926).[42] Reflecting the new jurisdictional intricacies, a significant number of the defendants appearing before the Free State courts on charges of smuggling resided in Northern Ireland; of twenty-five defendants before Monaghan District Court, at least eleven were persons residing in Northern Ireland (resulting in four convictions, the rest of the cases being withdrawn or dismissed without prejudice which may have reflected the difficulties of prosecuting defendants who resided in another jurisdiction). The proximity of the Border seems also to have afforded an opportunity for some defendants to abscond, such as in the case of Annie Magwood, outlined above. Although Annie was ultimately convicted, at one point it was noted that she had absconded to the six counties to avoid the summons.[43]

40 *Fermanagh Herald*, 3 Jan. 1925.
41 *Weekly Irish Times*, 7 Feb. 1925; *Northern Standard*, 30 Jan. 1925.
42 Patrick Collins (convicted 7 Aug. 1923) also seems to have been imprisoned, however, the prison committal register for Dundalk for this period was not present, as this prison was at this point under control of military authorities. General Prisons Board, Dundalk Prison Register 9 Nov. 1917 to 15 Apr. 1931, NAI PRIS 1/16/01.
43 Order Book, Monaghan District Court (12 Aug. 1924–22 May 1925), NAI CS/DC/MN/1.

A look at the newspaper reporting paints a picture of the smuggling cases heard in the District Court along the length of the new border. In October 1923, Ballyshannon District Court in Co. Donegal heard the first case of its kind, before District Justice Sean O'Hanrahan. Edward McAuley was fined five pounds for attempting to smuggle 6,300 cigarettes into the Free State. He was also ordered to pay customs duty of £32 6s. 2d.[44] Annie McAllister, of Belturbet, Co. Cavan, and her brother-in-law Michael McBrien, of Derrylin, Co. Fermanagh, were each fined two hundred pounds by Justice Hannan at Clones District Court in February 1925 for attempting to smuggle six pounds of tobacco across the border.[45] At Lifford District Court, Co. Donegal, before Justice Walsh, one unlucky defendant made the mistake of assuming that the customs officer would be at church on a Sunday morning, and was ultimately fined £1 14s. 4d. for attempting to smuggle fourteen pounds of sugar, a pound of tea, and two pounds of syrup.[46] Sarah Lyons on 15 May 1925, was, at Burnfoot District Court before Justice Walsh, fined £1 5s. 4d., with £1 costs, for attempting to take sugar from Derry to Donegal. She had told customs officers that the substance was flour, and explained to the court that she had lifted the sugar from the shop counter in Derry mistaking it for meal.[47]

The cases demonstrate the mundanity of much of the smuggling in these years. While some of the persons who appeared before the courts were charged with smuggling goods in large quantities, most answered charges of a much more minor nature. David Gardiner, a labourer from Ballindrait in Co. Donegal, found himself before Justice Sean O'Hanrahan, at Lifford District Court, on 3 November 1924, charged with trying to smuggle a pair of boots. The duty on this item would have been just 3s., and for his trouble, Gardiner was instead fined £3, receiving a reprimand from the judge: '[t]he magistrate said the defendant was very foolish to risk so much for so little.'[48]

The smuggling of cigarettes was often carried out in a somewhat organised fashion, with the involvement of local businessmen who sought to employ 'agents' in Northern Ireland to bring over goods which would then be sold in Free State shops.[49] In Clones District Court in the autumn of 1923,

---

44 *Weekly Irish Times*, 3 Nov. 1923. The following humourous exchange is recorded in the report from the *Donegal Democrat*, 26 Oct. 1926:
   Maguire (Defence): What led you to suspect these people?
   Civic Guard: We are always suspicious.
   Maguire: Are you always out at night?
   Civic Guard: Not every night.
   Justice O'Hanrahan: You need not give official information away.
45 *Irish Times*, 14 Feb. 1925.
46 *Weekly Irish Times*, 7 Mar. 1925; *Donegal News*, 28 Feb. 1925.
47 *Weekly Irish Times*, 16 May 1925; *Donegal News*, 16 May 1925.
48 *Irish Times*, 4 Nov. 1924; *Derry Journal*, 5 Nov. 1924.
49 This was suggested in the case of Edith Coulson, as well as in the case of Edward McAuley mentioned above.

'a respectably dressed young lady named Edith Coulson' was charged with attempting to smuggle 1,800 cigarettes across the border.[50] When the case was heard in November, before Justice Hannan at Clones District Court, Coulson pleaded guilty and received a fine of £11 3s. 10d. It emerged that Coulson was related by marriage to Clones shopkeeper, James Young, who took full responsibility for what had happened and received a similar penalty.[51]

The recency of both the new customs barrier and the new courts system sometimes created uncertainty. There was 'an unusual amount of public interest' at Castleblayney District Court when the court heard its first case under the new customs regulations. Justice Tyrrell (acting temporarily for Justice Goff) heard the case of a farm labourer, Patrick Collins, who was charged with attempting to smuggle tobacco and cigarettes into the Free State:

> At this stage, Mr Laverty [defending] raised a legal point as to the exact nature of the charge and the section under which the prosecution was brought. A lot of time was spent in controversy on this point. Mr Keenan [state solicitor] said the charge might be described as smuggling.[52]

Beyond these questions of terminology and charge, this case also raised awkward questions such as whether it would still be smuggling if the cigarettes had been purchased prior to 1 April in anticipation of the coming customs barrier, as was suggested by the defence. The District Court in these early years faced many novel issues, such as the question of jurisdiction which arose in an assault case at Monaghan District Court in May 1925. The problem was whether the defendant, residing in the Free State but alleged to have committed the assault in Northern Ireland, could be tried in Monaghan. Keenan, the state solicitor, said he was confident the court had 'ample jurisdiction', citing a rule that: '[w]here an offence was committed near the Border of an adjoining county or within 500 yards of the Border the case could be dealt with in the adjoining county.' As Justice Hannan reminded him, however: 'Fermanagh is no longer an adjoining county so far as we are concerned.' The hearing was adjourned, and at the next sitting, it was held that there was no jurisdiction to hear the case and defendant was discharged.[53]

Uncertainty is also evident in a 1926 case in which the possibility of appeal was seemingly in doubt. At Dundalk Circuit Court, Justice Doyle heard an appeal from conviction from James Bennett, a commercial traveller, and Edward Coleman, a railway guard. Both men had been convicted and fined £100 by Justice Goff at a recent District Court sitting for attempting to

50 *Northern Standard*, 5 Oct. 1923.
51 *Fermanagh Herald*, 17 Nov. 1923.
52 *Northern Standard*, 10 Aug. 1923.
53 Ibid., 5 June 1925.

smuggle dutiable handkerchiefs into the Free State. Hamill, the state solicitor, 'said there was a grave doubt as to whether there was a right of appeal at all in a customs case, but the case could easily be decided on its merits'.[54] In the end, the judge refused the appeal.

District justices found themselves in the front line of the state's criminal justice response to smuggling, in many cases offering their comments on the realities of the customs barrier. Justice Hannan presided over a sitting of the Monaghan District Court at which the first case of a mere user of an unapproved route was prosecuted and convicted. As was acknowledged, there had been no intention of smuggling on the defendant's part. Rather, the unapproved route saved the defendant a detour of thirty miles, which would have taken two days by horse and cart. Hannan 'had nothing but sympathy with him in the irksomeness, inconvenience and cost which observance of the customs regulations imposed upon him, as on other inhabitants of this particular locality'.[55] There was also evident sympathy in the case of Thomas Brown and James Finlay, heard by Justice Hannan at Clones District Court in November 1925. Hannan held the charge of failure to pay duty on a motorcar proved but dismissed the case, noting the 'extenuating circumstances', namely, that the men had been travelling from Northern Ireland to Cavan with the body of a family member who had died suddenly while north of the border.[56] These cases could not help but expose the inconveniences and ambiguities of the new border, as was clear in the case of Michael Hughes, convicted at Castleblayney on 1 June 1926 for travelling by an unapproved route. Justice Goff, acknowledging the case proved, adjourned the matter while the Revenue Commissioners considered designating the route in question as an approved one. Nonetheless, Goff, noting it as a 'hard case', fined Hughes a total of 8s.[57]

PATRIOTISM

One of the intriguing themes to emerge from these early smuggling cases was the extent to which the judges' views could on occasion be gleaned from their remarks, and the extent to which such cases provoked comment on the wider national question. As Mary Kotsonouris asks of these first District Court justices: 'Who were these men? They were a mixture of solicitors and barristers – most of whom were quite young, and none of whom had previous judicial experience, unless in Dáil courts.'[58] As the cases explored in this

54 *Sunday Independent*, 16 May 1926.
55 *Northern Standard*, 17 July 1925.
56 Clones District Court, Order Book (26 Sept. 192 –13 Aug. 1926) NAI CS/DC/CS/1.
57 *Dundalk Democrat*, 5 June 1926.
58 Mary Kotsonouris, *'Tis all lies, your worship': tales from the District Court* (Dublin, 2011), p. 11.

chapter show, many came to their role with firm principles of patriotism and had themselves played a role in the fight for Irish independence. Fiscal independence had been hard won, and smuggling, depending on the direction of travel, could either be perceived as unpatriotic or, as suggested in a report of the North East Boundary Bureau, it could actively work to bring about reunification. Under this view, the careful calibration of tariffs could: 'create and foster a great smuggling trade along the 240 miles of irregular and impossible Border from Saorstát into the six counties, much to the discomfit and commercial disorganisation of the latter'.[59] While smuggling *could* be made to work for the Free State, it was also the case that smuggling in the other direction, to the detriment of the new state, could be perceived as a deeply unpatriotic act.

Recalling the first smuggling case under the new customs regime, that of Lawrence Hoey in June 1923, District Justice Goff's comments to the court present an insight into how these cases were received initially.[60] Goff said that he looked upon the case as 'a most serious one', continuing:

> Hitherto they had been lax in paying their taxes to a foreign government, but now there was no excuse and it would be well that people should have clear ideas that they were morally bound to pay the taxes, and failure to do so was a matter for Catholics in confession. As to the patriotic aspect they all knew that the boundary question was not yet settled, and the matter of the customs duty and the enforcing of it was a very strong weapon on the side of the Free State to insist that the boundary question would be settled in accordance with the Treaty.[61]

The judge declined to hand down the maximum penalty, but fined Hoey £10 10s. and ordered the goods to be confiscated. He imposed an additional £1 for the offence of crossing the border after hours. 'In future cases', the judge warned, 'he would impose the maximum fine and would take no excuses for any offence which was at once illegal, immoral and unpatriotic'.[62] He also

59 'Boundary Commission', 'Customs – imperial preferences and the North-East', 23 Mar. 1923, NAI NEBB/1/6/3.
60 B.J. Goff had been a Dublin solicitor who occasionally acted as a temporary Circuit judge (see Niamh Howlin's chapter for discussion of Goff in the context of the Ballybay District Court). He was part of the committee established to consider how best to wind down the Dáil courts. See James Casey, 'Republican courts in Ireland, 1919–1922', *Ir. Jur.*, 5:2 (1970), 321–42. Goff went on to become minorly notorious as the judge in the 1937 'kissing case', in which a young woman was convicted for kissing her boyfriend in public. See Mark O'Brien, *The fourth estate: journalism in twentieth-century Ireland* (Manchester, 2017) and Michael Mary Murphy, 'How a public kiss in de Valera's Ireland caused a global sensation', RTÉ Brainstorm, 9 Nov. 2023. See Thomas Mohr's chapter for an overview of the Dáil courts.
61 *Dundalk Democrat*, 16 June 1923.
62 Ibid.

added an admonishment for the citizens of Northern Ireland: '[i]f the people of Newry once thought they could keep out of the Free State, and at the same time have the profit by defrauding the Free State, they might not be very anxious to come into it.'[63] In the judge's opinion, there were matters both moral and national at stake in the illicit business of cross-border smuggling. A later case showed that Goff's views were little altered. Michael Coogan, a Monaghan jeweller, and Francis Boylan, a local publican, were convicted before him at Castleblayney on 2 March 1926. The men had attempted to smuggle various items of clothing from Northern Ireland and were ordered to pay £9 4s. 4d. and £13 18s. 6d. respectively. Goff gave his view that: 'A deliberate offence of this kind was not only illegal, but was unpatriotic. It was unpatriotic for any citizen of the State to defraud his fellow citizen. It means that every rate-payer is defrauded of the amount of the duty, and the unemployed of work.'[64] Goff, a solicitor from Roscommon, had been interned during the War of Independence, and had served as a temporary judge in the Dáil courts.[65] His own patriotic past may have informed his opinions about the implications of smuggling.

The District Court therefore became an unlikely arena in which arguments for patriotism and unification could be made. This is further illustrated through the comments of Louis Joseph Walsh, a Donegal district justice.[66] Walsh argued that the Free State had finally realised its hard-won independence, and this included the independence to set its own customs tariffs. Walsh appeared affronted by the smuggling activities of citizens of the new state. Walsh himself had been a constitutional nationalist until the 1916 Easter Rising, an event which radicalised him and drew him towards militant republicanism. In 1921, he had been arrested and interned, first in Derry Gaol, and then in Ballykinlar internment camp. Having run unsuccessfully as a Sinn Féin candidate in the Northern Ireland elections of May 2021, he moved across the border to Letterkenny in Donegal where he became the first district justice appointed by the new Irish Free State.[67]

Walsh's views on partition and the political question of smuggling are evident in various of the cases he heard. At Donegal's Burnfoot District Court, Edward Deeney was fined £100 for attempting to smuggle 42 pounds of tobacco. Deeney was a commercial traveller for a well-known Derry wholesale tobacco merchant (ironically, also a noted Republican). On 7 September, on approaching the Free State customs, Deeney had declared that

63 *Irish Independent*, 16 June 1923.
64 *Dundalk Democrat*, 6 Mar. 1926.
65 Mary Kotsonouris, *The winding up of the Dáil courts 1922–1925: an obvious duty* (Dublin, 2004).
66 Nicholas Allen, 'Louis Joseph Walsh', *DIB*. See Thomas Mohr's chapter for mention of Walsh and his role on the Judiciary Committee.
67 District Justices (Temporary Provisions) Act 1923, sch. 3.

he had no dutiable goods and was subsequently searched. Although nothing was found on his person, tobacco was found in his motor car. Deeney attempted to talk his way out of the charge, claiming that the tobacco was an order for a customer based in Northern Ireland who had been not at home when Deeney called. Deeney further claimed that he had approached customs to obtain a special pass because he hoped to attend a dance in Donegal that Sunday. Contradicting this claim, however, was the fact that Deeney had approached customs with a pass for his motor car in his hand, signalling that he was indeed attempting to take the tobacco across the border without paying the duty owed. Judge Walsh was strong in his rebuke of the defendant, alleging that:

> One of the things they had fought for was the right to control their own finance, and no policy had been more justified by results than the use that they had made of the fiscal power that they now had. Since the customs barrier had been established, new factories had been springing up in the Free State, and in Inishowen [County Donegal] they had three new shirt factories.[68]

The goods and the car were both confiscated. Walsh, setting bail at £300 and two sureties at £150 each, denied that this was too great a sum, arguing that:

> the charge, if proved, would amount to one of fraud against the revenue of their own country and in the interests of the British Exchequer; and 'the predominant partner' had never been so generous in its financial relations with Ireland that he should feel bound in any way to facilitate unduly those accused of acting against their own country's financial upbuilding.[69]

These rationales, invoking patriotism and Ireland's 'financial upbuilding', were to recur in many subsequent cases before Walsh. Presiding over a sitting of the Newtown Cunningham District Court in September 1926, Walsh made a similar argument regarding the burgeoning Donegal shirt-making industry. At this sitting, one man was fined a hundred pounds for smuggling drapery goods into Donegal from Derry while another man was fined a hundred pounds for attempting to smuggle a portion of a suit. Walsh, in handing down the fines, 'said protection had resulted in half a dozen factories springing up in that county, and it was the duty of every public-spirited citizen to assist the government'.[70]

68 *Irish Times*, 9 Oct. 1925.
69 Ibid., 9 Sept. 1925.
70 *Northern Standard*, 24 Sept. 1926.

CONCLUSION

The introduction of the customs barrier in April 1923 imposed a new reality on the people who lived at the Border. The introduction of tariffs on a range of goods also, inevitably, created the conditions for the emergence of smuggling along the length of boundary, an illicit trade in which many 'ordinary' Irish citizens engaged. The newly constituted District Court was the arena in which this new breed of case was heard. In courtrooms the length of the border, a new class of criminal was made to answer charges of smuggling. Many of these cases exposed the difficulties and uncertainties of the new legal reality on the island of Ireland, on which two jurisdictions now co-existed. There were inevitable jurisdictional and procedural intricacies which emerged in the early years of partition, and which had their first airing in the District Court. There was also evident sympathy for Border-dwellers who found themselves before the courts on what amounted to little more than technical breaches of the regulations. The District Court assumed a role in communicating the significance of the new regulations and of the necessity of adhering to them. Yet in many of cases, particularly those of a more serious and organised nature, wider questions of patriotism were also on the agenda. The newly appointed district justices, many of whom had played an active role in the fight for independence, viewed smuggling as at once a moral matter *and* a matter of national significance. As some judges saw it, Ireland's independence had been hard won, and its subsequent fiscal independence was a vital prong in ensuring the financial security of the new state. The District Court therefore became a novel backdrop against which key questions of nationhood were considered.

CHAPTER THIRTEEN

'Twenty-six high courts': the Circuit Court, decentralisation and its opponents, 1924–34

KEVIN COSTELLO*

A couple of weeks before the 1932 general election, the Irish Free State government produced a glossy newspaper supplement celebrating the achievements of the new state. One of those accomplishments was the Circuit Court.[1] This court was described as an Irish judicature innovation: a sort of 'High Court in miniature' sitting outside Dublin to which jurisdiction previously belonging to the High Court had been devolved:

> in order that people living in the country districts who formerly had to bring their cases before a high court in Dublin might have the opportunity of going before a judge sitting in their own county ... in other words its main principle was the decentralisation of justice.

The idea of diverting legal business in Ireland away from the centre and towards local courts had underlain Austin Stack's scheme of underground Dáil courts.[2] Decree no. 5, session 1, provided for a county-wide system of District Courts with a jurisdiction in claims up to one hundred pounds[3] – twice that of the County Courts.[4] The success of the revolutionary District Court – convening in parish halls, school buildings and Sinn Féin clubs – was fresh in the minds of the Judiciary Committee. Submissions were received by the committee arguing that the success of the Republican courts system had proven the case for moving in the centre of gravity of legal activity away from the Four Courts. Judge Meredith wrote to the committee that the 'experience of the Republican courts [showed] that there is a large mass of business which has been kept out of [the High Court] by reasons of expense and delay'.[5] W.T.

---

* Associate Professor, Sutherland School of Law, University College Dublin.
1 *Irish Times*, supplement, Jan. 1932.
2 Mary Kotsonouris, *Retreat from revolution. the Dáil courts 1920–24* (Dublin, 1994), p. 31.
3 ibid.
4 County Officers Act 1877 (40 & 41 Vict., c. 56), s. 50.
5 22 Feb. 1923, NAI BR/DUB 151/22.

Cosgrave, in his briefing note to the committee, directed that one of the elements of the committee's judicature re-design should be the 'decentralization of the courts'.[6]

However, an expansion in the jurisdiction of the County Court, and the diversion of business from the Four Courts, would entail a cost for one constituency in particular: the Bar. A memorandum prepared by the Bar Council in March 1923[7] argued vehemently against any expansion in the jurisdiction of the County Courts. A network of mini 'district high courts' could make it profitable for barristers to set up business in county towns removed from the control and expertise of the law library. It would not be possible for every county to have a 'complete or sufficient library'. In the absence of access to more expert colleagues, or law reports, or statutes, cases would be argued by a legally ignorant local Bar. This could degrade the quality of justice. This, in turn, might even threaten the rule of law itself by reducing the pool of barristers sufficiently expert to be offered judicial office.[8] A further strain to the Bar Council's argument suggested that closing off access to the High Court in routine debt matters could be a threat to the national economy. Irish retail commerce depended on the supply of goods on credit by English wholesalers and factories to Irish country shops. There was a danger that, faced with the risk of relying on low quality local courts for the protection of that credit, such retail credit would be cancelled. If the English merchant 'knows that he must resort to some local venue he will be less inclined to give credit'.[9] Behind the Bar's objections of principle, lay some unspoken income-related concerns. If the jurisdiction of the local courts was expanded, barristers would face the choice of either remaining in Dublin, from where work had been diverted, or enduring the travelling and accommodation expenses and the reduced scale of fees[10] entailed in practising in the local courts. Either way, barristers' incomes could be affected.

GLENAVY'S 'GYRATIONS'

The Bar Council's attempt to dissuade the Judiciary Committee from the policy of decentralization failed. The Committee reported in late April 1923, recommending the establishment of a Circuit Court with a jurisdiction in tort and contract of three hundred pounds,[11] modelled on the District Court of New South Wales.[12] This was a six-fold increase on the jurisdiction allowed

6 (nd) 1923, UCDA P4/1090.
7 Bar Council to the Judiciary Committee, 2 Mar. 1923, NAI BR/Dub/151/16.
8 'Bar Council's Action. Proposed Amendment' *Irish Independent*, 9 Oct. 1923; *Report of the Committee on the Courts of Justice Act 1924* (Dublin, 1930), p. xiii.
9 Bar Council memo., 2 Mar. 1923, NAI BR/Dub/151/16.
10 See n. 68 below.
11 *Report of the Judiciary Committee* (Dublin, 1923), p. 15.
12 Report by A.F. Blood, 7 Dec. 1922, UCDA P4/1089 (6–7).

1 Hugh Kennedy and Lord Glenavy, early 1920s.
Courtesy of the National Library of Ireland.

2 'New Irish Courts', 1924. Courtesy of British Pathé.

3 The new judges arriving at Dublin Castle, 1924. Courtesy of British Pathé.

4 Christmas card sent by Hugh Kennedy from Dublin Castle. Courtesy of UCD Archives

5 Dun Emer Guild design for robes for Circuit Court judges. Courtesy of UCD Archives.

6 Dun Emer Guild design for robes for Supreme Court judges. Courtesy of UCD Archives.

7 Charles Shannon designs for the District Court and the Central Criminal Court. Courtesy of the Courts Service and Brian O'Connell.

8 Charles Shannon design for the High Court.
Courtesy of the Courts Service and Brian O'Connell.

9 District judges in 1926 wearing new robes. Courtesy of the *Daily Mirror*.

10 Hugh Kennedy holding his wig. Courtesy of UCD Archives.

11 Chief justice's seal. Courtesy of UCD Archives.

12 'Man Overboard'. Cartoon by Gordon Brewster regarding the Courts of Justice Act 1925. Courtesy of the National Library of Ireland.

13 'Kennedy Chief Justice'. Cartoon by Isa Macnie.
Courtesy of the National Library of Ireland.

14 A Century of Courts conference logo, depicting both Dublin Castle and the Four Courts.

15 Tralee courthouse with cannon.

16 Monaghan courthouse with its coat of arms still intact.

17 Cavan courthouse before the removal of its coat of arms.
Courtesy of the National Library of Ireland.

18 An Post stamp commemorating the Courts of Justice Act 1924. Courtesy of An Post.

to the old County Court.[13] By increasing the value of claims that could be sued for in the Circuit Court, the measure would expand the amount of business in the Circuit Court. This recommendation was then implemented by the bill that would become the Courts of Justice Act 1924. Cosgrave considered this the single 'most important feature'[14] of the entire scheme, with a Circuit Court providing inexpensive, localized justice to persons who previously could not afford High Court litigation and which could attend to 75% of the litigation generated within the country. An amendment proposed by William Redmond TD at committee stage which would have reduced the £300 jurisdiction to £100 was rejected; Cosgrave strongly endorsed the policy of 'popularising' the Circuit Court, saying that his personal preference had been to set the limit even higher at £400.[15]

The enactment of the 1924 Act did not, however, end the campaign of opposition to the enlarged jurisdiction. For the next ten years, the Bar and its allies engaged in a campaign to reverse the transfer of business from the High Court to the Circuit Court. As a gesture of assurance to the Southern Unionist community, the Executive Committee had invited, the septuagenarian former Conservative MP and Irish lord chancellor, James Campbell (now Baron Glenavy), to participate in the nation-building project by chairing the Judiciary Committee. While Glenavy had made clear his opposition to allowing the Circuit Court unlimited jurisdiction, he had expressly endorsed the Committee's unanimous proposal for a Circuit Court with a £300 jurisdiction.[16] Just eight months later, however, he attempted to subvert the £300 jurisdiction reform. In introducing the Courts of Justice bill in the Senate, Glenavy began by explaining that the proposal to increase the jurisdiction of the Circuit Court had the unanimous support of the committee. In the next sentence, he effectively invited the Seanad to step in and reverse the £300 proposal:[17] it was 'well worth consideration, whether in making the new departure the committee and the Dáil may not perhaps have gone a little too far in extending the limit from £50 to £300'. Encouraging the reopening of the £300 question, he described the measure as 'a matter which is capable of discussion, and, I am sure, will receive full discussion in committee'. Hugh Kennedy looked on, amazed at Glenavy's disloyalty to his own committee and his 'gyrations' in introducing, and then attempting to wreck, his own bill.[18] Glenavy was accused by one commentator of 'killing his own child in order to please the Irish Bar'.[19]

13 See above, text accompanying n. 4.
14 *Dáil Éireann deb.*, vol. 5, col. 7 (12 Oct 1923).
15 Ibid.
16 Glenavy to Kennedy, Mar. 1923, UCDA P4/1087.
17 *Seanad Éireann deb.*, vol. 2, col. 11 (16 Jan. 1924).
18 Kennedy to Walsh, 6 Feb. 1924, UCDA P4 1126.
19 'Correspondence. The Circuit Court', *Irish Statesman*, 25 Aug. 1928.

THE £300 JURISDICTION QUESTION, 1924 TO 1926. GLENAVY 'ON THE WAR PATH'

Glenavy's performance in the Senate in 1924 was not to be the last of his destructive efforts. In introducing the Courts of Justice bill, Cosgrave had explained that the statute was merely a 'framework',[20] which would be filled out by detailed Rules of the Circuit Court approved by the Oireachtas.[21] The rules were necessary to operationalize the £300 jurisdiction. Opposition to the Circuit Court Rules became a proxy for opposition to the £300 jurisdiction itself. Underlying the opposition's strategy was the idea that if the machinery for implementing the £300 jurisdiction could be obstructed, then the £300 jurisdiction itself might become impossible and fall away. It would take another seven years, and three postponements, for the Circuit Court Rules to be finally approved.

By 1925, unease was beginning to be felt at the long time it was taking to prepare the Circuit Court Rules.[22] The task of drafting the rules had been delegated to Edmond Lupton KC.[23] Lupton had to be prompted into finally completing his draft rules by July 1926.[24] Lupton's careful draft included a series of reforms,[25] one of which provided that all Circuit Court proceedings would be initiated by a summons that would include 'particulars' setting out the 'grounds of the claim'.[26] Proceedings in the old County Court had been initiated by a bill simply identifying the bare cause of action ('negligence' or 'work and labour', or 'goods').[27] Although there was no requirement that the plaintiff set out the actual details of the claim, the defendant could request full particulars.[28] The apparently innocuous adjustment in the status of particulars proposed in 1926 – from being detail which the defendant could request to detail which the plaintiff was required to provide – became the subject of the first battle of the Circuit Court Rules.

As soon as he read the provision for particulars in Rule 98, an unaccountably furious Glenavy went on the 'war path'.[29] He urgently contacted the rules committee to ask it to reconsider its proposal for, what he insisted on describing as, 'pleadings'.[30] In a note to Kevin O'Higgins, Glenavy

20 *Dáil Éireann deb.*, vol. 5, col. 1 (20 Sept. 1923).
21 Courts of Justice Act 1924, s. 101.
22 *Irish Statesman*, 10 Jan. 1925.
23 Note by T.A. Finlay, 15 June 1925, NAI JUS/H264/7; *I.L.T.&S.J.* 76 (1942), 296.
24 Finlay to J.J. Horgan, 11 Mar. 1925. Courts of Justice Act 1924, Rule-Making Committee. Circuit Court, NAI JUS/H264/7.
25 Lupton's draft included measures allowing public access to records (rule 13) and to assist access to litigation for poor persons (rule 72), Rules of the Circuit Court 1926.
26 Rules of the Circuit Court 1926, rule 98.
27 H.W. Rainey, *Handbook on the jurisdiction and practice of the Circuit Court* (Dublin, 1906), p. 8.
28 County Courts (Ireland) Orders 1890, order 3(7). Equity civil bills were required to set out the facts constituting the plaintiff's claim (order 3(5)).
29 Horgan to T.F. Coyne, 28 Feb. 1927, Rule-Making Committee, NAI JUS/H264/7.
30 *Seanad Éireann deb.*, vol. 7, col. 9 (22 July 1926).

argued – not entirely accurately – that the 'old County Court had acted without pleadings' and he 'never heard of any complaint of their absence'.[31] Mischievously terming particulars as 'pleadings', with its implication of ornate eighteenth-century special pleading, provided Glenavy with a means of framing his campaign in populist terms. Requiring poor litigants to pay for the drafting of pleadings was, he argued, a betrayal of the original democratic vision of the Circuit Court as an accessible popular tribunal. The archconservative Glenavy found an unlikely ally in the leader of the Labour Party, Thomas Johnson. Subjecting poor litigants to the formality and expense of pleadings was, Johnson implied, a betrayal of the original Republican vision of the Circuit Court as an accessible popular tribunal.[32] In the Senate the following day, Glenavy argued that the committee had misunderstood the uniquely informal character of the Circuit Court and its proposals would complicate the efficiency of Circuit Court litigation by imposing the 'whole machinery of the High Court'.[33]

Privately, O'Higgins was part-persuaded by Glenavy's objection, being 'greatly struck' by the impact upon the accessibility of the Circuit Court by the introduction of a requirement to formulate particulars.[34] O'Higgins agreed to withdraw the draft rules.[35] In its defence, the rules committee argued that the measure was a reasonable one and what 'some people' – referring to Glenavy – 'may regard as complicated procedures are necessary for the protection of the litigants themselves'.[36] Circuit Court judge John Wakely explained that it had 'always been a drawback' of the civil bill that 'the plaintiff does not know the defendant's case till he comes into court'.[37]

While Glenavy was busy trying to obstruct the completion of the Circuit Court, his nemesis, Hugh Kennedy, was strengthening the Circuit Court's £300 jurisdiction. The 1924 Act had not positively barred plaintiffs from ignoring the Circuit Court and suing in the High Court. Section 24 gave the High Court a discretion to remit cases back to the Circuit Court. In 1927 the discretion to remit was converted into a presumption in favour of remittal by the decision of the Supreme Court in *Hosie v. Lawless*.[38] In *Hosie*, Kennedy held that the power of remittal should be read in light of the Courts of Justice Act's policy of 'decentralisation of jurisdiction' to the Circuit Court.[39] Accordingly, cases must be remitted unless there were 'special circumstances' making it suitable for hearing in the High Court. The effect of *Hosie* was to

31 Glenavy to O'Higgins, 26 Nov. 1926, NAI JUS/H264/7, Annex 7.
32 *Dáil Éireann deb.*, vol. 16, col. 22 (21 July 1926).
33 *Seanad Éireann deb.*, vol. 7, col. 9 (22 July 1926).
34 O'Higgins memo., 15 Nov. 1926, NAI DJ/H/264, Annex 4.
35 *Dáil Éireann deb.*, vol. 16, col. 22 (21 July 1926).
36 Ibid.
37 J. Wakely, to sec. Dept. Justice, 3 Dec. 1926, Rule-Making Committee, NAI JUS/H264/7.
38 [1927] IR 464.
39 Ibid., at 471.

effectively close off the plaintiff's choice of suing in the High Court and to give the Circuit Court a practically exclusive jurisdiction in all cases within the £300 limit.

1928: '£300 HAS PROVED TO BE UNDULY EXCESSIVE'

The particulars row delayed the settlement of the Circuit Court Rules for a further two years. The rules committee spent two more years, between 1926 and 1928, preparing a second set of Circuit Court Rules, which was not much different from the earlier version. O'Higgins had predicted that the committee would not retreat from the proposal for particulars.[40] This proved accurate. The second version of 1928 made no concession on the requirement for particulars.[41] In order to settle the conflict, O'Higgins's successor as minister for justice, James FitzGerald-Kenney, proposed in May 1928 that the matter be referred to a joint committee of the Dáil and Seanad.

FitzGerald-Kenney's hope that the committee would find a compromise to the row about particulars, and that it would 'not be too keen on finding defects',[42] was misplaced. Diverting the dispute to a joint committee proved to be a disastrous strategy: the committee fell straight into the hands of Glenavy. It is difficult to understand how FitzGerald-Kenney did not anticipate that the ex-lord chancellor would, as the most eminent legal member the Oireachtas, have to be appointed to this committee. It is also difficult to see how FitzGerald-Kenney did not foresee that, once appointed, the forceful and motivated Glenavy would capture the committee. This is precisely what happened. The committee of selection announced the appointment of Baron Glenavy to the Circuit Court Rules Committee.[43] When the Circuit Court Rules Committee met, it appointed Glenavy as its chair.[44] The fate of the Circuit Court Rules was now in the hands of their most dedicated opponent.

Glenavy now took his opportunity to derail the rules. In a short thirteen paragraph report produced the following month, the committee set out the familiar objections to the 'elaborate system of pleadings, discovery of documents, particulars, admissions' provided for in the proposed rules.[45] The rules would increase the expense of litigating in the Circuit Court, and would make the Circuit Court more expensive by comparison with litigation in its English comparator, the County Court. However, the report went further than merely arguing for the rejection of the provisions regulating particulars.

40 O'Higgins memo., 15 Nov. 1926, NAI DJ/H/264, Annex 4.
41 Draft Circuit Court Rules 1928, Rule 98; *Irish Independent*, 23 Mar. 1928.
42 *Seanad Éireann deb.*, vol. 23, col. 8 (3 May 1928).
43 *Seanad Éireann deb.*, vol. 10, col. 15 (23 May 1928).
44 *Report of the Joint Committee on the Rules of the Circuit Court* (Dublin, 1928).
45 Ibid., proceedings, 28 May 1928, para. 3.

In a single blunt sentence, it called for the reversal of decentralisation and the return to the High Court of its traditional jurisdiction. The experience of the last three years had satisfied the committee 'that the extension of the former jurisdiction of the County Courts in actions on contracts or for damages from a maximum of £50 to £300 has proved to be unduly excessive'.[46] Glenavy had a reputation for being under-prepared in his contributions to the Oireachtas[47] and his casual approach to parliamentary work may have got the better of him. The breezy single-sentence claim that the new jurisdiction was 'unduly excessive' was not elaborated upon or further justified.

Glenavy's poorly argued report turned the tide, provoking an overwhelming defence of the Circuit Court. Resolutions passed by Limerick County Council, the Southern Law Association[48] and the Dublin Circuit Bar Association condemned the Glenavy proposal.[49] The Southern Law Association said that the business community of Munster would be put to enormous expense by restoration of High Court jurisdiction.[50] In a protest sent to W.T. Cosgrave, Cork Chamber of Commerce described the Glenavy recommendation as a reactionary attempt 'to force the repeal of the most important provision of the Courts of Justice Act 1924'.[51] The only support for Glenavy's proposal 'emanated from the senior members and some junior members of the Bar'.[52] There were also legal, as well as policy, objections to Glenavy's proposal. The joint committee's jurisdiction only extended to a review of the rules. It was not authorised to review – as Glenavy had done – the policy of the parent Act. The *Irish Statesman* argued that Glenavy, in recommending changes to the Act, was acting *ultra vires* the committee's terms of reference.[53]

THE 'COMEDY OF THE CIRCUIT COURT RULES', 1928–31

Glenavy's retirement from public life in November 1928[54] removed the principal leadership figure against the expanded jurisdiction of the Circuit Court. Notwithstanding the strong popular counter-reaction against the Glenavy proposal, and Glenavy's retirement, the 'Comedy of the Circuit Court Rules'[55] dragged on for another three years.

46 Ibid., para. 11.
47 Patrick Maume, 'Campbell, James Henry Mussen', *DIB*.
48 *Irish Independent*, 11 Jan. 1930.
49 10 Aug. and 29 Sept. 1928, Rule-Making Committee, NAI JUS/H264/7.
50 *Irish Examiner*, 11 Jan. 1930.
51 17 Dec. 1928, NAI JUS/H264/7, Annex 1.
52 O'Brien Moran to Roche, 14 July 1928, Rule-Making Committee, NAI JUS/H264/7.
53 *Irish Statesman*, 25 Aug. 1928; 'Circuit Court Rules', *Irish Independent*, 17 July 1928.
54 *Irish Times*, 28 Nov. 1928.
55 'From Dublin town', *Connacht Sentinel*, 18 Mar. 1930.

After yet another two-year delay a third draft was introduced in early 1930. A joint committee on the Courts of Justice Act 1924 had been established in October 1929, chaired by Daniel Morrissey TD.⁵⁶ This provided the opportunity for one final push against the £300 jurisdiction. The lawyer TDs William Redmond and Jasper Wolfe pressed the minister to adjourn the adoption of the rules until the Circuit Court question has been considered by the Committee on the Courts of Justice Act 1924.⁵⁷ There was a chance, they argued, that the committee might recommend changes to the Circuit Court that might affect the rules. The minister, James FitzGerald-Kenney, consented to this delay. This, after the earlier postponements in 1926 and 1928, was the third delay to the introduction of the rules. FitzGerald-Kenney was ridiculed as a 'weakling';⁵⁸ the real problem may have been that FitzGerald-Kenney, like many of his barrister colleagues, did not actually believe in a higher-capacity Circuit Court. In opposition, in 1935, he sponsored an amendment to the Courts of Justice Act that would have reversed the £300 jurisdiction.⁵⁹

The Morrissey Committee was already hearing submissions from senior members of the profession⁶⁰ who argued that the enhanced jurisdiction of the Circuit Court interfered with the constitutional right of the litigant to sue in the High Court. There was also some support from within the judiciary for the Bar's position. In 1929, the High Court judge Henry Hanna in his *Statute law of the Irish Free State* rehearsed the Bar's traditional anti-devolution argument. The Courts of Justice Act 1924 would bring about 'decentralization to … scattered Circuit Courts'. 'The effect of this', Hanna wrote, 'upon … the Bar, and its discipline, is a matter of much concern'.⁶¹ The ex-president of the Law Society, Dr Quirke, told the committee that the solicitors profession was split along Dublin/country lines: country members supported enlarged jurisdiction while the Dublin members, fearing the establishment of what it believed would become 'twenty six little high courts',⁶² opposed the £300 jurisdiction. However, a majority of witnesses who gave evidence to the Morrissey Committee favoured retention of the existing Circuit Court jurisdiction. The committee declined to recommend the restoration of the County Court jurisdictional limits.⁶³

56 *Dáil Éireann deb.*, vol. 32, no. 3 (25 Oct. 1929).
57 Ibid., vol. 33, no. 13 (12 Mar. 1930).
58 'The Circuit Court Scandal', *Nationality*, 8 Aug. 1931.
59 *Dáil Éireann deb.*, vol. 59, no. 8 (21 Nov. 1935).
60 *Report of the Joint Committee on the Courts of Justice Act 1924 and the civil jurisdiction of the courts* (Dublin, 1930), Evidence: William Carrigan KC, 4 Feb. 1930; F.W. Price, 6 Feb. 1930; Conor A. Maguire, 6 Feb. 1930.
61 *The statute law of the Irish Free State 1922 to 1928* (Dublin, 1929), p. 21.
62 *Report of the Joint Committee on the Courts of Justice Act 1924 and the civil jurisdiction of the courts*, Evidence 29 Dec. 1929.
63 Ibid., para. 13 and 15.

The Morrissey Committee's report of November 1930 appeared to remove the final opportunity to disrupt the decentralization project and to clear the way for confirmation of the rules. Yet, by the summer of 1931 there was still no sign of the rules being enacted. As the Supreme Court was about to rise for the 1931 long vacation, Kennedy CJ took the opportunity in *Quinn and White v. Stokes*[64] to aim a withering rebuke to those – like Glenavy, FitzGerald-Kenney and the Bar – who had been responsible for the delay. The 'failure', after seven years, to complete a set of rules of court had 'impeded the development of the court and [had] embarrassed everyone concerned in its administration'.[65] Kennedy's intervention had a galvanising effect: the 1930 draft was introduced to, and quickly approved by, the Oireachtas in October 1931.[66]

While the Bar had lost the £300 jurisdiction battle, the professions did manage to defeat a number proposals that might have damaged its interests. One was the Rule Committee's plan for a limited form of legal aid. The 1926 and 1928 draft rules[67] had provided that where the means of a plaintiff or defendant were less than £10, the Circuit Court judge could assign a solicitor and barrister to act for free. If the poor litigant's case failed, the unsuccessful plaintiff could not be charged by its lawyers. This novel form of forced contingency fee arrangement was deleted from the 1930 draft rules. The Irish Trade Union Congress paper, *The Watchword*, blamed the professions for the withdrawal of this attempt at a system of civil legal aid.[68]

THE BUSINESS OF THE CIRCUIT COURT, 1924–33

Shop debts incurred by customers remained a significant fraction of the business of the early years of the Circuit Court. In Nenagh Circuit Court, for instance, nearly fifty of the first hundred cases lodged with the court in December 1924 involved shop debts.[69] As well as being used by shops against customers, the court was also used by wholesalers to recover debts from shops which had been supplied with goods on credit. A concern that English

64 [1931] IR 588.
65 Ibid., at 562.
66 *Dáil Éireann deb.*, vol. 40, no. 5 (22 Oct. 1931).
67 1926 draft, rules 72–4; 1928 draft, rules 71–3.
68 'No free legal assistance for the poor', *The Watchword*, 24 Nov. 1931. The professions also managed to reduce the extent of state regulation of fees. The 1890 Schedule of Fees had subjected fees in all County Court claims, regardless of size, to state control (County Courts (Ireland) Orders 1890). In what may have been a concession to the professions, the 1930 rules kept fees in claims for more than £100 – the sort of cases in which barristers would have briefed – outside of the Schedule and outside of state control (Circuit Court Rules 1930, sch. 3).
69 Tipperary Circuit Court civil bills etc. judges' books 1924, NAI C/86/16.

wholesalers, deterred by the prospect of having to sue in the local Circuit Court, would withdraw from the Irish market had underlain one of the Bar's arguments against the enlarged jurisdiction of the Circuit Court.[70] In spite of these concerns, English wholesalers such as the Leyland and Birmingham Rubber Company[71] and J.S. Fry[72] continued to issue civil bills in Circuit Courts in the West of Ireland.

By the late 1920s, the Land Commission had replaced the retail trade as the most active user of the Circuit Court. Typically, Land Commission cases involved claims against small farmers who had defaulted in instalments for the purchase of farmland.[73] The Land Commission, which had inherited the debts of the Congested Districts Board, also sued defaulters for loans made by the Board for the purchase of cattle and fishing boats.[74] Over 60% of actions in the Circuit Court in Nenagh in 1925 were taken by the Irish Land Commission.[75] Soon after its establishment in 1927,[76] the Agricultural Credit Corporation began to use the Circuit Court to recover unpaid instalments.[77]

While the court was still overwhelmingly a small debts court, a smaller fraction of cases involved litigants taking advantage of the increased jurisdictional limit in tort cases. The expansion in car usage in 1920s Ireland brought about an increase in actions for personal injuries caused by cars and buses. About 6% of cases in Galway in 1929 involved actions arising out of injuries caused by cars.[78] The policy of decentralisation enabled rural litigants to avail of the Circuit Court, rather than the High Court, in order to sue local newspapers for libel and to sue the men who had impregnated their daughters.[79]

The cost of the social policy of enabling access to justice to persons living outside Dublin was borne by the Bar practising from the Four Courts. How much business was appropriated from the Four Courts by the new Circuit Court? Most of the claims heard by the Circuit Court in the 1920s were low-level disputes that would never have been suitable for the High Court. The Department of Justice collected figures showing that 77% of cases heard by the Circuit Court in the late 1920s involved claims under £50[80] – cases that would have fallen within the competence of the old County Court. The

70 See n. 7 above.
71 Galway civil bill papers 1923 to 1927, NAI IC/7120.
72 Ibid., 1926/7887.
73 *Ellis v. Irish Land Commission* (1925), ibid., 1925/7677.
74 Land Law (Commission) Act 1923, s. 8.
75 Tipperary Circuit Court civil bills etc. judges' books 1925, NAI 1C/134/36.
76 Agricultural Credit Act 1927.
77 Hilary 1929, Galway cause book in civil cases 1929–1933, NAI ID/73/61.
78 Ibid.
79 *Mahon v. Powell* (1932), Galway cause book in civil cases 1932–1934, NAI ID/73/60; *Curren v. Connolly* (1931), Galway cause book in civil cases 1929–1933, NAI ID/73/61.
80 *Report of the Joint Committee* (1930), para. 12.

balance, of course, was claims that would, but for the Courts of Justice Act 1924, have been processed by the High Court. In the legal years 1926, 1927 and 1928, the Circuit Court received almost 8,000 bills for sums above £50.[81] This amounted to a loss in the traffic of business to the Four Courts of almost 30%.[82] That was work that the Bar in the bleak late 1920s could have done with. On the other hand, the diversion of work to a higher capacity Circuit Court did not remove work from the Bar. Litigation was, instead, diverted from the Four Courts and dispersed throughout the country. The Bar, however reluctant, had no choice but to adapt. Barristers travelled from Dublin to Circuit Court sittings.[83] The Circuit Court registrar for Monaghan reported that barristers 'motored down from Dublin in the morning and they motor back'.[84] In the end, despite the catastrophising of the Bar Council, decentralization to the Circuit Courts did not affect the supply of English commercial credit; the £300 jurisdiction did not result in barristers permanently deserting the law library for a life of legal ignorance in backwater country towns, and the Four Courts did not disintegrate into 'twenty-six little high courts'.

81 Ibid., app. 3.
82 In the legal years 1926 to 1928 the High Court received over 20,000 plenary and summary summonses. Department of Industry and Commerce, *Statistical abstract 1931*, p. 117.
83 *Report of the Joint Committee* (1930), evidence 16 Jan. 1930.
84 Ibid., evidence of Henry Murphy, 14 Jan. 1940.

CHAPTER FOURTEEN

The expanding role of the Circuit Court judge

PATRICIA RYAN*

Under the Courts of Justice Act 1924, the old system of County Courts, Quarter Sessions and Assizes was replaced by a new District Court and a new Circuit Court.[1] However, both new courts had a wider jurisdiction than the County Court, dealing with a somewhat similar Circuit Court monetary ceiling in contract and tort cases, and dealing with all serious crime bar capital offences.[2] The 1924 Act created eight circuits.[3] In 1937 the number of circuits was increased to nine,[4] and in 1960 it was reduced to eight once more.[5] The Courts Act 1964 allowed for the renaming or reorganisation of circuits as needed, and several counties have been transferred from one circuit to another over the past century. At present, the country is divided into eight circuits with one judge assigned to each circuit except in Dublin, where ten judges may be assigned, and Cork, where there is provision for three judges.

JUDGES OF THE CIRCUIT COURT

Section 37 of the Courts of Justice Act 1924 stated that there would be eight Circuit Court judges – this meant that there was one judge per circuit. The role of president of the Circuit Court was formally created by section 9 of the Courts of Justice Act 1947,[6] and its first president was George William Shannon. This was aimed at addressing the uneven distribution of work among the circuits. The role of the president was to assess the situation in each circuit and organise the assignment of judges to provide assistance where

---

* President of the Circuit Court.
1 See Kevin Costello's chapter.
2 Ronan Keane, 'The Irish courts system in the 21st century: planning for the future', *Bar Review*, 6 (2001), 321–8, at 323.
3 Courts of Justice Act 1924, s. 37.
4 Circuit Court (New Circuits) Order 1937 (SI 309/1937), under the Courts of Justice Act 1936, s. 13.
5 Circuit Court (New Circuits) Order, 1960 (SI 70/1960), under the Courts of Justice Act 1953, s. 16.
6 S. 9(2) provided that the president of the Circuit Court should be 'ex-officio an additional judge of the High Court.' See Appendix 5 for a list of office-holders.

it was required.⁷ Section 4 of the Courts (Establishment and Constitution) Act 1961 provided that the Circuit Court would have a president and 'such number of ordinary judges as may from time to time be fixed by Act of the Oireachtas'. The Courts and Court Officers (Amendment) Act 2007 increased the number of ordinary judges from thirty-three in 2004 to thirty-seven in 2007. Though there was provision in the Personal Insolvency Act 2012 for the appointment of eight specialist (insolvency) judges, of which six were appointed in 2014, no specialist judges remained by mid-2022. This resulted in the number of Circuit Court judges remaining the same as it had in 2007, despite the substantial increase in population since then. The Circuit Court currently consists of the president and forty-five judges.⁸ The contrast between the initial number of judges appointed and the present count underscores the growth within both the legal system and society.

THE COURT'S JURISDICTION

This chapter focuses on a selection of areas which have fallen under the Circuit Court's civil jurisdiction over the past one hundred years. It includes a particular focus on jurisdiction which relates to family matters, financial difficulties, and workers. It then demonstrates that the court has taken on entirely new areas in recent years, including in the area of assisted decision-making, data protection, examinership and residential tenancies. Finally, it argues that the number of Circuit Court judges is inadequate to deal with the court's significantly increased responsibilities.

Upon its establishment, the Circuit Court had the following civil jurisdiction:

i) unlimited jurisdiction where all the parties consented in writing;
ii) contract and tort cases valued up to £300;
iii) land law matters (such as title to lands) valued up to £60;
iv) probate and administration matters, where the value of the personal property did not exceed £1000, and the land value did not exceed £60;
v) equity matters (including the winding up of companies), where the value of personal property did not exceed £1,000 and the value of land did not exceed £60, or where the issued capital of a company did not exceed £10,000 in value;
vi) bankruptcy matters; and
vii) proceedings initiated by the state, a minister or a government department to recover any sum not exceeding £300.⁹

7 *Dáil Éireann deb.*, vol. 106, col. 7 (28 May 1947).
8 Courts Act 2023, s. 5.
9 Courts of Justice Act 1924, s. 48.

Most of the Circuit Court's work can be divided into three main areas: civil, criminal and family law. The Circuit Court also has appellate jurisdiction of the District Court,[10] decisions of the Labour Court, the Unfair Dismissals Tribunal and the Workplace Relations Commission.[11] Among the current civil cases, the Circuit Court deals with family law;[12] personal injuries;[13] defamation, negligence and other tort and contract cases; equity disputes;[14] adverse possession disputes; claims under succession law;[15] licensing applications; examinership and various company matters; disputes between landlords and tenants and disputes under the Residential Tenancies Act 2004; injunctions under the Protected Disclosures Act 2014 and the Planning and Development Act 2000.[16] It also deals with applications under the 1999 Montreal Convention involving airline passengers' claims; appeals from mental health tribunals;[17] GDPR cases and appeals from decisions of the Data Protection Commission; certain employment matters under the Equal Status Acts 2000 to 2018 and applications under the Assisted Decision-Making (Capacity) Act 2015 and various motions and preliminary issues under the Statute of Limitations 1957. The current jurisdiction of the Circuit Court represents a significant expansion from its original scope under the 1924 Act.

The third schedule of the Courts (Supplemental Provisions) Act 1961 provided that the monetary jurisdiction of the Circuit Court was £1,000, and this was raised to £30,000 by 1991.[18] The monetary limit increased to claims not exceeding €75,000 and the market value not exceeding €3,000,000 in 2013.[19] The jurisdiction of the Circuit Court in relation to personal injuries actions is limited to €60,000.[20]

JURISDICTION IN FAMILY MATTERS

Historically, the jurisdiction of the Circuit Court in family law matters was more limited than its current jurisdiction. The Circuit Court had a longstanding role in handling familial disputes, including cases such as

10 Courts of Justice Act 1928, s. 28.
11 This replaced the Employment Appeals Tribunal under the Workplace Relations Act 2015.
12 Under the Family Law Act 1995.
13 Personal Injuries Assessment Board Act 2003 and the Civil Liability and Courts Act 2004.
14 E.g., constructive trusts or resulting trusts arising out of cohabitants or co-ownership disputes.
15 These include, e.g., claims for 'proper provision' under the Succession Act 1965, s. 117 and the Civil Partnership and Certain Rights and Obligations of Cohabitants Act 2010.
16 This includes s. 60 injunctions in relation to unauthorised development.
17 Mental Health Act 2001.
18 Courts Act 1991, s. 2.
19 Courts and Civil Law (Miscellaneous Provisions) Act 2013, s. 14.
20 Ibid., s. 16.

affiliation suits, actions for maintenance, bigamy cases, and injunctions relating to domestic violence. However, the jurisdictional basis of the Circuit Court increased significantly with the Family Law Act 1995, which provided it with its concurrent jurisdiction with the High Court. When dealing with family matters, the Circuit Court is now referred to as the Circuit Family Court.[21] Circuit Court judges can hear and determine applications for divorce, separation, nullity and appeals from the District Court (in which it can make orders for custody, access, and maintenance). They also have jurisdiction to deal with preliminary applications, interim applications, and applications for ancillary relief. Since the introduction of this legislation, the Circuit Court's involvement in family law issues has grown considerably.[22] One notable indicator of this is the ongoing increase in the number of divorces granted in Ireland, with a 5% increase seen between 2021 and 2022.[23]

In addition to the growth of family law cases the Circuit Court has acquired new powers under the Gender Recognition Act 2015 and the Domestic Violence Act 2018. The latter gives the Circuit Court unlimited powers to deal with domestic violence cases. More recently, the government received approval to publish the Family Courts bill 2022, which is currently before Seanad Éireann. As noted by the president of the District Court, Paul Kelly, the purpose of the bill is to provide for a more efficient and user-friendly family court system. The bill also recommends that judges will be assigned on a full-time basis to the Family Court divisions and that a family law rules committee or, alternatively, family law sub-committees of the existing court rules committees be established to ensure consistency across all levels of the family court.

JURISDICTION IN FINANCIAL MATTERS

As Kevin Costello points out in his chapter, the Circuit Court primarily functioned as a small debts court in its initial years, dealing with shop debt cases and also used by wholesalers to recover debts from shops. The court has continued to exercise jurisdiction in relation to debt and financial matters. The financial crisis that struck Ireland in 2008 uncovered the need for a proper legal framework to be put in place to deal with issues of personal insolvency. The Personal Insolvency Act 2012, and its successor, the Personal Insolvency (Amendment) Act 2015, introduced a regime whereby personal insolvency practitioners are tasked with facilitating a resolution process that is acceptable to both creditor and debtor. The Circuit Court has jurisdiction in personal insolvency cases where the debt liabilities are under €2,500,000

21 Family Law Act 1995, s. 38.
22 Carol Coulter, *Family law in practice: a study of cases in the Circuit Court* (Dublin, 2009).
23 Courts Service of Ireland, *Annual report 2020* (Dublin, 2020), p. 79.

and so deals with the vast majority of cases. Section 187 of the 2012 Act provides for the appointment of specialist insolvency judges who are trained and have an expertise in this area of law. The introduction of the Personal Insolvency Acts has expanded hugely the remit of work and expertise of the Circuit Court and its judges. In 2023, 2,365 personal insolvency cases were resolved by the Circuit Court.[24] In 2021, the Personal Insolvency (Amendment) Act 2021 brought further changes to the regime, including removing the cut-off date after which creditors were allowed to refuse a reasonable repayment proposal.[25]

JURISDICTION IN EMPLOYMENT MATTERS

In its early years, the Circuit Court played a pivotal role in handling cases related to workers and employment, particularly those falling under the purview of the Workmen's Compensation Act 1934. This act aimed to provide legal protections and compensation for workers who suffered injuries or accidents in the workplace. This early jurisdiction marked the Circuit Court as a significant institution in safeguarding the rights of the labour force during a time when labour protections and regulations were still evolving.

The Circuit Court now hears certain appeals relating to employment law under the Equal Status Acts 2000 to 2018, though since the repeal of certain parts of the acts, as well as the enactment of the Equality (Miscellaneous Provisions) Act 2015 and the Workplace Relations Act 2015, this jurisdiction has narrowed. However, the Circuit Court continues to act as appellate court for applications pursuant to section 9 of the Equal Status Acts on discriminating redress in respect of prohibited conduct under section 21 of the Acts, as an appellate court when a complaint is dismissed as frivolous by the Workplace Relations Commission under section 22 of the Acts, and as an appellate court for claims under section 25 of the Acts.[26]

In 2014, the government introduced a landmark piece of legislation, the Protected Disclosures Act 2014, to give protection to all workers who raised concerns about acts of penalisation by their employers. It also amended the Unfair Dismissals Acts 1977 to 2015 and provides that, if an employee is dismissed for having made a protected disclosure, it is considered as unfair dismissal. The 2014 Act provides that an employee can apply for interim relief to the Circuit Court and seek to procure an order against their employer.[27] The court can make an order for reinstatement or re-engagement of the employee on terms and conditions not favourable than those which would

---

24 Courts Service of Ireland, *Annual report 2022* (Dublin, 2023).
25 Personal Insolvency (Amendment) Act 2021.
26 Karl Martin and Susan Dowling, *Civil procedure in the Circuit Court* (Dublin, 2020), ch. 23.
27 Protected Disclosures Act 2014, s. 11 and sch. 1.

have been applicable to the employee if they had not been dismissed. If an employer is unwilling to do this, the court can make an order for the continuation of the contract of employment.[28] The protection of workers was further enhanced by the Protected Disclosures (Amendment) Act 2022. Under this Act, interim relief measures are extended to include acts of penalisation other than dismissal and workers can apply to the Circuit Court for interim relief within 21 days following the date of the last instance of penalisation or such longer period as the court may allow.

GROWTH AND DEVELOPMENT OF THE CIRCUIT COURT'S JURISDICTION

Since the turn of the twenty-first century, there has been a notable expansion of the Circuit Court's jurisdiction. During this period, various legal reforms and legislative changes have been introduced, conferring new powers and responsibilities upon this judicial institution. New jurisdictions have been granted to the Circuit Court, encompassing a wide range of areas including data protection, company law, residential law and assisted decision-making, as discussed below.

Data protection

The General Data Protection Regulations and the Data Protection Act 2018 provide for certain legal actions that can be instituted before the Irish courts arising out of a breach of a data subject's data protection rights. Under section 150 of the Act, the Circuit Court has concurrent jurisdiction with the High Court to hear appeal applications. It hears appeals from the Data Protection Commission and cases now come directly to the Circuit Court in view of backlogs in the Commission's office. Section 117 of the 2018 Act provides that jurisdiction for data protection actions is held by the Circuit Court concurrently with the High Court.[29] The Circuit Court also plays a role in confirming or annulling fines when administrative fines are imposed by the Data Protection Commission, where the initial fine is €75,000 or less.[30] The Circuit Court can hear appeals against a requirement specified in an enforcement or information notice,[31] a prohibition specified in a prohibition notice, a refusal by the Commission[32] and a decision of the commissioner in relation to a complaint.[33]

28 Frances Meenan, *Employment law* (2nd edn, Dublin, 2023), ch. 14.
29 The compensation recoverable in a data protection action in the Circuit Court is limited to the current monetary jurisdiction in tort as prescribed by law, which currently stands at €75,000.
30 General Data Protection Regulations and the Data Protection Act 2018, s. 142.
31 Data Protection Act 1988, s. 26 (as amended).
32 Ibid., s. 17.
33 Ibid., s. 10(1)(a).

Company law

In 2013, the Companies (Miscellaneous Provisions) Act 2013 provided an option for small companies to apply for examinership in the Circuit Court, as well as the High Court. Prior to the Act, there was no option for a company to apply directly to the Circuit Court for the appointment of an examiner, it was only if the High Court chose to remit the matter to the Circuit Court. The intention of this Act was to reduce the cost of seeking examinership protection, albeit that the work required to be done by the parties involved remained exactly the same as in the High Court.

Residential law

The Residential Tenancies Act 2004 has been affected by the Criminal Justice (Enforcement Powers) (Covid-19) Act 2020 and also by statutory instruments up to and including the rent pressure zone orders. Applications to the Circuit Court to confirm or refuse decisions and impose sanctions, for example on landlords, are frequent.[34] The Circuit Court can also hear appeals against a decision of the Residential Tenancies Board under sections 84 and 88 of the 2004 Act. The Board may apply to the Circuit Court for interim or interlocutory relief as it considers appropriate under section 189.[35]

Assisted decision-making

Another new area of jurisdiction was introduced by the Assisted Decision-Making (Capacity) Act 2015. This establishes a new legal framework for supported decision-making in Ireland. It allows people to make legal agreements on how they can be supported when making decisions about their welfare, property and affairs. While the 2015 Act was signed into law in December 2015, it was not brought into effect until the enactment of the Assisted Decision-Making (Capacity) (Amendment) Act 2022. Both pieces of legislation commenced on 26 April 2023.

Under section 4 of the 2015 Act, the Circuit Court has exclusive jurisdiction, except for reserved matters specified in the Act for the High Court.[36] There are now five roles for assisting and supporting decision-making in Ireland. Each role is determined by using a three-tier framework

---

34 See the Residential Tenancies Act 2004, s. 7A (as amended by the Residential Tenancies (Amendment) Act 2019, s. 28).
35 Martin and Dowling, *Civil procedure*, ch. 21.
36 The High Court exercises jurisdiction in the following matters: (1) any decision regarding the donation of an order from a living donor who lacks capacity; (2) withdrawal of life-sustaining treatment cases where the person lacks capacity; (3) applications in relation to advance healthcare directives, where it involves consideration of life-sustaining treatment; (4) applications under part 6 of the act, where the High Court made the order by virtue of which the ward is a ward; and (5) issues arising in relation to the validity of an enduring power of attorney.

for capacity. A person with capacity can avail of a designated healthcare representative and an enduring power of attorney, which can be activated once the person ceases to have capacity. If a person's capacity is diminished, they can avail of a decision-making assistant agreement and a co-decision maker. If a person lacks capacity, a decision-making representative can be appointed. While the decision-making assistant agreement and co-decision maker are dealt with without court intervention, they are subject to some regulatory requirements with the decision support service. Disputes concerning this may be referred to the Circuit Court. However, decisions concerning the appointment of the decision-making representative are made by the Circuit Court. One question for the Circuit Court to consider when making these decisions is whether a decision-making representative should be appointed, or if a less intrusive method would be more appropriate, such as the appointment of a co-decision making representative. Bearing in mind the guiding principles under section 8 of the 2015 Act, it is important that the will and preferences of the relevant person are, where possible, taken into account. This will result in specific orders, for example in care and various financial matters.

Under the legislation, the old wards of court system in Ireland is abolished. Under the 2015 Act, section 55A (review of declaration by wardship court as respects capacity) was inserted. Under this new section, the Circuit Court has jurisdiction to carry out capacity reviews within twelve months (or no later than three years) following the making of a declaration in respect of lack of capacity and discharge from wardship if satisfied that the previous ward is unlikely to recover capacity. It is anticipated that the 2015 Act will have a significant effect on the resources of the Circuit Court.

CONCLUSIONS

In the hundred years since the creation of the Circuit Court, its jurisdiction and the roles and responsibilities of Circuit Court judges have grown immensely.[37] Certain jurisdictions have vanished or diminished, making way for new areas of legal practice. Consequently, the responsibilities of a Circuit Court judge in 2024 differs significantly from those in 1924. Recently, a 2023 OECD report acknowledged the greater demands placed on our judges:

> Over the years, the judiciary in Ireland has shown great agility in covering resource demands across the country, especially in the two lower court levels, the Circuit Courts and District Courts, that are the primary courts serving provincial areas.[38]

---

37 See Kevin Costello's chapter.
38 OECD, *Modernising staffing and court management practices in Ireland* (Paris, 2023), p. 28.

It is clear that this growth in the quantity and diversity of cases before the Circuit Court reflects the complex needs of our society and its growing population.

In addition to the increase in court users, the expansion and complexity of new legislation has put a substantial strain on the Circuit Court. Consequently, the commitment in the programme for government 2020[39] and the subsequent formation of the judicial planning working group was welcomed by judges at all levels of the court systems, not least the Circuit Court. The report of the working group recommended the appointment of eight new judges to the Circuit Court.[40] The government has appointed three judges under the Assisted Decision-Making (Capacity) (Amendment) Act 2022,[41] and five judges under the Courts Act 2023.[42] It is clear that the increasing workload of the Circuit Court shows no sign of abating. As we commemorate this centenary, it is important to celebrate and appreciate where we came from, and how far we have come. I can only imagine what the next 100 years have in store.

---

39 *Programme for government: our shared future* (Dublin, 2020), p. 85.
40 Department of Justice, *Report of the judicial planning working group* (Dublin, 2022).
41 Assisted Decision-Making (Capacity) (Amendment) Act 2022, s. 98.
42 Courts Act 2023, s. 5.

CHAPTER FIFTEEN

The role of the president of the High Court

DAVID BARNIVILLE*

INTRODUCTION

The president of the High Court has onerous duties to perform. In the last eleven years he has had very onerous duties to perform. He is the head of the High Court, he has to attend to jury actions, he has to attend to appeals in the Circuit Court, he has to attend in Green Street at the Central Criminal Court, he has to sit in the Court of Criminal Appeal, he has to attend to certiorari, mandamus and State matters, and all matters that come before him. With all these onerous duties which he has had to fulfil in the last eleven years, we now propose in this bill ... to put further onerous duties on him of a very personal character, requiring personal contact with the individual patient, if the continuity of the tradition which has been maintained by the chief justice is to be kept up. We propose to put these very onerous duties on the president of the High Court for no reason that has been given and no reason that I can see.[1]

So said John A. Costello, when in opposition as a Fine Gael TD in the Dáil on 14 November 1935, in the resumed debate on the Courts of Justice bill 1934. He was speaking in opposition to the proposal in the bill (which was to become section 9 of the Courts of Justice Act 1936) to transfer to the president of the High Court the jurisdiction in 'lunacy and minor matters' which had been transferred to and vested in the chief justice by section 19(1) of the Courts of Justice Act 1924.

---

* President of the High Court since July 2022. I am very grateful to a number of people for their assistance in the research which has allowed me to prepare this paper. They are my judicial assistants, James Watson and Isobel Kenny; Orlaith Geaney and Heather Burke in the Courts Service Research Support Office; and Mr Justice Gerard Hogan for providing me with some invaluable original material relevant to the transfer of wardship functions from the chief justice to the president of the High Court. All errors are, however, mine and mine alone.

1 *Dáil Éireann deb.*, vol. 59, col. 6 (14 Nov. 1935).

Those comments were made prior to the transfer to the president of the High Court of the wardship jurisdiction under section 9 of the 1936 Act (and subsequently vested in the High Court, to be exercised by the president of the High Court, under section 9 of the Courts (Supplemental Provisions) Act 1961). This was a time when the High Court consisted of only six judges[2] in comparison with the 51 judges (including the president) sitting in the High Court today. Those comments were also made before the president of the High Court assumed all of the duties and obligations relating to the admission, supervision and disciplining of solicitors from the chief justice,[3] and before the High Court (usually through the president) was conferred with the powers and duties in relation to the disciplining and sanctioning of a whole range of statutorily regulated professions. They were also made before the establishment of bodies such as the Courts Service, the Judicial Appointments Advisory Board, and the Judicial Council, on whose boards the president of the High Court must also sit. If the duties of the president were, in the words of Costello, 'very onerous' (a description endorsed by Attorney General Conor A. Maguire, in the same debate in the Dáil), then one can appreciate, with the conferral of these various additional duties and obligations in the 90 years since those comments were made, that those duties have certainly become no less onerous. The position is, however, one of the more interesting positions, if not the most interesting position, in the Irish judicial system. Costello's description of the president's duties is relevant to one of the historical issues which I address in this chapter: the background to the transfer of the wardship jurisdiction from the chief justice to the president of the High Court in 1936. Before doing so, however, I should start at the start.

ESTABLISHMENT OF THE HIGH COURT AND THE OFFICE OF THE PRESIDENT

Article 64 of the Constitution of Saorstát Éireann provided for the establishment by the Oireachtas of courts comprising courts of first instance and a court of final appeal (to be called the Supreme Court). The courts of first instance included a High Court which was 'invested with full original jurisdiction in and power to determine all matters and questions whether of law or fact, civil or criminal ... with a right of appeal as determined by law'.

2 Although one of those judges, Wylie J, 'was in the extraordinary position whereby he only did land commission work and refused to perform the ordinary duties of a judge of the High Court, save in exceptional circumstances, and then only as a courtesy to the president of the High Court': see Gerard Hogan, 'Chief Justice Kennedy and Sir James O'Connor's application', *Irish Jurist*, 23:1 (1988), 144–58, at 157–8.
3 Under the Solicitors (Amendment) Act 1960, s. 25.

Article 65 provided that the judicial power of the High Court extended to the question of the validity of any law having regard to the provisions of the Constitution, and that in all cases in which such matters came into question, the High Court alone was required to exercise original jurisdiction. The Supreme Court was conferred, under article 66, with appellate jurisdiction from all decisions of the High Court.

The number of judges, the constitution and organisation of, and distribution of business of jurisdiction among the courts and judges, and all matters of procedure were to be prescribed by law.[4] Section 4 of the 1924 Act provided that the High Court would consist of not more than six judges (namely a president and five ordinary judges). Section 6 provided that the president of the High Court was to be *ex-officio* an additional judge of the Supreme Court (and the chief justice was to be *ex-officio* an additional judge of the High Court).

Section 9 of the 1924 Act dealt with the precedence between judges. The chief justice ranked first and next after him was the president of the High Court. After that, the ranking was the judges of the Supreme Court, according to priority of appointment, and next the ordinary judges of the High Court, according to the priority of appointment.

The precedence between judges was most recently significantly amended following the establishment of the Court of Appeal and the office of the president of that court under the Court of Appeal Act 2014. Section 28 of the 2014 Act provides for the precedence between judges of the Supreme Court, Court of Appeal and High Court by amending section 9 of the 1924 Act. The chief justice ranks first; the president of the Court of Appeal ranks next; then the president of the High Court; after that rank the judges of the Supreme Court who are former chief justices and so on down through the Supreme Court, Court of Appeal, High Court and the president of the Circuit Court.

Section 19 of the 1924 Act provided for the transfer to and the exercise by the chief justice of the jurisdiction in 'lunacy and minor matters', which were previously exercised by the lord chancellor of Ireland (and in 1924, exercised by the lord chief justice of Ireland), with provision being made for an appeal to the Supreme Court from the exercise by the chief justice of that jurisdiction. The existence of that right of appeal and its exercise proved to be somewhat controversial and was relied on as one of the reasons why the jurisdiction should be transferred from the chief justice to the High Court to be exercised by the president of that court under the 1936 Act.

Following the publication of the report of the Joint Oireachtas Committee on the Courts of Justice in November 1930,[5] various amendments to the 1924

---

4   1922 Constitution, art. 67.
5   *Report of the Joint Committee on the Courts of Justice Act 1924 and the civil jurisdiction of the courts* (Dublin, 1930).

Act were proposed in the Courts of Justice bill 1934, which became the 1936 Act. It made significant changes to the manner in which Circuit Court appeals were dealt with in civil cases by the High Court and provided for such appeals to be heard *de novo* by one High Court judge sitting on circuit as opposed to the position under the 1924 Act where two judges sat on those appeals which were not heard on a *de novo* basis.[6] Of most relevance for present purposes, however, was section 9, under which the jurisdiction transferred to and vested in the chief justice by section 19(1) of the 1924 Act was transferred to the High Court, to be exercised by the president of that court or, if the president so directed, by another ordinary judge of the High Court. That was the section which caused the greatest controversy during the debates in the Dáil leading to the enactment of the 1936 Act, in which Costello made the comments quoted at the outset of this chapter and to which I will return.

The courts established by the 1924 Act (under the Constitution of Saorstát Éireann) were continued in existence by article 58 of the 1937 Constitution. Those courts ceased to be established and the offices of the judges of those courts were abolished by section 7 of the Courts (Establishment and Constitution) Act 1961. The new courts provided for in Article 34 of the Constitution were then established by that Act. Section 2 provided for the establishment of the High Court and for that court to consist of the president and such number of ordinary judges as might from time to time be fixed by act of the Oireachtas. Section 2 provided that the chief justice and the president of the Circuit Court should also be *ex-officio* additional judges of the High Court. Section 1A of the Act[7] now provides that the president of the Court of Appeal is *ex-officio* an additional judge of the High Court.

Under the Courts (Supplemental Provisions) Act 1961, the number of ordinary judges of the High Court could be not more than six. As of April 2024, the total number of judges of the High Court, including the president and the ordinary judges, is fifty-one. The High Court exercising its criminal jurisdiction was first described as the 'Central Criminal Court' in the 1924 Act.[8] Section 11 of the 1961 Act made similar provision in respect of the new High Court exercising its criminal jurisdiction. It too would be referred to as the 'Central Criminal Court'. The jurisdiction of that court was to be exercisable by High Court judges nominated from time to time by the president of the High Court.[9]

Section 10(3) of the 1961 Act provided that the president of the High Court should 'arrange the distribution and allocation of the business of the High Court'. That remains one of the president's most important functions.

6   Courts of Justice Act 1936, s. 34.
7   Inserted by the Court of Appeal Act 2014, s. 6.
8   Courts of Justice Act 1924, s. 3.
9   Ibid., s. 11.

The business of the High Court is carried out by judges assigned to different lists (personal injuries, chancery, commercial, family, non-jury/judicial review and so on), with a judge being appointed by the president as the judge in charge of each of those lists. Judges are assigned by the president to the Central Criminal Court with a judge being appointed by the president as the judge in charge of that division of the High Court.

WARDSHIP JURISDICTION

Wardship jurisdiction originally vested in the chief justice. The first chief justice, Hugh Kennedy, exercised that jurisdiction for more than eleven years until his death in December 1936. He is generally regarded as having done so with great patience and dedication. Kennedy himself spoke about this work in his evidence to the Joint Committee on the Courts of Justice in February 1930.[10] He explained that he was only concerned, in his role, with wards who had property as the function of the court was to administer their property for their benefit. Accordingly, people with no property were not under his jurisdiction.[11] Quite different from the position in recent times, cases involving care, treatment or detention of persons lacking capacity were not regarded as part of the chief justice's wardship jurisdiction. Kennedy noted in his evidence that he was not aware as to whether any changes were being contemplated by the committee in the area of wardship but he, nonetheless, wanted to make clear that if a change were contemplated, 'this particular branch of work should be a one-man job'. He explained what he meant by that:

> one man should be always attached to this particular work. There is a very human element about it. A great deal of the work is done, not in court, but in chambers. There are a great number of conferences with relatives and so on, and in a great of many of the cases one requires more or less to be personally in touch. Again one often requires to be available in urgent cases.[12]

Kennedy confirmed that if a change was to be made 'only one judge should be attached to the position, and he should be made responsible for it'.

10 *Report of the Joint Committee on the Courts of Justice Act 1924 and the civil jurisdiction of the courts* (Dublin, 1930). Kennedy's evidence was given on 5 Feb. 1930: questions 4515–4777. His evidence in relation to wardship is at questions 4559–4591.
11 That ceased to be the position following the enactment of s. 9 of the Courts (Supplemental Provisions) Act 1961 as was made clear by the Supreme Court in *In Re D* [1987] IR 449. The Supreme Court confirmed that there is vested in the High Court a jurisdiction to take into wardship a person of unsound mind whose person requires protection and management even if that person does not have any property: see Finlay CJ at 454 and 456.
12 Question 4563.

Kennedy noted that an appeal lay from his decision in wardship cases to the Supreme Court. However, he pointed out that, by that stage, there had never been an appeal in 'lunacy cases' and there had only been two appeals in minors' cases. In his personal notes for his evidence for the Joint Committee, Kennedy noted that in both of those cases he was affirmed.[13] The day before the Courts of Justice bill 1934's second stage in the Dáil, Kennedy wrote to minister for justice P.J. Ruttledge, on a range of issues addressed in the bill. He touched on the issue of a possible transfer of wardship business to the High Court.[14]

Section 9 of the 1936 Act duly provided for the transfer of the chief justice's wardship jurisdiction to the High Court to be exercised by the president of the High Court or by an ordinary judge of the High Court for the time being assigned to that work by the president. That change had not been recommended by the joint committee which made no recommendations on the issue.[15] The rationale for the change given by the attorney general at the second stage of the debate in the Dáil was twofold. First, he said that the 'chief justice's time was so intimately associated with the work of the Supreme Court that any special duty thrown upon him must necessarily delay the work of the Supreme Court generally'. Second, he said that it appeared to be 'not altogether proper or elegant that an appeal should lie, even in theory from the decision of the highest judge in the State'. It was noted that Kennedy CJ had no objection to the proposal 'subject to certain safeguards as regards the privacy of the work and the adequacy of the High Court personnel to cope with the extra work'.[16]

The debate in relation to this provision of the 1934 bill proved to be highly contentious. Prominent in the debate were Conor A. Maguire (attorney general), John A. Costello (a former attorney general and future taoiseach) and Patrick McGilligan (a former minister for industry and commerce and external affairs, future attorney general and, of course, father of Declan Costello, a future president of the High Court). The rationale for the change was disputed by the opponents of the bill. Costello described it as a 'vicious

13 UCDA P4 1247(7). I am very grateful to Mr Justice Gerard Hogan for providing me with a copy for the purposes of this paper. Kennedy was subsequently reversed by the Supreme Court in two high-profile minor wardship cases which were decided in 1933 and 1934: *In Re Westby, Minors (No. 2)* [1934] IR 311 and in *Re McLorinan, A Minor* [1935] IR 373.
14 He also pointed out that if such a transfer was to proceed, there would have to be, at least, one additional judge appointed to the High Court. However, that did not happen in the 1936 Act.
15 The Law Reform Commission in its *Consultation paper on consolidation and reform of the Courts Acts* (LRC CP 46 – 2007) suggested at para. 2.125 that the committee had recommended the transfer of wardship jurisdiction from the chief justice to the president of the High Court. However, that does not appear to have been the case as was stated by the attorney general (Conor A. Maguire) when moving the second stage of the bill in the Dáil on 20 Feb. 1935.
16 *Dáil Éireann deb.*, vol. 54, col. 13 (20 Feb. 1935).

proposal' and 'one of the worst sections in the bill'. He could see no reason for the transfer and described it as 'entirely unsound and uncalled for when a practice has grown up in an office of this nature, of the delicate kind required in connection with these matters, over a period of eleven years, suddenly to change that entire procedure and practice and to transfer it from one judge to another.' He described Kennedy, as chief justice, as having 'revolutionised the entire practice' in wardship and that he had a 'very busy time' with that work. He continued:

> We all know that he sits there on a Friday – sometimes until 6 or 7 o'clock in the evening – and that after court every evening he interviews people in connection with these lunacy and minor matters. He has a peculiar and personal knowledge of each individual case that has gone through his office and that is in his office at the present moment. That is all going to be taken away at one stroke by one section in this bill and transferred to a man who has not been dealing with such matters, who cannot have the same intimate knowledge, who has been out of touch and too busy to give the same personal attention as the chief justice has been able to give and who, because of the additional duties that will be imposed on him by this bill, will be unable, in my view, at all events, to give the same personal attention as the chief justice gave.[17]

Costello described the stated rationale of the undesirability of permitting an appeal from the chief justice to his colleagues in the Supreme Court as 'absurd'. He dismissed the argument that the other members of the Supreme Court (at a time when its membership was three) had nothing else to do on the Friday on which Kennedy was dealing with wardship matters, noting that when he was doing this work, his two colleagues 'were engaged together working on the cases standing at that day and preparing their judgments and that, when they had prepared them, they all three sat on Saturday to confer on the judgments that were awaiting determination.' Notwithstanding those objections, however, the bill passed and included what became section 9 of the 1936 Act.

Two wardship cases that were decided by Kennedy after his evidence before the Joint Committee and in which he was overturned by the Supreme Court bear further consideration, not only for the fact that he was reversed in those cases but also for the remarkable terms in which he was overturned in one of the cases[18] and for the particular facts of those cases, which definitely belong to another era.

In Re Westby, Minors (No. 2)[19] concerned a minor ward (aged 12) who was being educated in a preparatory school in England, funded by his grandfather

17 *Dáil Éireann deb.*, vol. 59, col. 6 (20 Feb. 1935).
18 *In Re Westby, Minors (No. 2)* [1934] IR 311.
19 Ibid.

with the intention that he would be subsequently sent to a public school in England. His father had died a number of years previously and the grandfather died shortly after he had started in the school. On his death, the minor became entitled to a life interest in considerable settled trust funds (largely made up of the proceeds of sale of large estates in Co. Clare) and to an estate in tail in Roebuck Castle in Co. Dublin. The minor's mother was his guardian of the person and joint guardian of his fortune. She had previously lived with her husband in Ireland but moved to England wishing to be near her father and the minor while he was at school there. The question of a home being provided for the minor in Ireland was raised before the chief justice. The mother stated that although she was Irish and had a great love for Ireland, she could not make her home here as she had been living in a house in Dublin in 1920 where six men were shot, which led to her suffering a nervous breakdown and she did not wish to risk another one. The mother applied to the chief justice to permit the minor to remain at the preparatory school and when finished there to move on to a public school in England, where his father and other relatives had been educated.

The chief justice was prepared to allow the minor to remain in the preparatory school in England for the remainder of the school year but directed that he should then attend school in Dublin and be brought back to Ireland so that arrangements could be made for establishing a home for him in this jurisdiction. He decided that the education of the minor was to be directed towards his entering and graduating from the University of Dublin. He rejected the proposal put forward by the mother, which he described as being part of a scheme to bring up and educate the minor wholly in England and to make his home in that country bringing with him the benefit of the Irish property. He rejected the suggestion that there was no school in Ireland to which 'Irish Protestants of the middle class ... can send their boys to be educated suitably in accordance with their station and life'.[20] He rejected that contention in the following terms:

> I cannot, as I have said, accept that proposition and for the very good reason that, with my experience here for the past nine years, I know it to be untrue. I have known Protestant wards educated here who would reflect credit on any school anywhere. I was asked to accept it as the case that every Irish Protestant who can afford it would send his boys to be educated in England, but I cannot suppose that our Protestant population which has, as we all know, shown itself loyal to the Saorstát really, desires to be a kind of foreign body in the body politic, to be in the State but not of it, and tries to preserve an alien identity.[21]

20 Ibid., at 315.
21 Ibid.

The mother appealed successfully to the Supreme Court (FitzGibbon and Murnaghan JJ with Sullivan P dissenting). The judgment of FitzGibbon J is notable for its remarkably caustic terms.[22] He described the principles applied by the chief justice in reaching his decision as being

> supposed to necessitate ... that except in abnormal cases, a ward who is called by the chief justice 'a Saorstát national', whose father's domicile was in the Saorstát, must be educated as a prospective citizen of the Saorstát, 'and will therefore be provided with his or her general education according to the means of the ward in suitable schools and (in a proper case) university in the Saorstát'.[23]

FitzGibbon strongly disagreed. He referred to 'other principles of equal cogency', which he said seemed to have 'escaped' the notice of the chief justice including the significance of the express desire and intention of the father of the minor that he be sent to a preparatory school in England and to a public school there subsequently. FitzGibbon J continued:

> I see no ground for the assumption, which the chief justice says he is compelled to make, that the life of the minor is to be cast in Ireland. It was true of his forebears that 'their roots were in this country where their homes were' but of the vast possessions in the County Clare which made Frances Valentine Westby the third largest landowner in that county, and one of the limited number in all Ireland who owned over 25,000 acres, I understand that not a rood remains in the possession of his grandson. The duties imposed upon the owner of such an estate no longer remain to be performed, and where the minor's ancestors filled the offices of deputy lieutenant, high sheriff, grand juror or justice of the peace, the policy of successive governments which has transferred the land to its occupiers, has left people in the position of the Westbys without employment for their energies. There is no ground for wonder if the ambitious among them turn their attention to the wider stage of the great commonwealth of nations of which the Saorstát is only one member, with all its colonies and dependencies throughout the world, on which so many Irishmen have found honour for themselves and have enhanced the reputation of their native land. We know well that genuine Irish patriotism is not incompatible with distinguished service and exalted position in the colonies and dependencies beyond the seas, and I cannot assume that every Irishman must, as a matter of necessity or should as a matter of duty, limit his ambition to a career in the twenty-

---

22 See the discussion of this case and of *The State (Ryan) v. Lennon* [2935] IR 170 in Hogan, 'Chief justice Kennedy', at 156–7.
23 *In Re Westby, Minors (No. 2)* [1934] IR 311, at 323.

six counties which compose the Saorstát, nor am I prepared to lay down as a general principle that his education should be regulated with that objective alone in view.[24]

Having then set out the limitations of Protestant boarding schools in Ireland, FitzGibbon J observed that it would be in the interest of the minor 'having regard to the ample means at his disposal, that he should be sent to one [an English public school] for his education and that he should not be put off with anything less than the best that his income can procure for him'.[25]

He concluded that the minor should be allowed to remain at his preparatory school and then proceed to 'one of the first class English public schools for which his name has been or should at once be entered', and that he should continue to reside during his holidays with his mother in England. Murnaghan J agreed that the appeal should be allowed but in somewhat less trenchant terms. He felt that in the absence of any pronouncement by the legislature on the issue, the court should, as far as possible, comply with the wishes of the parents and near relatives of the minor. He felt that the court should not 'on an assumption of national policy force children to be educated in a way which the parents do not approve'.[26]

Sullivan P (who had to sit on the Supreme Court in place of the chief justice) dissented and agreed that the chief justice was 'right in saying that in the normal course a ward of his Court who is a Saorstát national, would get his general education in the Saorstát, and that that course should be followed unless in a particular case the benefit of the ward required that he should receive his general education abroad'.[27]

Hogan has referred to *Westby* as an example of a case where a 'profound clash in judicial attitude – between what might conveniently be described as the enthusiastic nationalism of Kennedy CJ and the pessimistic scepticism of FitzGibbon J' ultimately came to a head.[28]

In Re McLorinan, A Minor[29] is notable first for the fact that the chief justice was again reversed by the Supreme Court, this time in a judgment delivered by Sullivan P, and also its rather unusual facts.[30] The appellant was formerly a minor and was a ward of court in circumstances where on the death of her mother she became entitled to property of some considerable value. While a minor ward (in the words of Sullivan P) 'she then was, or subsequently became intimate with a chemist's assistant ... and the intimacy

24 Ibid., at 324–5.
25 Ibid., at 326.
26 Ibid., at 331.
27 Ibid., at 321.
28 Referring also to *the State (Ryan) v. Lennon* [1935] IR 170: see Hogan, 'Chief Justice Kennedy', at 156–7.
29 [1935] IR 373.
30 It is also notable for the fact that John A. Costello appeared for the appellant.

led to misconduct which resulted in her pregnancy'.[31] This was described by the chief justice in his judgment as a 'great outrage' committed against the court but, having become aware of events and having ascertained that the parties were anxious to marry, the chief justice caused inquiries to be made with a view to arranging a marriage on terms he could sanction. However, the minor was a Catholic and the man was not and refused to provide the undertakings then required in the case of marriages between Catholics and non-Catholics. He also refused to bring anything of value to the marriage in the event that it was sanctioned. The minor then took the view that she would not marry the man at that point but would wait until she came of age. Her attitude was described by the chief justice as being 'generally one of defiance'. While steps were being considered against the man (and against the woman) for his 'gross contempt of court' he left the country and went to England. A few days after the minor came of age, she married the man in England and a few weeks later gave birth to a child. An application was made on her behalf to be discharged from wardship on an urgent basis so that she could obtain access to her funds. The chief justice directed that a settlement of the ward's property be made. He concluded his judgment as follows:

> Marriage with a female ward of court without the consent of the court is grave a contempt, which will be visited by punishment, and, in particular, by exclusion of the man from any benefit in the ward's property. In my opinion there can be no more grievous contempt of the court than the violation of its ward. If the contempt is to be purged by merely marrying the ward on her attaining full age, then every female ward with property is exposed to any penniless scoundrel who can take advantage of her with a view to marriage immediately she comes of age and capture of her property or living on it as long as it lasts. In the present case the ward herself was a party to the contempt as efforts were made, but in vain, to dissociate her from [the man]. I have not in any way condoned the gross contempt, but, while I desired to take care that [the man] should not derive any benefit from his offence, I had been unwilling that the ward and her child should ultimately have to suffer the whole punishment which would be the indubitable result of handing out her property to her without more ado. I chose the course of having a settlement as the best course in her interest and that of her child and the most merciful in all the circumstances.[32]

The Supreme Court unanimously reversed the chief justice. It held that the law was well settled that the court had no jurisdiction to compel a ward to

---

31 [1935] IR 373, at 378.
32 Ibid., at 376–7.

execute a settlement of her property. It rejected the contention that where the ward has committed a contempt of court, the court as a punishment for the contempt may refuse to part with possession of the ward's property on her marriage unless a settlement is executed. FitzGibbon J did not deliver a judgment on the appeal.

Those two cases present an interesting backdrop to one of the reasons advanced by the government for the transfer of wardship jurisdiction from the chief justice to the High Court to be exercised by the president; namely, that it was unseemly to have provision for an appeal from the chief justice to his colleagues in the Supreme Court. That problem was removed by the enactment of section 9(1) of the 1936 Act, which vested in the High Court jurisdiction in wardship matters. Section 9(2) provided that such jurisdiction was to be exercisable by the president of the High Court or, where he or she so directs, by an ordinary judge of High Court assigned on that behalf by the president.[33] Section 9 of the Courts (Supplemental Provisions) Act 1961 continued this arrangement. The continued exercise of wardship jurisdiction by the president instead of the chief justice was not controversial in 1961, unlike the transfer of that jurisdiction from the chief justice to the president in 1936.

The president's role in dealing with wardship matters (adults lacking capacity and minors) is probably their most important function. The president typically sits personally, in court and in chambers, most days to deal with wardship matters and, because of the volume of work involved (particularly in more recent times), has required the assistance of one or more other High Court judges in the discharge of that function.

It is work involving deeply personal human-interest issues. While the Assisted Decision Making (Capacity) Act 2015 (as amended) abolished the concept of wardship for new cases when it came into force on 26 April 2023, the jurisdiction continues to apply to existing cases. The 2015 Act requires the High Court to review and discharge all existing wards from wardship within a three-year period from the commencement of the new legislation. The 2015 Act is expressly stated not to affect the inherent jurisdiction of the High Court to make orders for the 'care, treatment or detention of persons who lack capacity'.[34] A large number of applications come before the court for orders for the care, treatment or detention of vulnerable persons lacking capacity who require the intervention of the court to ensure the defence and vindication of their constitutional rights, including their rights to life and

---

33   The basis for the High Court's wardship jurisdiction and its constitutional underpinning has been explored in several cases including *In Re D* [1987] IR 449; *In Re FD* [2015] IESC 83; [2015] 1 IR 741; *In Re Francis Dolan* [2008] IEHC 264, [2008] 1 ILRM 19; *AM v. HSE* [2019] IESC 3, [2019] 2 IR 115; *A.C. v. Cork University Hospital* [2019] IESC 73, [2019] 2 IR 38; *In Re JJ* [2021] IESC 1; *In Re KK (No. 1)* [2023] IEHC 306.
34   Assisted Decision Making (Capacity) Act 2015, s. 4(5).

bodily integrity. It has therefore been necessary to establish a new list of the High Court to deal with such applications (the inherent jurisdiction (capacity) list), on which the president and two other High Court judges now routinely sit.

As we have seen, the wardship jurisdiction has principally been exercised by the president in the period from 1936 onwards. The president is entitled to assign other judges of the High Court to assist in carrying out that work. Because of the volume and complexity of wardship related applications, many of which concern the care, treatment and detention of vulnerable adult wards, wardship applications are heard every day in the High Court and I am assisted by two other High Court judges in carrying out that work. As well as that, the president deals with non-contentious wardship matters in chambers and has regular contact with the Registrar of Wards of Court and the Office of Wards of Court in relation to wards. Notwithstanding the abolition of wardship by the 2015 Act, the court continues to exercise its wardship jurisdiction in respect of existing wards pending their discharge from wardship (which must take place within three years of the Act's commencement). Due to the curtailment of the Court's wardship jurisdiction, the court is now required to exercise its inherent jurisdiction in the case of persons lacking capacity where treatment, care or detention is necessary to defend and vindicate their constitutional rights.

With the work arising from the wardship list, applications under the 2015 Act to review and discharge adult wards from wardship and applications under the court's inherent jurisdiction, there remains an enormous amount of work for the High Court to do to protect the interests of vulnerable persons lacking capacity. This area remains the most significant, important and rewarding work carried out by the president of the High Court.

OTHER FUNCTIONS OF THE PRESIDENT OF THE HIGH COURT

The president of the High Court has a whole range of other functions, both court and non-court related. I will touch on those functions relatively briefly in the remaining part of this chapter.

Solicitors

Those powers and functions in relation to solicitors that had been exercised by the lord chancellor and then by the lord chief justice of Ireland were transferred to the chief justice by section 19(1) of the 1924 Act. That jurisdiction was not changed by the 1936 Act, and remained with the chief justice under the Solicitors Act 1954. The chief justice was responsible for admitting persons as solicitors,[35] and for exercising statutory-disciplinary

---

35 S. 10.

jurisdiction over solicitors.[36] An appeal lay from the decision of the chief justice in the exercise of that statutory disciplinary jurisdiction. The seminal case of *In Re Solicitors Act 1954*[37] is an example of one in which the Supreme Court determined an appeal from a decision of the chief justice (Maguire CJ) on an appeal from a decision of the Disciplinary Committee of the Law Society.

Those functions exercised by the chief justice in relation to solicitors were transferred to the president of the High Court under the Solicitors (Amendment) Act 1960.[38] The president is now responsible for the admission of persons as solicitors and must sign certificates of admission in respect of all solicitors entered on the roll of solicitors. Rules of court have been made in relation to applications for such admission.[39] In the area of discipline, the president appoints members of the Solicitors Disciplinary Tribunal.[40] The High Court has inherent jurisdiction to discipline solicitors by reason of the fact that they are officers of the court. That jurisdiction is additional to the statutory jurisdiction provided for under the Solicitors Acts. In disciplinary cases, where the Solicitors Disciplinary Tribunal decides that serious sanctions should be imposed on a solicitor, it must refer the matter to the High Court, and does so by way of a report prepared on completion of an inquiry. Where a Tribunal finds that there has been misconduct on the part of the solicitor and where it does not itself make any order imposing one of the less severe sanctions which it may impose, the Tribunal must set out in its report (a) its opinion as to the fitness or otherwise of the solicitor to be a member of the solicitor's profession having regard to the findings of the Tribunal, and (b) its recommendations as to the sanction which, in its opinion, should be imposed. The Law Society is required to bring that report before the president of the High Court.[41] The president of the High Court has also issued a practice direction in respect of professional disciplinary applications including those relating to solicitors.[42] The Solicitors (Amendment) Act 1960 (as amended) confers extensive powers on the court (generally exercised by the president) arising from a report of the Tribunal. Those powers include the power to strike the name of the solicitor off the roll, to suspend the solicitor, to prohibit the solicitor from practising on his own account as a sole practitioner or in partnership and so on.[43]

36 Solicitors Act 1954, ss 6, 14 and 23.
37 [1960] IR 239.
38 S. 25.
39 Order 53 of the Rules of the Superior Courts (as most recently amended and substituted by SI 196/2021).
40 Under the Solicitors (Amendment) Act 1960 (as amended), s. 6.
41 This is all provided for in the Solicitors (Amendment) Act 1960 (as amended) and in order 53B of the Rules of the Superior Courts.
42 Practice Direction HC 115, professional disciplinary list (14 Oct. 2022).
43 See, for example, the discussion in *Law Society of Ireland v. Coleman* [2018] IESC 71.

The involvement of the High Court in the regime for the disciplining of solicitors (and, indeed, other regulated professionals) and, in particular, the president is essential to ensure the constitutionality of the regime in light of the decision of the Supreme Court in *In Re Solicitors Act 1954*.[44] It is also open to the Law Society to make applications directly to the High Court, generally to the president in relation to solicitors, including applications for orders prohibiting solicitors from contravening provisions of the Solicitors Acts.[45] Quite an amount of time is spent by the president in dealing with applications in relation to solicitors.

Legal practitioners

The Legal Services Regulation Act 2015 introduced a new legislative regime for the regulation and disciplining of legal practitioners (solicitors and barristers) and replaces much of the regime provided for in the Solicitors Acts. Space does not permit an extensive examination of the new regime. However, the president of the High Court has a number of important functions under that Act. They include the appointment of the members of the Legal Practitioners Disciplinary Tribunal which hears disciplinary proceedings against legal practitioners. Jurisdiction is vested in the High Court to hear and determine appeals by legal practitioners from adverse decisions of the Disciplinary Tribunal and applications to confirm recommendations as to serious sanctions to be imposed on legal practitioners in the case of misconduct.[46] Section 86 of the 2015 Act provides that that jurisdiction must be exercised by the president of the High Court or by another judge of the High Court assigned on that behalf by the president. The High Court is also given jurisdiction to order a legal practitioner to comply with certain directions, determinations or orders of the Legal Services Regulatory Authority or other bodies established under the legislation.[47] While the 2015 Act has not expressly specified that those applications are to be dealt with by the president, as a matter of course they are dealt with by him or her.

Other professions

As well as dealing with disciplinary matters involving solicitors and legal practitioners, the president also deals with similar applications in relation to a whole host of other statutorily regulated professions. They include doctors,[48]

44 [1960] IR 239.
45 Solicitors (Amendment) Act 2002 (as amended), s. 18.
46 Legal Services Regulation Act 2015, ss 82–5.
47 Ibid., s. 90.
48 Medical Practitioners Act 2007 (as amended).

nurses,[49] dentists,[50] pharmacists,[51] veterinary practitioners,[52] teachers,[53] property service providers,[54] health and social care professionals, which includes dieticians, dispensing opticians, medical scientists, occupational therapists, optometrists, physical therapists, physiotherapists, podiatrists and chiropodists, radiographers, radiation therapists, social workers, speech and language therapists and social care workers.[55]

The High Court has several different roles under the statutory provisions in respect of these professions. While the legislation applicable to each profession is not identical, typically it confers a jurisdiction on the High Court to suspend the registration of a professional on an interim basis, to hear and determine appeals by a professional from an adverse decision of a professional regulatory body and to hear applications for confirmation of serious sanctions by the relevant body. While the legislation does not normally expressly require the president of the High Court to deal with these types of applications, typically the president does deal with them, drawing on assistance from other High Court judges, where necessary.[56] Needless to say, with an ever-expanding list of professions being subject to legislative regulation along similar lines involving the court, this type of work has become a very significant feature of the work of the president of the High Court.

Arbitration Act 2010

The Arbitration Act 2010 adopted the UNCITRAL Model Law into Irish law and gave force of law in Ireland to various international conventions. The 2010 Act, combined with the relevant provisions of the Model Law, made provision for a single judge to hear and determine most arbitration related cases and applications. Section 9 of the 2010 Act, and article 6 of the Model Law, read together, provide that the president of the High Court, or another designated High Court judge, must deal with most arbitration related matters coming before the court.[57] The practice adopted by the presidents has differed in respect of this role. I was previously designated as the arbitration judge in

49 Nurses and Midwives Act 2011 (as amended).
50 Dentists Act 1985 (as amended).
51 Pharmacy Act 2007 (as amended).
52 Veterinary Practitioners Act 2005 (as amended).
53 Teaching Council Act 2001 (as amended).
54 Property Services (Regulation) Act 2011 (as amended).
55 Health and Social Care Professionals Act 2005 (as amended). Shortly to be added to that list are clinical biochemists, orthopaedists, psychologists and psychotherapists.
56 The procedures for such applications are set out in order 95 of the Rules of the Superior Courts and in Practice Direction HC 115, professional disciplinary list (14 Oct. 2022).
57 The relevant rules are provided for in order 56 of the Rules of the Superior Courts (as amended) and further required procedures are set out in Practice Direction HC 116, arbitration list (14 Oct. 2022).

2018 on the request of the then president (Peter Kelly) when an ordinary judge of the High Court and resumed that role following my appointment as president in July 2022.

Other functions

The president of the High Court has many other non-court and administrative functions. The president is a member of the Council of State under article 31.2 of the Constitution. The president is also a member of several other boards and committees including the board of the Courts Service;[58] the board of the Judicial Council;[59] the Judicial Appointments Advisory Board;[60] the Superior Courts Rules Committee;[61] and the Advisory Committee on the Grant of Patents of Precedence.[62] The president is also, with the chief justice and the attorney general, a member of the committee provided for in section 56 of the Courts (Supplemental Provisions) Act 1961 which considers whether to continue in office a county registrar who is about to reach the age of 65 in office. The president is also a member (with the chief justice and president of the Society of Chartered Surveyors Ireland) of the Reference Committee (reconstituted by the Acquisition of Land (Reference Committee) Act 1925), which appoints property arbitrators to determine compensation under the Acquisition of Land (Assessment of Compensation) Act 1919. In addition, the president, by virtue of section 105 of the Planning and Development Act 2000 (as amended) and the Planning and Development Regulations 2001–2023, is a member of, and chairs, the committee to select candidates for appointment by the relevant minister as chairperson of An Bord Pleanála.

Finally, the president chairs the investment committee of the Courts Service, which comprises members of the judiciary, court officers, Courts Service officials and independent external members. The investment committee meets on a regular basis each year, and its main function is to devise investment policy for the investment of court funds based on advice from independent investment advisors, to oversee the implementation of investment strategies and to ensure compliance with best practice in the management of court funds. The total value of funds overseen by the investment committee was €2.486 billion at the year ending 30 September 2023 (which is made up mainly of funds of adult and minor wards of courts).

Doubtless I have overlooked other significant aspects of the role of the president of the High Court but I can confirm that, from my own experience

58 Courts Service Act 1998, s. 11(1).
59 Judicial Council Act 2019, s. 8(1).
60 Courts and Court Officers Act 1995, s. 13(1).
61 Court of Justice Act 1936, s. 67(3).
62 Legal Services Regulation Act 2015, s. 172(2).

and from that of my predecessors with whom I have spoken about the issue, it is undoubtedly one of the most interesting, varied and rewarding positions in the Irish legal and judicial system, notwithstanding the 'very onerous duties' that Costello described as being inherent in the role back in November 1935.

CHAPTER SIXTEEN

Who would be a chief justice?

DONAL O'DONNELL*

The clock struck 9.00. Sarah reappeared in the hall.
'Was you all just talking of the chief justice? Bovill?'
William frowned perplexedly at his wife. 'Cockburn's the justice'.
'Who's Bovill then?'
'William Bovill? chief justice of the Common Pleas. Different job.'
'Well, it's him who'll hear the Tichborne case!'
'That so! Poor man. Who'd be a chief justice?'[1]

This passage in a recent book by Zadie Smith, which includes an account of the sensational case of the Tichborne claimant, caught my eye for perhaps understandable reasons. However, it is also interesting because it draws attention to the fact that, before the Judicature Acts, there was in England and Wales not just one lord chief justice but two (and one lord chief baron), yet none were the head of the judiciary. Lawyers tend to reason by analogy, and insomuch as we think about these things at all, there is a dim understanding that the position in Ireland was similar, and that today the position of chief justice of Ireland is essentially similar to the position of lord chief justice of England and Wales (or now lady chief justice) or perhaps the president of the Supreme Court of the United Kingdom. In addition to this general understanding of the history, we have a sense that change came about in 1922 or, more accurately, in 1924 which was when, in some of the more romantic accounts, hopes of a more truly radical and indigenous legal system harking back to the Brehon law were dashed. Instead, the common law system was continued with some superficial cosmetic changes in an exercise akin to that which the late John Kelly described as an approach of changing the colour of the post-boxes. Like most simplified accounts, this contains some element of truth, but the detail is more complex and, to me at least, more interesting.

---

* Chief justice of Ireland since October 2021, having been appointed to the Supreme Court in January 2010.
1 Zadie Smith, *The Fraud* (London, 2023), p. 86.

THE EMBEDDING OF COMMON LAW IN IRELAND

The coming of the common law to Ireland is beautifully surveyed by one of the first judges of the Free State, an interesting man in his own right, William Johnston.[2] In an article published in the *Law Quarterly Review* in 1920,[3] he observed that it is perhaps an error to seek to identify some formal moment when the common law can be said to have officially arrived in Ireland. Arguably, it could be said to have followed from the very fact that Henry II planted his flag in Ireland and claimed lordship over the country in addition to his position as king of England and Wales. The king's law was then going to apply, at least insofar as the king's writ ran. As Johnston observes, it existed for the benefit of the colonists alone, and to resolve disputes between themselves and between them and the Crown. The unfortunate *Hibernici* were not considered and had 'neither the benefit of the common law nor the effectual means of administering and executing their own Brehon laws'.[4]

From the very start, there was by definition an inherent tension in the relationship of the common law with Ireland, which already had its own indigenous body of law. Henry VIII in due course claimed to be king of Ireland, but there were only limited areas of the country in which that could be said to be borne out in reality. Throughout the rest of the country, Brehon law applied. That was, by the standards of its time, a well-developed and sophisticated system, but it reflected a decentralised and essentially rural society in contrast to the more unified common law system. Interestingly, Sir Henry Maine noted that, over time, there likely would have been a unified corpus of Brehon law:

> If the country had been left to itself, one of the great Irish tribes would almost certainly have conquered the rest. All the legal ideas which, little conscious as we are of their source, come from the existence of a strong central government lending its vigour to the arm of justice would have made their way into the Brehon law.[5]

In so much as the common law embodied the imposition of English law upon Ireland, it was likely to lead to dissatisfaction and resentment. However, in so much as it was a body of law well adapted to a developing society and capable of providing a satisfactory method of dispute resolution, it could be effective. Thus, on the one hand, Edmund Spenser was able to acknowledge

---

2   Donal Coffey considers Johnston the strongest judge of the Free State era: see Donal K. Coffey, 'The judiciary of the Irish Free State', *Dublin University Law Journal*, 33 (2011), 61.
3   W.J. Johnston, 'First adventure of the common law', *Law Quarterly Review*, 36 (1920), 9.
4   Ibid., at 10.
5   Henry Sumner Maine, *Lectures on the early history of institutions* (London, 1875), pp 54–5, cited in Johnston, 'First adventure', at 9.

that the laws of England 'worke not that good which they should, and sometimes also that evill that they would not', a problem he attributed not to the law, but rather to those to whom it was being applied, describing the Irish as 'being a people very stubborne and untamed'.[6] On the other hand, Sir John Davies, not otherwise a sympathetic observer of Ireland, could say:

> There is no nation of people under the sun that doth love equal and indifferent justice better than the Irish, or will rest better satisfied with the execution thereof, although it be against themselves; so that they may have the protection and benefit of the law when upon just cause they do desire it.[7]

The *Case of Tanistry* in 1607 is traditionally identified as the point of triumph of the common law over Brehon law in Ireland.[8] In fact, a more accurate point is perhaps the proclamation of King James I in 1603 purporting to abolish the Brehon law, and, with the Flight of the Earls and the plantation of Ulster, that decree was capable of being enforced throughout Ireland. One might also say that it was not until 1612 that the Brehon law was truly suppressed,[9] when the Irish parliament passed a statute declaring that:

> All the natives and inhabitants of this kingdome, without difference and distinction, are taken into his Majestie's gratious protection, and doe now live under one law as dutiful subjects of our Soveraigne lord and Monarch.[10]

The common law could be said to have occupied the field and copied the development in England. The Court of Common Pleas was, according to Johnston, undoubtedly the first of the four courts in Dublin that had a separate and distinct existence.[11] Richard De Exeter was a member of a Norman family settled in Connacht at the time of Henry III who, under the name of Jordan, became more Irish than the Irish themselves, and was identified as holding office as chief justice of the Court of Common Pleas in

---

6   Edmund Spenser, *A view of the present state of Ireland* (Dublin, 1633), cited in Johnston, 'First adventure', at 9.
7   Sir John Davies, *A discovery of the true causes why Ireland was never subdued and brought under obedience to the Crown of England until the beginning of his majesty's happy reign*, ed. James P. Myers, Jr (Washington, 1969). But see: Sean Patrick Donlan, '"Little better than cannibals": Sir John Davies and Edmund Burke on property and progress', *Northern Ireland Legal Quarterly*, 54:1 (2003), 1, at 4, who considers this was largely a rhetorical statement and that Davies shared the view of the Irish as barbarous wild and uncivilised.
8   (1607) Dav. 28, in which Davies appeared for the defendant.
9   Albert Keating, 'The demise of Brehon law', *Irish Law Times*, 30 (2012), 184.
10 11, 12 & 13 Jac. I, c. 5.
11 Johnston, 'First adventure', at 16.

1326.[12] While sitting as a justice in eyre (i.e., a judge on circuit) in Ardfert in Co. Kerry, he was called upon to hear a plea as to whether a whale cast up on the lands came within the terms of royal grant of 'wreck of the sea'.[13] The intermixing of the cultures can be seen in the fact that the chief justice of Common Pleas in 1597 received an enviable bardic encomium which read: 'Justice Walsh would not give a corrupt judgment for any consideration of wealth; his rather is a true pure blameless judgment from the best of intellectual discourses'.[14]

The King's Bench, according to Johnston, became definitively established as an independent court at some point between the years 1323 and 1351. It had its own lord chief justice and came to be seen as the most senior common law court.[15] The Exchequer was originally an administrative department responsible for the finances of the kingdom, but, as in England, it developed the fiction whereby the Exchequer acquired a general jurisdiction in respect of all civil actions on the basis that if it was established or even alleged that a plaintiff owed a debt to the king, the suit became one in which the king was interested and the king's Exchequer, as a consequence, became entitled to investigate the matter. The Exchequer was overseen by a chief baron of the Exchequer. There was also a Chancery Division presided over by a lord chancellor who, like his English counterpart, had both an executive and judicial function, and a master of the rolls.

This system of common law courts with overlapping jurisdictions was borrowed from the structure in England and Wales. While the Court of King's Bench in England claimed and exercised, in some cases, a right to review the decisions of the Irish courts, the distance from London and the different circumstances in Ireland led almost inevitably to distinct developments in Ireland. Thus, the Irish House of Lords between 1783 and 1801 claimed and exercised a jurisdiction as an appellate court.[16] It was noted that this was fitting because statutes passed by the legislature would be more appropriately interpreted by Irish courts, 'moreover, the courts in Ireland had developed doctrines which were not understood by the British House of Lords'.[17]

In 1800, just prior to the enactment of the Act of Union, the Court of Exchequer Chamber was reimagined as a Court of Appeal having appellate jurisdiction from all common law courts. It was to be presided over by the

12 Ibid.
13 Ibid., at 19.
14 W.N. Osborough, *An island's law: a bibliographical guide to Ireland's legal past* (Dublin, 2013), p. 88.
15 Johnston, First adventure', at 19.
16 Andrew Lyall, *The Irish House of Lords: a court of law in the eighteenth century* (Dublin, 2013).
17 Ibid.

chief justice of the King's Bench, the chief justice of the Court of Common Pleas, the chief baron of the Exchequer and the puisne justices and barons. Lyall comments that 'it seems clear that the real function of the new Irish court was to enable the Irish common law judges, after the union, to retain control over appeals before they went to the British House of Lords'.[18] This development, driven by a political necessity, nevertheless preceded the establishment of a court of appeal in England and Wales.

Once enacted, article 8 of the Act of Union 1800 guaranteed the status quo and provided that 'all the courts of civil and ecclesiastical jurisdiction within the respective kingdoms, shall remain as now by law established within the same'.[19] However, it also provided that appeals 'shall from and after the union be finally decided by the House of Lords of the United kingdom',[20] a position that endured until 1922. During this time, there were separate common law courts (and a court of equity) with separate lord chief justices (or in the case of Exchequer, a lord chief baron). At a point I cannot precisely identify, the position of lord chief justice of King's Bench became that of lord chief justice, but none of the lord chief justices or lord chief barons, while occupying the senior position in their own courts, could be said to be the head of the Irish judiciary.

LORD CHIEF JUSTICE OF IRELAND

The next significant change was introduced by the Supreme Court of Judicature Act (Ireland) 1877.[21] That Act again followed the precedent of England and Wales and established a structure in which the lord chancellor was the overall head of the judiciary and the courts system. Section 6 of the Act preserved the pre-existing offices of the lord chancellor, lord chief justice, lord chief justice of Common Pleas, master of the rolls and lord chief baron, and the lord chief justice was defined in section 3 of the Act as 'lord chief justice of Ireland'. Section 6 also provided that the lord chancellor would be president of the new High Court of Justice, and that the lord chief justice, the second most senior judge, would act as president in his absence. The courts were accordingly reorganised into a single High Court with a number of divisions, being the Chancery Division (presided over by the lord chancellor), the Queen's Bench Division (presided over by the lord chief justice), the Exchequer Division (presided over by the lord chief baron), the Common Pleas Division (presided over by the lord chief justice of Common Pleas) and

18   Ibid., p. 138.
19   Act of Union (Ireland) Act 1800 (40 Geo. III, c. 38), art. 8.
20   Ibid.
21   40 & 41 Vic., c. 57.

the Probate and Matrimonial Division.[22] The existing offices were continued but the precedence between them was illustrated by section 18 of the 1877 Act which provided that the lord chief justice was to receive the princely salary of £5,000 while the lord chief justice of Common Pleas and the lord chief baron were to receive the not inconsiderable but lesser sum of £4,600.

It was ten years later that section 1 of the Judicature Act of 1887 provided that the title of lord chief justice of Common Pleas and, from the first vacancy after the passing of the Act, the title of lord chief baron of the Exchequer, would be abolished and their offices reduced to an equality with the puisne judges of the High Court. By section 3 of the 1887 Act, the lord chief justice was empowered to exercise all powers and authorities exercised by the law or custom by the lord chief justice of Common Pleas and, similarly, in the case of the chief baron on the occurrence of the next vacancy in that office. The first schedule to the Statute Law Revision Act 1894[23] repealed all the references in the Act of 1877 to the lord chief justice of Common Pleas, and so, in 1894, that office slipped from the statute books and into history. It was 1916 before section 1 of the 1887 Act took effect in relation to the title of chief baron of Exchequer with the retirement of Christopher Palles.

A Court of Appeal was constituted under section 10 of the 1877 Act, originally comprising the lord chancellor, the lord chief justice, the master of the rolls, the lord chief justice of Common Pleas, the chief baron of Exchequer and two ordinary members. The lord chancellor for the time was to be president of the Court of Appeal and, under section 22, retained the jurisdiction of the lord chancellor over, among other things, the custody of estates, and wardship, and what was expressed in the language of the time as 'the custody of the person and estates of idiots, lunatics, and persons of unsound mind' and any right as a visitor to any college or any charitable or other foundation.

For our purposes, the most significant point to note is that although there was a lord chief justice of Ireland, he was only the second-most senior figure in the judiciary; the lord chancellor was the head of the judiciary both nominally and functionally and presided in the Court of Appeal.

The first holder of the office of lord chief justice after 1877 was George Augustus Chichester May who had been the lord chief justice of the Queen's Bench. He was succeeded by Sir Michael Morris (1887), Peter O'Brien (1889), Richard Cherry (1914), James Campbell (1916) and, finally, Sir Thomas Molony (1918).

---

22 S. 34.
23 57 & 58 Vic., c. 56.

LORD CHIEF JUSTICE OF SOUTHERN IRELAND

The next significant development was brought about by the Government of Ireland Act 1920, that separated Ireland into the political units of Southern Ireland and Northern Ireland. The Supreme Court of Judicature in Ireland, established in 1877, was replaced by the Supreme Court of Judicature of Southern Ireland and the Supreme Court of Judicature of Northern Ireland respectively. Section 38 of the Act of 1920 established a High Court of Appeal for Ireland – a short lived but interesting body – to have appellate jurisdiction in both Southern and Northern Ireland.

The Supreme Court of Judicature of Southern Ireland was to consist of two divisions: a High Court of Justice in Southern Ireland, with the lord chief justice of Southern Ireland as its president, and a Court of Appeal in Ireland, also presided over by the lord chief justice. Section 44(2) provided that the lord chancellor would retain functions as a visitor to any college and other charitable institution, but otherwise the lord chancellor was not to exercise 'any executive functions' and the lord chancellor would cease to be the keeper of the great seal of Ireland which would pass to the lord lieutenant. Similarly, the jurisdiction of the master of the rolls with respect to public records would transfer to the lord lieutenant. The lord chancellor still retained a judicial role as the presiding judge in the High Court of Appeal for Ireland.

In December 1922 on the establishment of the Free State, the office of lord chancellor of Ireland was abolished altogether,[24] leading to the lord chief justice of Ireland becoming the head of the judiciary. There is an irony in this because, only a couple of years earlier, the Government of Ireland Act 1920 had abolished the position of lord chief justice of Ireland, and the only office which existed was that of the lord chief justice of Southern Ireland. However, the holder of the office of lord chief justice, Sir Thomas Molony, fought a strenuous battle to retain the title, even if the jurisdiction was limited to the position of lord chief justice of Southern Ireland – this episode was well described in an article by the late Nial Osborough.[25] Molony was an interesting character, who was described by Osborough as a 'home ruler of the old stamp'. He had been a member of the Royal Commission on the disturbances in Dublin at the time of the Howth gun-running that had been critical of the actions of the army and effectively forced the reinstatement of two policemen who had been dismissed for refusing to act against the Irish Volunteers who were parading from Howth with the newly landed weapons.[26] Those policemen had questioned why similar action had not been ordered in

---

24 Irish Free State (Consequential Provisions) Act 1922, which also abolished the High Court of Appeal in Ireland.
25 W.N. Osborough, 'The title of the last lord chief justice of Ireland', *Ir. Jur.*, 9:1 (1974), 87.
26 Part of the *Royal Commission on the circumstances connected with the landing of arms at Howth on 28 July 1914*, HC (1914–16) xxiv (821), Cmnd. 7649.

respect of the more serious Loyalist gun-running at Larne, Bangor and Donaghadee, a point the Commission appeared to feel had some merit. Molony, while at the Bar, had contributed an essay titled 'The judiciary, the police and the maintenance of law and order' to a series of essays edited by Professor J.H. Morgan on the 1912 Home Rule bill,[27] strongly defending the provisions in the bill from criticisms voiced by, among others, J.H. Campbell, a leading Unionist who was to become lord chief justice in 1914 before going on to hold the position of Baron Glenavy, the second last lord chancellor and, later again, the first chair of the Senate of the Irish Free State.

While Molony's campaign against the provisions of the Government of Ireland Act 1920, which would have abolished the position of lord chief justice, was ultimately unsuccessful, he did secure a transitional position, maintaining his entitlement to continue to use the title. This was, after all, consistent with the practice from the time of the Judicature Act whereby the holder of an office would retain the title and position until retirement notwithstanding the statutory abolition of the office.

This campaign reached the House of Lords where Lord Phillimore proposed an amendment to the Government of Ireland Act reserving to the lord chief justice of Ireland the position he presently enjoyed in relation to non-political academic and other bodies and that he should continue to hold and exercise all non-judicial offices and duties annexed to or appertaining to the office of lord chief justice of Ireland.

F.E. Smith, who was by now lord chancellor, was sympathetic to the first proposal acknowledging that:

> after all, mankind is very much influenced by titles, especially when they have their roots in history. The title of the lord chief justice of Ireland[28] has been a distinguished title and, if the present holder of the office would feel some solace in the face of the changes by which he is confronted, I would certainly make a great effort to meet the views of the noble and learned lord.[29]

Lord Birkenhead, however, considered that while the lord chief justice should continue to be able to exercise any function of visitor to any college or other charitable foundation, it should not extend to exercising all non-judicial offices and duties annexed to the position of lord chief justice of Ireland as that might encroach the jurisdiction of the new lord chief justice of Northern Ireland. Accordingly, a compromise amendment was proposed and included in the seventh schedule to the Act:

27 J.H. Morgan, *The new Irish Constitution* (London, 1912).
28 Presumably Smith was tracing the title back to the lord chief justice of King's Bench, and not to the 1877 Act.
29 Osborough, 'The title of the last lord chief justice.'

The existing lord chief justice of Ireland, if he becomes lord chief justice of Southern Ireland, shall, so long as he holds that office, be entitled to retain the rank and title of lord chief justice of Ireland, and to exercise any jurisdiction in respect of and on behalf of his majesty as a visitor to any college or other charitable foundation exerciseable by him on the appointed day.

Perhaps the most notable feature of the development of the position of lord chief justice was the care that was taken to maintain the various judicial offices once created, to only abolish such offices on the retirement or vacation of office by the existing holder, and ensure the continuation of the statutory functions attached to such offices, even when the titles were abolished and the court system reformed.

The Irish Free State Constitution of 1922 contained a provision in Article 69 that judges appointed under the Constitution should be independent and hold no other position of emolument and could not be a member of either House of the Oireachtas. It appears that this was designed to preclude the type of mixed judicial, administrative, and executive role that hitherto had been carried out by the lord chancellor. It might have been expected that the new constitutional setting would sweep aside the existing judiciary to which there was considerable antipathy on both sides of what was to become the Civil War divide, but article 75 of the Constitution contained transitional arrangements which provided that the existing courts system would remain in place until replaced by courts established under the Constitution. It might not have been anticipated either that it would take so long to set up the new courts envisaged by the Constitution, or that the period would be as troubled for the courts both in terms of the significance of the cases coming before them, and the conditions in which the work had to be done.

The antipathy towards Crown judges was expressed by two of the most significant figures in the new legal order. Both Hugh Kennedy and George Gavan Duffy were extremely strong in their criticism. This hostility was rooted in the view they had formed as to the decisions of the courts on *habeas corpus* applications during the War of Independence and, in particular, *R v. Allen*,[30] a judgment that Leo Kohn considered 'truly revolting', but which R.F.V. Heuston referred to as 'masterly'. The intensity of the emotion was understandable, particularly from participants in the applications where the consequence of a failed application for *habeas corpus* was trial before a military tribunal and execution. What is striking, however, is that judges like Molony considered that they were under attack for having upheld the law, whereas Kennedy and Gavan Duffy criticised them bitterly for, in their view, having failed to do so. Kennedy wrote of the 'bad repute of the Anglo-Irish bench

---

30 *R v. Allen* [1921] 2 IR 241. See the chapters by Bláthna Ruane and Maurice Collins.

and its position as an enemy institution in the eyes of the people ...', where a position was 'reserved as payment for political industry, sometimes it was blood-silver for a nationalist Judas'. Gavan Duffy spoke of the need to 'comb out the worst of the judges whose corruptness forced us to set up civil courts, men who had repeatedly proven themselves crooked on the very subject of *habeas corpus*'.[31] On the other hand, Gerald FitzGibbon, a member of the Oireachtas for Trinity College and later to become a member of the new Supreme Court, said that none of the judges he knew were 'capable of being false to his oath or duty as an administrator of law or that he would act on the orders of any paymaster in Dublin Castle or elsewhere'.[32] Darrell Figgis observed that at least some of the Crown judiciary 'were persons of accepted standing in their country and district; men who did stand on good relations with their neighbours; men whose judgment was known to be impartial; men who sought, at any rate, to deliver justice to the best of their ability'.

Hugh Kennedy played a significant role in the establishment, not just of the courts system, but of the State itself. He was only 44 years of age when appointed the first chief justice, and we are fortunate that such a talented, energetic and forceful person held that role. He was determined not only to establish a truly independent courts system, but also to demonstrate that while it represented a decisive shift from the pre-existing system, it would hold itself to the highest standards. As was said by the *Sunday Independent* on the occasion of his death when aged only 57: 'Mr Kennedy became chief justice following the passage of [the 1924] Act and he presided over the Supreme Court since with dignity and marked ability'. There is no doubt that his dissenting judgment in *State (Ryan) v. Lennon*[33] had a dramatic and largely positive impact in establishing the importance of constitutional law in the State, even if its reasoning and reliance on natural law now looks less persuasive. As Tom Daly has written, 'he was evidently not perfect, and his legacy remains contested'[34] and, in my view at least, if we were fortunate that the first chief justice had such a strong sense of cultural nationalism and a determination to see it expressed in the law, we were also fortunate that his views were tempered by his two colleagues on the first Supreme Court, Gerald FitzGibbon and James Murnaghan.[35] Nevertheless, the Act of 1924 was a monument to his practical skills as a lawyer and his determination to

---

31 David Foxton, *Revolutionary lawyers: Sinn Féin and Crown courts in Ireland and Britain, 1916–23* (Dublin, 2008).
32 Ibid., p. 21.
33 *State (Ryan) v. Lennon* [1935] IR 179.
34 Tom Gerard Daly, 'Hugh Kennedy: Ireland's (quietly) towering nation-maker' in Rehan Abeyratne and Iddo Porat (eds), *Towering judges: a comparative study of constitutional judges* (Cambridge, 2021).
35 I have discussed this elsewhere: see Donal O'Donnell, 'The sleep of reason', *Dublin University Law Journal*, 40:2 (2017), 191 and Donal O'Donnell, 'Irish legal history of the twentieth century', *Studies*, 105 (2016), 98.

establish a fully independent courts system. It would come to be a clear and decisive break with the colonial system that had existed before then, and the success of this endeavour was recognised at the time. The judgment of Nicholas Mansergh, an acute contemporary observer, is instructive:

> The nature of the revision of the Irish judicial system indicates that its main objective was the decentralisation of justice. In this there is little doubt but that the intention of the Oireachtas has been fulfilled. The advantages of the change are beyond question. The most outstanding success has been the District Court ... The district justices are trained in the law ... The extensive jurisdiction of the Circuit Courts permits the decision on the bulk of cases in the provincial Courts. The simplification of the judicial process has given widespread satisfaction.[36]

The fact that the system created in 1924 remains the essential structure for the courts in Ireland today is its own tribute to this remarkable man. It was also a fusing of the best of the old system and some novel ideas. As Mansergh said, 'a comprehensive reconstruction of the British judicial system did not imply a break from the principles by which it is inspired. On the contrary those principles were strengthened and confirmed'. When Hugh Kennedy died, it was not surprising that he was praised by his former colleagues in the first government of the Free State, but the new president of the Executive Council, Éamon de Valera, also paid him a generous compliment:

> The late chief justice was recognised as a great lawyer and a great judge. He was also a patriotic Irishman who gave fine service to his country. His death is a loss to the bench and the nation. Go ndéana Dia trócaire ar a anam.

The fact that the Free State was established without the new courts system envisaged by the Constitution in place and that that system took much longer to establish than might have then been anticipated gave rise to the unusual circumstance that Molony found himself, as lord chief justice, for the first time, to be the most senior judge in the State and the head of the judiciary and holding office under article 75 of the new Constitution. The new Provisional Government found itself in the unusual and somewhat uncomfortable position of having to rely on the judiciary that some of its most influential members had attacked so bitterly.

The conduct of the existing judiciary in remaining in office and continuing the business of the courts in response to the occupation of the

---

36 Nicholas Mansergh, *The Irish Free State: its government and politics* (London, 1934), pp 292, 297–8.

Four Courts and its subsequent destruction perhaps contributed, almost immediately, to a more nuanced view. In 1928, Denis Gwynn recorded admiringly the steadying influence of Molony in keeping the courts going and overseeing their transfer to the King's Inns following the occupation of the Four Courts:

> A special tribute is due to Sir Thomas Molony, who was lord chief justice when the Free State came into existence. He held that position when the Four Courts were forcibly occupied by the irregular forces under Rory O'Connor; and the work of Dublin courts had to be transferred to the building of the King's Inns. Confidence was utterly shaken during those momentous days, and it looked as though anarchy was to gain control. But the firmness and dignity of the lord chief justice when he established his own court at the end of a large room and allotted their respective cases to the other courts, did as much as anything else to restore a sense of security. And his personal example in arriving punctually at his work regardless of all threats of assassination, that as much as that of any man to strengthen the morale of the country.[37]

When the Courts of Justice bill came before the Dáil in 1923, W.T. Cosgrave struck an altogether more conciliatory note, commenting that: 'the bench in Ireland had the most distinguished and able jurists and conscientious law-givers ... we have endeavoured so to regulate these necessary alterations with as little disturbance and as free from offence as was possible in the circumstances'.[38] However, by then the new government had decided that it was necessary to wind up the Dáil courts that had been established during the War of Independence.[39] In truth, the die may have been cast earlier when article 64 of the 1922 Constitution provided for the establishment of a High Court and Court of Appeal to be called the Supreme Court.

CHIEF JUSTICE OF IRELAND

In 1923, the decision to wind up the Dáil courts system was put into action with the appointment of commissioners to complete the work. Subsequently, in 1925, the jurisdiction of the commissioners' work was transferred to the new High Court. The chief judicial commissioner was James Creed Meredith,

---

37 Denis R. Gwynn, *The Irish Free State 1922–1927* (London, 1928) pp 168–9.
38 *Dáil Éireann deb.*, vol. 4, col. 21 (31 July 1923).
39 See Thomas Mohr's chapter.

a man with a colourful past.[40] On 12 June 1924, the *Irish Times* recorded that the chief judicial commissioner stepped out of his court in Dublin Castle and, in the presence of the new chief justice, Hugh Kennedy, made the declaration provided for under section 99 of the Courts of Justice Act 1924 and was sworn in as a judge of the High Court in the new system.

The new chief justice had been the first attorney general of the Irish Free State and was heavily involved in both the drafting of the 1924 Act and its navigation through some heated debates, both in the Dáil and in the Senate. An engaging portrait of Kennedy can be found in the memoir by C.P. Curran, a contemporary at UCD of both Kennedy and James Joyce and who later became the registrar of the Supreme Court. Kennedy came from a comfortable background. He did not attend at any secondary school, but was educated by his father, a surgeon. The family lived in North Great Denmark Street, and Curran was able to say that as 'a schoolboy, like all the natives of that Northside area, I was familiar with the appearance of a future chief justice, a chubby faced boy returning on his pony in the afternoons from the Phoenix Park'.[41] In UCD, he became auditor of the Literary and Historical Society defeating James Joyce, who may have gotten his revenge by appropriating the name of his pious proper university opponent, Hugh Boyle Kennedy, for Hugh Boylan, as Blazes Boylan, the vulgar villain of Ulysses.

Curran describes the work of Kennedy on the courts of justice system, noting that the lawyers had their own obsolescent and honourable loyalties, and almost timidity and ingrained professional conservatism:

> They knew little of the quiet revolutionary in their midst and the resolute thoroughness with which, supported by John O'Byrne and John Costello, his axe would be laid to their upas tree. That axe was ground not in Trinity but in University College, through which the Greenwich Meridian did not run. From the outset he gave full legal effect to the revolution won by arms, establishing a wholly new legal system. He placed it in proper relation with the people by its efficient and modern structure, the elimination of all royal titles and pompous irrelevancies, and by the use of the Irish language in the courts.[42]

It is interesting to compare Kennedy and Molony as they were in many ways similar. They were both devout Catholics from the northside of Dublin and supporters of Home Rule. Curran describes Kennedy as a Redmondite and an orthodox home ruler who came into touch with Sinn Féin. Molony, for his

---

40 See Donal O'Donnell, 'A partial or uneven administration of the law: lawyers, the law and the importation of arms into Ireland, 1914', *Ir. Jur.*, 53 (2015), 100. See also Robert Marshall's chapter.
41 C.P. Curran, *Under the receding wave* (Dublin, 1970), p. 118.
42 Ibid., p. 123.

part, stood as a liberal candidate for the West Toxteth parliamentary division of Liverpool. He was described as a protégé of both John Redmond and John Dillon.[43] There were only twelve years between them, and it seems unlikely that their paths would not have crossed in what was a relatively small Catholic middle class in Dublin and at the Bar. Kennedy was a contemporary at UCD with a stellar group including Tom Kettle and Francis Sheehy Skeffington. In August 1916, Molony was appointed to the Royal Commission of Inquiry into the shooting of Sheehy Skeffington by a British officer and concluded that it constituted the offence of murder.

Molony was an ardent royalist and went to Trinity where he was an outstanding student. Kennedy attended UCD, and Curran describes him as more expressly nationalist than Skeffington, but as radical as him. It seems, however, that prior to the War of Independence, they would have occupied points on a spectrum of opinion within the Home Rule movement. It appears to have been the War of Independence and, more specifically, the litigation that it generated, that drove them on such separate courses, although their paths crossed in other ways. On the establishment of the Free State, Kennedy found himself defending *habeas corpus* applications, invoking some of the jurisprudence of which he had been so critical. In *The King (O'Brien) v. The Governor of the Military Internment Camp and Another*,[44] Kennedy sought to defend the detention of Republican prisoners, however the contention was scathingly rejected by the Court of Appeal, comprising Lord Chief Justice Molony and Lord Justice Ronan.

It does not appear that Molony was present on 11 June 1924 when the new courts were established, and his position as the last lord chief justice of Ireland and the first and only lord chief justice of Southern Ireland was abolished. He retired to England where he was made a Baronet in 1925. In 1931, he became vice chancellor of Trinity College. Under article 10 of the Treaty, retiring judges were to be provided with a pension, however that pension was to be paid by the new Free State and the retiring judges were concerned as to the security of that source of income. They claimed compensation from the British government and had to go through a procedure of making claims for compensation before a committee of senior British judges, comprising the lord chief justice of England, the master of the rolls and a judge of the Supreme Court nominated by the lord chancellor. The Treasury, predictably, argued that judges retiring younger, such as Molony, should receive less compensation because they had an opportunity of other employment. A memorandum of the hearing by a Treasury official named J.M. Trickett – described, in my view, correctly, by Bláthna Ruane as 'clearly

---

43 Bridget Hourican, 'Molony, Sir Thomas Francis', *DIB*.
44 [1924] 1 IR 32.

not a neutral observer'[45] – recounts Molony's appearance at the committee as having unfavourably impressed them with his 'bitter and prolix advocacy' and 'a medley of diatribe against the Treasury and Irish anecdote'. On his retirement as lord chief justice, Molony was presented by the solicitors' profession with a magnificent Orpen portrait that still hangs in the King's Inns. It shows him with the chain of office, which he left in the care of Trinity College to stay in its custody 'until such time as the office of lord chief justice of Ireland shall be restored'.

There was thus a very brief period during which the position of lord chief justice (or lord chief justice of Southern Ireland) was in fact the most senior position in the Irish judiciary. However, when the Courts of Justice Act 1924 came into effect, the system was quite radically restructured with the establishment of a Supreme Court to be presided over by a chief justice as the head of the judiciary.

As is well known, the Act of 1924 was the product of work of the Judiciary Committee established in January 1923. The then president of the Executive Council wrote to the committee in terms that suggest perhaps that it was drafted by Kennedy, referring to the 'body of laws' which were 'English (not even British) in their seed, English in their growth, English in their vitality'.[46] The suggestion that the common law system had not taken root in Ireland and the more romantic claims that a new system could be established reviving the Brehon law and, like the Dáil courts, prepared to accept any precedent other than those of the courts of England and Wales, were unrealistic, but that should not distract from the fact that the Act of 1924 was quite revolutionary. With the transfer of the jurisdiction of the Dáil courts first to the Commission and then to the High Court, and with the establishment of a new court system staffed by professional judges at every level and the adoption of a new Constitution, it can be said that the common law system was moulded and adapted into a distinctively Irish model which has continued to evolve over the last century.

Section 5 of the Courts of Justice Act 1924 established a Supreme Court consisting then of 'three judges, of whom the president (who is hereinafter called "the chief justice") shall be styled in his appointment "chief justice of the Irish Free State" or "Prímh-Bhreitheamh Shaorstát Éireann"'. Section 19 provided that there would be transferred to the chief justice and exercised by him all such jurisdictions in lunacy and minor matters lately exercised by the lord chancellor and, at the passing of the Act, exercised by the lord chief justice of Ireland. Similarly, the jurisdiction in respect of solicitors lately exercised by the lord chancellor and, at the passing of the Act, exercised by

---

45 Bláthna Ruane, 'Régime change: the fate of the senior Crown judiciary following the Anglo-Irish Treaty 1921', *Ir. Jur.*, 54:2 (2015), 96.
46 See the text of the letter in Niamh Howlin, 'Reflecting on a century of Irish courts', p. 2.

the lord chief justice, was to be transferred to the chief justice. Under section 19(3), the appointment of notaries public and commissioners to administer oaths was also transferred to the chief justice.

Section 20 of the 1924 Act adapted the provisions of the Finance (1909–10) Act 1910 so as to provide that the reference committee for the appointment of arbitrators for assessing compensation for compulsory acquisition would henceforth comprise the chief justice and the president of the High Court (in lieu of the lord chief justice and master of the rolls) and the chair of the Surveyors Institution, a committee which still exists.

The number of judges in the Supreme Court was increased to five by section 4 of the Courts of Justice Act 1936.[47] Section 9 of that Act transferred to the president of the High Court the jurisdiction conferred by the Act of 1924 in respect of lunacy, wardship and solicitors' matters. This, so far as I am aware, is the only example of a statutory reduction in the tasks to be performed by the chief justice since the foundation of the State. Notwithstanding that, it was a case of taking away with one hand and giving with the other. Section 67 of the Act of 1936 created a Superior Courts Rules Committee and further designates the chief justice as both an *ex officio* member and chairman of the committee.

The practice of adding functions to the role of the chief justice gathered pace during the twentieth century. Article 34.5.2° of the 1937 Constitution prescribes that the president of the Supreme Court shall be called the chief justice. Article 34.6.2° requires that the chief justice make the declaration provided for in article 34.6.1° before the president of Ireland, and that all other judges of the Supreme Court, Court of Appeal, High Court and of every other court shall make the same declaration in the presence of the chief justice or the senior available judge in the Supreme Court, in open court. Pursuant to article 12.8, the chief justice is required to administer the oath of office to the president of Ireland, and article 14 designates the chief justice a member of the presidential commission which exercises the powers and functions of the president in his/her absence. Pursuant to article 31 of the Constitution, the chief justice is an *ex officio* member of the Council of State.

Section 21 of the Courts of Justice (District Court) Act 1946 permits the minister for justice to request the chief justice to appoint a judge to investigate the condition of health, physical or mental, or to inquire into the conduct of a judge of the District Court. Section 10 of the Courts (Supplemental Provisions) Act 1961 continues the jurisdiction of the chief justice in respect of notaries public and commissioners to administer oaths and all other jurisdictions previously vested or capable of being exercised by the existing chief justice. Section 10(4) also permits the chief justice, where of the opinion that the conduct of a judge of the District Court has been such as to bring the

---

47 See Gerard Hogan's chapter.

administration of justice into disrepute, to interview the judge privately and inform him of such an opinion.

Section 56 of the Courts (Supplemental Provisions) Act 1961 contains an unusual and now quite anomalous[48] provision that establishes a committee consisting of the chief justice, the president of the High Court and the attorney general which, acting by a majority of its members, may if satisfied that a county registrar about to reach the age of 65 is not suffering from any disability which would render him/her unfit to discharge efficiently the duties of office, and after consultation with the minister, continue them in office for one year, commencing on the date on which he/she will attain the said age. This provision was introduced in the Act of 1961 and patterned on a similar provision in respect of judges of the District Court provided for by section 2 of the Courts of Justice (District Court) Act 1949, but which has now been repealed by virtue of the statutory extension of the retirement age of district judges to 70. This makes the provision in relation to the extension of time for county registrars even more anomalous.

The Prosecution of Offences Act 1974 created the position of the director of public prosecutions, and section 2(7) of that Act creates a committee tasked with selecting candidates for appointment to the office of the director and informing the taoiseach of those candidates and of their suitability for such appointment. This committee comprises the chair of the Council of the Bar of Ireland, the president of the Law Society, the secretary to the government, the senior legal assistant in the Office of the Attorney General and is chaired by the chief justice. This process, which was last undertaken in 2021, now involves a substantial amount of time to make such an appointment. The Court and Court Officers Act 1995 designates two further roles to the chief justice. It confirms under section 8 that it is the function of the chief justice to arrange the distribution and allocation of business of the Supreme Court and, on the establishment of the Judicial Appointments Advisory Board under section 13, it assigns the role of chairperson of that board to the chief justice. That Act, like many others, does not provide for the nomination of an appropriate substitute. As the number of judges to be appointed has increased over time, so too has the onerous work of this board. In recent years, the government has adopted an *ad hoc* model for the recommendation of candidates for appointment as presidents of the High Court and Court of Appeal, and the chief justice has been nominated as a member of the panel.

The Courts Service Act 1998 established the Courts Service, the statutory independent agency responsible for the administration and management of all courts in Ireland, and provides in section 11(1) that the chief justice (or a judge of the Supreme Court nominated by the chief justice) shall be a member of the board. Section 11(4) further dictates that the board shall be

---

48 By virtue of the Courts Act 2019, s. 4.

chaired by the chief justice (or the judge of the Supreme Court so nominated by the chief justice). However, with that position comes additional roles including membership of the Finance Committee and chairmanship of the Modernisation Committee of the Courts Service. The Courts Service is a substantial organisation currently having a budget of approximately €180 million and a staff of approximately 1,200 people.

Part 12 of the Legal Services Regulation Act 2015 establishes a procedure for the grant of patents of precedence. Section 172 creates an advisory committee which, in effect, gives binding advice to the government on the grant of a patent of precedence. By now it is perhaps unsurprising that the chief justice is designated both a member of the committee and chair under section 172(2)(a) of the Act of 2015.

The Judicial Council Act 2019 created, for the first time, a Judicial Council and section 8(4) of that Act provides that the chief justice will be the chair of the Council. The membership of the board of the Judicial Council is outlined in section 12 of the Act and section 12(2)(a) further provides that the chief justice shall be a member of the board and act as chair. Section 12(3) provides that an *ex officio* member of the board, including the chief justice, may nominate in writing another judge of the court of which he/she is chief justice to perform the functions of such *ex officio* member 'during such period or on such occasion or occasions as are specified in the nomination'. Section 44 of the Act provides that the chief justice shall be a member of the Judicial Conduct Committee and, pursuant to section 44(2)(a), shall once again chair that committee. Section 44(3) permits what appears to be an ad hoc nomination of a substitute from the Supreme Court 'during such or in respect of such occasion or occasions as are specified in the nomination'.

Most recently, the Judicial Appointments Commission Act 2023 has been enacted. This significantly expands the procedure for the appointment of judges. For the first time, the statutory procedure will apply to all appointments including promotions and appointments to the Court of Justice of the European Union and the European Court of Human Rights. Pursuant to section 9(1)(a), the chief justice is designated a member of the Commission and, by section 9(4), the chair. There is no procedure to allow for this function to be carried out by a nominated substitute. Section 16 of the Act permits the Commission to establish one or more committees, and section 16(3) provides that the chair of the committee shall be the chief justice, or such member of the Commission as the chief justice may determine.

In addition to the aforementioned statutory roles, the chief justice also performs a number of non-statutory functions such as chairing the chief justice's Access to Justice Working Group, which was established in 2021 to bring together members of the judiciary and key stakeholders with an interest in advancing access to justice, and which has since held conferences in 2021 and 2023. The chief justice has also chaired the courts' Decade of Centenaries Committee that oversaw the organisation of events in connection with the decade between 2012 and 2022. A new off-shoot sub-committee has since been established to coordinate a number of events and projects to commemorate the centenary of the Courts of Justice Act 1924 that the chief justice also chairs. There is also an informal group of court presidents, which is chaired by the chief justice. In addition, the chief justice performs a ceremonial function in respect of calls to the outer Bar, calls to the inner Bar, and in the granting of patents of precedence under the Act of 2015.

In addition to all the foregoing, Ireland's place in Europe has meant that the number of bilateral engagements carried out by the Supreme Court and, of necessity, led by the chief justice has mushroomed. The chief justice is a member of the Network of the Presidents of Supreme Judicial Courts of the European Union and a member of the board of that body. The Supreme Court is also a member of the Association of the Councils of State and Supreme Administrative Jurisdictions of the European Union, the Superior Courts Network operated by the European Court of Human Rights, the Judicial Network of the European Union, the World Conference on Constitutional Justice, the Venice Commission's Joint Council on Constitutional Justice and more.

CONCLUSION

It is not, I hope, special pleading to observe that this process of statutory accretion of roles, together with the expansion of the Supreme Court's international obligations and range of other outreach and *ad hoc* engagements, creates unrealistic and unsustainable expectations of the holder of the office who is still expected to play a full role as the presiding member in the Supreme Court. It is also inefficient, since there are many judges in the courts system who could perform some of the specific roles currently assigned to the chief justice. This would also have the beneficial effect of spreading the leadership roles across an expanded judiciary. I have suggested permitting the chief justice to nominate any serving judge to perform some of the statutory roles currently assigned to the chief justice. This would, however, require legislative change. In the short term, and in light of the significantly increased burden of establishing the Judicial Appointments Commission, I have exercised the power available under section 11(1) of the Courts Service Act 1998 and nominated a member of the Supreme Court, Ms Justice Elizabeth Dunne, as chair of the Courts Service Board. It is clear to me, however, that the role of chief justice today and the support necessary to perform it, requires comprehensive review and reform.

Among the non-judicial functions of the chief justice that Lord Chief Justice Molony was so exercised about is the position as a governor of Marsh's Library. This position dates back indeed to 1707 but in due course, in 1924, when Hugh Kennedy as the new chief justice wrote to the governors of Marsh's Library expressing his pleasure and anticipation at performing this function, he received the rather brusque and perhaps not entirely politic reply, dated 6 November 1924, that the statute of 1707 provided that the governors should include 'the lord chief justice of her majesty's Court of Chief Place in Ireland' and 'the lord chief justice of her majesty's Court of Common Pleas in Ireland'. The lord chief justice of her majesty's Court of Chief Place was the lord chief justice of Queen's Bench. As we know, the impact of the Judicature Acts in the period between 1877 and 1916 had the effect that the lord chief justice of Ireland was a governor of the Library as holding the office that had once been the lord chief justice of Chief Place, and who moreover by section 3 of the 1887 Act was entitled to exercise the functions of the lord chief justice of Common Pleas and the lord chief baron. However, the letter pointed out that the office of lord chief justice of Ireland had now been abolished by the Act of 1924 and the governors, considering that the position of chief justice of the Free State was not identical with that office, had not considered him to be a governor and therefore had not summoned him to their meetings. There may have been some legal merit in this argument, considering that the Acts between 1877 and 1920 had been careful to maintain the office and ensure the transfer of all existing jurisdictions, duties and privileges, whereas section 19 of the Act of 1924 only transferred the specific jurisdictions in relation to solicitors, wardship and the appointment of notaries and commissioners for oaths.[49] It was only in the 1960s that the governors thought it appropriate to accept that the transfer of jurisdiction under the Act of 1924 might be taken to have added this important function to the duties of the chief justice of Ireland. Perhaps this exchange of correspondence 100 years ago was the first occasion, but certainly not the last, when a chief justice of Ireland had reason to ask, 'Who'd be a chief justice?'

---

49 Section 20 of the 1924 Act also adapted the membership of the reference committee under the Finance Act 1910.

CHAPTER SEVENTEEN

The Supreme Court and the winter of 1936–7

GERARD HOGAN*

The months of November 1936, December 1936 and January 1937 have a significance in the history of the Supreme Court which is, perhaps, not sufficiently appreciated, not least because it was during this period that the composition of the court was extended from three to five members. The sudden resignation of Mr Justice Wylie from the High Court in July 1936 presented the Fianna Fáil government[1] with its first opportunity to make a judicial appointment to either the High Court or the Supreme Court since it had first taken office in March 1932. That vacancy was duly filled with the appointment of the attorney general, Conor A. Maguire SC, as an ordinary judge of the High Court on 2 November 1936. But there were then a series of other developments that significantly changed the composition of the High Court and (especially) the Supreme Court.

That composition had remained remarkably stable in the preceding decade.[2] The promotion of Murnaghan J from the High Court to the Supreme Court on 1 May 1925 following the sudden resignation of O'Connor J on the previous day had represented the only change in the composition of the Supreme Court in the previous eleven years. And there had been only two previous appointments to the High Court during this period following the establishment of that Court in June 1924; namely, Hanna J on 1 May 1925 (to replace O'Shaughnessy J who had retired on 23 December 1925) and O'Byrne J on 9 January 1926 (to replace Murnaghan J following his promotion to the Supreme Court).

---

* Judge of the Supreme Court. I should record my thanks to the UCD Archives for permission to quote from the Hugh Kennedy papers. I should also thank Dr Kevin Costello for drawing my attention to the article regarding Kennedy's death in the *Sunday Independent*, 12 Dec. 1936. I am also grateful to my judicial assistant, Oisín Mag Fhogartaigh, for accessing this article.

1 Or 'Executive Council' as it was formally known under the Constitution of the Irish Free State.
2 See generally Hugh Geoghegan, 'Three judges of the Supreme Court of the Irish Free State' in F.M. Larkin and N.M. Dawson (eds), *Lawyers, the law and history* (Dublin, 2013).

The next of these developments was an unexpected one. On Saturday 12 December 1936 the first chief justice, Hugh Kennedy, died after a sudden illness at the relatively young age of 57.[3] Kennedy had been such a dominant force in the momentous changes in the legal system from the days of the Civil War through the very establishment of the court system that it must have been almost hard at the time to visualise the Supreme Court without his forceful presence. This immediately left the government with an important choice to make as to his successor as chief justice. In addition, however, the Courts of Justice Act 1936 had been signed into law by the governor general on 28 November 1936 in what would also prove to be one of the last official functions ever performed by the three holders of that office. As part of the spillover effects of the abdication crisis in Britain, de Valera would seize the opportunity to abolish the governor general and all references to the Crown in the then Constitution of the Irish Free State with effect from 11 December 1936 through the mechanism of ordinary legislation passed by the Dáil as the (then) unicameral Oireachtas.[4] Following the amendment of article 68 of the Irish Free State Constitution, judges would now henceforth be appointed 'on the authority of the government', a situation which obtained until September 1961 when the new courts contemplated by article 34 of the Constitution were finally established by the Courts (Establishment and Constitution) Act 1961.[5] Section 4(1) of the 1936 Act had, however, expanded the composition of the Supreme Court from three judges to five.

---

[3] 'The chief justice's last appearance at the courts of justice was on the Thursday prior to his death. On that night he became unwell. On the following day the chief justice was confined to his home and was apparently making good progress under the care of his doctor, but on Saturday a serious relapse with a heart attack proved the heralds of death': 'The honourable Hugh Kennedy, chief justice of Saorstát Éireann', *I.L.T.&S.J.*, 70 (1936), 341. Other contemporary newspaper accounts corroborate this account, saying that Kennedy died 'at his residence' in Clonskeagh and that 'his last appearance at the Four Courts was on Thursday on which night he took suddenly ill': 'First chief justice of Saorstát dead', *Sunday Independent*, 13 Dec. 1936. Ruth Cannon's informative blogpost, 'The mysterious folding doors of the Supreme Court, 1937–73', ruthcannon.com, 11 Nov. 2021, quotes Coghlan, *The Evening Echo*, 8 Jan. 1973 as saying: 'In December 1936 during the Edward VII–Mrs. Simpson debacle a bell was rung in the law library, and all listened to the announcement: "the chief justice will not sit tomorrow". "Has he abdicated too?" asked one of the members. It was an unconsciously grim jest, for the Hon. Hugh Kennedy, chief justice died unexpectedly next day.' There are features of this account which, perhaps, do not quite hang together. According to the *Irish Law Times and Solicitor's Journal*, Kennedy CJ became ill on the Thursday night, so if this is correct the announcement must have been made on Friday 11 Dec. The Supreme Court would not have been sitting on the Saturday.

[4] See generally, Donal K. Coffey, 'British, Commonwealth and Irish responses to the abdication of King Edward VIII', *Ir. Jur.*, 44 (2009), 95–122.

[5] See generally the discussion of this point in *The State (Killian) v. Minister for Justice* [1954] IR 207 at 21–3, per Murnaghan J.

All of this left the government with important judicial choices to make. De Valera first paid tribute in the Dáil[6] in generous terms to Hugh Kennedy, who was a Cumann na nGhaedheal stalwart who had served as legal adviser/ attorney general during the Civil War and had later served as a TD between 1923 until 1924. The government chose Timothy Sullivan, then president of the High Court, as Kennedy's replacement and he made his declaration of office on 17 December 1936. This must have come as something of a surprise given that Sullivan had absolutely no connections with Fianna Fáil and he, if anything, came from an Irish Party background. Conor A. Maguire, on the other hand, had impeccable revolutionary credentials. He had been a judge of the Dáil courts[7] and was later counsel for Erskine Childers, and he had been appointed as attorney general in March 1932 on Fianna Fáil first entering government. He was then chosen in turn to be the president of the High Court.

The two new vacancies on the Supreme Court were filled by Mr Justice Meredith of the High Court and James Geoghegan TD. Meredith also had impeccable revolutionary credentials, having been one of the chief organisers of the Kilcoole gun-running in July 1914 and later having served as president of the Dáil Supreme Court from August 1920 until it was wound up in July 1922.[8] James Geoghegan TD had served as a minister for justice in the first Fianna Fáil administration in March 1932 and was later appointed attorney general in November 1936 to replace Conor A. Maguire.

The chief justice's death just as the composition of the Supreme Court was about to be extended had a certain poignancy. Kennedy had long pressed for the membership of the court to be extended. In what appears to be extensive handwritten notes prepared by him for his presentation to the Oireachtas Judiciary Committee in 1930, Kennedy noted that the 'present number of three was adopted by the Judiciary Committee in 1923[9] from motives of economy against my urging that the number should be five.' He continued:

> The former Court of Appeal consisted of three members (sometimes four when lord chancellor sat) but it was not a final Court of Appeal because [an] appeal lay as of right to the final Court of Appeal which was [the] House of Lords. Query whether any other country has so small a court as a final appeal court.

---

6 *Dáil Éireann deb.*, vol. 64, col. 10 (12 Dec. 1936), quoted in Donal O'Donnell's chapter. De Valera and several government ministers were reported as having attended Kennedy's funeral on Monday 14 Dec. 1936: see *I.L.T.&S.J.*, 70 (1936), 340 at 343.
7 Gerard Hogan, 'The Count Plunkett *habeas corpus* application and the end of the Dáil Supreme Court', *Ir. Jur.*, 68 (2022), 25–49, at 27.
8 Ibid., at 28.
9 Kennedy had a pronounced dislike for Glenavy: see R. MacCormaic, *The Supreme Court* (Dublin, 2016), pp 23–5.

Having itemised the position in Canada (including the appellate courts in the Canadian Provinces), Australia, the South of Africa and the United States of America, Kennedy then went on to say:

> *Disadvantages of having court of three only:*
> 1. No margin for sickness, other work etc.
> 2. Not sufficient weight for obviously final decisions.
> 3. In case of disagreement, if majority reverse, then [in that] event minority opinion may prevail, e.g., if court of two High Court judges are reversed.
>
> *Advantages of four or five member court:*
> 1. Margin for sickness or work etc. (e.g., Court of Criminal Appeal)
> 2. Greater weight and prestige of judgment. Bringing conviction of soundness to [the] minds of litigants and of public,
> 3. Greater variety of knowledge and outlook.[10]

He went on to add that:

> Four may be [a] better number than five if, on equal division, it is laid down that [the] original decision should stand, as then every decision must be a majority decision. If five be the number adopted. It should be provided that four at least should be a quorum to constitute the court: then if one [judge] has an interest or be or otherwise engaged (as in Court of Criminal Appeal or in Lunacy business etc.), the court can go on with its work.[11]

Kennedy had previously noted the increase in business, with 103 appeals in 1927, 86 appeals in 1928 and 101 appeals in 1929. He observed:

> There has been a great increase in business in the number of bona fide appeals as compared with the former Court of Appeal, though there have disappeared:
> (1) Northern appeals.
> (2) *Ex parte* appeals, e.g., service out of the jurisdiction, remittals, discovery, garnishee and receivers by way of equitable execution.
> (3) Appeals for time; formerly the time for final appeals was one year and much injury resulted in holding up the administration of estates. Now, three weeks from [the] perfection of [the] order.[12]

---

10 UCDA P4/1224.
11 Ibid.
12 Ibid.

The Oireachtas Committee duly recommended an increase in the numbers from three to five members. These recommendations were reflected in the original Courts of Justice bill 1934 which provided for the appointment of two additional judges of the Supreme Court, but whose principal work seemed to be in the High Court itself. Kennedy wrote to the minister for justice, P.J. Ruttledge,[13] on 18 January 1935 to protest:

> the view which was put before the Joint [Oireachtas] Committee that the Supreme Court should have at least five judges would not be met by appointing two Supreme Court judges who would be occupied in the business of the High Court. The proposal was to strengthen and enhance the prestige of the Supreme Court and [to] avoid certain considerations as to majority and minority opinions, in view of the finality about to be secured to the decisions of the Supreme Court. What would in effect amount to the conferring on two High Court judges the description, status and salaries of Supreme Court judges would not in the least give effect to the views of the Joint Committee. It would however defeat the policy of the Courts of Justice Act 1924 that the final appellate tribunal should be a complete self-contained Court and that the damage and inconvenience of judges with the High Court should be eliminated.

Kennedy later wrote to Ruttledge on 19 February 1935 pointing out that 'power to lend a judge from one court to the other to meet an occasional and purely temporary emergency as in the case of illness, is of course a matter entirely outside the foregoing observations.' In the end following further correspondence with the minister over a protracted period, a satisfactory compromise was achieved. As Ruttledge explained to the Dáil on the final stage of the Courts of Justice bill 1935:

> We have a Supreme Court in this country that is the final court of appeal, and it is necessary that that court should be in such a position that it would possess the confidence of the people of the country or any other people interested in litigation that might arise in this country. We have the recommendation of the joint committee which was set up in 1929 and which reported in 1930, or 1931, that the judges of the Supreme Court should be increased in number. Another ground that

---

13 There was here a certain irony in that here were Civil War adversaries – as an anti-Treaty officer Ruttledge had been severely wounded in the course of the Civil War – having what appears at least outwardly to have been a civilised dialogue. Ruttledge would write to Kennedy towards the end of this protracted correspondence on 22 Oct. 1936 assuring him that in these matters 'the views of yourself and of the Judges of the Supreme Court and the High Court ... must necessarily carry very great weight': UCDA P4/1225.

might be urged as showing the necessity for an increase is that we are going to have a new system of appeals, that is, the re-hearing system, and it will be conceded, I think, that that will entail extra work for the judges.

At the time that committee was dealing with this matter, they not only recommended that there should be an increase in the Supreme Court for the purpose of strengthening that court, but also an increase in the number of High Court judges, and I think that, with the new system of appeals, under which judges have to go on circuit to hear appeals, you would have to have an increase in the number of High Court judges at any rate. We have taken what is called the middle course, as described by the attorney-general on second reading. We are appointing two judges to act in the Supreme Court, but they will be available to do ordinary High Court work. In that way, we hope to avoid the expense that would be incurred in having to appoint Supreme Court judges at the same time as appointing High Court judges. We are trying to get over the expense of having to appoint additional High Court judges.[14]

All of this found expression in sections 4 and 5 respectively of the Courts of Justice Act 1936. Section 4 provided that appeals could be 'heard and determined' by not less than three and not more than five judges of the Supreme Court. Section 5(1) enabled these additional judges of the Supreme Court to sit as High Court judges where due to illness 'or for any other reason', the full number of High Court judges was not available or 'on account of the volume of business to be transacted in the High Court' or for 'any other reason ... it is expedient to increase temporarily the number of judges available for the purposes of the High Court', the chief justice might request a judge of the Supreme Court to sit as a judge of the High Court.

Tuesday, 12 January 1937, is perhaps a now forgotten date in the history of the Supreme Court. Yet that date is not without its own importance, since it was the first day on which the court sat as a court of five judges. The day was marked without any special fanfare and the *Irish Law Times and Solicitors' Journal* simply recorded the fact that 'the newly constituted Supreme Court of the Irish Free State sat for the first time on the 12inst. The court consisted of chief justice Sullivan, Mr Justice FitzGibbon, Mr Justice Murnaghan, Mr Justice Meredith and Mr Justice Geoghegan.'[15] Apart from a number of applications in respect of part-heard cases, the business of the day was the hearing of the appeal in the case of *Attorney General (Fahy) v. Bruen (No. 2)*.[16] It was a further step in the direction of the modern court that has

14 *Dáil Éireann deb.*, vol. 64, col. 7 (26 Nov. 1936).
15 *I.L.T.&S.J.* 71 (1937), 21.
16 [1937] IR 125.

evolved over the last 100 years from the simple three judge appellate court model on its establishment in June 1924 to the modern day court which now often sits as a court of seven judges and increasingly has the feel of something approximating a constitutional court.

While *The Irish Reports* version of the judgment in this case does not quite say so in such terms, the judgment of FitzGibbon J reveals that the composition of the court in respect of that appeal had been reconstituted. It had already sat for three days on Tuesday, 8 December 1936, Wednesday, 9 December 1936 and Thursday, 10 December 1936 with the previous composition of the court, namely, Kennedy CJ, FitzGibbon J and Murnaghan J. Since, however, Kennedy CJ had died suddenly on the morning of Saturday, 12 December 1936, the appeal could not have been determined save with the consent of the parties.[17] The *Irish Law Times and Solicitors' Journal* painted an interesting account of that hearing, saying:

> At the end of the third day, when the court rose, the arguments and submissions of learned counsel on both sides had not concluded and the court announced that the hearing would be resumed on Monday, 14 inst. The two double-sized tables which are available to that court for the use of senior counsel were literally strewn with textbooks, law reports, and dictionaries, and the senior counsel on behalf of the appellant occupied the attention of the court for two-and-a half days in his citations from the mass of literature in front of him ... The judgment of the Supreme Court was being awaited with interest, particularly having regard to the fact that the number of licence-holders for the sale and supply of intoxicating liquor in the Saorstát is well over 10,000. Death's sad intervention has postponed the determination of the

---

17 'The appeal ... had been heard in part by a court consisting of the late chief justice, my brother Murnaghan and myself when a premature end was put to the argument by the death of the chief justice': [1937] IR 125 at 146, per FitzGibbon J. The *Irish Law Times and Solicitors' Journal* reported: 'One or two applications were made in reference to cases in which the late Chief Justice Kennedy had been a member of the Court and in which judgment had been reserved. One was the case of *Fegan and others against the Great Northern Railway*. Counsel on both sides agreed to accept the decision of Mr. Justice FitzGibbon and Mr. Justice Murnaghan as arbitrators but FitzGibbon J intimated that their decision would not be binding on anyone except the parties in the case.' *I.L.T.&S.J.*, 71 (1937), 21. As it happens, Murnaghan J delivered the judgment in *Fegan v. Great Northern Railway Co.*, on 19 March 1937 holding that the plaintiffs were not entitled to invoke a national agreement concerning the resolution of a railway strike as they were based outside the Irish Free State. He noted that the parties had agreed to accept arbitration by the two surviving members of the court. By contrast it may be noted that in *O'Reilly v. Gleeson* [1975] IR 258 the Supreme Court found itself in a similar situation when FitzGerald CJ died suddenly on 17 October 1974. The parties agreed to be bound by the judgments of the other two members of the court, Henchy and Griffin JJ: see [1975] IR 258, at 268.

question.[18]

The court then re-assembled on 12 January 1937 with three new members, namely, Sullivan CJ, Meredith and Geoghegan JJ.

The issue that was presented in *Bruen* was not itself without interest, concerning as it did the meaning of that hallowed phrase in licensing laws, the concept of the 'bona fide traveller'. The defendant in that case was the proprietor of a licensed premises in Rosses Point. He held public dances in a hall which formed part of the licensed premises, but which was structurally separated from it. The premises were more than five miles distant from Sligo town and a special bus 'runs to and from Sligo for the convenience of persons attending the dances'.[19] Certain patrons were then given a special pass that enabled them to enter the licensed premises where they were then served with alcoholic drinks. Were these patrons 'bona fide travellers' for the purposes of section 15(1) of the Intoxicating Liquor Act 1927?

In the District Court the district justice found that the travellers were bona fide travellers in this sense and dismissed the summons. The prosecutor appealed this decision by way of case stated to the High Court under section 2 of the Summary Jurisdiction Act 1857. In the High Court, Hanna J held[20] that the defendants were not bona fide travellers in this sense. They had made two journeys and during these journeys the privilege conferred by the 1927 Act duly applied. It did not, however, apply to the interval of several hours spent at the dance.

The defendant sought to appeal this decision to the Supreme Court, but they were met with two objections. First, it was said that an appeal was barred by section 83 of the Courts of Justice Act 1924 which had stated that the 'determination of the High Court ... shall be final and conclusive and not appealable'. But Murnaghan J held in *Bruen (No.1)* that since the district justice had delivered his decision, the case stated was governed by the Summary Jurisdiction Act 1851 'and not under section 83 of the Court of Justice Act 1924 which provides for a new, consultative case stated before determination.'[21] The second objection was that section 50 of the Supreme Court of Judicature (Ireland) Act 1877 had precluded appeals from any decision of the High Court 'in any criminal cause or matter.' Murnaghan J noted that the effect of article 66 of the Irish Free State Constitution – which corresponds to the present constitutional provisions governing the right of appeal from the High Court to the Court of Appeal in article 34.4.1° – was that 'such exception must be found in a law made subsequent to the adoption of the Constitution.' It followed that 'the previous limitation on appeal'

18 *I.L.T.& S.J.*, 70 (1936), 339.
19 *Attorney General (Fahy) v. Bruen* [1936] IR 750, at 751.
20 *Attorney General (Fahy) v. Bruen (No.2)* [1937] IR 125.
21 [1936] IR 750, at 764.

contained in section 50 of the 1877 Act was 'thus abrogated'[22] and that Bruen was entitled to maintain his appeal.

It was thus the reconstituted Supreme Court of five judges that heard the appeal on the merits. Following a detailed exposition of the law in this area, the Court reversed the conclusions of Hanna J and held that the defendants were indeed bona fide travellers for the purposes of the section. While section 15 of the 1927 Act was itself repealed by section 3 and the schedule to the Intoxicating Liquor Act 1960, the judgments in *Bruen* are still of some interest. First, FitzGibbon J's judgment is of interest in that it applies the principle that when a court has pronounced definitively on the meaning of a statutory phrase and this phrase is subsequently used in a statute *in pari materia*, the Oireachtas is presumed to have adopted the meaning of that phrase as previously judicially interpreted.[23] Meredith J also sought to provide guidance on the concept of 'bona fide' used in conjunction with traveller. In this situation Meredith J suggested that the person concerned 'must be undertaking the purposive action, that makes the description applicable, in good faith with the legislature, and, therefore, not for the mere purpose of evading the provisions of the legislature'.[24]

As it happens, the Supreme Court delivered 37 reserved judgments in 1937, of which 18 involved the entire ordinary composition of the court;[25] 9 had a court of four and a further 10 simply had a court of three. The practice of sitting as a court of four was always going potentially to be problematic given the risk of the court dividing evenly. This first came to pass on 20 October 1937, when the Supreme Court was evenly divided in *Re Earle*,[26] an important contempt case. This question of a Supreme Court consisting solely of four members undoubtedly gave rise to problems from time to time. On 23 November 1949 the then minister for justice (General MacEoin TD) agreed in response to a Dáil question that it was:

> undesirable that the [Supreme] Court should ever be constituted of an even number of judges if it can possibly be avoided, and that in all circumstances a court of three is to be preferred to a court of four. But I recognise that valid objections may be urged against a court of three and that, in fact, it was because of these objections that the law with

22 Ibid.
23 See *Cronin v. Youghal Carpets (Yarns) Ltd* [1985] IR 312 at 32 for the application of this principle by Griffin J, but without, however, any reference to *Bruen*.
24 [1937] IR 125, at 171.
25 i.e., not including the president of the High Court as an *ex-officio* member.
26 [1938] IR 485. FitzGibbon and Meredith JJ were in favour of affirming the High Court order directing an order of attachment in respect of the mother of a young child, the subject of a *habeas corpus* application, whereas the Murnaghan and Geoghegan JJ considered that the order was irregular for want of service of the motion for attachment. As the court was evenly divided the order was affirmed.

respect of the composition of the Supreme Court was changed in 1936. If there were to be legislation [prohibiting four judge courts] the position would be, as experience has shown, that more frequent recourse would have to be made to a court of three, which, save for special and limited purposes, it was the object of the Act of 1936 to get away from.[27]

In the end the change in respect of uneven numbers of judges would only come about with section 7(3) of the Courts (Supplemental Provisions) Act 1961.[28] Yet the winter of 1936–7 is notable for the fact that the extension of the composition of Supreme Court from three to five members – a long held ambition of Hugh Kennedy – happened to coincide with Kennedy's death. This visionary judge thus unfortunately never got to see the realisation of his dream.

---

27 *Dáil Éireann deb.*, vol. 118, col. 9 (23 Nov. 1949).
28 Now as substituted by the Courts and Court Officers Act 1995, s. 7. Art. 26.2.1 of the 1937 Constitution requires a court of five judges when considering the constitutionality of a bill referred by the president and the Courts (Supplemental Provisions) Act 1961, s. 7(5) (as substituted by the Courts and Court Officers Act 1995, s. 7(5)) requires a court of five judges in cases involving a question 'of the validity of a law having regard to the provisions of the Constitution.'

CHAPTER EIGHTEEN

Where were the women?

NIAMH HOWLIN* AND MARK COEN**

The revolutionary zeal of the 1920s did not extend to ensuring that women had a significant presence in the new courts system. Despite the Sex Disqualification (Removal) Act 1919, the reality was that courts remained a male-dominated space until quite late in the twentieth century. However, that is not to say that women were entirely absent from the courts which were established in 1924. As this chapter illustrates, women's voices were heard, albeit faintly, in courthouses in Dublin and around the country. To varying degrees, they participated as barristers, solicitors, judges, jurors, witnesses and litigants, as well as the stenographers, civil servants, probation officers, interpreters and legal secretaries who helped to keep the machinery of justice moving.

WOMEN IN THE COURTS BEFORE 1924

Before 1924, it was not entirely unknown for women to be seen working in the courts in various capacities. The Sex Disqualification (Removal) Act 1919 had removed the legal barrier to women qualifying and practising in the legal professions.[1] The first women were called to the Bar in 1921[2] and the first women solicitors were appointed in 1923.[3] Early women barristers had practices around the country; for example, Frances Kyle practised on the Northern circuit; Mollie Dillon-Leetch on the Western circuit; Kathleen

---

* Associate professor at the Sutherland School of Law, University College Dublin.
** Associate professor at the Sutherland School of Law, University College Dublin.
1 See Niamh Howlin, *Barristers in Ireland: an evolving profession since 1921* (Dublin, 2023), ch. 9.
2 These were Francis Kyle and Averil Deverell. See Erika Rackley and Rosemary Auchmuty (eds), *Women's legal landmarks: celebrating the history of women and law in the UK and Ireland* (Oxford, 2019); Howlin, *Barristers*, ch. 9.
3 These were Mary Dorothea Heron, Helena Mary Early and Dorothea Mary Browne. See Rackley and Auchmuty, *Women's legal landmarks*; The Law Society of Ireland, *Celebrating a century of equal opportunities legislation: the first 100 women solicitors* (Dublin, 2019); Mary Redmond, 'The emergence of women in the solicitors' profession in Ireland' in Eamonn Hall and Daire Hogan (eds), *The Law Society of Ireland 1852–2002: portrait of a profession* (Dublin, 2002); John Garrahy, 'Heron, (Mary) Dorothea', *DIB*.

Phelan on the Southern circuit and Averil Deverell worked mainly in Dublin and on the Eastern circuit. There was a higher attrition rate for women than for men at the Bar, and many women either left upon marriage,[4] sought disbarment in order to practise as solicitors,[5] or forged alternative careers.[6]

Georgina Frost in Co. Clare was the first woman in the United Kingdom to be officially appointed as a Petty Sessions clerk in 1920, having previously carried out the duties for a number of years.[7] A number of women had been appointed to the magistracy before Independence. These included, in January 1920, Lady Rachel Beattie as a justice of the peace for the city of Dublin[8] and Lady Arnott, Lady Redmond, Lady Dockrell and Miss Palles as justices of the peace for the county of Dublin.[9] In April the *Irish Times* reported that Lady Dockrell 'was heartily welcomed' by the two other magistrates when she sat for the first time at Cabinteely Petty Sessions.[10] Margaret Dockrell had been active in the suffrage movement and was one of the first women elected to local government in Ireland. Her later election as chairman of Blackrock Urban District Council had drawn attention to the exclusion of women from the magistracy, as a man in her position would have automatically become a justice of the peace.[11] In May 1920 Lady Agnes Nash was appointed to the magistracy in Limerick.[12]

During the revolutionary period, women served as judges in the Dáil courts. As Ward points out, while the Dáil Department of Home Affairs accepted 'a form of appointment by local bodies, trade unions, Sinn Féin, Volunteers and clergy, "women eligible" was only tacked on at the end', and women were only appointed to the lower courts.[13] Hanna Sheehy Skeffington sat in south Dublin.[14] She recalled:

4   E.g., Mollie Dillon-Leetch, called to the Bar in 1923, and Antonia McDonnell, called in 1925. One of McDonnell's male contemporaries commented that 'marriage swallowed up the profession and a woman whom one knew very well and deserved to do well in her professional life was heard of no more except in terms of family life.' P.J. McEnery, 'Look back in love: conversations by an English fireside', UCDA P74/2, p. 205.
5   Howlin, *Barristers*, p. 180.
6   These included roles in the civil service, including the Department of Foreign Affairs.
7   Pádraig de Bhaldraithe, 'The Sixmilebridge clerks of petty sessions', *The Other Clare*, 11 (1987), 22–5 details Georgina Frost's legal battle. See Maria O'Brien, 'Frost, Georgina ('Georgie')', *DIB* and Ivana Bacik, Cathryn Costello and Eileen Drew, *Gender Injustice* (Dublin, 2003), pp 52, 54. An Post issued a commemorative stamp incorporating a photograph of Frost in 2000.
8   'Lady magistrate for the Borough of Dublin', *Irish Times*, 30 Jan. 1920.
9   Four photographs of the newly appointed magistrates appeared on the front page of the *Weekly Irish Times*, 31 Jan. 1920.
10 'Lady Dockrell J.P.', *Irish Times*, 8 Apr. 1920. No cases were heard that day, according to the report.
11 'Should Lady Dockrell be a J.P.?', *Irish Independent*, 8 Feb. 1906.
12 'Lady Magistrate for County Limerick', *Irish Times*, 5 May 1920.
13 Margaret Ward, *Unmanageable revolutionaries: women and Irish nationalism* (London, 1983), p. 141.
14 See Sheehy-Skeffington papers, NLI MS 33,621 (15); Hanna Sheehy Skeffington, '1918 –

We had no knowledge of law, but registrar supplied that and there was appeal to Supreme Court. Many well known lawyers ... pleaded in our courts and firms such as Barnardo applied ... Usually the women sat in cases regarding women. The decrees were respected, fines collected and often agreement arrived at by consensus (in marriage disputes). Courts were cheap, business done expeditiously and they were popular and respected. They did more to undermine British legal business in Ireland. We could hear lorries of Tans flashing by in the street outside as we met and were all liable to arrest were we caught in the act. But we were never given away. We had no real power to punish or to enforce our judgments but they were respected.[15]

Jenny Wyse Power,[16] Kathleen Clarke[17] and Margaret Buckley[18] served on courts in Dublin's north inner city. Maude Gonne also served in Dublin,[19] and Kathleen Barry was a judge in the Dáil courts as well as working in the Dáil Department of Home Affairs.[20] A Mrs McKean acted as a judge in Co. Kerry.[21] Áine Ceannt was appointed a district justice in 1920, and served as co-trustee of the funds of the Rathmines and Rathgar Dáil District Courts.[22] Helena Molony[23] and Áine Heron[24] also sat on the Rathmines Dáil District Court. Molony later wrote:

Treaty', handwritten manuscript, cited in Margaret Ward, *Hanna Sheehy Skeffington, suffragette and Sinn Féiner: her memoirs and political writings* (Dublin, 2017), p. 27. She wrote, 'my area was South City with D. Figgis, Neill Watson, Mme MacBride, two priests, Barrd and another.'

15 Handwritten manuscript, cited in Ward, *Hanna Sheehy Skeffington*, p. 27.
16 Frances Clarke, 'Clarke, Kathleen (Caitlín Bean Uí Chléirigh)', *DIB*.
17 Ibid.
18 Frances Clarke, 'Buckley (Goulding), Margaret ('Maggie'; 'Margaret Lee')', *DIB*.
19 Margaret Ward, *Maud Gonne: Ireland's Joan of Arc* (London, 1990), pp 126–7.
20 Lawrence William White, 'Moloney, Helen', *DIB*. See further Kathleen Barry Moloney papers, UCDA P94. Her statement to the Bureau of Military History relates only to her brother, Kevin Barry: Bureau of Military History (BMH) ws 731.
21 BMH ws 418, Mrs Austin Stack, p. 22.
22 Frances Clarke, 'Ceannt, Áine', *DIB*. Also mentioned in Mary Kotsonouris, *Retreat from revolution: the Dáil courts, 1920–24* (Dublin, 1994), p. 126. The Ceannt and O'Brennan papers in the National Library of Ireland contain letters, invoices and receipts relating to the costs of running the Republican court in Rathmines. E.g., see Áine Ceannt to Gearóid Ua Tuathail, 30 Mar. 1922 (enclosing a cheque for his salary as registrar): NLI MS 41,482/21. See also Áine Ceannt to min. finance, 31 Jan. 1934 (enclosing a cheque for the balance of funds of the Rathmines and Rathgar Republican District Courts): NLI MS 41,480/4/9.
23 Central Statistics Office, 'Life in 1916 Ireland: stories from statistics': www.cso.ie/en/releasesandpublications/ep/p-1916/1916irl/.
24 BMH ws 293. She recalled, p. 8: 'I was selected by the Pembroke Comhairle Ceanntair of Sinn Féin to act as Justice at the Sinn Féin Courts. The Pembroke and Rathmines Courts combined under the chairmanship co-trustees of Erskine Childers. Mrs. Ceannt and I were co-trustees of the moneys of the Court.' Ward notes that Ceannt and Heron 'sometimes sat together' in Rathmines-Pembroke. Ward, *Unmanageable revolutionaries*, p. 141.

I acted as a district justice in the Rathmines area. Lily Brennan got me into that. I was on the Courts, which I think were held at intervals. I do not think they were held weekly at the Town Hall. I think once a month was as much as I went. The cases I dealt with were mostly trivial crime and small debts, ordinary police court cases. The interesting thing about it was that the people did come to the Courts, and acknowledged their jurisdiction, and mostly obeyed their judgments.[25]

Other women worked in the Dáil courts as officials, lawyers and stenographers. Examples include Sighle Dowling, a stenographer in the Dáil courts in north Dublin city;[26] Patricia Hoey, secretary to the Dáil courts on Henry Street;[27] Marion Duggan, who worked as a Dáil court official,[28] Mary Herlihy, a parish clerk in Co. Cork[29] and Nellie Dillon from Co. Kildare, who 'acted in the Republican courts'[30] during the Truce.

Still others supported in the Dáil courts in other ways. Lena Brennan was involved in 'keeping watch' during Republican court sessions in Co. Clare,[31] while Catherine O'Leary drove IRA officers to the Dáil courts in Co. Limerick.[32] Frances Campion was involved in organising Dáil courts in Co. Laois.[33] Brigid McGeehan's uncle was a Dáil court judge in Co. Kildare. The sessions were 'always very late at night', and she had to stay up late waiting for his return 'and cook for any prisoners detained at the Sinn Féin Courts'.[34] Kate MacHale's home was used as a venue for Dáil courts in Co. Mayo,[35] as was Jennie Hoey's in Co. Monaghan,[36] Mary Lynch's in Waterford,[37] Mary

25 BMH ws 391, pp 51–2. Ward, *Unmanageable revolutionaries*, pp 141–2 notes that Albinia Broderick was elected to Kerry County Council. Her entry in the DIB does not make reference to this, but she was active in other parts of the Revolution: see Frances Clarke, 'Brodrick, Albinia Lucy (Gobnait Ní Bhruadair)', *DIB*.
26 Lawrence Wiliam White, 'Dowling, Sheila (Sighle)', *DIB*. She also worked for solicitor Michael Noyek, was an organiser for the Irish Women Workers' Union and later helped to found revolutionary leftist political party Saor Éire.
27 Military Service Pensions Collection (MSPC), 24SP13691. Her application refers to her role, inter alia, as 'Secretary to the South Dublin Courts (Henry Street).' See also Niav Gallagher, 'Hoey, Patricia', *DIB*.
28 Kotsonouris, *Retreat*, p. 126 and Howlin, *Barristers*, p. 298.
29 BMH ws 1461, Cornelius Hogan.
30 MSPC, MSP34REF7 (unsuccessful application). Papers in this file include a request to attend 'a meeting of justices here in Maynooth ... to receive instructions from registrar re working of courts'. Listing the various intelligence activities in which she was engaged, she finished her letter of appeal with the statement 'If these don't count as active services then I don't know the meaning of the term.'
31 MSPC, MSP34REF4027.
32 MSPC, MSP34REF44995.
33 MSPC, 49SP7070.
34 MSPC, MSP34REF36199.
35 MSPC, MSP34REF51346.
36 MSPC, MSP34REF45341.
37 MSPC, MSP34REF57423.

Bracken's in Co. Offaly[38] and Sarah O'Kelly's in Dublin.[39] In his account of his time as a judge of the Dáil courts, Chief Justice Conor A. Maguire mentioned Kathleen Devaney (later Kathleen O'Doherty), describing her as a member of staff at headquarters in Talbot Street, Dublin.[40] Kevin O'Sheil, judicial commissioner of the Dáil Éireann Land Courts, recalled 'two lady typists', one of whom was Kathleen.[41] The second was Eileen Barry, another sister of the famous patriot Kevin Barry.[42]

WOMEN, THE JUDICIARY COMMITTEE AND THE 1923 BILL

Although few women's voices were heard during the 1923 bill's passage through the Dáil and Seanad,[43] several women and women's groups made impactful submissions to the Judiciary Committee. For example, the Rathmines and Rathgar Branch of Cumann na Saoirse requested

> the government to include in the work of the proposed judicial commission a full inquiry into the working of juvenile courts in the USA and other countries, with a view to adopting modern methods of juvenile crime to Irish conditions.[44]

Louie Bennett also wrote, in her capacity as secretary to the Irish Women Workers' Union, urging the establishment of a juvenile court.[45] Replying to her, Hugh Kennedy wrote:

> I note that your Union, in addition to recommending the establishment of such a court, are willing to send a deputation to the Judiciary Committee of the government to discuss the matter. I shall be most happy to bring the resolution and your offer before the Judiciary Committee, which at the moment is breaking the ground ...[46]

---

38 MSPC, MSP34REF24675.
39 MSPC, MSP34REF56760.
40 Conor Maguire, 'The Republican Courts', *Capuchin Annual* (1969), 378, 388.
41 O'Sheil spells her name 'Devanny' but this appears to be a mistake.
42 BMH ws 1770.
43 Only Alice Stopford Green and Eileen Costello contributed to the debate in the upper house: *Seanad Éireann deb.*, vol. 2, col. 20 (6 Mar. 1924). They both commented in relation to language issues. Stopford Green suggested that 'breithimh' referred to a jurist, not a judge, citing the work of Eoin MacNeill.
44 Helen Curran to Judiciary Committee, 13 Jan. 1923, UCDA P4/1092 (2). The resolution was proposed and passed 'by Mrs Curran BA and Miss A. Bonham' at a meeting on 11 Jan. chaired by Marion Duggan LLB.
45 Letter enclosed in Smidic to Kennedy, 28 Feb. 1923, UCDA P4/1085 (22).
46 Kennedy to Bennett, UCDA P4/1092 (3).

Although the IWWU did not ultimately send a deputation to the Judiciary Committee, the Committee recommended the establishment of a Children's Court in Dublin, to be presided over by 'one or other of the two junior metropolitan justices, with an assessor selected from a panel of women who consent to act.'[47] This echoed the Juvenile Court provided for in section 111 of the Children Act 1908.

Originally the Courts of Justice bill 1923 provided for a Children's Court for Dublin city only. However, section 80 as enacted provided for weekly sittings by district justices in Dublin, Cork, Limerick and Waterford,[48] to deal with 'all charges against children'. The recommendation of having assessors taken from a panel of women did not make it into the bill, despite being described as 'exceedingly valuable' by Professor Magennis in the Dáil.[49]

Although the Judiciary Committee had suggested that the Children's Court should deal with all charges 'except those of an aggravated or heinous nature', the 1923 bill as introduced referred to everything except 'charges of a trivial nature.' This wording was objected to in the Dáil,[50] and section 80 as enacted therefore referred to the district justice exercising these powers except in relation to 'charges which by reason of their gravity or other special circumstances he shall not consider fit to be so dealt with.'[51]

Kennedy accepted the limitations of the proposed Children's Court, and described it as 'providing a hearing for cases against children in special surroundings other than the formal courts and have them dealt with in a paternal rather than a judicial manner'.[52] Independent TD John Good suggested that further steps ought to be taken to accommodate children in court:

> it would be very desirable if any arrangements could be made, when it is necessary to bring children and their mothers to court, whereby there should be the absence of any connection with the criminal proceedings in this court, so that there should be no mixing up of criminals and children and their mothers in the same court.[53]

---

47 *Report of the Judiciary Committee* (Dublin, 1923), p. 14.
48 Courts of Justice Act 1924, s. 80.
49 *Dáil Éireann deb.*, vol. 5, col. 9 (1 Nov. 1923).
50 Ibid., Thomas Johnson.
51 Ibid., and vol. 15, col. 17 (4 Dec. 1923).
52 Ibid., vol. 5, col. 9 (1 Nov. 1923).
53 Ibid. Cumann na nGaedheal TD George Woulfe commented 'I have a long experience, of between 30 and 40 years, of jurors' and grand jurors' work in county towns, and I have been shocked, beyond measure, on many occasions, by seeing children brought for trial before crowded courts, upon cases varying from trivial things to very heinous offences. I thought long ago, and I think still, that it has a most demoralising effect on them and on their after life.'

Although it was not practicable to legislate for this at a national level, evidently the practice by many district judges was to deal with minor cases involving children less formally or separately where possible.

WOMEN JUDGES

The various contributions by women to the smooth operation of the machinery of justice during the Revolution were quickly forgotten. This was part of a wider trend. Irishwomen, whose contribution to the struggle for independence had been significant, would have their public role curtailed by successive governments.[54] One of the first instances of this occurred in relation to jury service, discussed below. The appointment of the first judges was an important moment for the new state as it would signal those who embodied justice in the new order. Political inclusivity was evident in the appointment of several former Crown judges to the new judiciary.[55] The message in relation to women could not have been more stark; none were appointed. As we have seen, women had been appointed to the magistracy in the pre-Independence period. They would serve in this role in significant numbers in England and Wales from the 1920s on. In a lecture to the Statistical and Social Inquiry Society of Ireland in 1921, Lord Chief Justice Molony spoke approvingly of the advent of women magistrates, lawyers and jurors. He added that he hoped he would see a woman appointed to the High Court before he retired.[56] A wait of 80 years would be required.

From the passing of the Courts of Justice Act 1924, forty years elapsed before a woman was appointed as a judge. Hanna Sheehy Skeffington, writing in 1936, remarked that despite the roles played by women in the Dáil courts,

> [t]here is yet no woman justice or district justice in the Free State, though one would have thought that a sufficient time had elapsed to entitle a woman barrister to promotion there being a number of distinguished women lawyers, though these do not actually practice in the criminal courts, which is to be regretted.[57]

54 See, e.g., Maryann Valiulis, 'Neither feminist nor flapper: the ecclesiastical construction of the ideal Irish woman' in Mary O'Dowd and Sabine Wichert (eds), *Chattel, servant or citizen: women's status in church, state and society* (Belfast, 1995), p. 168; Caitriona Beaumont, 'Women, citizenship and Catholicism in the Irish Free State, 1922–1948', *Women's History Review*, 6 (1997), 563–85; Maryann Valiulis, 'Virtuous mothers and dutiful wives: the politics of sexuality in the Irish Free State' in Maryann Valiulis (ed.), *Gender and power in Irish history* (Dublin, 2008), p. 100; and Maryann Valiulis, *The making of inequality in the Irish Free State, 1922–37: women, power and gender ideology* (Dublin, 2019).
55 Bláthna Ruane, 'The challenge of creating a new judiciary 1922–1924' in Eoin Carolan (ed.), *Judicial power in Ireland* (Dublin, 2018), pp 20–2. See also Robert Marshall's chapter.
56 'Prevention of crime: lord chief justice on causes and remedies', *Irish Independent*, 14 Jan. 1921.
57 Hanna Sheehy Skeffington, 'Women in the Free State: a stocktaking', *The New English Weekly*, 19 Mar. 1936, cited in Ward, *Hanna Sheehy Skeffington*, p. 335.

Eileen Kennedy, who qualified as a solicitor in 1947, was appointed to the District Court bench in 1964.[58] A second woman was not appointed to the bench until 1975, when Agnes Cassidy was appointed a temporary district justice.[59] It was not until 1992 that women were appointed as judges in courts at all levels.

WOMEN JURORS

Women first sat as trial jurors in Ireland in January 1921, in a medical negligence case at Green Street courthouse.[60] As in England, both the national and provincial press were obsessed with the novelty of the 'lady jurors' and reported in detail on their appearance and conduct in court.[61] While some judges welcomed the new jurors, others, in particular Mr Justice Dodd, were openly hostile.[62] After an initially promising start, by 1923 lawyers were routinely objecting to women jurors; William Carrigan KC was particularly fond of using challenges to achieve all male juries in criminal cases.[63] Lorcan Sherlock, the Dublin city sub-sheriff, was opposed to women jurors and lobbied the government for reform.[64]

Reform came in the Juries (Amendment) Act 1924, which permitted women who satisfied the property rating qualification for jury service to claim an exemption from serving.[65] The measure was motivated by the belief that women should not be exposed to the 'distasteful'[66] details of court cases, particularly criminal cases, and that in any case their proper place was at home with their children. Women availed of the opt-out in the 1924 Act in large numbers, achieving the government's desired outcome of exclusively male juries. However, O'Higgins could not resist returning to the issue of women's jury service. He introduced a bill that would have removed women from the jury system completely, by limiting eligibility to male citizens who had the requisite interest in property.[67] The proposal met with strong opposition from

58 Marie Coleman, 'Kennedy, Eileen', *DIB* and Miriam Hederman, 'Children in court', *Irish Press*, 14 Dec. 1967. Kennedy was given particular responsibility for the Children's Court, and later chaired a committee to examine the reformatory and industrial schools system: *Report of committee on reformatory and industrial schools* (Dublin, 1970). Before her appointment to the bench she had served as coroner for South Monaghan in the early 1960s, and was responsible for presiding over inquests. See Paul Kelly's chapter.
59 'Second woman district justice', *Irish Times*, 1 Feb. 1975.
60 Mark Coen, 'Through a narrow window: women's jury service in Ireland, 1921–1927', *law&history*, 9:2 (2022), 32–63, at 43.
61 Ibid., at 43–7 and 51–3.
62 Ibid., at 58–9.
63 Ibid., at 58.
64 Ibid., at 59–60.
65 Juries (Amendment) Act 1924, s. 3.
66 *Dáil Éireann deb.*, vol. 6, col. 22 (5 Mar. 1924), Kevin O'Higgins.
67 Juries bill 1927, s. 3.

women's organisations including the National Council of Women of Ireland and the Irish Women's Citizens Association.[68] The government backed down and amended the legislation so that women could apply to serve as jurors if they wished.[69] The concession meant little in practice but it did enable campaigners Beatrice Dixon and Kathleen Swanton to apply and serve in the late 1950s.[70] It would take the decision of the Supreme Court in *de Búrca and Anderson v. Attorney General*[71] in the mid 1970s to force the Oireachtas to provide for equal liability for jury service between men and women. It is interesting to note that while this was relatively late by international standards, it was by no means a complete outlier.[72]

WOMEN IN OTHER ROLES

Section 63 of the Courts of Justice bill provided for the appointment of stenographers. Appeals from the Circuit Court would be based on their official reports, rather than having appeals heard *de novo*. It was estimated that eight stenographers would need to be appointed for the Circuit Court.[73] Speaking in the Dáil, Kevin O'Higgins commented on the unsuitability of women for this role:

> I had to consider lately the question of ... stenographers in the courts, and the question arose would we have women stenographers in the Central Criminal Court and in the Circuit Courts throughout the country ... I took the decision that women stenographers would be unsuitable ... Extremely unpleasant cases come before the courts, cases of indecent assault, of rape, and, occasionally, of sodomy, and so on, and I would not take the administrative decision of subjecting women officials to a task of taking down verbatim evidence ... in cases of that kind.[74]

Such attitudes prevailed for another decade or so. In 1932 Daniel McMenamin TD asked the minister for justice, James Geoghegan,

---

68 Maryann Gialanella Valiulis, 'Defining their role in the new state: Irishwomen's protest against the Juries Act 1927', *Canadian Journal of Irish Studies*, 18 (1992), 43–60.
69 Juries Act 1927, sch. 1, pt. ii.
70 Coen, 'Through a narrow window', at 35. See Linde Lunney, 'Dixon, Beatrice Maureen', *DIB*.
71 [1976] IR 38.
72 Andrew L.-T. Choo and Jill Hunter, 'Gender discrimination and juries in the 20th century: judging women judging men', *International Journal of Evidence and Proof*, 22 (2018), 192–217, at 205.
73 *Dáil Éireann deb.*, vol. 5, col. 4 (3 Oct. 1923), Kevin O'Higgins.
74 Ibid., vol. 18 col. 5 (15 Feb. 1927).

> whether it is proposed to appoint girl stenographers to take verbatim reports of the evidence in trials for immoral and unnatural offences, and, if not, what arrangement he proposes to make for the taking of evidence in such cases if girls are appointed as official stenographers in the courts.[75]

The minister replied: 'I certainly do not propose, in any contingency to employ girls to report indecent cases in the Criminal Courts nor can I imagine any responsible person contemplating such a policy.' However, a few years later when the Special Criminal Court was established by the Offences Against the State Act 1939, women were appointed as stenographers. The minister for justice Gerald Boland stated in the Dáil:

> All the proceedings of the Special Criminal Court, since its institution, including the trial of many very serious offences, have been reported by two women verbatim reporters, both civil servants. The arrangement has worked very well and I would be reluctant to disturb it except in the event, which has not yet occurred, of cases of an indecent nature. I may perhaps point out that women are entitled to be present at all trials as barristers, solicitors and journalists and I do not see any logical reason for making an exception in the case of official stenographers.[76]

It thus appears that by the late 1930s, women were no longer necessarily seen as being too delicate for this kind of work.

Women also supported the operation of the courts by working as registrars[77] or in court offices.[78] They worked in court-adjacent roles as law reporters, clerks and legal secretaries. In 1928, for example, Marion Duggan was the first woman to be appointed as a law reporter by the Incorporated Council for Law Reporting Council.[79]

As will be demonstrated in Úna Ní Raifeartaigh and Róisín Costello's chapter, the idea of having courts in which proceedings could be conducted entirely through Irish was unrealistic and ill thought-out. It was necessary to appoint Irish-language interpreters, some of whom were women. For example,

---

75 Ibid., vol. 44, col. 7 (2 Nov. 1932).
76 Ibid., vol. 95, col. 3 (19 Oct. 1944).
77 Ita Heslin worked in the High Court office, and as assistant examiner, registrar of wards of court, and registrar of the Supreme Court. She had been called to the Bar in 1951. Kenneth Ferguson, *King's Inns barristers, 1868–2004* (Dublin, 2005), p. 206.
78 Onora Ní Shúilleabháin worked in the central office of the Four Courts and in the probate office. She was called to the Bar in 1972: Ferguson, *King's Inns barristers*, p. 364.
79 She was appointed on probation, which was unusual, and was pressured to resign in 1934: Eamon G. Hall, *The superior courts of law: 'official' law reporting in Ireland, 1866–2006* (Dublin, 2007), p. 150.

a Miss A.M. Sharkey provided interpretation services at Lifford Circuit Court in Donegal.[80]

Women were frequently in court in their capacity as probation officers or social workers,[81] both before and after the passing of the Courts of Justice Act 1924. The pre-Independence Dublin probation service staff 'comprised one official probation officer, Miss Dargan, assisted by an unpaid volunteer, Miss O'Brien.'[82] Kathleen Sullivan was appointed in 1926 and Miss O'Brien was given full recognition as a probation officer. Evelyn Caroll was later appointed in 1936, followed by Bridget Murphy and Mary E. Ryan. McNally notes that until 1936, all probation officers in Ireland were women,[83] and that '[d]espite their limited numbers and lack of resources, the probation officers exercised significant influence and authority, not just in court but also in wider policy and practice arenas.'[84]

It was not until 1959 that women were appointed to An Garda Síochána, although a small number of women had been appointed as police assistants as early as 1917.[85] The Carrigan committee recommended the appointment of at least twelve 'women police' in the Dublin Metropolitan Police District.[86] Kennedy describes how, in the official repression of the Carrigan recommendations and findings, a government memorandum questioned whether women police officers and probation officers were 'of any real value'.[87] Hanna Sheehy Skeffington pointed out in 1936 that 'There are ... women solicitors and a number of women probation officers, but as yet only a few women police (without uniforms and without power to effect arrest).'[88]

80 *Sunday Independent*, 9 Feb. 1936. We are grateful to Dr Mary Phelan for this reference. Miss Sharkey was described as the 'Irish instructress at the Letterkenny Technical School'.
81 See Caroline Skehill, *The nature of social work in Ireland: a historical perspective* (New York, 1999).
82 Gerry McNally, 'Probation in Ireland: a brief history of the early years', *Irish Probation Journal*, 4:1 (2007), 5–24, at 7.
83 Ibid., at 7.
84 Ibid., at 9. He gives the example of probation officer Kathleen Sullivan intervening on behalf of Mary Cole, who had been convicted of murdering her two children and had her sentence commuted to imprisonment in Mountjoy. Sullivan negotiated for Cole to be taken in by the Sisters of Charity of St Vincent de Paul, on Dublin's Henrietta Street.
85 See further Catherine Clancy, '50 years later: women in policing', *Communiqué* (Dec. 2009), 22–30.
86 *Report of the Committee on the Criminal Law Amendment Acts (1880–85) and Juvenile Prostitution* (Dublin, 1931), p. 41. There were two women on the committee: V. O'Carroll, matron of the Coombe hospital, and Jane Power, a commissioner of the Dublin Union. Women who testified before the committee included Dorothy Stopford Price from the Irish Women Doctors Committee; Edith Tancred of the Women's Police of Great Britain and representatives from several women's organisations. See Finola Kennedy, 'The suppression of the Carrigan Report: a historical perspective on child abuse', *Studies*, 89 (2001), 354–63.
87 Kennedy, 'The suppression', p. 357, citing a memo. from the Dept. Justice, 27 Oct. 1932. The minister for justice was James Geoghegan.
88 Sheehy Skeffington, 'Women in the Free State'.

Hugh Kennedy engaged with the all-women Dun Emer Guild when it came to proposing designs for new judicial robes in the 1920s, though the designs were not ultimately adopted.[89]

WOMEN IN THE CRIMINAL COURTS

While women did not serve as judges or jurors in the courts for several decades after the passage of the Courts of Justice Act, they were present in other capacities, in particular as victims and defendants.

Victims

Section 77B(iii) of the Courts of Justice Act 1924 provided that indecent assault cases in the District Court should be heard *in camera* and that 'if the assaulted person is a female, one other female person nominated by the assaulted person shall be entitled to be present in court during the whole hearing of the case.' Although the *in camera* hearing of sexual cases was proposed by the Judiciary Committee, the provision relating to having a female friend was a parliamentary addition. When Cumann na nGaedheal TD Daniel Morrissey suggested it in the Dáil, Hugh Kennedy was not immediately receptive:

> I do not know whether it is proposed that a person should be there for hire or on voluntary terms. Is it intended that someone should be invited in from the road to hear the case? As put in the amendment the thing is impracticable ... It would really amount to having a wardress in court all the time.[90]

It was generally agreed that the *in camera* rule, if enforced, might mean that a female complainant in an indecent assault case could be the only woman in court: in the words of Labour's Thomas Johnson, 'you would have the person preferring a charge present in the company of a man hearing a case of this kind, and no woman present except herself.'[91]

When Kennedy came back with an amendment along the lines Morrissey had proposed, Johnson objected to the wording 'one other female person nominated by the assaulted person.' He wished to confer on the court the power to nominate someone in case the complainant was 'quite careless, or ignorant enough' not to nominate someone, but Kennedy pointed out that 'it

---

89 An exhibition featuring these designs, as well as those of Charles Shannon, was displayed at the 'Century of Courts' event in Dublin Castle on 12 April 2024, and at an event in the Four Courts to mark the centenary of the Supreme Court on 28 May 2024.
90 *Dáil Éireann deb.*, vol. 5, col. 9 (1 Nov. 1923).
91 Ibid.

would compel the woman to have someone in court when she would not want it and when she might desire the case heard completely *in camera*.'[92] The Women's Independent Association pointed out that the provision would not have been necessary if women were not being prevented from acting as jurors, and called for half the jury to be women in such cases.[93]

Criminal defendants

Women appeared in the courts as criminal defendants. The crime of infanticide has been a particular focus for scholars.[94] The conviction rate for women accused of homicide generally was lower than that for men. The higher acquittal rate for women may not have been grounded in gender alone; as Brennan has demonstrated, there were often evidential deficiencies, particularly when it came to killings (notably by poison) that took place in the privacy of the home.[95]

Juries that convicted women often added riders to their verdicts, urging the judge to be lenient when sentencing.[96] The underlying assumption was that 'women should be treated more leniently than men because they were less rational or autonomous in their actions'.[97] Where men and women had convicted offences together it was common for juries to emphasise in a rider that the men were more culpable, and had 'influenced or dominated the women.'[98]

In criminal cases, Magdalene laundries and other institutions were routinely used as judicial alternatives to sending women to prison.[99] Some

---

92 Ibid., col. 17 (4 Dec. 1923).
93 'Women on juries', *Irish Times*, 9 Nov. 1923. This provision was repealed by the Criminal Justice Act 1951, and replaced by more extensive provision for the exclusion of members of the public and restrictions on reporting (s. 20).
94 See Karen Brennan, '"A fine mixture of pity and justice": the criminal justice response to infanticide in Ireland, 1922–1949', *Law and History Review*, 31:4 (2013), 793–841; Karen Brennan, 'Social norms and the law in responding to infanticide', *Legal Studies*, 38:3 (2018), 480–99; Clíona Rattigan, *'What else could I do?' single mothers and infanticide, Ireland, 1900–1950* (Dublin, 2012); Clíona Rattigan, '"Done to death by father or relatives": Irish families and infanticide cases, 1922–1950', *The History of the Family*, 13:4 (2008), 370–83.
95 Karen Brennan, 'Murder in the Irish family, 1930–1945' in Niamh Howlin and Kevin Costello (eds), *Law and the family in Ireland, 1800–1950* (London, 2017).
96 Mark Coen and Niamh Howlin, 'The jury speaks: jury riders in the nineteenth and twentieth centuries', *American Journal of Legal History*, 58 (2018), 505–34. At 505, we explain that riders were 'a device through which the jury could comment with great freedom on myriad matters, including issues that influenced its reasoning, troubled its members or, in the jury's opinion, required remediation by the authorities.'
97 Coen and Howlin, 'the jury speaks', at 527.
98 Ibid.
99 See generally, Ian O'Donnell, *Coercive confinement* (Manchester, 2012); Lynsey Black, *Gender and punishment in Ireland: women, murder and the death penalty, 1922–64* (Manchester, 2022) and Lynsey Black, Louise Brangan and Deirdre Healy (eds), *Histories of punishment and social control in Ireland: perspectives from a periphery* (Bradford, 2022).

women who should have served finite sentences in the care of the state saw out their days behind convent walls.[100] In the case of Mary Lucy, a domestic servant convicted of the larceny of items from her employer, the judge gave her a choice between two years 'in a home' (a euphemism for a religious institution) or six months in prison. She chose prison.[101] Father Anthony Gaughan recalls in his memoirs that he attended the Central Criminal Court at Green Street on behalf of the Sisters of Charity, 'with a message from the Sisters to the judge'[102] stating that a woman convicted of infanticide should be sent to the Magdalene laundry run by them at Donnybrook instead of prison, on the basis that that approach represented 'her best chance of being rehabilitated'.[103] It appears his entreaty was successful on this, and other, occasions.[104]

Executions of women were rare. One woman was executed post-Independence; this was Annie Walsh in 1925.[105]

REPUBLICAN WOMEN

Many high-profile women who had been prominent in the struggle for independence opposed the Treaty and became 'very publicly and visibly associated with the Republican side.'[106] Some of them engaged in anti-Free State activities that brought them before the courts. In the 1920s women were charged with offences including possession of revolvers and ammunition and assisting in the maintenance of a military organisation not recognised by law.[107] Those involved in subversive activity did not recognise the courts. They generally refused to plead and a separate jury had to be empanelled to determine the preliminary issue of whether they were 'mute of malice or by the visitation of God'.[108] A jury having determined that they were capable of

100 Lynsey Black, '"Women of evil life": Donnybrook Magdalene and the criminal justice system' in Mark Coen, Katherine O'Donnell and Maeve O'Rourke (eds), *A Dublin Magdalene laundry: Donnybrook and church-state power in Ireland* (Dublin, 2023), pp 188–9.
101 'Prison preferred to a home', *Weekly Irish Times*, 29 Nov. 1924.
102 Anthony Gaughan, *At the coalface: recollections of a city and country priest, 1950–2000* (Dublin, 2000), p. 73.
103 Ibid.
104 Ibid.
105 Ian O'Donnell, *Justice, mercy and caprice* (Oxford, 2017), pp 30–1.
106 Louise Ryan, '"Furies" and "Die-hards": women and Irish republicanism in the early twentieth century', *Gender & History*, 11:2 (1999), 256–75, at 264.
107 See e.g., 'Woman and revolver', *Irish Times*, 5 May 1928.
108 See e.g., 'Mute of malice: girl who refused to recognise the court', *Irish Times*, 15 Nov. 1928. The requirement that a jury be sworn to determine this issue was removed by the Juries (Protection) Act 1929, s. 6, with the function given to the trial judge. The 1929 Act was a temporary measure, the duration of which was extended until 30 September 1933, by the Juries (Protection) Act 1931, s. 1. The requirement for a jury determination in respect of a person standing mute was permanently removed by the Courts of Justice Act 1936, s. 80.

communicating and therefore mute of malice, a plea of not guilty would be entered on their behalf.

Republican women engaged in a variety of disrespectful behaviours that served both to demonstrate their non-recognition of the courts and to generate publicity for their activities. Their tactics while in the dock included reading aloud from books, singing rebel songs,[109] conversing with each other as if the proceedings were not happening, 'shouting in high falsetto tones'[110] and invoking the names of famous Irish rebels such as Wolfe Tone.[111] In a 1928 case two women – who refused to give their names – 'laughed heartily'[112] when brought before the District Court on charges of posting notices that contained seditious libels and incited the murder of the governor general. When the district justice sent them forward for trial to the Circuit Court, one of them told him he was 'only wasting his time' and it would not stop them doing the same thing again 'until we kick everything British out of this country'.[113]

The most significant aspect of Republican women's interactions with the courts in the decade after the enactment of the Courts of Justice Act 1924 was their coordination of a campaign of jury intimidation. This involved sending anonymous circulars (often signed 'Ghosts') to potential jurors, urging them to acquit Republican men and women if they were empanelled to try them. In a number of different trials, Sighle Humphreys, Helena Molony, Máire Comerford and Florence McCarthy were convicted of the common law offence of embracery (seeking to influence a juror by means other than the evidence) and served sentences of imprisonment. The campaign destabilised the jury system and led to the enactment of the Juries (Protection) Act 1929.[114]

Leading members of the Women's Prisoners' Defence League, including Maud Gonne MacBride, Charlotte Despard and Hannah Sheehy Skeffington, attended cases involving male and female Republicans as observers.[115] Their presence was often included in press reports, their names listed as persons 'in sympathy with the accused.'[116] Further details were sometimes provided; for example that Maud Gonne 'took copious notes during the hearing'[117] or presented a prisoner in the dock with flowers.[118] Her watching brief on the

109 'Scene in Dublin court', *Cork Examiner*, 2 Mar. 1928.
110 'Women billposters', *Irish Times*, 2 Mar. 1928.
111 'Court ignored', *Irish Independent*, 27 Oct. 1926.
112 'Seditious posters', *Irish Times*, 3 Feb. 1928.
113 Ibid.
114 For a detailed discussion of the campaign and its consequences, see Mark Coen '"The work of some irresponsible women": jurors, ghosts and embracery in the Irish Free State', *Law and History Review*, 38:4 (2020), 777–810.
115 See, e.g., 'Death of Kevin O'Higgins: ten men again in the dock on conspiracy charge', *Evening Herald*, 18 July 1927; 'Dublin court turmoil', *Irish Times*, 9 Sept. 1933.
116 'Dublin scenes: sequel to search for firearms', *Cork Examiner*, 8 Feb. 1930.
117 'The Tipperary treason charges', *Leitrim Observer*, 21 Feb. 1931.
118 'Mute prisoners', *Kerry News*, 23 July 1928.

criminal courts evidently caused annoyance in official quarters. A civil servant wrote privately:

> Loitering in the neighbourhood of courts should undoubtedly be made an offence. This would enable us to deal appropriately with Mrs Gonne McBride and other harpies of her ilk.[119]

Sometimes these Republican observers interjected during proceedings and were silenced.[120] On one occasion Judge Davitt acceded to a Garda application seeking the exclusion of Hanna Sheehy Skeffington on the basis that she was a journalist with the Republican newspaper *An Phoblacht*.[121] Before exiting she addressed the following remarks to the judge: 'This is a Star Chamber proceeding. Remember your father, Michael Davitt. This is a Star Chamber Court and you can commit me for contempt if you wish.'[122]

WOMEN IN THE PUBLIC GALLERY

Mulcahy argues that scholars, including feminist scholars, have overlooked the role women assumed in court proceedings by attending as observers.[123] She notes that when official court roles were denied to women, or were not commonly occupied by them, their ability to attend in the public gallery involved an important assertion of a public role.[124] Her research on women as spectators in British courts in the Victorian period found little mention of them in the *Times* newspaper.[125] The situation in Ireland from 1924 onwards was quite different; the presence of women in significant numbers at any case invariably attracted press comment and was often part of the scene-setting in reportage. For example, an account of a 1926 breach of promise of marriage case began: 'A crowded court, including a good sprinkling of the fair sex, laughed heartily …'.[126]

However, women did not confine themselves to attending quaint cases. Indeed, they appear to have been just as interested as men in sensational and grisly criminal trials. This is noteworthy given that the unsuitability of

119 NAI JUS/8/685.
120 For an instance where Hanna Sheehy Skeffington did so and was told to be silent by Mr Justice Hanna, see 'Charges against civic guards', *Irish Times*, 16 Nov. 1927.
121 The application was most likely made under the Juries (Protection) Act 1929, s. 7(5).
122 'More treason charges', *Evening Herald*, 10 July 1931.
123 Linda Mulcahy, 'Watching women: what illustrations of courtroom scenes tell us about women and the public sphere in the nineteenth century', *Journal of Law and Society*, 41:1 (2015), 53–73, at 54–5.
124 Ibid.
125 Ibid., at 55, n. 8.
126 'Match-making in Longford', *Weekly Irish Times*, 6 Nov. 1926.

criminal courts as an environment for women was emphasised for many decades as a reason why women should not be jurors. It also appears to contradict official claims that women were not interested in the administration of justice.

The 1926 trial of Henry McCabe for the murder of six people at a mansion called 'La Mancha' in Malahide attracted enormous public interest. The *Irish Independent* correspondent observed of the spectators: 'Of those in the public galleries fully 50 per cent were women, some of whom came ... with sandwiches, holding firmly to their seats from morning till night.'[127] When ten people appeared before Waterford District Court charged with the murder of Lawrence Griffin (the so-called 'missing postman' case), 'ladies in a big majority crowded the grand jury gallery' above the judge's bench.[128] Similarly, members of the public attending the prosecution of Mamie Cadden for abandoning an infant were predominantly female.[129] At the trial of Bernard Kirwan for the murder of his brother Laurence there was 'a scramble at the gates' of Green Street courthouse in which 'fashionably dressed ladies vied with members of the unemployed for a seat in the public gallery.'[130] In May 1950 Kathleen Harmon, a 17-year-old girl who worked as a maid in Templeogue, was tried for the murder of Penelope Willoughby, aged four. Members of the public in attendance were predominantly female: 'The public galleries were crowded, mostly by elderly women ... after the luncheon interval women queued on the stairs inside the courthouse.'[131]

The emotional responses of female onlookers, often relatives of convicted persons, provided the press with elements of human interest and colour. A mother pleaded unsuccessfully with Judge Davitt not to send her two sons to prison and borstal respectively. The *Evening Herald* reported: 'Mrs Maher broke down and went sobbing from the court. Three or four women in the public gallery also wept and went out.'[132] When Christopher Crowe was sentenced to four years penal servitude for a series of thefts, 'a woman in the public gallery began to scream, and had to be removed by a guard.'[133] The passing of death sentences was often reported as being accompanied by audible crying from women in the public gallery.[134] The sentencing of Patrick Boylan by O'Byrne J for the murder of Norah Whelan followed this pattern:

127 'A verdict of guilty', *Irish Independent*, 15 Nov. 1926.
128 'The missing postman', *Munster Express*, 7 Mar. 1930.
129 'Dublin matron's statements in baby case', *Irish Times*, 4 Aug. 1938.
130 'Murder trial ends', *Westmeath Independent*, 13 Feb. 1943.
131 'Kathleen Harmon 1½ hours in witness box', *Irish Times*, 5 May 1950.
132 'Weeping women in Dublin court', *Evening Herald*, 9 June 1939. See also 'Women in court weep', *Irish Press*, 10 June 1939.
133 'Station bag thief gets penal servitude', *Irish Times*, 12 Feb. 194.
134 'Irish farm murder', *Irish Times*, 18 Nov. 1932; 'Cork murder trial', *Irish Times*, 10 Apr. 1937; 'Miss Cadden found guilty of Mrs. O'Reilly's murder', *Irish Times*, 2 Nov. 1956; 'Hopkins sentenced to die for murder of fiancee', *Irish Times*, 27 Feb. 1953.

'The judge then donned the black cap. A woman's sobs punctuated the stillness of the court.'[135]

The presence of women could attract adverse judicial comment. Judge Sheehy stated in the Circuit Court at Carrick-on-Shannon that it was disgusting to see so many women attending an indecent assault trial.[136] Women were sometimes instructed to leave the court, an approach taken by Judge McElligott at Ennis Circuit Court when, in the words of the *Nenagh Guardian*, 'a certain case was called'.[137] The fact that the newspaper could not bring itself to name the crime involved suggests that the case was sexual in nature, most likely homosexual. Justifying his expulsion of women, Judge McElligott stated that the day before 'there were a lot of women grinning and grimacing when there was a shocking case being heard.'[138]

WOMEN'S DRESS AND APPEARANCE

Newspaper reports of court cases often contained comments on the physical appearance of women, whether they were on trial, witnesses or members of the public. Sometimes headlines highlighted this issue, such as 'Well dressed woman pleads duress'.[139] On other occasions physical descriptions, including 'respectable looking', were contained in the text.[140] While examples can be found of similar descriptions of male accused persons and witnesses,[141] the physical appearance of women in court seemed to exercise a particular fascination, and extended to descriptions of female spectators. References to the 'presence of many well-dressed women in court'[142] and the 'lavish application of face powder and lipstick' by female onlookers bear this out.[143]

The question of whether women could be compelled to wear hats in court was discussed in the press, initially because judges in Northern Ireland and England stated that women must cover their heads.[144] Inevitably, the issue then arose in the twenty-six counties. District Justice Mangan believed that the covering of a woman's head was required when taking the oath.[145] The *Irish Independent* explained the rationale to its readers:

135 'Dublin death sentence', *Irish Times*, 8 Mar. 1937.
136 'Verdict of acquittal', *Anglo-Celt*, 2 Dec. 1933.
137 'Judge McElligott rebukes Ennis women', *Nenagh Guardian*, 14 Oct. 1933.
138 Ibid.
139 *Connacht Tribune*, 29 Sept. 1928.
140 Alleged brush larceny', *Roscommon Herald*, 30 Nov. 1940; 'Goats the cause of trouble', *Evening Echo*, 3 July 1953; 'Theft of rings from Dublin jewellers', *Dublin Evening Mail*, 24 Oct. 1932.
141 See, e.g., '£100 for one day at Omeath', *Dundalk Democrat*, 12 Sept. 1932.
142 'The missing postman', *Munster Express*, 7 Mar. 1930.
143 'A verdict of guilty', *Irish Independent*, 15 Nov. 1926.
144 'Women in court: order of lord chief justice of Belfast', *Evening Echo*, 26 Feb. 1931; 'Must women wear hats in court?', *Evening Herald*, 26 May 1939.
145 'Even fashion bows to the law!', *Irish Independent*, 18 Sept. 1943.

It was stated in legal circles that women should wear some form of headgear in court to show respect for the law, just as hats are deemed necessary for women in catholic churches as an outward sign of reverence to God. St. Paul, in one of his Epistles to the Corinthians, speaks of men praying to God with heads uncovered and women with heads covered to show reverence to the creator.[146]

On a subsequent occasion the same district justice asked a female witness if she had a hat to cover her head while taking the oath. When she said that she did not, he asked if she had a handkerchief. Receiving another reply in the negative, he instructed her to put a coat on her head.[147]

WOMEN IN CIVIL LITIGATION

Some of the most high-profile constitutional cases in the twentieth century were taken by female litigants. Gladys Ryan,[148] Mairín de Búrca,[149] Kathleen Byrne,[150] Johanna Airey,[151] Mary McGee[152] and Patricia McKenna[153] took cases which were extremely significant in the development of constitutional jurisprudence on fundamental rights, state liability and the separation of powers.[154] Marie O'Donoghue[155] and Kathryn Sinnott[156] sued the State on behalf of their children to establish the State's obligations to educate children with disabilities.[157]

146 Ibid.
147 'Coat as hat', *Evening Herald*, 22 Sept. 1944.
148 *Ryan v. Attorney General* [1965] IR 294.
149 *De Búrca and Anderson v. Attorney General* [1976] IR 38. Several years later, reflecting on her decision to take the case, Mairín de Búrca stated that while it was 'a fascinating experience', it was also difficult: 'It took five years of my life, and it was daunting.' Ivana Bacik and Mary Rogan (eds), *Legal cases that changed Ireland* (Dublin, 2016), p. 19.
150 *Byrne v. Ireland* [1972] IR 241.
151 *Airey v. Ireland* (1979) 2 EHRR 305.
152 *McGee v. The Attorney General* [1973] IR 284.
153 *McKenna v. An Taoiseach (No. 2)* [1995] 2 IR 10.
154 See Máiréad Enright, Julie McCandless and Aoife O'Donoghue, *Northern/Irish feminist judgments: judges' troubles and the gendered politics of identity* (Oxford, 2017) for alternative feminist judgments in relation to some of these cases.
155 *O'Donoghue v. Minister for Health* [1996] 2 IR 20.
156 *Sinnott v. Minister for Education* [2001] 2 IR 505.
157 Women were also involved in cases taken against Ireland at the European Court of Human Rights, including *Open Door and Dublin Well Woman v. Ireland* [1992] ECHR 68; *Airey v. Ireland* [1981] 3 EHRR 592, which led to the introduction of a scheme of civil legal aid and advice covering family-law matters; *A, B and C v. Ireland* (2011) 53 EHRR 13, which led to a legal and regulatory framework for establishing whether a woman satisfies the statutory conditions for an abortion in Ireland; and *O'Keeffe v. Ireland* [2014] 59 EHRR 15, which dealt with state liability for the sexual abuse of children in schools.

Aside from pushing the boundaries of constitutional rights and obligations, women were also involved in other kinds of civil litigation.[158] Some civil actions were notably gendered. Actions for breach of promise of marriage were taken until the abolition of this action in 1981.[159] Gendered civil litigation included the outdated 'crim con' or 'criminal conversation' action, which allowed a cuckolded husband to seek damages from his wife's lover.[160] The voice of the wife in such actions was notably absent. Urquhart charts the role of feminist groupings in campaigning for the abolition of this action,[161] which was proposed by the Law Reform Commission in 1980[162] and effected in 1981.[163]

CONCLUSION

The new Irish state envisaged almost no public role for women, and the courts system reflected that reality. The Courts of Justice Act was passed in the same year as legislation designed to end jury service by women. No female judges were appointed under the Act, even though female magistrates had been appointed prior to Independence. Describing official responses to inter-family violence and sexual abuse in the Free State, Earner-Byrne makes the point that there was 'an official insistence that there was no need for women in the justice system'.[164] Women were supposed to be at home, in accordance with Catholic social teaching. Nevertheless, women could not be completely prevented from interacting with the court system. Republican women were highly disruptive of court proceedings, especially in the first decade after Independence. When on trial they defied male authority and engaged in publicity-seeking behaviour. They also opposed the legal system in a more

---

158 E.g., Eileen Flynn sued the Sisters of the Holy Faith after being dismissed from her teaching post due to her relationship with a married man: *Flynn v. Power* [1985] IR 648. Marjorie O'Byrne took a case claiming that her late husband, as a judge, ought to have been exempted from paying income tax on his judicial salary: *O'Byrne v. Minister for Finance* [1959] IR 1.
159 Family Law Act 1981, s. 2. See Law Reform Commission, *Breach of promise of marriage* (LRC 4-1978) and Michael Sinnott, 'The action for breach of promise of marriage in nineteenth-century Ireland' in Howlin and Costello, *Law and the family*.
160 In one 1970s case, *Braun v. Roche*, Butler J commented that a wife was 'something that the husband owned', and that he ought to be compensated for her loss 'just as you would compensate him for a thoroughbred mare or cow.' *Irish Times*, 22 June 1972.
161 See Diane Urquhart, 'Ireland's criminal conversations', *Études Irlandaises*, 37:2 (2012), 65–80.
162 Law Reform Commission, *First Report on Family Law* (LRC 1-1980).
163 Family Law Act 1981, s. 1. See Niamh Howlin, 'Adultery in the courts: damages for criminal conversation in Ireland' in Howlin and Costello, *Law and the family*.
164 Lindsay Earner-Byrne, '"Behind closed doors": society, law and familial violence in Ireland, 1922–1990' in Howlin and Costello, *Law and the family*.

organised way, by intimidating juries. More generally, women appeared as accused persons and witnesses. Women also worked as clerks and probation officers. With the passage of time the roles they played increased in variety and status. They also attended trials as members of the public – an important dimension of their engagement with the administration of justice that has been overlooked to date.

CHAPTER NINETEEN

The Courts of Justice Act 1924 and the Irish language in the courtroom

ÚNA NÍ RAIFEARTAIGH* AND
RÓISÍN Á. COSTELLO**

The declaration by the Constitution that the national language of the Saorstát is the Irish language does not mean that the Irish language is, or was at that historical moment, universally spoken by the people of the Saorstát, which would be untrue in fact, but it did mean that it is the historic distinctive speech of the Irish people, that it is to rank as such in the nation, and, by implication, that the state is bound to do everything within its sphere of action (as for instance in state-provided education) to establish and maintain it in its status as the national language and to recognise it for all official purposes as the national language'

Kennedy CJ, *Ó'Foghludha v. McClean* [1934] IR 469

INTRODUCTION

Prior to Independence, the law and the legal system of Ireland were hostile to the Irish language. For several centuries, the exclusion of the Irish language from official settings by legislative measures that prohibited its use in those settings, coupled with a more general antipathy towards the language, resulted in a monolingual and Anglophone system of government. This status quo was maintained primarily by the Administration of Justice (Language) Act (Ireland) 1737,[1] which required the legal branch of the state to conduct its affairs in English only.[2] The result was that English was, in

---

* Judge of the European Court of Human Rights.
** Assistant professor of EU law, Trinity College Dublin; Barrister at Law.
1 11 Geo. II, c. 6.
2 This followed earlier efforts effected through the Statutes of Kilkenny (1366) and An Act for the English Order, Habit, and Language 1537 (28 Hen. VIII, c. 15) [Ir.]. For a brief overview of this history see Tony Crowley, 'Language, politics and identity in Ireland: a historical overview' in Ray Hickey (ed.), *Sociolinguistics in Ireland* (Basingstoke, 2016); Tony Crowley, *The politics of language in Ireland 1366–1922: a sourcebook* (Dublin, 2000). For an

effect, the sole official language of the state and of the law within the jurisdiction.³

In 1922, article 4 of the Constitution of the Irish Free State effected a significant, formal reversal of this position by elevating the Irish language to the position of the national, and one of the two official, languages of the state.⁴ The Constitution further provided, in article 42, that two copies of all laws were to be made: one in Irish and another in English. One of those copies was to be signed by the representative of the Crown in Ireland, and it was this signed copy that acted as conclusive evidence regarding the provisions of every such law in cases of dispute. The state thereby pronounced a constitutional commitment to a bilingual legal system, and one in which those wishing to use the Irish language would be as at home as those wishing to use the English language. This vision was continued by article 8 of the 1937 Constitution.

The first, and enduring, piece of legislation intended to impose some practical reality on this new constitutional landscape was the Courts of Justice Act 1924. However, the provisions of that Act were limited in scope and fell far short of providing a detailed, practical framework that would set the tone and provide the necessary scaffolding for the construction of a new system in which the Irish language would take its place within the courtrooms of the nation.

DRAFTING AND DEBATE

Given the high constitutional status of the Irish language in the new State, one of the most surprising features of the drafting of and debate on the Courts of Justice Act 1924 is how little the Irish language featured within them. The text of the Courts of Justice bill 1923 was initially introduced in

---

examination of the provision actually made for language rights in court, see Mary Phelan, *Irish speakers, interpreters and the courts, 1754–1921* (Dublin, 2019), pp 12–13.

3 The particular institutional view of the language during this period is typified by the judgment delivered by the King's Bench in Dublin in the 1906 decision in *Mac Giolla Bhríde v. Mac Gamhna (McBride v. McGovern)* [1906] 1 IR 181. This was, incidentally, one of only two cases in which Pádraig Pearse appeared as counsel, the other being *Buckley v. Finnegan* (1906) ILTR 76. See Ruairí Ó hAnluain, 'Tuairiscí speicialta 1980–1998' in *Tuairiscí Éireann/ The Irish Reports* (1999). On the carts litigation see also, Colum Kenny, 'Legible letters: the cases of Patrick Pearse and the "English" alphabet' in Adam Hanna and Eugene McNulty, *Law and literature: the Irish case* (Liverpool, 2022). For those interested in the well-known macaronic song based on the case see, Róisín Á. Costello, 'The Barbarian and the cart: law, citizenship and linguistic identity in Irish macaronic verse', *Law and Humanities* 15:2 (2021), 219.

4 On the position of the Irish language under the 1922 Constitution, see Róisín Á Costello, 'The National language and article 4 of the 1922 Constitution' in Laura Cahillane and Donal K. Coffey (eds), *The centenary of the Irish Free State Constitution* (London, 2024).

the second Dáil but was not passed, and was re-introduced in September 1923.[5] The bill referenced the Irish language only indirectly, with section five providing that the chief justice was alternatively titled 'chief justice of the Irish Free State' or 'príomh-bhreitheamh Saorstáit Éireann', and sections 36(v), 67 and 92 providing that the rules of the High, Circuit and District courts respectively could make provision for 'the use of the national language'.

On its re-introduction, President W.T. Cosgrave noted that the Act would represent 'a passing away of what might be called the old landmarks and the establishment of a new system ... to suit the needs of the country.'[6] Despite this, debate concerning the place and role of the national language remained piecemeal and sporadic throughout the legislative process. Major Bryan Cooper noted the need for paid stenographers at a circuit and an appellate level because of the unreliability of recorded testimony in cases where no official transcript existed.[7] If no paid stenographers were permitted, Cooper feared that Irish-speaking witnesses would be required, on appeal, to rely on judges' notes or other secondary records to prove the events of the trial, and could suffer a detriment as a result. Yet Cooper did not make any reference to the need for judges with a competence in Irish.[8] Indeed, it was only at the prompting of Attorney General Hugh Kennedy during consideration of section 91 of the bill that the matter of linguistic competence emerged – and even then only in the context of the need for the rule-making body for the District Court to include members who would 'have a knowledge of the language which is so largely used in a proportion of the country in which the courts are functioning'.[9] Despite this, no provision was made in the final text for Irish-speaking members of the body.

The text of the bill, as subsequently amended in committee, retained the references to Irish as introduced in the initial text, moving the relevant sections to 37(v), 68 and 93, but did not otherwise augment the legislative treatment of the language or make provision for Irish-speaking judges.[10] Deputy McGoldrick noted, in the context of an amendment in respect of the constitution of the rule making body of the District Court, that while the proposed amendments were welcome, they did not ensure that Irish-speaking judges would be appointed to the relevant districts. He remarked that,

> There is nothing that has given such satisfaction to the community ... as the appointment of district justices who have a knowledge of the Irish

5   *Dáil Éireann deb.*, vol. 5, col. 2 (20 Sept. 1923).
6   Ibid., W.T. Cosgrave.
7   Ibid., col. 7 (12 Oct. 1923).
8   Ibid.
9   Ibid., col. 9 (1 Nov. 1923).
10 See the remarks of the attorney general regarding amendment 21, ibid., col. 17 (4 Dec. 1923).

> language especially in counties and districts where Irish is the only language understood and spoken ... It is to be feared ... that there will not be the same advantages in this respect in the Circuit Courts. I would ask the Government to take good care when they are making appointments of Circuit Court judges ... in counties like Tírconaill, Galway and Kerry, all of which are Irish speaking counties, that the judges appointed will have a good knowledge of Irish and will be competent to deal with all cases which come into their courts.[11]

Despite this, the later text of the bill continued to omit any provision in respect of Irish-speaking judges. Instead, the bill retained a discretionary power to make court rules providing for the use of the language in sections 35(v), 64 and 88. A further addition was made in the final draft as passed by the Dáil in December: section 63 provided that the Circuit Court's rule-making committee would include at least two members with an 'adequate knowledge of the Irish language'.

Senator Patrick W. Kenny emphasised the risk of injustice where judges in Irish-speaking – and particularly western – districts were not Irish-speaking. He remarked that

> ... it is up to us to meet the just requirements of these people in the interest of justice, and also in the interest of the language. If the language is to make any definite progress in this country we must press into service the schools, the courts of law, the pulpit and the forum. These are the four great agencies, and now we have the opportunity in the reconstruction of these courts to press this point, and to ask the government to make some provision whereby this long-deferred want will be supplied to these unfortunate litigants in the predominantly Irish speaking districts in the West.[12]

The text of section 44 as it would eventually appear (concerning the appointment of Irish language competent Circuit Court judges to Gaeltacht areas) was proposed by the government as an amendment to the Act.[13] The Dáil subsequently approved that amendment, and sections 71 and 88 in respect of District Court judges and peace commissioners[14] appear in the final version of the Act, as it was passed on 3 April 1924.

---

11   Ibid.
12   *Seanad Éireann deb.*, vol. 2, no. 11 (16 Jan. 1924).
13   Ibid., no. 19 (5 Mar. 1924).
14   Ibid., vol. 6, no. 35 (22 Apr. 1924).

THE TEXT OF THE COURT OF JUSTICE ACT 1924

The resulting text of the 1924 Act thus provided for the integration of the Irish language into courtroom settings through three provisions – in sections 44, 71 and 88(2) provided that any Circuit or District Court judge or peace commissioner (respectively) 'shall, so far as may be practicable having regard to all relevant circumstances', possess sufficient knowledge of Irish to enable them to consider disputes before them without an interpreter. It may be noted that these provisions applied, and continue to apply, only to areas 'where the Irish language is in general use' and were therefore very limited in scope: effectively restricted to Gaeltacht areas.

Beyond these provisions, section 36(v) provided that rules could be made in respect of the use of the national language including for the High Court and Court of Criminal Appeal, while section 65 provided for Irish-speaking members of the Circuit Court's rule making body, and section 66 provided that Circuit Court Rules should be made regarding the use of the Irish language.[15] This latter requirement was mirrored in section 91 in respect of the use of Irish in the District Court.[16]

Subsequent to these provisions, order 29 of the Rules of the High Court and Supreme Court 1926 required that official interpreters for both courts could be appointed, and summonses and notices served in the Gaeltacht were to be provided in Irish translation if the original was in English while the same documents served elsewhere were to be provided in English translation if the original was in Irish.[17] Order 1, rule 4 of the Circuit Court Rules 1928 similarly provided that 'either the national language or the English language may be used in the proceedings in the court'.

The effect of these provisions, read in light of article 4 of the 1922 Constitution, was positive for the Irish language insofar as it sought to effect some practical accommodation of Irish speakers in courtroom settings in contradistinction to the position prior to the Act.[18] However, the scope of the provisions was limited. For example, nothing was said about the use of the Irish language generally by a litigant in a courtroom (including courtrooms outside the Gaeltacht), nor was there any mention of connected practicalities such as interpretation. The Act also made no mention of the translation of written sources of law and neither the 1924 Act nor the rules of court provided that any proportion of judges appointed be able to speak or understand Irish. Indeed, it is also noteworthy that the Act did not contain any general statement of the basic right to conduct one's side of the case in

---

15 On the drafting of the Circuit Court Rules more generally see Kevin Costello's chapter.
16 Now supplemented by Courts (Supplemental Provisions) Act 1961, s. 52(1).
17 Leo Kohn, *The Constitution of the Irish Free State* (London, 1932), p. 25.
18 See Phelan, *Irish speakers*.

Irish. These, as we shall see, proved to be significant omissions, and formed the basis of litigation during the following century.

While the 1937 Constitution subsequently replaced the provisions of articles 4 and 42 with articles 8 and 25.5, the 1924 Act's provisions were not supplemented until the Official Languages Act entered into force in 2003. One has only to contrast the detailed provisions of current Official Languages legislation[19] with the spartan provisions in the 1924 Act to see how limited the Act was in terms of providing support for the Irish language.

The framework provided by the 2003 and 2021 legislation covers such important matters as the use of the official languages in the houses of the Oireachtas, the translation of Acts of the Oireachtas, the use of the Irish language in the courts (including the matter of interpretation), duties placed on public bodies with regard to the use of the Irish language (including advertising and publication of certain documents), and the establishment of the office of An Coimisinéir Teanga. The stark contrast between the detailed provisions of the 2003 and 2021 Acts and the limited provisions in the 1924 Act points out eloquently the scant attention paid to the Irish language by the latter.

It is perhaps surprising that so little in the way of support for the Irish language found its way into the 1924 Act. Hugh Kennedy, then attorney general and later to become chief justice, was the son of a native Irish speaker from Donegal and himself a strong proponent of the language and its place within the institutions of the new state, going so far as to hope that with the formation of the new system the time had come when, at last, 'the voice of the Gael' would be heard in Irish courts.[20]

Kennedy made vigorous attempts to author and/or support a series of foundational legal texts in bilingual format,[21] as well as to make the Irish language compulsory for members of the Bar (through attempts to change the rules of admission to the King's Inns,[22] and later the Legal Practitioners

19   Official Languages Act 2003 as amended by s. 62 of the Civil Law (Miscellaneous Provisions) Act 2011 and the Environment (Miscellaneous Provisions) Act 2011, s. 48; Official Languages (Amendment) Act 2021; SI 312/2002 Official Languages Act 2003 (Establishment Day) Order 2022; SI 313/2002 Official Languages (Amendment) (Commencement) Order 2022; SI 511/2022 Official Languages (Amendment) Act 2021 (Commencement) (No. 2) Order 2022; SI 90/2023 Official Languages (Amendment) Act 2021 (Commencement) Order 2023.
20   On Kennedy's attempts to shape a new, distinctively Irish system of justice following independence see Ronan Keane, 'The voice of the Gael: Chief Justice Kennedy and the emergence of the new Irish court system 1921–1936', *Irish Jurist*, 31:1 (1996), 205–25. On Kennedy's attempts to foster an academic and legal literary culture which advanced these aims see, Thomas Mohr, 'The influence of Chief Justice Hugh Kennedy on Irish legal scholarship and publishing', *Irish Jurist*, 64 (2020), 97–137.
21   Mohr, 'The influence of Chief Justice Hugh Kennedy', at 127.
22   In Oct. 1925, for example, Kennedy proposed that a sub-committee of the King's Inns benchers be established to consider what changes to the rules of admission would be

Qualification Act 1929). But these had little impact on the institutions that they sought to change. Subsequent efforts after his death, such as the creation of the Irish Legal Terms Advisory Committee by the Irish Legal Terms Act 1945, fell similarly flat[23] despite the need for a vocabulary of legal technical terms in the Irish language as identified in Kennedy CJ's own judgment in *O'Foghludha v. McClean*.[24]

There was, therefore, some degree of commitment in the 1924 Act to supporting the Irish language, but it was not accompanied by any detailed legislative commitment to building the linguistic and human resources necessary for ensuring that the constitutional and political aspirations that contextualised the Act could be secured. Indeed, the limitation of sections 44 and 71 of the Act by reference to efforts being made 'so far as may be practicable having regard to all relevant circumstances' could be read as a recognition of this failure, and the same provisions have continued to limit the capacity of courts, including in Gaeltacht areas, to operate in a manner that facilitates Irish speakers on a more proactive basis.

THE CASE LAW FOLLOWING THE 1924 ACT

Given the limited nature of the 1924 Act's provisions concerning the Irish language, it is perhaps not surprising that the courts tended to draw greater strength from the constitutional provisions than from the Act when seeking to support the Irish language. Thus, in *Attorney General v. Joyce and Walsh*,[25] the Court of Criminal Appeal emphasised the special position of the Irish language and remarked that those who had given evidence through the Irish language had 'a double right to do so: first on general principles of natural justice as their vernacular language; and secondly, as a matter of constitutional right'.[26] The court's distinction between the two different rationales for their conclusion may be noted.

required so that 'no one should be admitted to the degree of Barrister-at-Law without possessing a competent knowledge of the Irish language, Irish history and of the constitution and government of Ireland', Benchers of the King's Inns, Minutes for 1925.

23 Note that SI 130/1961, Rules of the High Court and Supreme Court mode of address rules provided that the judges of the Supreme Court, the High Court (including the Central Criminal Court) and the Court of Criminal Appeal may be referred to in Irish as 'an Chúirt' or in English as 'the court'. This repealed order 30, rule 1 of the 1926 Rules which had provided that every Judge of the Supreme Court and the High Court may be addressed therein in the manner at present in use, or by the Irish equivalent thereto.

24 These remarks concluded with the memorable sentence: 'We are particularly rich in legal literature in the Irish language, and a committee of competent lawyers with the assistance of scholars should be able to produce a genuine Irish legal vocabulary without resorting to the tying of Gaelic tails to English heads'.

25 [1929] IR 526.

26 Ibid., at 581.

In *Ó'Foghludha v. McClean*,[27] Kennedy CJ remarked that the declaration in the 1922 Constitution to the effect that the Irish language was the national language of the State did not mean that it was 'at that historical moment, universally spoken by the people' but that it was 'the historic distinctive speech of the Irish people' and was 'to rank as such in the nation'.[28] The chief justice found that the State was therefore bound to do 'everything within its sphere of action to establish and maintain it in its status as the national language.'[29] Other remarks of Kennedy CJ's in the judgment seem to indicate a hope and indeed an expectation that the State was strongly committed to realising a bilingual legal system and that such a future was not only imminent but in some manner inevitable.

This was not to be. While the statements of Kennedy CJ in *Ó'Foghludha v. McClean* constituted powerful expressions of support for the language, in keeping with the chief justice's attitude to the language more generally, the jurisprudence that followed illustrated repeated instances of the State authorities falling short of doing 'everything within their sphere of action' to establish and maintain the Irish language within the courts and the legal system more generally. Throughout the twentieth century and even today, the Irish language was not, and is not, used regularly within the Irish legal system.

Further, it is arguable that the absence of a detailed legislative framework, leaving the courts to fall back on the rather open-textured nature of article 8 which was open to differing interpretations, hindered the development of a consistent and coherent set of principles in this area. A full discussion of the case law is not possible in this context and we merely highlight some of the

---

27 [1934] IR 469.
28 Ibid., at 493.
29 Ibid. The outcome of the case was unfavourable to Connradh na Gaedhilge (as it was spelled in the judgment). The court held that order 30, rule 1 of the 1926 Rules of the Superior Courts was not incompatible with the Constitution insofar as it required an originating summons in the Irish language to be accompanied by an English language translation (whether prepared by the plaintiff or prepared officially in the Central Office). Kennedy CJ said that 'the hard fact remains, and must of stern necessity remain at least for a generation, that of the adult population a number, decreasing as time goes on but even still perhaps a majority, not because of perversity nor of their own fault (because they did not prescribe the course of their own education), is unable to read or understand a summons or notice written only in the Irish language, or to glean from it that something is required on the part of the person served within a limited number of days at the risk of certain consequences in default.' As long as this 'hard fact' subsisted, natural justice imposed a duty on the rule-making authority, a duty to make special provision for this fact. Otherwise, the service would amount in effect to serving 'an envelope which the person served is quite unable to open'. The Rules of the District Court did not refer to the use of Irish in court forms and documents, a point which was relied upon by the High Court (O'Hanlon J) in *An Stát (MacFhearraigh) v. Breitheamh Dúiche Neilan* [1984] IRSR 38 in reaching a conclusion adverse to an individual in the Gaeltacht area of An Fál Carrach who had received an English language summons in a road traffic case and claimed his constitutional rights had been violated on that ground.

leading cases with respect to two significant issues: (1) the translation of sources of Irish law into the Irish language; and (2) the use of the Irish language in the courtroom.[30]

TRANSLATION OF SOURCES OF LAW

To take one example, regarding the most basic of matters, during the twentieth century the translation of legal sources fell into a state of serious neglect. While the practice of publishing Irish-language versions of Acts of the Oireachtas persisted until about 1980, it changed in the early years of that decade and publication largely occurred in the English language alone from that point,[31] generating an increasing number of cases that focused on the state's failure to translate various sources of law.

In *Ó'Beoláin v. Fahy*,[32] the Supreme Court granted a declaration regarding the translation of certain Road Traffic Acts and District Court Rules. The majority judgments of McGuinness and Hardiman JJ were highly critical of the state's neglect of its constitutional duty to translate legislation into Irish. McGuinness J, in particular, stated it was 'clear that the state is simply unwilling to provide the resources to fulfil its clear constitutional duty' and that 'the state has been flagrantly and over a long period of time in breach of this constitutional duty.'[33] Hardiman J delivered a characteristically trenchant judgment in the case, containing strong statements concerning the need to ensure that persons desirous of using the Irish language as a means of communication should not be precluded from, or disadvantaged in, so doing in any national or official context.[34]

In a blistering condemnation of the state's inaction, Hardiman J noted the state's 'failure to provide the most basic materials ... [which was] at its grossest in the most recent times' and condemned some of the arguments made by the State in the case as 'unworthy.'[35] In a section of his judgment entitled 'Effective official neglect' Hardiman J said that the case established that 'a situation has developed over a period of twenty years or so in which

---

30 For more detailed treatments of the case law, see Mark de Blacam, 'Official language and constitutional interpretation', *Irish Jurist*, 52:2 (2014), 90–114; Daithí MacCarthaigh, *An Ghaeilge sa Dlí* (Dublin, 2020); S. Ó Tuathail, *Gaeilge agus an Bunreacht* (Baile Átha Cliath, 2002); Seán O'Conaill, 'The Irish language and the Irish legal system, 1922 to present' (PhD, University of Cardiff, 2013); Niamh Nic Shuibhne, 'State duty and the Irish language', *Dublin University Law Journal*, 19 (1997), 32–49.
31 See Hardiman J in *Ó'Beoláin v. Fahy* [2001] 2 IR 279, at 324.
32 [2001] 2 IR 279.
33 Ibid., at 308.
34 Ibid., at 311 onwards.
35 Ibid., at 346. See also his comment that 'the State has taken up some positions which are narrow, legalistic, petty fogging and reductionist'.

important legal materials have been provided in Irish only haphazardly and in many cases in response to litigation or threats of litigation', which meant that 'only a person of unusual independence of mind and pertinacity will attempt to conduct his or her legal business through the medium of Irish.'[36] The judge went on to note that it was 'no wonder that the Irish language and Irish speakers have made little progress in the routine use of the national language in the courts'.[37]

Despite the subsequent enactment of the Official Language Act 2003, the state's commitment to the Irish language continued to be challenged – in particular the state's failure to translate statutory instruments into Irish.[38] In *Delap v. Minister for Justice*,[39] a declaration had been granted that an Irish translation of the Rules of the Superior Courts should be provided. However, O'Hanlon J did not base this decision on article 8 but rather on rights derived from articles 34 and 40.

In *Ó'Murchú v. An Taoiseach*[40] this reasoning was followed and it was held that the scope of the obligation in article 25.4.4 did not extend to statutory instruments. Nonetheless the court granted a declaration that there was a constitutional duty to provide this particular applicant with all of the rules of court in Irish because the absence of these 'constitute an impediment on a solicitor ... having a significant clientele wishing to undertake their legal affairs in Irish'. As in *Delap*, this was derived from articles 34 and 40 rather than articles 8 or 25. More recently, in the *Glann Mór Céibh Teoranta v. Minister for Housing*,[41] the Supreme Court confirmed there was no general obligation to translate statutory instruments, save for those instruments made pursuant to section 3 of the European Communities Act 1972. It is notable that Hogan J in his judgment remarked that, as of the date of the case, approximately 450 Acts were awaiting translation, which he equated to approximately ten years of arrears. He described the situation as one of 'anxious concern' and referred to 'manifest non-compliance by the state with an express constitutional obligation.'[42]

36 Ibid., at 349.
37 Ibid., at 350. O'Conaill has described the decision in *O'Beoláin* as the 'high water-mark' of the jurisprudence concerning the Irish language and some of the subsequent jurisprudence as containing unduly restrictive interpretations of art. 8 and creating an indefensible distinction between the right to present one's case in court in Irish and having access to the necessary legal tools to do so. See O'Conaill, *The Irish language and the Irish legal system*, ch. 3. He describes the further development of language rights as having been 'halted' by the judiciary, although it may be noted that the dissertation was written some ten years ago.
38 Interestingly, in the *DPP v. Billings* [2019] IECA 149 case (see below), the Court of Appeal held that the Explosive Substances Act 1883, as a pre-Independence statute, did not fall within the constitutional translation obligation.
39 [1990] IRSR 116.
40 [2010] 4 IR 484.
41 [2022] IESC 40.
42 Ibid., at para. 61.

The remarks of Hogan J in *Glann Mór Céibh Teoranta* demonstrate clearly that the state faces significant practical problems in providing Irish language translations of Acts of the Oireachtas. Nor is the backlog being helped by the increasing trend of Irish-proficient lawyers to seek work as lawyer-linguists within the institutions of the European Union, rather than in domestic institutions or roles. The provision of Irish-language translation of statutory instruments – that is not encompassed within the general constitutional obligation which applies to legislation – would only add further to this burden.

This is not to say that such translations should not be made available but to highlight the practical difficulties in making a more linguistically integrated legal service, and judicial branch, a reality in Ireland a century after the 1924 Act entered into force. The opportunity presented by the 1924 Act was not capitalised on early in the history of the state, and the decisions that followed in the intervening century have shone sporadic light on how much ground has been lost by failing to make incremental advances through clear legislative provision in that period.

Other cases concerning the translation of documents connected with court proceedings have generally been unsuccessful.[43] Perhaps most strikingly, in a case with echoes of *O'Foghludha*, the High Court in *MacAodháin v. Coiste Rialacha na nUaschúirteanna* held that order 120(2) and (3) of the Rules of the Superior Courts (concerning the different translation requirements in respect of English and Irish versions of any summons, petition or notice) were neither unconstitutional nor in breach of section 8(6) of the 2003 Act.[44]

IRISH LANGUAGE HEARINGS IN COURT

In perhaps the first significant language rights case following the passage of the 1924 Act, *R (Ó'Coileáin) v. Crotty*,[45] the appellant had been charged with an offence contrary to the Finance (New Duties) Act 1916 and sought to give evidence in his defence and to conduct all cross-examination of witnesses through Irish. Crotty J, in the Circuit Court, found that none of those appearing in support of the prosecution spoke Irish, and while it appeared the judge himself could speak and understand Irish, did not consider it proper to act as interpreter. As the accused declined to use English, he did not present a defence, and was fined £50, which fine he appealed.

---

43 See *Ó Gribín v. An Comhairle Mhúinteoireachta* [2007] IEHC 454 (translation of an official report concerning the establishment of the Teaching Council); *Ó Gríofáin v. Éire* [2009] IEHC 199 (translation of a printout from intoxyliser machine in a 'drunk driving' case); *DPP v. Avadenei* [2018] 3 IR 215; *O'Conaire v. MacGruairc* [2010] 3 IR 30 (translation of witness statements in a 'drunk driving' case).
44 *MacAodháin v. Coiste Rialacha na nUaschúirteanna* [2010] 2 IR 678.
45 (1927) 61 ILTR 81.

O'Sullivan P in the High Court quashed the fine and confirmed that the defendant enjoyed a constitutional right to conduct his case in Irish under article 4 which had been disregarded by the trial judge. While the decision does not cast any great light on the scope of the 1924 Act as interpreted by the courts, it does offer an insight into the position of Irish speakers in the Saorstát, as a constitutionally protected but practically overlooked group.[46] The principle established in *Ó'Coileáin* and reiterated since is that in both judicial and quasi-judicial settings[47] a person is entitled to conduct their side of a case in the Irish language, but cannot deprive any other party of their right to conduct their portion of proceedings in English.[48] Interestingly, this basic principle had never been set out in the 1924 Act.

The right to conduct one's own side of the case in the Irish language is one thing; but having a decision-maker (judge or jury) who understands that part of the case in Irish directly and without the aid of an interpreter is another. It was in the two decisions of *Ó'Monacháin v. An Taoiseach*[49] and *Ó'Cadhla v. An tAire Dlí agus Cirt*[50] that the 1924 Act, and its relevance for Irish-language hearings came before the courts for specific consideration in this context. Both cases concerned the assignment of a district judge with sufficient proficiency in the Irish language as to be capable of hearing the trial of a summary criminal offence (in which all or part of the evidence would be given in the Irish language) without the assistance of an interpreter. In *Ó'Monacháin*, reliance was placed on section 71 of the 1924 Act, whereas in *Ó'Cadhla*, the applicant relied directly on article 8 of the Constitution.

The plaintiff in *Ó'Monacháin* had been found guilty, twice, in the Donegal District Court in respect of planning offences. During the trial of both offences the relevant district judges relied on an interpreter in court. The plaintiff appealed the findings of both judges and in doing so queried whether section 71 of the 1924 Act placed an absolute obligation on the minister to appoint an Irish speaking Judge to those districts where the language was in general use, and in addition whether it obliged a district judge to hear a case through Irish without the assistance of an interpreter. The court in *Ó'Monacháin* found the obligation in respect of appointment under section 71 was not absolute but bound the minister 'only insofar as is practicable' and that no party had the power to compel a judge to hear an entire case in Irish. The latter point was the subject of some critical comment in *Ó'Cadhla*, on the basis that the applicant in *Ó'Monacháin* had never sought an entirely Irish-language hearing.

---

46 See also, *State (Buchan) v. Coyne* 70 ILTR 185 (1936).
47 In *An Stát (MacFhearraigh) v. MacGamhna* [1998] IRSR 29, the High Court (O'Hanlon J) held that the right to conduct one's side of the case in the Irish language applied to proceedings before the Employment Appeals Tribunal.
48 *Ó'Griofain v. Éire* [2009] IEHC 188; *Ó Beoláin v. Fahy* [2001] 2 IR 279, 343.
49 [1986] ILRM 660.
50 [2019] IEHC 503.

In any event, it appears to have been common practice to assign a bilingual district judge to hear a case in which a litigant wished to conduct his or her part of the case in Irish where this was possible, and indeed, there was affidavit evidence from solicitors in Donegal, Galway and Dublin to this effect in *Ó'Cadhla*. This may be why there are few reported decisions on section 71 of the 1924 Act. The availability of bilingual judges was not, however, due to any formal or institutional training or support. If judges had sufficient proficiency in the Irish language to conduct cases in that language, it was because of their upbringing or personal interest. Interestingly, in *Ó'Cadhla*, the state argued that while there was a practice of nominating bilingual judges, this was not underpinned by any constitutional obligation, and produced evidence that the practice was not invariable and that sometimes interpreters were used instead.

In *Ó'Cadhla*, the district judge before whom the case had first come dismissed the idea of sending the case to a bilingual judge, stating, in effect, that he knew the applicant and that the latter spoke English. The High Court (Ní Raifeartaigh J) held that the state had a constitutional duty to make reasonable efforts to find a bilingual judge, and that it was not sufficient for the district judge to dismiss the application for a bilingual judge summarily on the basis that the applicant understood English. There was no appeal from the decision of the High Court in *Ó'Cadhla* and therefore neither the Court of Appeal nor the Supreme Court have confirmed whether or not the High Court was correct in its criticisms of *Ó'Monacháin* or in its constitutional analysis more generally. The analysis in *Ó'Cadhla* sought to contrast 'due process' issues (under article 38 of the Constitution) with 'language right' issues (under article 8), and to tease out some of the issues concerning Irish language in the courtroom which are apt to be conflated and confused.

Finally, the issue of the availability of an Irish-language jury in criminal cases came to the fore in *MacCarthaigh v. Éire*[51] and *Ó'Maicín v. Éire*,[52] which latter case arguably contains the most significant modern judicial discussion of issues relating to the Irish language.[53] In *Ó'Maicín* the majority found that the applicant was not entitled to a bilingual jury, in the context of a Gaeltacht-based case, noting that any language right arising from article 8 was to be balanced against the constitutional imperative of a representative jury, and finding that this representative aspect could not presently be achieved in view of the statistics before the court outlining the number of Irish speakers in the relevant geographical area.

Hardiman J's dissent in *Ó'Maicín* was notable for its strong emphasis of the State having been constituted on the basis of a constitutionally enshrined

---

51 [1999] IR 200.
52 [2014] 4 IR 583.
53 For a discussion of the case, and the right to an Irish speaking jury see, Dáithí Mac Cárthaigh and Seán Ó'Conaill, 'Aguisíní le breithiúnas Hardiman BRMH in *Ó'Maicín v. Éire*', *Irish Judicial Studies Journal*, 2 (2020), 148.

policy of bilingualism as part of which article 8 obliged the courts to treat Irish as the national and first official language not only in aspirational terms but as a matter of fact. The dissent, authored some 90 years after the 1924 Act, and 80 years after the remarks of Kennedy CJ in *Ó'Foghluadha,* is striking for its exposition of the basic failures of the legal system of the independent Irish state – of which the 1924 Act was intended to serve as a lynchpin – to advance a truly bilingual state, or, at least, to secure for Irish speakers the practical guarantees of their constitutional rights in their interactions with the legal system.

THE FUTURE OF 'THE DISTINCTIVE SPEECH OF THE PEOPLE'

Section 71 and other provisions of the 1924 Act were intended to provide some degree of legislative underpinning for the constitutional status of the Irish language in the Free State Constitution. However, the provisions themselves were limited in both scope and content. This, no doubt in combination with other factors on the ground, led to a situation where the quotidian position was that the Irish language remained isolated and unsupported. Indeed, the century since the passage of the Courts of Justice Act 1924 has witnessed a steady accumulation of precedents which illustrate, to a greater or lesser extent, the unfulfilled promise of the 1924 Act and the absence of any institutional build-out to achieve even its minimal undertakings in respect of Irish speaking judges at a local level.

From the Irish-language point of view, the 1924 Act lacked detail and its key guarantees were heavily qualified, so that its impact on advancing the use of the language within the legal system was minimal. Developments in the twenty-first century have given more cause to be optimistic about the future of the Irish language within the legal system.

The Official Languages legislation is much broader in scope than the 1924 Act. In addition to the provisions noted earlier, public bodies are under a statutory duty to provide a scheme detailing the service they will provide through Irish. The fourth such scheme has been produced by the Court Service and features on its website, and the Attorney General's Office has similarly produced a scheme.

The influence of the European Union's recognition of Irish as an official language[54] has also done much to re-centre Irish as a language of the law. A

---

54 Irish has been a Treaty language of the European Union since 1973. In 2007, at the request of the Irish government, Irish became an official and working language of the European Union, with a derogation which provided that Ireland was to gradually phase in the translation required by this status over time. This derogation ended on 1 January 2022. The European Commission, in a report from 2021, confirmed sufficient resources across the Union's institutions to provide for comprehensive translation into and from Irish. See,

number of university and professional training courses have been created, with the aim of producing bilingual lawyers.[55] The work of the next century may be to continue this development towards an integrated, bilingual legal system as foreseen by the Constitution, with timely translations of important sources of law, and a sufficient number of legal practitioners, judges and court personnel fluent in Irish to accommodate those who wish to conduct their legal business through the Irish language. In other words, that the State will do everything within its sphere of action to realise the constitutional aspirations for the language, as explained and articulated by Kennedy CJ ninety years ago.

Report from the Commission to the Council on whether the Union institutions have sufficient available capacity for the Irish language: COM/2021/315 (21 June 2021).

[55] At present, Clár na Gaeilge / The Irish Language Register, maintained by the King's Inns pursuant to the Legal Practitioners (Irish Language) Act 2008 and which records those barristers competent to practise through Irish, lists fifty seven barristers. However, there is no requirement to be registered in order to practise through the medium of Irish. The Law Society of Ireland also maintains a Clár na Gaeilge / The Irish Language Register pursuant to the same legislation and lists 238 solicitors though, similarly, there is no requirement to be registered in order to practise through the medium of Irish. The King's Inns provides an Advanced Diploma in Lawyer-Linguistics and Legal Translation, and an Advanced Diploma in Legal Practice through Irish. Some universities provides options to study law with Irish; UCD (Law with Irish, commenced 2017); UCC (Law and Irish, commenced 1999) and an MA in Irish Language and European Law; UCG (Specialist Stream in Legal Irish as part of the BCL); UL (Bachelor of Laws (Law Plus), commenced 2007); Maynooth (BCL in Law and Arts, commenced 2016).

CHAPTER TWENTY

Section 29 of the Courts of Justice Act 1924 and the certification process: a long-lasting legacy

HILARY BIEHLER*

INTRODUCTION

Section 29 of the Courts of Justice Act 1924 regulated the circumstances in which an appeal might be taken from the Court of Criminal Appeal to the Supreme Court. Although this provision has been repealed[1] and the former court has been replaced by the Court of Appeal, the legacy of the certification process remains. The principle that the Supreme Court,[2] and now the Court of Appeal,[3] only have appellate jurisdiction 'subject to such regulations as may be prescribed by law' is a consistent one having been enshrined in the Constitution of Saorstát Éireann 1922 and the Constitution of Ireland 1937. However, the mechanism for regulating the bringing of such appeals set out in section 29 of the Courts of Justice Act 1924 has also had an enduring legacy. It has provided the template for similar schemes in other legislation enacted over the last century and many of the principles which developed in interpreting its provisions have been applied in a variety of contexts. The process of certification of appeals where the issues at stake are of public importance and it is in the interests of justice that they be heard also now forms the basis for the jurisdiction of the Supreme Court in so-called 'leapfrog' appeals pursuant to article 34.5.4° of the Constitution. Section 29 can, therefore, be characterised as having had a long-lasting legacy a century after the enactment of the Courts of Justice Act 1924.

---

* Professor of public law at the Law School of Trinity College Dublin.
1 Court of Appeal Act 2014, s. 1(2), s. 73 and sch. 1.
2 Constitution of Ireland 1937, art. 34.5.3° and art. 34.5.4°.
3 See art. 34.4.1°.

CONSTITUTIONAL ARCHITECTURE GOVERNING APPEALS

Article 66 of the 1922 Constitution provided that the Supreme Court of Saorstát Éireann 'shall, with such exceptions (not including cases which involve questions as to the validity of any law) and subject to such regulations as may be prescribed by law, have appellate jurisdiction from all decisions of the High Court.' Article 34.4.1° of the 1937 Constitution now provides[4] that the Court of Appeal shall, 'with such exceptions and subject to such regulations as may be prescribed by law, have appellate jurisdiction from all decisions of the High Court'.[5] So, as was explained in the Supreme Court determination in *Fox v. Mahon*,[6] '[t]he main consequence of the 33rd amendment to the Constitution which brought about that change is that the fundamental right of appeal from the High Court is now to be found in an appeal to the Court of Appeal.'[7] More specifically, where a limitation was set out in legislation in respect of an appeal to the Supreme Court, this limitation now applies to the equivalent appeal to the Court of Appeal unless the context otherwise requires.[8] The changes effected by the 33rd amendment also mean that the appellate jurisdiction of the Supreme Court, in addition to being subject to such regulations as may be prescribed by law, now only applies in relation to decisions made by the Court of Appeal and the High Court where the criteria as set out in the provisions of article 34.5.3° and article 34.5.4° respectively, considered below, are met.

THE CERTIFICATION MECHANISM SET OUT IN SECTION 29 OF THE COURT OF JUSTICE ACT 1924

Section 29 of the Courts of Justice Act 1924 as originally enacted provided that:

> The determination by the Court of Criminal Appeal of any appeal or other matter which it has power to determine shall be final, and no appeal shall lie from that court to the Supreme Court, unless that court or the Attorney-General shall certify that the decision involves a point of law of exceptional public importance and that it is desirable in the public interest that an appeal shall be taken to the Supreme Court, in

---

4 This replaces art. 34.4.3° in its original wording.
5 It should also be noted that art. 34.4.2° and art. 34.5.5° provide that no law can be enacted excepting from the appellate jurisdiction of the Court of Appeal and Supreme Court respectively cases which involve questions as to the validity of any law having regard to the provisions of the Constitution.
6 [2015] IESCDET 2 at para. 12.
7 Court of Appeal Act 2014, s. 74(1), s. 74(3) and sch. 2.
8 Ibid., s. 75(b). See also *Grace v. Bord Pleanála* [2020] 3 IR 286, 293–4.

which case an appeal may be brought to the Supreme Court, the decision of which shall be final and conclusive.

Perhaps the most important case in which section 29[9] has been considered is *People (AG) v. Conmey*,[10] in which Walsh J set out the now well established 'clear and unambiguous' principle. He expressed the view that 'any statutory provision which had as its object the excepting of some decisions of the High Court from the appellate jurisdiction of [the Supreme] Court, or any particular provision seeking to confine the scope of such appeals within particular limits, would of necessity have to be clear and unambiguous.' He added that the appellate jurisdiction of the Supreme Court from decisions of the High Court flowed directly from the constitution and that any diminution of that jurisdiction 'would be a matter of such great importance that it would have to be shown to fall clearly within the provisions of the Constitution and within the limitations imposed by the Constitution upon any such legislative action.'[11]

A number of significant other points of interpretation relating to section 29 were established over the years which have also been applied to subsequent legislation containing similar certification mechanisms. These include that the appellate court had no jurisdiction to grant a certificate,[12] that the onus was on the appellant to establish that there is a point of law of exceptional public importance and that it is desirable in the public interest that an appeal be taken to the appellate court[13] and that it 'should give as much assistance as possible in clarifying the law and should not regard itself as imprisoned within the particular facts upon which the point referred is first raised.'[14] However, while section 29 has been interpreted as not limiting the appellate court to consideration of the issue or issues certified by the court below,[15] this principle has not been universally applied in other statutory schemes.

APPLICATION TO OTHER STATUTORY SCHEMES

The certification process set out in section 29 of the 1924 Act formed a template for similar provisions in a number of other statutory schemes, many of which regulate the availability of judicial review proceedings. These schemes involve the regulation of appellate jurisdiction from decisions of the

9 As re-enacted by the Courts (Supplemental Provisions) Act 1961, s. 48.
10 [1975] IR 341, at 360.
11 Ibid.
12 *Attorney General v. Murray (No. 2)* [1926] IR 300, at 301.
13 *People (DPP) v. Littlejohn* [1978] ILRM 147, at 148.
14 *People (DPP) v. Lynch* [1982] IR 64, at 78.
15 *People (AG) v. Giles* [1974] IR 422, 429. *People (DPP) v. Shaw* [1982] IR 1, at 48.

High Court by legislation which provides that no appeal shall lie, formerly to the Supreme Court, and now to the Court of Appeal, except where a decision is certified as involving a point of law of exceptional public importance and where it is desirable in the public interest that an appeal be taken. Reflecting the earlier jurisprudence relating to s.29,[16] it was made clear by the Supreme Court in *Irish Asphalt Ltd v. An Bord Pleanála*[17] that the High Court alone has power to issue such a certificate and so the Court of Appeal has no jurisdiction to hear an appeal from a refusal to grant one. Therefore, if a certificate is not obtained in the High Court, it cannot be granted and any attempted appeal cannot be entertained by the appellate court.[18]

The schemes that have been most frequently used in practice relate to planning and immigration law and are contained in sections 50 and 50A of the Planning and Development Act 2000[19] and section 5 of the Illegal Immigrants (Trafficking) Act 2000[20] respectively. As Fennelly J noted in *Clinton v. An Bord Pleanála*,[21] the provisions limiting the appellate jurisdiction found in these schemes are in virtually identical terms to that contained in section 29 of the 1924 Act and similar principles apply.

Some differences in approach are noteworthy, for example, in relation to whether the appellate court is limited to considering the issues certified by the court below. In the context of the certification mechanism contained in section 5(3) of the Illegal Immigrants (Trafficking) Act 2000, it has been held that once a point of exceptional public importance is certified for appeal pursuant to that section, the appellant is not confined to arguing only that point.[22] The position in relation to the planning scheme of statutory judicial review has evolved over time. In *Clinton v. An Bord Pleanála*,[23] in which the Supreme Court had to examine the scope of an appeal brought pursuant to section 50(4)(f) of the Planning and Development Act 2000,[24] Denham J

16 *Attorney General v. Murray (No. 2)* [1926] IR 300, at 301.
17 [1996] 2 IR 179. See also *Irish Hardware Ltd v. South Dublin County Council* [2001] 2 ILRM 291.
18 See *Minister for Justice, Equality and Law Reform v. Adach* [2010] 3 IR 402.
19 As amended by the Planning and Development (Strategic Infrastructure) Act 2006, s. 13; the Planning and Development (Amendment) Act 2010, s. 32 and the Environment (Miscellaneous Provisions) Act 2011, s. 21.
20 As amended by the Employment Permits (Amendment) Act 2014, s. 34. See also the Waste Management Act 1996, s. 43(5)(c)(i); the Irish Takeover Panel Act 1997, s. 13(6); the Fisheries (Amendment) Act 1997, s. 73(3); the Transport (Railway Infrastructure) Act 2001, s. 47A(7), as amended by the Planning and Development (Strategic Infrastructure) Act 2006, s. 49; the Aviation Regulation Act 2001, s. 38(5)(a); the Fisheries (Amendment) Act 2003, s. 19(3); the National Asset Management Agency Act 2009, s. 194.
21 [2007] 1 IR 272, 294.
22 See *Balc v. Minister for Justice and Equality* [2018] IECA 76 at para. 6; *S.T.E. v. Minister for Justice and Equality* [2019] IECA 332 at para. 7.
23 [2007] 1 IR 272.
24 However, now see the Planning and Development Act 2000, s. 50A(7) and (11), as substituted by the Planning and Development (Strategic Infrastructure) Act 2006, s. 13.

referred to the *Conmey* principles and concluded that, as there was a degree of ambiguity, the applicant was entitled to advance other grounds of appeal which properly arose from the decision of the High Court. Fennelly J also referred to *Conmey* and found that the applicant was not confined to arguing the certified point of law.[25] However, section 50A(11) of the Planning and Development Act 2000,[26] as inserted by the Planning and Development (Strategic Infrastructure) Act 2006, which replaced the earlier provision, provides that the Court of Appeal only has jurisdiction to determine the point of law that has been certified and to make only such order in the proceedings as follows from such determination.[27] It is intended that this statutory scheme will be replaced by the provisions of part 9, section 1 of the Planning and Development bill 2023. Section 259(1) of this bill provides that the determination of the High Court in judicial review proceedings brought pursuant to the legislation 'shall be final and no appeal shall lie from the decision of that court to the Court of Appeal.' This means that the only option for a litigant who wishes to appeal a decision of the High Court in this context will be a leapfrog appeal to the Supreme Court where the criteria set out in article 34.5.4° are met.[28]

ADAPTATION TO LEAPFROG APPEALS

When the changes to the constitutional architecture of appeals from the High Court were introduced in the wake of the 33rd amendment to the Constitution and the establishment of the Court of Appeal, the following limitations were placed on the appellate jurisdiction of the Court of Appeal and the Supreme Court.

Article 34.5.3° provides as follows:

> The Supreme Court shall, subject to such regulations as may be prescribed by law, have appellate jurisdiction from all decisions of the Court of Appeal if the Supreme Court is satisfied that:
> (i) the decision involves a matter of general public importance, or
> (ii) in the interests of justice it is necessary that there be an appeal to the Supreme Court.

---

25 See also *Talbot v. An Bord Pleanála* [2009] 1 IR 375, 385. See further *Dellway v. National Asset Management Agency* [2010] IEHC 375 at para. 7.3 in the context of the National Asset Management Agency Act 2009, s. 194 and *Minister for Justice, Equality and Law Reform v. Connolly* [2014] 1 IR 720, 730 in the context of the European Arrest Warrant Act 2003, s. 16(11), as amended.
26 As inserted by the Planning and Development (Strategic Infrastructure) Act 2006, s. 13 and adapted by the Court of Appeal Act 2014, s. 74(1).
27 See also *L.O'S. v. Minister for Health and Children* [2015] IESC 61 at para. 3.15 in the context of the Hepatitis C Compensation Tribunal Act 1997, s. 5(19).
28 Planning and Development bill 2023, s. 259(2).

Whereas article 34.5.4° provides:

> Notwithstanding section 4.1 hereof, the Supreme Court shall, subject to such regulations as may be prescribed by law, have appellate jurisdiction from a decision of the High Court if the Supreme Court is satisfied that there are exceptional circumstances warranting a direct appeal to it, and a precondition for the Supreme Court being so satisfied is the presence of either or both of the following factors:
> (i) the decision involves a matter of general public importance, or
> (ii) the interests of justice.

While the threshold for the leapfrog mechanism is somewhat lower in one respect than that originally set out in section 29 of the Courts of Justice Act 1924, requiring only that an issue of *general* rather than *exceptional* public importance arises, it is also necessary to establish that there are exceptional circumstances justifying such an appeal and the bar for obtaining leave to bring an appeal remains high.[29]

The Supreme Court has provided some guidance in its determinations and judgments in relation to how the criteria that a decision involves 'a matter of general public importance' or that it is necessary in the interests of justice that there be an appeal may be met. It is beyond the scope of this chapter to examine these in detail but some useful indicators of the court's views on this issue are set out in its determination in *B.S. v. Director of Public Prosecutions*[30] and in a unanimous judgment of a full court delivered by O'Donnell J in *Quinn Insurance Ltd v. PricewaterhouseCoopers*.[31] In the latter case, O'Donnell J made it clear that to satisfy the test of 'general public importance', it is necessary that the point be stateable and that it should normally have the capacity to be applicable to cases other than that under consideration. In relation to the criterion that leave should be granted in the interests of justice, he said that it is best viewed as a residual category and he rejected the argument that a broad interpretation should be taken towards it which in his view would erode any conceptual distinction between error and injustice. O'Donnell J considered these criteria further in his judgment in *Odum v. Minister for Justice and Equality*,[32] where he stated as follows:

> The interests of justice criterion speaks for itself and, in some cases, may be limited to the resolution of the issue in the specific case. However, the majority of appeals in which leave is granted to this Court

---

29 Note that a similar leapfrog mechanism exists in Northern Ireland, examined by Brice Dickson in his chapter.
30 [2017] IESCDET 134, at para. 5.
31 [2017] 3 IR 812, at 820–1.
32 [2023] IESC 3, at para. 35.

from the Court of Appeal under article 34.5.3° or the High Court under article 34.5.4° are those which satisfy general public importance standard. The fact that the importance is described as both general and public suggests that the issue transcends the particular case and the private dispute of the parties. Indeed, it is the importance of resolving that issue in the public interest which justifies the second-tier appeal in such cases.

Clarke J confirmed in *C.C. v. Minister for Justice and Equality*[33] that the only grounds on which an appeal may be brought to the Supreme Court are the grounds specified in the determination in which the court certifies that the constitutional threshold has been met. It has been accepted that it is open to the case management judge to refine the grounds of appeal in the course of the case management process[34] and that 'there may be a legitimate refinement of the precise argument put forward on appeal provided that it can fairly and properly be said that the argument comes within the general ambit of the grounds on which leave to appeal was granted'.[35] While it has been suggested that 'the court should not adopt an overly technical approach to the precise boundaries of the issue or issues in respect of which leave to appeal was granted'[36] and that limitations on the scope of an appeal should not be inflexibly applied,[37] it has also been stressed that a court 'should not lightly depart from the scope of appeal which originally led to the grant of leave.'[38]

DIFFERENCES IN THE CERTIFICATION THRESHOLD

There has been some debate about the changes to the certification threshold from 'exceptional public importance' to one of 'general public importance'. In *Grace v. An Bord Pleanála*,[39] Clarke and O'Malley JJ pointed out that the thresholds for certifying an appeal in the High Court and for bringing an appeal to the Supreme Court are not the same and that it was possible to envisage cases where the High Court had correctly refused a certificate but the Supreme Court would find that the constitutional threshold had been met. They expressed the view that the certification threshold 'is undoubtedly somewhat higher'.[40] Conversely, it was observed by the Supreme Court in its determination in *Callaghan v. An Bord Pleanála*[41] that the decision by the

33 [2016] 2 IR 680, at 686–7.
34 *Wansboro v. Director of Public Prosecutions* [2017] IESCDET 115, at para. 8.
35 *Director of Public Prosecutions v. O'R* [2016] 3 IR 322, at 330.
36 *Callaghan v. An Bord Pleanála* [2017] IESC 60, at para. 2.1.
37 *Fitzpatrick v. An Bord Pleanála* [2018] IESC 60, at para. 4.7.
38 Ibid.
39 [2020] 3 IR 286.
40 Ibid., at 295.

High Court that a point of law was within the scope of the certification scheme does not of itself meet the constitutional threshold for leave to appeal to the Supreme Court. In this case the Supreme Court concluded that the single point of law certified by the High Court did not meet the criteria for leave to appeal to the Supreme Court and that the constitutional threshold for leave to appeal from the High Court directly to the Supreme Court had not been met. One clear outcome of the changes set out in section 259 of the Planning and Development bill 2023 will be greater clarity as it will no longer be possible to seek to pursue parallel or sequential appeals in this context.

CONCLUSIONS

The key questions to address in assessing the legacy of the certification process in section 29 of the Courts of Justice Act 1924 are how effective it has been and whether it has achieved an appropriate balance in permitting appeals where necessary and appropriate whilst avoiding the appellate courts becoming overburdened. The process itself has stood the test of time relatively unchanged, which in itself suggests that it has provided an effective mechanism for filtering appeals. While the wording of the criteria in the context of appeals to the Supreme Court has changed slightly since the original test set out in section 29 was formulated, the key yardsticks of public importance and public interest or the interests of justice remain of significance in current legislative and constitutional provisions.

As regards the second question, it is crucial that any certification process achieves an appropriate balance in preserving access to justice for litigants while avoiding the spectre of an appellate court being overwhelmed with appeals of a relatively routine nature. The criterion of permitting appeals where, in the wording used in section 29 of the 1924 Act, 'it is desirable in the public interest' captures both considerations which have to be weighed in the balance in this regard. It is of fundamental importance to the fair and effective administration of justice that appeals be permitted where significant matters of public interest need to be clarified. It is also in the public interest that litigants can have confidence that the courts' appellate structures will adequately safeguard their entitlement to access to justice. However, it should also be recognised that access to justice is a concept that applies to defendant and respondents as well as plaintiffs and appellants. This point was made by Clarke CJ in *Quinn Insurance Ltd v. PricewaterhouseCoopers*,[42] where he suggested in the context of applications for security for costs, that, 'just as the cost of bringing certain types of proceedings may prove a barrier to those who

---

41 [2015] IESCDET 60, at para. 39.
42 [2021] 2 IR 70, at 99.

might have a good claim being able to vindicate their rights, so also can the cost of defending proceedings be a barrier to the rights of defence and the ability of parties sued to vindicate their right to have the claim determined by a court of competent jurisdiction on the merits or at least not to be forced to compromise the case on a skewed basis because of their exposure to costs.'[43] A well-balanced certification process can play a crucial role in avoiding the spectre of unnecessary appeals and the incurring of an excessive costs burden in this regard.

A nuanced approach to the question relating to the balancing process is also necessary and clearly the context of the various statutory schemes may have an impact on the level of appeals considered appropriate. The fact that all appeals to the Court of Appeal are ruled out by the provisions of the Planning and Development bill 2023 is consistent with the purpose which lies behind this bill of reducing the delays which protracted litigation involving appeals may bring. However, in other contexts such as immigration law, while a relatively strict approach has been adopted towards the construction of the certification test, it appears to have played a useful role in clarifying issues which might otherwise have led to unnecessary litigation whilst also controlling the volume of appeals.

Nearly a decade has now passed since the introduction of the certification process for appeals to the Supreme Court. It is possible at this remove to form a view on whether the bar for obtaining leave to appeal has been set at too high a level. The answer appears to be that it has not, and an effective filter mechanism is clearly necessary to avoid appellate processes being overwhelmed. Whilst it has clearly at times placed a significant burden on the Court of Appeal, the certification process has allowed the Supreme Court to focus on the interpretation and clarification of legal issues. The resources of the courts are finite and it must surely be in the broader public interest to have a filter mechanism which allows appellate courts, and particularly the Supreme Court, to focus on clarifying the law.

It is unlikely that the far-reaching impact of devising a certification procedure in section 29 of the Courts of Justice Act 1924 could have been envisaged at the time of the drafting process a century ago. However, it can now be said with the benefit of hindsight that the certification process for appeals set out in that section must rank as one of the procedural innovations in the Act with the most far-reaching legacy.

---

43 Ibid., at 98.

CHAPTER TWENTY-ONE

Appeal routes in Northern Ireland

BRICE DICKSON*

When the jurisdiction of Northern Ireland was created in 1921 the court system largely inherited the appeal routes previously in place for the whole of Ireland, which to a considerable extent replicated those available in England and Wales. In Northern Ireland there was no completely fresh start such as was provided for in the Irish Free State by the Courts of Justice Act 1924. Even the reforms introduced by the Judicature (NI) Act 1978 did not significantly alter the appeal system. This chapter summarises the current state of play and touches upon 'alternatives' to appeals, namely judicial reviews and references. It seeks to demonstrate how complicated and anomalous the appeal system is. It rests on two principles, rarely expressly articulated: first, that every litigant is entitled to one appeal but thereafter has to justify why a second appeal should occur; second, that an appeal court has all the powers of the court appealed against. The chapter proceeds by considering appeal routes based on where a case begins.

CRIMINAL CASES BEGINNING IN A MAGISTRATES' COURT

Relatively minor criminal cases are tried summarily in Magistrates' Courts by district judges. Defendants who are convicted can appeal against their conviction or their sentence to a County Court,[1] and the County Court judge can award any punishment, whether more or less severe than that awarded by the Magistrates' Court, up to the limit of the latter court's jurisdiction.[2] Alternatively, defendants who lose in the Magistrates' Court, *and the prosecution*, can appeal directly to the Court of Appeal on a point of law, using the 'case stated' procedure.[3] Defendants who appeal to the County Court but lose can also appeal from there to the Court of Appeal by way of case stated, this being a huge exception to the statutory provision

---

* Emeritus professor of international and comparative law, Queen's University Belfast. I am grateful to Niamh Howlin and Conor McCormick for their comments on a draft of this chapter. Remaining shortcomings are solely my responsibility.
1 Magistrates' Courts (NI) Order 1981, art. 140(1).
2 County Courts (NI) Order 1980, art. 28(3).
3 Magistrates' Courts (NI) Order 1981, art. 146(1).

that County Court decisions on appeals from Magistrates' Courts are 'final and conclusive'.[4]

The 'case stated' is a longstanding procedure, still used in the rest of Ireland and in England and Wales, whereby specific legal questions are transmitted to the Court of Appeal so that it can clarify the law for the benefit of future litigants. If used successfully by the prosecution the defendant's acquittal in the Magistrates' Court may be overturned. In Northern Ireland an application for a case to be stated by a Magistrates' Court must be made within fourteen days of the decision being appealed and the district judge can refuse to state it only if the application is 'frivolous'.[5] The judge must then state the case within three months from the date of the application, failing which the applicant can apply to a judge of the Court of Appeal for an order directing the district judge to state a case within a specific time limit.[6] In the County Court the applicant has twenty-one days to apply for a case to be stated and the case to be stated must be sent to the judge within two months of the judge directing that this should happen. The judge then has a further two months to formally state the case. The judge can refuse to state a case if of the opinion that it is 'frivolous, vexatious or unreasonable', but again the applicant can then apply directly to the Court of Appeal for an order directing the County Court judge to do so.[7]

The theory is that the case stated procedure facilitates the *supervision* of inferior courts, as opposed to the *correction* of their decisions, but as the Court of Appeal's powers when dealing with a case stated are so very extensive that distinction has become blurred. The Court of Appeal can exercise all the powers of a Magistrates' Court and can affirm, reverse or vary that court's decision or remit the case for rehearing by the original district judge or a different district judge in accordance with whatever directions the Court of Appeal thinks proper.[8] The same applies in relation to cases stated by a County Court judge.[9]

Generally speaking, decisions by the Court of Appeal in appeals by way of case stated are final,[10] but there are exceptions. Criminal appeals *can* be further appealed to the Supreme Court, by either the defendant or the prosecution.[11] However, as in all criminal appeals to the Supreme Court, the Court of Appeal has a veto power in that it must certify that a point of law of

---

4   County Courts (NI) Order 1980, arts. 28(1) and 61(1).
5   Magistrates' Courts (NI) Order 1981, art. 146(2) and (4).
6   Ibid., art. 146(6) and (7); Magistrates' Courts Rules (NI) 1984, rules 158–60. For an example, see *Parker v. Chief Constable of the PSNI* [2018] NICA 17.
7   County Courts (NI) Order 1980, art. 61(1), (2), (4) and (6); County Court Rules (NI) 1981, order 32, rules 4–6.
8   Magistrates' Courts (NI) Order 1981, art. 147(1).
9   County Courts (NI) Order 1980, art. 64.
10 Magistrates' Courts (NI) Order 1981, art. 147(2); County Courts (NI) Order 1980, art. 61(7).
11 Judicature (NI) Act 1978, s. 41(1).

general public importance is involved. Only then can permission to appeal be requested from the Court of Appeal and/or the Supreme Court.[12] It might be argued that the rationale for this appeal route is that a person's liberty could be at stake, but that does not explain why the prosecution can appeal. A criminal case which begins in a Magistrates' Court might therefore be appealed three times – to a County Court, to the Court of Appeal and to the Supreme Court. A recent example is *Public Prosecution Service of Northern Ireland v. Elliott and McKee*. The defendants were convicted of theft in a Magistrates' Court but acquitted on appeal to the County Court because the judge found that the machine used to take their fingerprints had not been officially approved, as statutorily required.[13] The prosecution then requested a case to be stated to the Court of Appeal, where the judges held that the lack of official approval of the machine did not mean that its results were inadmissible against the defendants.[14] The defendants' further appeal to the Supreme Court was unsuccessful.[15]

Magistrates' Courts in Northern Ireland often play a role at the beginning of serious criminal cases which, if they eventually go to trial, are dealt with by the Crown court. These are called committal proceedings.[16] If the defendant is committed there is no appeal available against that decision and if there is no committal the prosecution can likewise not appeal. But the prosecution can instead ask a judge of the High Court or Crown court to permit the prosecution to proceed in the absence of any committal, a procedure know as a 'voluntary bill of indictment'. Moreover, a person directly affected by a decision not to commit the defendant, such as the victim of the alleged crime, can challenge that decision by applying for judicial review in the High Court.

All applications for judicial review are considered to be civil proceedings, but if they relate to 'a criminal cause or matter' they are dealt with by three (sometimes two, or even just one[17]) High Court or Court of Appeal judges sitting in a divisional court.[18] They sometimes occur in the aftermath of a criminal conviction.[19] Whereas appeals against decisions in judicial review applications can normally be made by either side to the Court of Appeal, appeals in reviews involving a criminal cause or matter are appealable directly

---

12 Ibid., s. 41(2).
13 Under the Police and Criminal Evidence (NI) Order 1989, art. 61(8b).
14 [2011] NICA 61, [2012] NI 154.
15 [2013] UKSC 32, [2013] 1 WLR 1611.
16 Provision has been made for 'direct committal', effectively making the proceedings before the Magistrates' Court a relative formality, but it is not yet in force: Justice Act (NI) 2015, s. 9, as substituted by Criminal Justice (Committal Reform) Act (NI) 2022, s. 4.
17 As in *Ward v. Police Service of Northern Ireland* [2007] UKSC 50, [2007] 1 WLR 3013.
18 Rules of the Court of Judicature (NI) 1980, order 53, rule 2(7).
19 E.g., *Gaughran v. Chief Constable of the PSNI* [2015] UKSC 29, [2016] AC 345. See too *Gaughran v. UK* App 45245/15, judgment of 13 Feb. 2020.

to the Supreme Court but *only by the Crown*, only if the divisional court certifies that a point of law of general public importance is involved and only if the divisional court or the Supreme Court grants leave.[20] There is no obvious justification for distinguishing between the way judicial reviews in civil and criminal matters are processed. The situation is clearly anomalous. Treating appeals against judicial review decisions the same way in all cases makes more sense, especially as it avoids disputes over what exactly constitutes a criminal cause or matter.[21] A further anomaly is that no leave at all is required for an appeal to the Supreme Court against a High Court decision on a criminal application for *habeas corpus*.[22]

CRIMINAL CASES BEGINNING IN THE CROWN COURT

These are trials on indictment and a defendant can appeal against conviction or sentence to the Court of Appeal provided leave is first obtained. The test for granting leave is whether arguments have been made indicating that the conviction may be unsafe. Leave to appeal against a conviction can in theory be granted by the trial judge through a certificate that the case is fit for trial,[23] but in practice this never occurs. Instead leave is sought from the Court of Appeal itself[24] and in appeals against sentence it is only the Court of Appeal that can grant leave.[25]

In acknowledgment of the significance of these appeals, defendants are allowed two attempts to obtain leave.[26] They can first apply to a single judge of the Court of Appeal[27] and if leave is refused a second application can be made to the full court,[28] which will comprise two or three judges.[29] The single judge or full Court can grant an extension to the 28-day period during which leave should be sought, and will do so if there appears to be merits in the grounds of appeal. If it seems that an application for leave to appeal indicates no substantial ground of appeal, the master of the appeals office in the Court of Judicature can refer the application to the Court of Appeal for summary dismissal if they consider the application to be frivolous or vexatious.[30]

20 Judicature (NI) Act 1978, ss. 41(1)(a) and 41(2).
21 See, e.g., *Re McGuinness's Application for Judicial Review* [2020] UKSC 6, [2021] AC 392.
22 Judicature (NI) Act 1978, s. 45(3).
23 Criminal Appeal (NI) Act 1980, s. 1(b). The certificate must be granted within 28 days from the date of the conviction.
24 Ibid., s. 1(a).
25 Ibid., ss 8, 9 and 10(1).
26 The European Convention on Human Rights confers no right to appeal against a court's decision. Protocol 7, art. 2, does so in criminal cases, but the UK has not ratified that protocol.
27 Criminal Appeal (NI) Act 1980, s. 45(2)(a). A single judge can also grant an extension of time to appeal against conviction, as in *R v. Adams* (n. 38 below).
28 Ibid., s. 16(1). Again, the time limit is 28 days.
29 Ibid., s. 44(1) and (2).
30 Ibid., s. 18.

In Crown court trials where there is no jury, there is usually an automatic right of appeal to the Court of Appeal, without any need for leave.[31] The prosecution has the right to appeal against rulings made by judges during trials on indictment, such as that there has been an abuse of process or that reporting restrictions should be imposed, but, unlike through cases stated in the Magistrates' Courts or County Courts, the prosecution cannot appeal against an acquittal, even on a point of law.[32]

When the Court of Appeal hears a criminal appeal against a conviction it can allow the appeal only if it decides that the conviction is 'unsafe'.[33] In certain circumstances it can substitute convictions for alternative offences[34] and it can also impose alternative sentences after hearing an appeal against conviction, whether more or less severe than the lower court's sentence (so long as it does not increase any sentence on the basis of evidence not given at the trial).[35]

Decisions by the Court of Appeal in appeals relating to trials on indictment can be further appealed to the Supreme Court, provided again that the Court of Appeal certifies that a point of law of general public importance is involved[36] and that permission to appeal is then granted by either Court.[37] It is very rare for the Court of Appeal to grant permission, but the Supreme Court does so regularly. Recent examples include *R v. Adams*, where in 2020 Gerry Adams successfully appealed against his conviction in 1975 for escaping from detention[38] and *R v. Maughan*, where the defendant unsuccessfully argued that the discount he received for pleading guilty should not have been reduced just because he was caught red-handed.[39]

---

31 Justice and Security (NI) Act 2007, s. 5(7). Juryless trials usually relate to the Troubles in Northern Ireland. They can also occur in non-terrorist cases if there is alleged jury-tampering, but leave *is* then required for an appeal: Criminal Justice Act 2003, ss 44–50.
32 Criminal Justice (NI) Order 2004, part iv (ss 16–33) and the Criminal Appeal (Prosecution Appeals) Rules (NI) 2005. See, e.g., *R v. JM* [2013] NICA 64.
33 Criminal Appeal (NI) Act 1980, s. 2(1)(a).
34 Ibid., s. 3.
35 Ibid., s. 4(2). In England and Wales the Court of Appeal cannot increase a sentence when hearing an appeal.
36 This caused controversy in *R v. Hayes and Palombo* [2024] EWCA Crim 304, where two bankers lost their appeal against convictions for conduct deemed to be fraudulent in the UK but not in the US; see Joshua Rozenberg, 'Who has the last word?', available at https://rozenberg.substack.com/p/who-has-the-last-word.
37 Criminal Appeal (NI) Act 1980, s. 31(1) and (2). Under the Appellate Jurisdiction Act 1876, s. 10, appeals to the House of Lords in criminal cases were possible only if the attorney general granted permission. This power was not extended to the attorney general for Northern Ireland in 1920, so criminal appeals from Northern Ireland to the House of Lords became possible only when the Administration of Justice Act 1960 was passed (see s. 18 and sch. 2).
38 [2020] UKSC 19, [2020] 1 WLR 2077.
39 [2022] UKSC 13, [2022] 1 WLR 2820.

CIVIL CASES BEGINNING IN A MAGISTRATES' COURT

As with criminal cases, many civil cases beginning in a Magistrates' Court can be fully appealed (this time by either side) to a County Court,[40] where the decision is again 'final and conclusive',[41] or by way of the case stated procedure, raising only a question of law, directly to the Court of Appeal.[42] The powers of the Court of Appeal in such appeals are as extensive as in criminal cases.[43] At that point, the general rule applies that no further appeal can be taken to the Supreme Court,[44] the underlying principle being *interest reipublicae ut sit finis litium* (there is a public interest in putting an end to litigation). But, as shall see in the next section, there is a small exception to that rule.

CIVIL CASES BEGINNING IN A COUNTY COURT

These can be fully appealed to the High Court, the decision of which is normally final,[45] but as in criminal cases it is possible to appeal directly to the Court of Appeal via the case stated procedure.[46] Moreover, if the decision of the County Court is appealed to the High Court that court can also state a case for the opinion of the Court of Appeal on a point of law, though this is rare.[47]

In both scenarios the general rule is that the decision of the Court of Appeal is final but, as mentioned above, there is an exception. There can be an appeal to the Supreme Court if the civil case 'involves a decision of any question as to the validity of any provision made by or under an Act of the Parliament of Northern Ireland or a measure of the Northern Ireland Assembly',[48] and a later statute provides that those words should be taken as including Orders in Council made for Northern Ireland and Acts of the current Assembly.[49] An interesting example of the exception being applied is the so-called 'gay cake' case, *Lee v. Ashers Baking Company Ltd*,[50] where the Supreme Court reversed the Court of Appeal and held that there had been no unlawful discrimination of any kind.

40 Magistrates' Courts (NI) Order 1981, art. 143.
41 County Courts (NI) Order 1980, art. 28(1).
42 Magistrates' Courts (NI) Order 1981, art. 146(1).
43 See the text at n. 8 above.
44 Judicature (NI) Act 1978, s. 42(6).
45 County Courts (NI) Order 1980, art. 60.
46 Ibid., art. 61(1) and (2).
47 Ibid., art. 62. See, e.g., *DMcA v. A Health and Social Services Trust* [2017] NICA 3.
48 The Assembly in question was in place between 1973 and 1975.
49 Northern Ireland Act 1998, s. 95(5) and sch. 12, para. 3.
50 [2018] UKSC 49, [2020] AC 413. See too the text at nn. 78 and 79 below.

CIVIL CASES BEGINNING IN THE HIGH COURT

These cases can be appealed, *generally without leave*, to the Court of Appeal. In the rare cases where leave is required, such as when the appeal is against an interlocutory order, the test for deciding whether to grant it is whether there is 'a prima facie case of error; or a question of general principle not already decided; or a question of importance upon which further argument and a decision of the Court of Appeal would be to the public advantage' and in cases not involving a point of general principle or public advantage, the appellant must show 'an arguable case with a reasonable prospect of success that the trial judge had gone plainly wrong'.[51] If the High Court refuses leave that decision can itself be appealed to the Court of Appeal. Alternatively, the would-be appellant can apply directly to the Court of Appeal for leave.

The decision of the Court of Appeal can be appealed provided that either that court or the Supreme Court grants leave and, unlike in criminal cases, there is no requirement that the Court of Appeal first certifies that a point of law of general public importance is involved. Today it is uncommon for the Court of Appeal to grant leave since the Supreme Court has implied that it would prefer to have the final say over which appeals it hears.[52] An exception occurred in 2019 in a case on the legality of the Ireland / Northern Ireland Protocol to the EU-UK Withdrawal Agreement.[53]

It is also possible for an appeal to bypass the Court of Appeal and go straight from the High Court to the Supreme Court. This so-called 'leapfrog' procedure, which now has an analogue in the Republic of Ireland,[54] permits the High Court to certify that the case involves a point of law of general public importance (another example of a veto power) and that it either relates to the construction of legislation or is one on which there is a binding precedent of the Court of Appeal or of the Supreme Court.[55] Leave must still be granted by the Supreme Court. It seems that the leapfrog procedure has never been activated in Northern Ireland, but it is used every couple of years or so in England and Wales.[56]

---

51 *Department of Finance, Land and Property Services v. Foster* [2022] NICA 19.
52 See, e.g., *Kinloch v. HM Advocate* [2012] UKSC 62, [2013] 2 AC 93.
53 *Re Allister's Application for Judicial Review* [2023] UKSC 5, [2023] 2 WLR 457.
54 Courts (Supplemental Provisions) Act 1961, s. 7B, inserted by the Court of Appeal Act 2014, s. 9. See too art. 34.5.4° of the 1937 Constitution and Hilary Biehler's chapter.
55 Administration of Justice Act 1969, ss 12–16, esp s. 12(3) and (3A). See too the Tribunals, Courts and Enforcement Act 2007, s. 14A, which permits leapfrog appeals from the Upper Tribunal to the Supreme Court.
56 See, e.g., *Financial Conduct Authority v. Arch Insurance (UK) Ltd* [2021] UKSC 1, [2021] AC 649.

THE CENTRALITY OF THE COURT OF APPEAL IN NORTHERN IRELAND

The stand-out point emerging from this review of appeal routes in Northern Ireland is that the Court of Appeal plays a central role.[57] The court was created by the Government of Ireland Act 1920 and was allocated 'all such jurisdiction as is now exercised by his majesty's Court of Appeal in Ireland'.[58] The 1920 Act also created a short-lived High Court of Appeal in Ireland, which could hear appeals from both the Court of Appeal in Northern Ireland and the Court of Appeal in Southern Ireland. Provision was even made for yet a further appeal from that Court to the House of Lords,[59] meaning it was possible for an initial court decision to be appealed no fewer than four times.[60]

At its launch the Court of Appeal was not explicitly conferred with criminal jurisdiction. In England and Wales 'appeals' in serious criminal cases had been dealt with by the Court for Crown Cases Reserved[61] but that court was replaced by the Court of Criminal Appeal in 1907.[62] The Government of Ireland Act 1920 transferred the jurisdiction of the Court for Crown Cases Reserved to the High Court of Appeal in Ireland and on that Court's demise the jurisdiction defaulted, in Northern Ireland, to the Court of Appeal.[63] The Criminal Appeal (NI) Act 1930 then transferred the jurisdiction to a new Court of Criminal Appeal, mirroring what had been done for England and Wales, but it was staffed by the same judges as those sitting in the Court of Appeal, whose workload around that time was described by a subsequent lord chief justice as 'very light'.[64] Eventually the Judicature (NI) Act 1978 incorporated the Court of Criminal Appeal into the Court of Appeal.[65] Over the years the jurisdiction of the Court of Appeal has been further extended by making it the appellate court for several tribunals and statutory bodies.[66]

---

57 See, generally, Conor McCormick and Brice Dickson, *The Court of Appeal in Northern Ireland* (Bristol, 2024, forthcoming).
58 Government of Ireland Act 1920, s. 40(1); the Court of Appeal in Ireland was established by the Supreme Court of Judicature Act (Ireland) 1877 (40 & 41 Vic., c. 57).
59 Ibid., ss 42, 43 and 49. The High Court of Appeal survived for just under 12 months.
60 See, e.g., *Boggan v. Motor Union Insurance Co* [1923] 2 IR 136. For more on the High Court of Appeal see the chapter by Maurice Collins.
61 Established by the Crown Cases Act 1848 (11 & 12 Vic., 78). For a fascinating account of the way in which criminal appeals developed in Ireland see Desmond Greer, 'A security against illegality? The reservation of Crown cases in nineteenth-century Ireland' in Norma Dawson (ed.), *Reflections on law and history* (Dublin, 2006), pp 163–202.
62 Court of Criminal Appeal Act 1907 (7 Ed. VII, c. 23).
63 Irish Free State (Consequential Provisions) Act 1922, sch. 1, para. 6.
64 See Robert Carswell, 'Founding a legal system: the early judiciary of Northern Ireland' in Felix M. Larkin and Norma Dawson (eds), *Lawyers, the law and history* (Dublin, 2013), at p. 17.
65 Judicature (NI) Act 1978, s. 34(2) and (3).
66 See, e.g., Lands Tribunal and Compensation Act (NI) 1964, s. 8(6); Social Security Administration (NI) Act 1992, s. 22; Industrial Tribunals (NI) Order 1996, art. 22; Tribunals, Courts and Enforcement Act 2007, s. 13(12).

REFERENCES

To complete the picture of how questions of law can be dealt with by higher courts in Northern Ireland it is important to note that issues can sometimes be 'referred' to them. Four types of reference can be made to the Court of Appeal, the first three of them in criminal cases and the fourth in criminal *or* civil cases:

(1) the director of public prosecutions can refer sentences to the Court of Appeal if he or she thinks they are unduly lenient, a step which is taken several times a year;[67]
(2) the DPP can refer a question of law to be considered by the Court of Appeal after a defendant's acquittal, but that Court cannot alter the acquittal;[68]
(3) the Criminal Cases Review Commission can refer a conviction or a sentence to the Court of Appeal when it considers that there is a real possibility that the conviction or sentence would not be upheld;[69] in recent years several convictions dating from the Troubles have been overturned due to this mechanism;[70]
(4) lower courts and tribunals can refer 'devolution issues' to the Court of Appeal.[71] A devolution issue is defined as one which raises a question about the legislative competence of the Northern Ireland Assembly or the executive competence of a minister or a department.[72]

In all of these situations the opinion of the Court of Appeal on the referred matter can then be further appealed, by either side and with leave, to the Supreme Court.[73]

In addition, three types of reference can be made to the Supreme Court:

---

67 Criminal Justice Act 1988, s. 36. This (and the next) power were formerly exercisable by the attorney general.
68 Criminal Appeal (NI) Act 1980, ss. 15 and 34.
69 Criminal Appeal Act 1995, ss. 10(1) and 13(1).
70 See, e.g., Marny Requa, 'Revisiting the past: miscarriages of justice, the courts and transition' in Anne-Marie McAlinden and Clare Dwyer (eds), *Criminal justice in transition: the Northern Ireland context* (Oxford, 2015).
71 Northern Ireland Act 1998, sch. 10, paras. 7 and 8. No such reference has yet been made.
72 Ibid., sch. 10, para. 1.
73 See, e.g., *R v. Z (Attorney General for Northern Ireland's Reference)* [2005] UKHL 35, [2005] 2 AC 645, on whether, as a question of law, 'the Real IRA' could be treated as 'the IRA'.

(1) the Court of Appeal can refer a devolution issue to the Supreme Court.[74]
(2) both the advocate general and the attorney general for Northern Ireland can refer to the Supreme Court the question whether a provision of a bill is within the legislative competence of the Northern Ireland Assembly.[75]
(3) the attorney general for Northern Ireland or for England and Wales and the advocate general for Northern Ireland or for Scotland can require any court or tribunal in Northern Ireland to refer to the Supreme Court any devolution issue which has arisen in proceedings before it to which they are a party or indeed any devolution issue which is not the subject of proceedings at all.[76] In 2016, when Maguire J held in the High Court that nothing in the Northern Ireland Act 1998 prevented the UK government from notifying the EU of its intention to leave that organisation, the attorney general for Northern Ireland required the judge to refer four questions to the Supreme Court and on appeal the Court of Appeal referred a fifth question.[77] In the 'gay cake' case the Court of Appeal refused the attorney general's request that it refer a devolution issue to the Supreme Court,[78] but after the Supreme Court granted leave to appeal it ruled that the Court of Appeal's refusal had been wrong.[79]

CONCLUSION

The appeal routes currently in place in Northern Ireland can be divided into several binary categories: civil and criminal appeals, appeals requiring leave and those not requiring leave, appeals on points of law and those on points of facts, and appeals that are final and those that are not. Within each of these categories there are sometimes sub-categories, such as criminal appeals by defendants and those by the prosecution or appeals on points of law and those on points of law of general public importance. There may be rationales for all

---

74 Northern Ireland Act 1998, sch. 10, para. 9. No such reference has yet been made.
75 Ibid., s. 11.
76 Ibid., sch. 10, paras. 33 and 34 (the latter power overlaps with the s. 11 power). For an example of a para. 34 reference see *Reference by the Attorney General for Northern Ireland – Abortion Services (Safe Access Zones) (Northern Ireland) Bill* [2022] UKSC 32, [2023] AC 505.
77 *McCord's (Raymond) Application* [2016] NIQB 85. The Supreme Court unanimously held that three of the questions had been superseded and that the answer to the other two was 'no': *R (Miller) v. Secretary of State for Exiting the European Union* [2017] UKSC 5, [2018] AC 61 at paras. 126–52.
78 [2016] NICA 39 and 55.
79 See the text at n. 50 above.

of these distinctions, but they are rarely articulated or re-assessed. And then there are mechanisms that seem to have the same objective as an appeal – namely the correction of an injustice – but which are processed instead through judicial reviews or references. The present system has developed by accretion over decades, leading not just to complexity but also to inefficiency. It may not require a complete overhaul but it certainly deserves some focused reconsideration.

CHAPTER TWENTY-TWO

The Courts of Justice Act in comparative perspective: Friedrich Carl von Savigny, Irish nationalism, and 'transplanted Britons'

DONAL K. COFFEY*

In June 1922, the Four Courts complex was bombed. Although the event is now commonly analysed either as the opening stanza of a brutal Civil War, or as the moment in which Irish historiography lost irreplaceable records, there is a third dimension worth considering: the courts themselves. Completed in 1802, the building housed the administration of justice for just over a century at the outbreak of the Civil War. Yet, there had been increasing dissatisfaction with this administration in the years prior to the bombing, and a corresponding belief that it was increasingly admixtured with the executive, at least as regards to certain judges.[1] It was, in a sense, grimly ironic that the damage done to the Four Courts necessitated the carrying out of judicial business in Dublin Castle. Nonetheless, the question of what was to be done with the administration of justice in the new Free State took place against a unique backdrop amongst Dominions. In no other jurisdiction were the judiciary viewed with such suspicion as they were in Ireland.[2] Admittedly, there were disagreements about the remit of the apex imperial court in jurisdictions such as Australia as a result of cases like *Webb v. Outrim*,[3] but these criticisms were typically confined to the Judicial Committee of the Privy Council, rather than the indigenous court structure.

It is in this context that we must consider the reconstruction of the courts system in the new State. The legislation itself was understood at the time to

---

* Assistant professor, Maynooth University.
1 See, e.g., Ronan Keane, 'The voice of the Gael: Chief Justice Kennedy and the emergence of the new Irish court system 1921–1936', *Ir. Jur.*, 31 (1996), 205–25, at 218–19. The article contains a good overview of the background to the Act.
2 See the chapters by Bláthna Ruane, Laura Cahillane and Robert D. Marshall. It is also noteworthy that the age of the bench at Independence was a concern; see Daire Hogan's chapter.
3 [1907] AC 81 (PC).

be particularly significant. In Dáil Éireann on 3 October 1923, the president of the Executive Council stated 'the constitution is not yet complete without it.'[4] This is perhaps the most striking element of the bill from a comparative perspective; that it was viewed as so important.[5]

The consolidation of court structures took place with some regularity in the time period under consideration in different jurisdictions. For example, in 1912 the Australian states of Queensland and New South Wales introduced District Court bills to consolidate the operation of that level of the judiciary. These were, however, regarded as being relatively uncontroversial in terms of legislative impact – in New South Wales, for instance, the bill's second reading and committee stage were dispensed with in the Lower House in ninety minutes, along with another twenty-two bills in the same time period.[6] In fact, the introduction of the Courts of Justice bill on 31 July 1923 was accompanied by a request by the president of the Executive Council that the legislation might be dealt with within one week.[7] This was resisted by Thomas Johnson, leader of the Labour Party, and Gerald FitzGibbon, then a TD for Dublin University, on the grounds that it could tend to entrench errors that may prove costly to remedy. As it was, the general election of 1923 intruded, the bill lapsed, and was re-introduced before the new Oireachtas on 20 September. It did not become law until April 1924.

What accounts for the fact that the bill was claimed to be both so important and yet also capable of passage relatively swiftly? In part, it reflects the manner of its drafting. The Judiciary Committee fits well with Osborough's description of the judiciary after the establishment of the Free State: 'erstwhile enemies of the Irish people' found themselves forced, among their other duties, to help consolidate the political authority of a government composed of former 'rebels against the crown'.[8] Glenavy appears to have understood the task as being of first-rate importance, writing a cover letter with the *Report of the Judiciary Committee* in which he noted:

> the difficult task with which your colleagues in the government and yourself are confronted, and upon which so largely depends the future peace and prosperity of our country, the establishment of a judiciary

---

4 Hogan also ranks the legislation as 'perhaps ... the most important' constitutional statute: Gerard Hogan, 'Irish nationalism as a legal ideology', *Studies*, 75:300 (1986), 528–38, at 529.
5 Brice Dickson has drawn attention to the relative absence of judicial review of legislation at the time of the establishment of the Free State, but that falls outside the remit of this consideration as it was provided for under art. 64 of the Constitution, rather than the Courts of Justice Act. Brice Dickson, *The Irish Supreme Court: historical and comparative perspectives* (Oxford, 2019), ch. 2.
6 'Quick Work', *Evening News* (Sydney), 9 Nov. 1912.
7 *Dáil Éireann deb.*, vol. 4, no. 21 (31 July 1923).
8 W.N. Osborough, 'The title of the last lord chief justice of Ireland' in W.N. Osborough, *Studies in Irish legal history* (Dublin, 1999), p. 315.

which will command the confidence and respect of every class in the community.⁹

It was unquestionably an important piece of legislation, yet attention to the debates around this legislation disclose a dimension not limited to the minutiae of jurisdiction and term limits; it encompassed questions about the nature of the relationship between law and nation in the nascent Irish State. In order to critically analyze the nature of the debate in the Free State, we must turn to the previous century and the work of the great Prussian jurist Friedrich Carl von Savigny.

FRIEDRICH CARL VON SAVIGNY

In English, Savigny's theory is generally remembered as the theory of the *Volksgeist*, the spirit of the nation, a word which he neither popularised nor used originally in the exposition of his ideas.¹⁰ What is more relevant to the discussion of the Free State is the manner in which he explained his concept of jurisprudence and its striking parallels with the language used to justify the Courts Act. In 1814 Savigny weighed into a debate about the benefits of codification of law that was then raging in the states of Germany. Savigny was firmly opposed to this movement and it is his theory of law that we are concerned with. This theory, which he called the 'historical school', was most clearly developed in a book which its English translator entitled *Of the vocation of our age for legislation and jurisprudence*.¹¹

The historical school, according to Savigny, believed that the substance of law is given by the entire past of a nation, 'from the innermost essence of the nation itself and its history'.¹² From Savigny's point of view, therefore, the development of law was intimately bound up with the development of national identity. He claimed that when the nation loses its identity, the law dies out between the members of that nation.¹³ He also distinguished between two forms of the existence of law: (i) between members of the community, (ii) as a particular scientific discipline as developed by jurists as law becomes more complex.¹⁴

9 Glenavy to president of the Executive Council, undated, NAI TSCH/S1739.
10 See Ernst von Moeller, 'Die Enstehung des Dogmas von dem Ursprung des Rechts aus dem Volksgeist' in Mitteilungen des Instituts für Österreichische Geschichtsforschung (Innsbruck, 1909), pp 2–4.
11 Friedrich Carl von Savigny, *Of the vocation of our age for legislation and jurisprudence*, tr. Abraham Hayward (London, 1831).
12 Friedrich Carl von Savigny, 'Über den Zweck dieser Zeitschrift', *Zeitschrift für Geschichtliche Rechtswissenschaft* (1815), 6.
13 Friedrich Carl von Savigny, *Vom Beruf unsrer Zeit für Gesetzgebung und Rechtswissenschaft* (Heidelberg, 1814), p. 11.

In Savigny's account, these developments proceeded in the same direction. What the Irish example provided, however, was a possible disjunction between these two forms of law. The Irish experience, as envisaged by the nationalist ideal, was confronted with a difficulty in relation to this bifurcated relationship between law and jurist: what if the form of law that the juristic community developed was antithetical to the expression of the spirit of the law as it existed between the members of the community? This, in essence, was the question that confronted the new Irish state upon its inception. One answer to this question was given by Patrick Pearse in his essay 'The sovereign people', an essay deeply steeped in a nationalist ideology that would have been familiar to Savigny. Pearse argued:

> the people are the nation; the whole people, all its men and women; and that laws made or acts done by anyone purporting to represent the people but not really authorised by the people, either expressly or impliedly, to represent them and to act for them do not bind the people; are a usurpation, an impertinence, a nullity.[15]

He specifically stated that this applied to, among others, a 'government of lawyers'.[16] It is no coincidence that one of the proponents of the bill was Hugh Kennedy, who Thomas Mohr has linked to the concept of the *Volksgeist*.[17] As a student, he co-founded a magazine and wrote in the first editorial about the ideal of university life:

> But, in our opinion, however broad be the basis of an university, or college ideal, it should not embrace cosmopolitanism; it should have an individuality developed from within itself. Hence, the ideal at which we shall aim will be a distinctively Irish one; from others we may – we ought to – learn, but imitation is incompatible with true culture.[18]

Similarly, as Mohr notes, the opening paragraph of the letter from W.T. Cosgrave to the Judiciary Committee is infused with the ideas of nationality infusing the consciousness of the people.[19] It is difficult to conceive of an articulation that could be more in tune with Savigny's theory of law itself than

---

14 Ibid., p. 12.
15 Patrick Pearse, 'The sovereign people' in Richard Bourke and Niamh Gallagher (eds), *The political thought of the Irish Revolution* (Cambridge, 2022), p. 239.
16 Ibid. It is possible that he was specifically referring to the executive branch here, but it seems more plausible that he was referring to the state as a whole.
17 Thomas Mohr, 'Law in a Gaelic utopia: perceptions of Brehon law in nineteenth and early twentieth century Ireland' in Oliver Brupbacher et al. (eds), *Remembering and forgetting* (Oxford, 2007).
18 Hugh Kennedy, Editorial, *St. Stephen's: A Record of University Life*, 1:1 (1901), 1–3, at 2.
19 The text is set out in Niamh Howlin's chapter, 'Reflecting on a century of Irish courts', p. 2.

one which endorses a view of law as 'part of the living national organism'. Moreover, the appeal to an 'alien' system of law and governance can here be seen as one in which a professional caste imposed a new system of law, in line with the model outlined above, but one in which the nation as the bedrock of Irish intellectual and cultural life continued to exist and had not been supplanted.

These views were relatively widespread and help explain the key comparative difference between the Free State and other Dominions. In the *Official handbook of the Free State*, the chapter on the constitution begins by noting that the constitution had its basis in popular authority and went on to note the difference between the settler colonies of the Commonwealth and Ireland: '[t]his was the home of an ancient nation drawn from divers racial elements but, basing itself on a Gaelic stock.'[20] In contrast, the *Official yearbook of Australia* published contemporaneously with the establishment of the Free State noted baldly: '[t]he Australian, at present, is little other than a transplanted Briton'.[21] The adoption of a new legal structure would therefore appear to be based on an underlying idea of the difference of Irish people, who comprised a distinct nation, from the rest of the Commonwealth, who had their basis in settler colonies. In these circumstances, a legal regime which was appropriate between members of essentially the same nation was inappropriate amongst the members of a different nation.

Nor, indeed, was the scheme for the new courts viewed in these terms simply by ardent nationalists. In a piece published in 1920, William Johnston recounted the arrival of the common law in Ireland in terms of a clash between civilisations, because Johnston, always a supremely confident writer, argued: '[l]aw is civilisation in the concrete'.[22] He continued his account of the common law, here and in other work, as an account of the introduction of a civilisational standard to a 'primitive' people.[23] In this, he was following in ideological currents that were then well-established; Henry Maine, for example, specifically referred to the Brehon law in his 'Theories of primitive society'.[24] What occurred in Ireland, according to Johnston?

> And so the common law came to Ireland. It came as an essential art of the accoutrement of King Henry II and his knights and clerics when they set out with jingling spur and clanking armour on their march from

20 E.M. Stephen, 'The Constitution' in *Saorstát Éireann/Irish Free State: official handbook* (Dublin, 1932), p. 72.
21 *Official yearbook of the Commonwealth of Australia* (Melbourne, 1920), p. 91.
22 W.J. Johnston, 'The first adventure of the common law', *Law Quarterly Review*, 36 (1920), 9–30.
23 W.J. Johnston, 'The parliament of the Pale', *Law Quarterly Review*, 34 (1918), 291–303.
24 Henry Maine, 'Theories of primitive society' in Henry Maine, *Dissertations on early law and custom* (London, 1883), p. 195. Maine was extremely interested in Brehon law: see Henry Maine, *The early history of institutions* (7th edn, London, 1914), pp 1–63.

Waterford to Dublin in November, 1171. The primitive people in the midst of whom they passed gazed open-mouthed at the gay cavalcade and then resumed their daily toil, unconscious for the moment of the new influence that had come into their lives.[25]

Johnston went on to note the displacement by the common law of the 'older and less complex code that hitherto sufficed for the simple needs of the native Irish',[26] but also noted that the development of that code of law was primarily in the hands of people who knew nothing of the social needs of Ireland.

It is also noteworthy that opposition to the 1923 bill was phrased in a manner which was consistent with the dynamic outlined above. It might be thought that the internal organisation of the judicial system of a Dominion wouldn't elicit much opposition. The *Morning Post*, however, did not agree and published a caustic editorial decrying the new innovations that mirrored the themes we find in proponents of the scheme:

> Juridically speaking, there was not the slightest necessity for any such a bill, the judicial system obtaining in Ireland before the Free State swam into exultant life being as good a thing of its kind as could be found in any civilised country in the world. Its continued existence, however, was impossible for two reasons. It was not Gaelic, and the Irish Free State is not a civilised country.[27]

Here we can see the civilisational and nationalist ideals being deployed by opponents of the new scheme. Kennedy also explicitly foresaw a reunification of the two parts of Savigny's ideal, the new courts structure would put law as a scientific discipline back in tune with the ideology of the nation:

> it would be for them in these newly-established courts to enshrine the ancient inspiration and to evoke again the dormant reverence for the judgment by establishing confidence in its fearless and impartial justice, and the assured expectation that as the law is made by the people, so shall be the judgment.[28]

The question as to how precisely this was to be done was, however, not fully developed. One possibility would be to re-adopt the system of Brehon law that had been in use before the imposition of the 'alien' system of the common law. This might seem to be the most logical method and, indeed, the Dáil courts had the ability to use Brehon law as a form of persuasive

---

25 See above, n. 16, p. 30.
26 Ibid.
27 'Irish political jobbery', 26 Sept. 1923, NAI AGO/2002/14/1396.
28 'The new Free State judiciary' *I.L.T.&S.J.*, 58 (1924), 152.

precedent.[29] Nonetheless, by 1923, the Dáil courts were in the process of being wound up, although Kotsonouris recounts the unease that the re-introduction of the British court structure would bring.[30] It might be surmised, therefore, that Brehon law fell out of favour as a by-product of its association with the Dáil courts. A more compelling argument against the use of Brehon law is, however, contained in an article published by John A. Costello in 1913.[31] The article, entitled 'The leading principles of the Brehon laws', was initially a prize-winning essay for the Law Students Debating Society and was written while he was an undergraduate student.[32] Costello was to devil for Hugh Kennedy and later succeed him in office as attorney general of the Irish Free State, after the interregnum of John O'Byrne. Costello's article engages directly with Maine's work, but is more clearly in line with Savigny's. He refers to the law as a 'living organism' because of its connection to the people and suggests a bifurcated structure with a professional class of lawyers responsible for the articulation and development of the general principles.[33] Costello's explanation for the demise of Brehon law, however, provides an indication for why it could not be re-introduced – it rested upon a societal matrix which broke down in the aftermath of the seventeenth century.[34] In his conclusion, Costello compares the Brehon laws to Dún Aonghasa: '[Dún Aonghasa] contemplates a civilization which has not kept pace with modern progress, and the Brehon laws stood for centuries in their primitive state, and forgot that the world went round.'[35]

This suggests a rather more prosaic reason for the lack of adoption of the Brehon laws as a code for the new state – they were regarded as being out of touch with modern jurisprudence.[36] Once that argument is conceded, however, it is clear that the Courts of Justice Act could not hope to satisfy some of the hopes of wilder opponents of the British system. It also hints, however, at a complication in Savigny's theory – the law as between members of the community had changed since the eighteenth century and the socio-legal national settlement. While the professional British judges were not trusted with the administration of justice, the underpinning legal structure could nonetheless form a bedrock for a new national consensus, once it had, in Pearse's ideal, received national authorisation, in this case provided by the new Free State Constitution.

29 James Casey, 'Republican courts in Ireland 1919–1922', *Ir. Jur.*, 5:2 (1970), 321–42, at 329.
30 Mary Kotsonouris, *The winding up of the Dáil courts 1922–1925: an obvious duty* (Dublin, 2004), p. 25. See also Thomas Mohr's chapter.
31 John A. Costello, 'The leading principles of the Brehon laws', *Studies*, 2:8 (1913), 415–40.
32 Charles Lysaght, 'Costello, John Aloysius', *DIB*.
33 Costello, 'The leading principles', at 416–17.
34 Ibid., at 416.
35 Ibid., at 400.
36 This did not mean that Brehon law was not relevant in certain circumstances: see Thomas Mohr, *Guardian of the Treaty: the Privy Council appeal and Irish sovereignty* (Dublin, 2016), p. 136.

THE COURTS OF JUSTICE ACT AND BUNREACHT NA HÉIREANN

One other interesting argument made in relation to the Courts of Justice Act was by Arthur Berriedale Keith in 1932.[37] This was a response to the proposal by the new Fianna Fáil government to remove the Oath from the 1922 Constitution. Keith argued that the Oireachtas, as a body constituted under the terms of the constitution, had no legal authority to amend or repeal the constituent act which gave the force of law to that constitution. Keith argued that because the judiciary had sworn to uphold the constitution by virtue of section 99 of the Courts of Justice Act 1924, they could not simultaneously accept the argument put forward by Fianna Fáil and be loyal to their oaths. This position was substantially accepted by the Irish Supreme Court in *State (Ryan) v. Lennon*.[38] Gerald FitzGibbon confirmed as much in a letter to Keith in December 1937, after he had taken an oath to uphold the new Constitution:

> I have just returned from taking the declaration of allegiance to the new constitution, and I confess that my conscience is much relieved thereby. You have noted that I and one of my colleagues held the view, (with which you did not agree) that the Treaty was binding on the Oireachtas, and that any legislation contrary to the terms of the Treaty was *ultra vires* of the Oireachtas. I have been in dread that some patriot might challenge in the courts the validity of the new constitution, and I am not prepared like a politician or a member of the Judicial Committee of the Privy Council, to eat my own words whenever political expediency demands. Now, however, I consider that I have been absolved from my former obligation to uphold the late Constitution, which Mr. de Valera claims has been superseded by the new one, in accordance with a national plebiscite.[39]

CONCLUSION

Writing in the immediate aftermath of the passage of the Courts of Justice Act, Hanna claimed it 'effectually secures the complete disruption of the system of British courts in the Saorstát and introduces most striking changes both in establishment and administration.'[40] Interestingly, he did not share

---

37 Arthur Berriedale Keith, 'Notes on imperial constitutional law', *Journal of Comparative Legislation and International Law*, 14:4 (1932), 255–82.
38 [1935] IR 170.
39 FitzGibbon to Keith, 31 Dec. 1937, University of Edinburgh, Keith papers, Gen 145/3/114.
40 H. Hanna, 'Saorstát Éireann (Irish Free State) 1922–1924', *Journal of Comparative Legislation and International Law*, 8:2 (1926), 19–53, at 38.

the government's view about the intimate connection between the Act and the Constitution, as he did not discuss it under 'Constitutional laws', in comparison to, for example, the Adaptation of Enactments Act 1922.[41] Looking back with further remove, Delany, however, concluded that 'there was very little change in the principles involved'.[42] Of the two, Delany appears to have been more vindicated. Keane notes that this may have been due to the personnel who took part in the Glenavy committee, dominated by members of the legal community, who would have regarded sweeping changes as being too radical.[43] Kennedy appears to have believed more was possible, and noted in his inaugural speech that 'the voice of the Gael' would be heard in Irish courts.[44] By the 1930s, however, Kennedy's increasing irritation with the Irish legal community can be seen; initially with the universities and finally with his colleagues.[45] It stemmed in large part, it would seem, from his frustration with the failure of the new constitution and courts structure to introduce a new legal order deriving its vitality and scientific impetus from the Irish nation. In this, it should be noted that the failure of this movement, if it was a failure, rested largely in his own hands – he was involved in drafting the Free State Constitution, he sat on the Glenavy Committee and drafted the Courts of Justice bill, and he was then appointed as chief justice of the new judiciary. The difficulty Kennedy appears not to have considered is that while Irish people in the 1920s were not, as were Australians, 'transplanted Britons', they had been the subject of a far more insidious transplant – the common law.

41 Ibid, at 21.
42 V.T.H. Delany, 'The Constitution of Ireland: its origin and development', *University of Toronto Law Journal*, 12:1 (1957), 1–26, at 13.
43 Keane, 'The voice of the Gael', at 215.
44 This striking phrase was the source of the title of Keane's excellent article.
45 See, e.g., preface to Leo Kohn, *The Constitution of the Irish Free State* (Dublin, 1932) and *State (Ryan) v. Lennon* [1935] IR 170.

CHAPTER TWENTY-THREE

'A new order in this country': symbolism and the new courts

MARK COEN*

In May 1931, the county councillors of Cavan unanimously decided that the royal coat of arms should be removed from its prominent position atop Cavan courthouse.[1] The councillors also directed the removal from outside the building of a Russian cannon captured in the Crimean War. Describing the presence of the coat of arms as 'a shame', Mr Ernest McDonnell, a Fianna Fáil member of the council, called for it to be removed 'at no matter what cost'. Turning to the cannon, he characterised it as 'a memento of a not very pleasant age.' Mr Patrick Farrell (independent) asked: 'Are these things we could sell?' Meanwhile, Mr Eugene Carroll of Fianna Fáil suggested that the harp, shamrock and round tower would make fitting replacement emblems. At the August meeting of the county council Mr McDonnell demanded to know why the offending symbols had not been removed.[2] By October the coat of arms was gone, broken up when no purchaser could be found.[3] It appears that the cannon was not taken away until August 1934; it was sold to a man from Bailieborough for £3.[4]

Courts are hugely symbolic entities. They not only reflect the laws applied within them; they contribute significantly to the image and spirit of the state that enshrines those laws. The structural features of a courts system, its underlying culture and the way in which it is perceived by the public combine to create narratives about the rule of law, state legitimacy and national identity. The physical architecture, emblems, rituals and conventions of courts play important roles in projecting these narratives.[5]

The symbolism of the British Crown was strongly entrenched in the pre-Independence legal system. Accused persons were prosecuted in the name of

---

* Associate professor at the Sutherland School of Law, University College Dublin.
1 'Symbols of sovereignty', *Meath Chronicle*, 23 May 1931.
2 'Courthouse coat of arms', ibid., 29 Aug. 1931.
3 'British coat of arms', *Donegal News*, 10 Oct. 1931.
4 'Cheap artillery', *Dundalk Democrat*, 25 Aug. 1934.
5 See further Linda Mulcahy, *Legal architecture: justice, due process and the place of law* (Oxford, 2011) and Rahela Khorakiwala, *From the colonial to the contemporary: images, iconography, memories, and performances of law in India's High Courts* (Oxford, 2021).

the monarch. The oath taken by jurors included a reference to 'our sovereign lord the king'. Senior barristers were styled king's or queen's counsel. The royal coat of arms was displayed on the exterior of courthouses and over the judge's bench in courtrooms. The king's judges conducted travelling assize courts in every county, impressing the arrival of the king's justice on the people by shows of 'judicial grandeur' and 'royal splendour'.[6] Royal symbols in courthouses had been vandalised during the War of Independence; the royal coat of arms in Belturbet courthouse in Cavan was tarred 'beyond recognition' in 1919,[7] while the coat of arms in Kinsale courthouse was removed without authorisation in 1920.[8] Reform of the courts after 1922 presented an opportunity to eliminate monarchical symbols from an important area of Irish life.

This chapter considers the symbolism of the new courts. It will argue that their symbolic potential was considerable but that it was not fully realised. Far-reaching changes to the structure of the courts were not accompanied by a coherent scheme of distinctively Irish symbols and practices, thereby frustrating the decolonising potential of the 1924 Act.

SYMBOLISM AND NATION-BUILDING

The achievement of a country's independence and the subsequent nation-building period is associated with the creation and embedding of new symbols.[9] As Morris states: 'To contribute to debates about national symbols ... is to participate in the imagining of the nation.'[10] The question of symbols was particularly fraught in the Irish Free State. Symbols had loomed large in disagreements over the Treaty; 'the Republic – the symbol of separation and independence'[11] had been denied and the 'qualified autonomy'[12] on offer was accompanied by 'the maintenance of the odious symbols of the British monarchy, including the governor general and the oath of allegiance'.[13]

Among the myriad challenges facing the Cumann na nGaedheal government in the aftermath of the Civil War was an intangible, albeit hugely significant one; there was a question mark over its 'ability to convincingly

6   W.E. Vaughan, *Murder trials in Ireland, 1836–1914* (Dublin, 2009), pp 260–3.
7   'Royal coat of arms tarred', *Cork Examiner*, 3 Nov. 1919.
8   'Kinsale courthouse: coat of arms removed', *Evening Echo*, 15 May 1920.
9   Gabriella Elgenius, 'National museums as national symbols' in Peter Aronsson and Gabriella Elgenius (eds), *National museums and nation-building in Europe, 1750–2010* (Abingdon, 2004), pp 145, 145–6.
10 Ewan Morris, *Our own devices: national symbols and political conflict in twentieth-century Ireland* (Dublin, 2005), p. 10.
11 Frank Pakenham, *Peace by ordeal* (London, 1935), p. 112.
12 John M. Regan, *The Irish counter-revolution, 1921–1936* (Dublin, 1999), p. 31.
13 Ibid.

embody national sovereignty.'[14] Republicans condemned Free State ministers as 'the errand boys of England'[15] for accepting Dominion status and dishonouring the Republic. They drew attention to anything that could be characterised as demonstrating British influence in Ireland or – even better for propaganda purposes – Free State mimicry of British customs.[16] Some historians argue that the government cleaved too closely to British conventions and too readily adopted British institutional models in the civil service, policing and the courts.[17] Others emphasise the significant decolonising work that was done in the first decade of the new state. The painting of the postboxes green is the symbolic change most people associate with the advent of the Irish Free State, probably because of its high visibility and perceived superficiality.[18] However, Cumann na nGaedheal made significant inroads in decolonizing the state in its 10 years in office, as Morris has shown:

> [T]he Irish Free State was the only dominion to completely remove the king's head from stamps, coins and banknotes; to choose a non-heraldic state seal rather than a coat of arms; to use a non-English language alone on its stamps, coins and state seal; to have a national flag which bore no trace of the Union Jack; and to make no official use whatsoever of the Union Jack and 'God Save the King.'[19]

Despite these significant assertions of nationhood and independence, for many, decolonisation did not happen at sufficient speed. McGarry puts it strikingly, observing that Cumann na nGaedheal was ultimately 'undone by the importance of symbols'[20] in circumstances where it 'never resolved the contradiction between its unwavering defense of the Treaty settlement, which bound the state to the empire, and its desire to maximize Irish sovereignty.'[21]

---

14 Fearghal McGarry, 'Southern Ireland, 1922–32: a free state?' in Alvin Jackson (ed.), *The Oxford handbook of modern Irish history* (Oxford, 2014), p. 649.
15 'What are the Free State ministers?' 1923 handbill, NLI https://catalogue.nli.ie/Record/vtls000508823.
16 E.g., *An Phoblacht* ridiculed the court dress worn by President Cosgrave to a Buckingham Palace dinner: 'Cosgrave in tights,' *An Phoblacht*, 12 Nov. 1926.
17 McGarry, 'Southern Ireland', pp 653–4; Diarmaid Ferriter, *The transformation of Ireland, 1900–2000* (London, 2004), pp 304–5.
18 Anon., 'Ireland as it is', *The Round Table*, 13:50 (1923), 254–72, at 246 ('Far too much time has been wasted on … trivialities like the colour of the pillar boxes'); Ferriter, *Transformation*, p. 304.
19 Morris, *Our own devices*, p. 173. As early as July 1923 Lord Oranmore and Brown stated in the House of Lords: 'One by one every symbol that we valued and that attached us to the past has vanished'. *Hansard 5 (Lords)*, vol. 54, col. 1225 (23 July 1923).
20 McGarry, 'Southern Ireland', p. 665.
21 Fearghal McGarry, 'Independent Ireland' in Richard Bourke and Ian McBride (eds), *The Princeton history of modern Ireland* (Princeton, 2016), pp 109, 121.

The Courts of Justice Act 1924 should be considered against this backdrop of a government engaged in decolonisation but struggling – then and now – to convince many that that was in fact what it was doing.

THE 1924 ACT: DECOLONISING INTENTIONS

A consideration of symbolism includes, but is not limited to, visual signs or emblems.[22] According to the social anthropologist Anthony Cohen, '[m]ost symbols do not have visual or physical expression but are, rather, ideas'.[23] It is clear that the Executive Council of the Irish Free State regarded the replacement of the British courts as a priority, and part of a wider decolonising initiative. The instructions of Cosgrave to the Judiciary Committee, drafted by Hugh Kennedy,[24] could scarcely have been more ethnonationalist in tone.[25] It is noteworthy that the head of government of the fledgling state identified the legal system as the institution most associated by the populace with its unhappy colonial experience.

What Henchy J would later call 'the bitter Irish race memory'[26] of the British courts was deeply ingrained. In similar vein, Kotsonouris referred to '[t]he folk-memory of the resident magistrate ... forever at the bidding of government.'[27] The names of 'Peter the Packer' (later Lord O'Brien, lord chief justice of Ireland) and Justice William Keogh were invoked during Oireachtas debates on the Courts of Justice bill, lest the judicial abuses of the past be forgotten.[28]

Cosgrave and Kennedy wanted to see substantive changes to the legal system that would result in more just outcomes and attract the support of the people. But that was not all; Cosgrave's letter also indicates that both men were also highly conscious of the symbolic importance of devising a new courts system for the new state. However, in choosing Baron Glenavy to chair the Judiciary Committee they seemed to prioritise inclusivity in public life over radical reform of the legal system.[29] Despite Glenavy's conservatism, significant if not revolutionary, changes were made in the 1924 Act. As will be seen below, they were sufficient to cause irritation in the United Kingdom.

22 Anthony P. Cohen, *The symbolic construction of community* (Abingdon, 2001), p. 18.
23 Ibid.
24 Thomas Towey, 'Hugh Kennedy and the constitutional development of the Irish Free State, 1922–1923', *Ir. Jur.*, (ns) 12:2 (1977), 355–70, at 364.
25 See Niamh Howlin, 'Reflecting on a century of Irish courts', where the relevant passage is reproduced.
26 *People (DPP) v. O'Shea* [1982] 1 IR 384, at 432.
27 Mary Kotsonouris, *Retreat from revolution: the Dáil courts, 1920–1924* (Dublin, 1994), p. 115.
28 *Seanad Éireann deb.*, vol. 2, col. 15 (30 Jan. 1924), John Thomas O'Farrell.
29 John Joseph Lee, *Ireland 1912–1985* (Cambridge, 1989), pp 128–9; Bláthna Ruane, 'The challenge of creating a new judiciary 1922–1924' in Eoin Carolan (ed.), *Judicial power in Ireland* (Dublin, 2018), pp 1, 12–3.

Hugh Kennedy's reference to the 1924 Act ending 'the silence of the Gael in courts of law' at the ceremony opening the new courts is well known. At the same event, Attorney General John O'Byrne, who had also been a member of the Judiciary Committee, stated that their establishment 'constituted a culminating factor in the inauguration of a new order in this country.'[30] The reference to 'a new order' rather than 'a new legal order' was presumably deliberate, underlining the centrality of a courts system in the apparatus of state power.

From the standpoint of symbolism, the main significance of the Act was that it asserted the independence and sovereignty of the new state, and in particular its separation from the United Kingdom. The mindset of British imperialists was that 'their institutions had not only led them to world power but could be put at the service of all mankind'.[31] In the case of Ireland, this benevolent gift included a courts system very similar to that which pertained in Britain, albeit with important modifications including stipendiary magistrates and the suspension of normal trials in cases of executive decreed emergency.[32] The speed with which the Irish Free State sought to depart from the machinery of justice it had inherited, and the criticisms of British justice aired while doing so, did not escape unnoticed. Cosgrave's characterisation of the system as 'a standing monument to alien government' particularly rankled, with the *Belfast Telegraph* describing it as 'very insulting'.[33] The London *Times* countered the slur by contending: 'The British legal system in Ireland was recognised, even by its greatest enemies, as scrupulously fair.'[34] A columnist in the *Sunday Pictorial*, referring to the anticipated cost of the reforms, adopted the tone of a weary parent: 'The Irish Free State seems able to find an abundance of new troubles.'[35] Some publications resorted to racist mockery while discussing the proposed changes. The derision of Cosgrave's directions to the Judiciary Committee in the *Morning Post* was particularly extreme:

> The idea of the assassinating, land-grabbing, creditor-bilking, customer diddling, gombeening, cattle driving, chicken stealing, loot-hungry native of Southern Ireland regarding any administration of justice with confidence and affection is simply too funny for words.[36]

30 'The Irish Free State judiciary: new courts opened', *I.L.T.&S.J.*, 58 (1924), 151–2, at 152.
31 Krishan Kumar, 'Empire and English nationalism', *Nations & Nationalism,* 12:1 (2006), 1–13, at 9.
32 Niamh Howlin, 'The prehistory of the Offences Against the State Act' in Mark Coen (ed.), *The Offences Against the State Act 1939 at 80: a model counter-terrorism act?* (Oxford, 2021), pp 7–21; Ruane, 'The challenge', at 4.
33 'The Free State courts', *Belfast Telegraph*, 27 Sept. 1923.
34 'Wigs and gowns: Free State controversy', *The Times*, 13 Oct. 1923.
35 'Costly judicial change', *Sunday Pictorial*, 18 Nov. 1923.
36 'Irish political jobbery – mockery of justice', *Morning Post*, 26 Sept. 1923.

The anonymous correspondent of *The Round Table*, the commonwealth journal ('an Irishman'), sneered:

> [The] mania for giving new titles to everything has led to some amusing complications. For instance, the rules for the new courts provide that a High Court judge may be addressed as *A Heerna*, which, being literally translated by an Irish-speaking peasant, means an invocation to the Deity ('O Lord').[37]

While not all reportage in Britain on the new courts was hostile, and in many cases was confined to factual reports of the changes involved,[38] Hugh Kennedy acknowledged the potential for specifically English annoyance in the opening words of an article in the *Law Journal*:

> Englishmen, who are so justly proud of their jurisprudence and of their ... institutions of law and justice, will be, perhaps, not a little surprised that the Irish people should ... brush aside a judicial system bearing a close external resemblance to that of England and to construct from the foundations a new judicial organisation.[39]

His efforts to diplomatically explain the changes to a British audience faltered when he referred to the judges of the *ancien régime* as 'distant strangers deriving their appointments and their authority from alien sources'.[40] Kennedy's speech at the Dublin Castle ceremony opening the new courts met with an unenthusiastic response in the same journal a few months later, with an unnamed 'member of the Irish Bar' disputing the veracity of his claim about Gaelic silence:

> [I]n point of fact, the Irish Courts have for many generations been presided over exclusively by Irishmen, and the law therein has been adapted to the peculiar needs of the country, while the people, being a litigious race, have thronged the courts and fought their cases with vigour, so that 'the silence of the Gael in courts of law' has never been remarked on before.[41]

---

37 Anon., 'The Irish scene 1925', *The Round Table*, 15:60 (1925), 749–68, at 765.
38 See, e.g., 'A Supreme Court for the Free State', *Manchester Guardian*, 22 Sept. 1923; 'The Free State judiciary: new appointments', *The Times*, 6 June 1924; 'Judge's speech in Irish', *Daily Telegraph*, 12 June 1924.
39 Hugh Kennedy, 'Judicial reorganisation in the Irish Free State', *The Law Journal*, 9 Feb. 1924, p. 70.
40 Ibid., at 71.
41 Anon., 'The legal revolution in the Irish Free State', *The Law Journal*, 12 July 1924, pp 435–6.

While bemoaning the fact that criminal prosecutions would no longer be brought in the King's name and that the judges were not required to swear an oath to him, the writer nonetheless conceded that the Courts of Justice Act 1924 contained some measures that had merit, notably the wide jurisdiction of the Circuit Court, which they felt would render the administration of justice more efficient and affordable.

HOW NEW WERE THE NEW COURTS?

The symbolic impact of the new courts was contingent on the degree to which they could be said to be different to the old courts. The rhetoric of Cosgrave and Kennedy had promised an indigenous court system unconnected with and untainted by the past. While the decentralisation of justice, particularly in civil matters, has long been highlighted as a major – perhaps the major – innovation of the 1924 Act,[42] the very significant changes it made to the administration of criminal justice have arguably been overlooked. Misdemeanours would no longer be tried before magistrates in Petty Sessions but before a professional judge in the District Court.[43] Grand juries would no longer be summoned to determine if indictments disclosed offences that should be sent forward for trial.[44] The person convicted of an indictable offence could now appeal to the Court of Criminal Appeal (a facility that had existed in England and Wales since 1907).[45] These changes clearly 'effected a very considerable re-organisation of the courts system'.[46] They would be accompanied by related changes in the Criminal Justice (Administration) Act 1924, including the prosecution of criminal cases in the name of the attorney general rather than the monarch[47] and the removal of the reference to the monarch in the juror's oath.[48] Although the Courts of Justice Act provided for

42 James O'Connor, 'The decentralization of the Free State courts', *Solicitors' Journal and Weekly Reporter*, 13 Oct. 1923, p. 24; Gerald Horan, *The Courts of Justice Act 1924* (Dublin, 1924), p. v; Nicholas Mansergh, *The Irish Free State: its government and politics* (London, 1934), p. 297.
43 Courts of Justice Act 1924, part iii.
44 Ibid., s. 27.
45 Ibid., s. 8. See Brice Dickson's chapter.
46 Gerard Hogan, 'Hugh Kennedy, the Childers *habeas corpus* application and the return to the Four Courts' in Caroline Costello (ed.), *The Four Courts: 200 years: essays to commemorate the bicentenary of the Four Courts* (Dublin, 1996), pp 177, 206.
47 Criminal Justice (Administration) Act 1924, s. 9.
48 Ibid., s. 14. For criticism of the elimination of the king's name from indictments and the juror's oath see 'Disloyalty in the Irish Free State', *The Scotsman*, 16 Sept. 1924. The changed juror's oath was referred to with dismay in the House of Lords in July 1923. This suggests that the new form of oath contained in the Criminal Justice (Administration) Act 1924 was in use before it was provided for by statute. See *Hansard 5 (Lords)*, vol. 54, col. 1225 (23 July 1923).

a system of travelling High Court judges similar to the pre-Independence assizes, the provision was never used and was repealed in 1926.[49] It can thus be seen that criminal trials were changed quite drastically by the 1924 Act, giving rise to a strong argument that the new judicial system represented a clean break with past practice.

However, there were significant barriers to achieving this clean break and, perhaps more importantly, the perception of a clean break among the population at large. Chief among them was the fact that the state would remain a common law jurisdiction with pre-Independence precedents and legislation remaining in force. Keane points out that the Constitution of the Irish Free State already provided for this, meaning that the Judiciary Committee could not have recommended the adoption of a civil law system.[50] Even if it was constitutionally possible, the financial, social and other problems facing the government made abandoning the common law unfeasible.[51] Surveying the first four decades of post-Independence Irish law, Hogan characterises them as a period of legal stagnation. He identifies the 1924 Act as the only notable legislative innovation of that period. The presence of the harp on Acts of the Oireachtas 'was ... the legal equivalent of painting the post boxes green instead of red.'[52] English case law was hugely influential and there was often an assumption that it would be followed as a matter of course.[53] As the *Law Times* remarked in the early 1950s: '[T]he common law, transplanted to the other side of the Irish Sea, has flourished.'[54] Changing the courts structure while maintaining in force the laws of the oppressor severely diluted the symbolic potential of the new courts as manifestations of self-determination.

A second difficulty was resistance to change among the legal profession. Trained in the common law tradition, the Bar in particular was a powerful bulwark against reforms to the legal system. The rejection of Hugh Kennedy's proposed new judicial robes is a celebrated example of this culture in operation. Described in stark terms as 'one of the very few senior members of the Irish Bar who welcomed independence',[55] Kennedy wrote in the aftermath of the judicial attire controversy: 'The legal profession is still, by a large majority, of the old school and very conservative.'[56] That legal

49 Courts of Justice Act, 1924 s .3, repealed by Courts of Justice Act 1926, s. 2.
50 Ronan Keane, 'The voice of the Gael: Chief Justice Kennedy and the emergence of the new Irish court system 1921–1936', *Ir. Jur.* (ns) 31 (1996) 205–25, at 214–15.
51 Ruane, 'The challenge', at 14.
52 Gerard Hogan, 'Mr Justice Brian Walsh: the legacy of experiment and the triumph of judicial imagination', *Ir. Jur.*, (ns) 57:1 (2017), 1–13, at 1.
53 Ibid., at 2.
54 'The jury during the hearing: some recent Irish decisions', *The Law Times*, 12 Oct. 1951.
55 Gerard Hogan, 'Irish nationalism as a legal ideology', *Studies*, 75:300 (1986), 528–38, at 528.
56 UCDA P4/1166, quoted in Keane, 'The voice of the Gael', at 222.

community could not conceive of law administered in an environment devoid of the trappings to which it was long accustomed, including the wearing of wigs and addressing judges as 'my lord'. It conceived of such features as essential to a courts system, providing it with a dignity that ensured popular respect. Their removal would represent a downgrading of the law, and critically, the status of those who participated professionally in its mysteries.

Third, the courts of the new state were targets of Republican activism and propaganda in the same way as the British courts had been during the War of Independence. While there was no establishment of guerilla courts as had occurred during that conflict, Republicans unsurprisingly characterised the courts of the Irish Free State as potent symbols of continuing British rule in Ireland. Their incendiary newspaper, *An Phoblacht*, referred to 'his majesty King George's criminal courts in Dublin'[57] and urged its readers to treat members of the judiciary as 'social pariahs'.[58] While the audience for these niche forms of propaganda was probably relatively limited, especially as the 1920s progressed, a narrative that the courts were not truly Irish was nevertheless in circulation. This critique increased the need for the courts to look and feel Irish, a fact appreciated by Kennedy.[59]

A fourth challenge to the decolonising potential of the new courts was that from the beginning there was disagreement, including among lawyers, on the extent to which the 1924 Act represented a radical new departure. Horan, in his commentary on the statute, stated that it 'made a clean sweep of the old tribunals and set up an entirely new Judiciary system.'[60] Hanna struck a similar note with his reference to 'the abolition of the British judiciary and system of courts.'[61] However, Sir James O'Connor gave a pithy, contrasting analysis: 'The new judicial system differs little from the old.'[62] An anonymous writer had previously observed that apart from the introduction of the Circuit Court with its wide jurisdiction, the Act 'left the courts practically as they were under English rule, but camouflaged under new names.'[63] O'Síocháin, writing almost 30 years after the passage of the legislation, described it as 'a scrappy and unsatisfactory recast of the old judicial system ... without any notable change.'[64] Osborough's assessment was more measured in its language but perhaps no less damning: 'The new system ... was less different from the old than might be supposed.'[65]

57 'Sheila Humphries tried again', *An Phoblacht*, 30 June 1928.
58 'Boycott them', ibid., 20 June 1931.
59 Towey, 'Hugh Kennedy', at 355. See also Morris, *Our own devices*, p. 17.
60 Horan, *The Courts of Justice Act*, p. v.
61 Henry Hanna, *The statute law of the Irish Free State 1922 to 1928* (Dublin, 1929), p. 17.
62 James O'Connor, *A history of Ireland* (London, 1929), p. 67.
63 'The Irish scene 1925', at 765.
64 P.A. O'Síocháin, *The criminal law of Ireland* (3rd edn, Dublin, 1952), p. 4. Similar comments are made throughout Liam Ua Cadhain, *The law courts in Éire* (Dublin, n.d. [1943]).
65 W.N. Osborough, 'Law in Ireland, 1916–1926', *N.I.L.Q.*, 23:1 (1972), 48, at 59.

Many eminent historians of twentieth-century Ireland also say that the courts system continued with very minimal change. Lee describes the changes as 'very limited.'[66] McGarry identifies a 'remote legal system' as one of the features of the Irish Free State that suggested continuity with the pre-Independence administration.[67] Fanning emphasises visual manifestations of similarity between the two systems: 'Irish law remained wedded to British traditions. Cases were heard in the same courtrooms, often conducted by the same lawyers in the same antique garb of wig and gown.'[68] In circumstances where legal commentators have disagreed on the extent to which the 1924 Act set in train substantial reforms, it is unsurprising that historians have looked to visual cues and concluded that little had changed. The failure to underscore the changes to the courts system with strong visual symbolism had real consequences – it meant that the decolonising intentions underpinning the 1924 Act were not fully realised.

SYMBOLISM AND THE NEW COURTS

Initially it appeared that the new courts would cast off the outward symbols of the old courts, at least in matters of dress. The anonymous 'member of the Irish Bar' writing in the *Law Times* characterised the procession of newly-appointed judges at Dublin Castle as having 'no majesty and not much dignity' and was particularly disapproving that they had 'discarded their robes as relics of English influence'.[69] The writer regretted that the Irish legal system was being politicised; pressed into service 'as an outward expression of distaste for the monarchist principles of England.'[70] Their horror that the judges were merely wearing top hats and tails, the quintessential formal attire of the English upper class, seems hard to believe at a distance of 100 years.

The initial signs that the legal system might move away from the rituals and practices of their predecessors quickly evaporated. Realising that the judges would not adopt his proposed new robes, Kennedy wrote to Cosgrave that the courts, which he hoped 'were to be distinguished as the national courts', were instead 'to have the symbols of the old time servitude imposed upon them.'[71] There was some adoption of Kennedy's judicial attire by district justices.[72] The English *Daily Mirror* published a photograph in March

66 Lee, *Ireland*, p. 128.
67 McGarry, 'Southern Ireland', at 650.
68 Ronan Fanning, *Independent Ireland* (Dublin, 1983), p. 67.
69 Anon., 'The legal revolution in the Irish Free State', *The Law Journal*, 12 July 1924, p. 435, at 435–6.
70 Ibid.
71 UCDA P4/1166, quoted in Keane, 'The voice of the Gael', at 222.
72 Keane, 'The voice of the Gael', at 222–3.

1926 of District Justice Little and District Justice Cussen wearing the distinctive headdress. In retrospect it bears more than a passing resemblance to the nuns' veils introduced after the Second Vatican Council.[73] Keane recounts District Justice Reddin wearing the headdress in the 1950s.[74] A *Daily Mail* columnist of 1928 advocated the wearing of gowns by English magistrates, and cited Irish practice as a model to follow:

> During a recent visit to the Irish Free State I was impressed by the dignity of the district magistrates [*sic*], who wore gowns similar to those worn by English county court judges. The Irish magistrates are also equipped with queer-looking hats, which they invariably throw under their seats immediately they enter the court.[75]

Apart from the District Court, wigs were worn by counsel and judges in Irish courts until the second decade of the twenty-first century.[76] There were spirited debates about their desirability from the 1920s onwards, but they proved very enduring.[77] During a Dáil debate on what became the Criminal Evidence Act 1992 Michael Bell TD decried them as 'a hangover from the colonial days of British rule'.[78]

There were other hangovers too, most obviously the mode of judicial address. District Justice Ua Cadhain criticised what he termed the 'antiquated or efféte' titles applied to judges, including 'your honour', 'your worship' and 'your lordship.'[79] In 1970 District Justice de Búrca stated at Thurles that he found himself repeating that 'your worship' had ceased to be appropriate in 1923.[80] The judge was fighting a lost cause; he had to regularly reiterate his point, including at Thurles again in 1975[81] and at Nenagh in 1980.[82] In the Circuit Court and the superior courts judges were addressed using the 'ludicrous'[83] forms of 'my lord' and 'your lordship', and an attempt to change this by statute in the late 1950s was strongly – and successfully – resisted by the Bar Council.[84] The practice continued into the twenty-first century. It was

73 'New robes for judges', *Daily Mirror*, 15 Mar. 1926. The photograph appeared at the bottom of the women's fashion page, presumably as a sartorial curiosity.
74 Keane, 'The voice of the Gael', at 223.
75 'Gowns for magistrates', *Daily Mail*, 10 Mar. 1928.
76 Carol Coulter, 'Judges to end tradition of wearing wigs in court today', *Irish Times*, 14 Oct. 2011.
77 Niamh Howlin, *Barristers in Ireland: an evolving profession since 1921* (Dublin, 2023), pp 94–7.
78 *Dáil Éireann deb.*, vol. 416, col. 1328 (3 Mar. 1992), Michael Bell TD.
79 Ua Cadhain, *Law courts in Éire*, p. 47.
80 '"Your worship" – very annoying says D.J.', *Evening Echo*, 9 Nov. 1970.
81 'Don't "worship" me, says justice', *Tipperary Star*, 14 June 1975.
82 '"Your worship" went out in 1923', *Nenagh Guardian*, 16 Feb. 1980.
83 Hogan, 'Mr Justice Brian Walsh', at 1.
84 Howlin, *Barristers in Ireland*, pp 352–4.

redolent of the British class system, evinced servility and symbolised all that was archaic in the legal system.

Judicial behaviour could also be lordly. Judges interviewed for a study on jury trials in 2017 and 2018 recalled judges from their time in practice who had left a lasting negative impression. In the words of three different judicial interviewees, some judges of the past were 'very stern ... extraordinarily cross', 'terrifying' and 'had pretensions to "majesty"'.[85] Another interviewee recalled a courtroom atmosphere of 'pomp',[86] a word associated in England with royal ceremonial. Obsequious forms of address and the social chasm between superior court judges and most of the population fuelled God complexes in some quarters. Several judges who participated in the study stated that they had made conscious efforts to behave with greater courtesy and humility on the bench as a result of what they had experienced as young practitioners.[87]

Wigs, lordly appellations and majestic conduct were not the only pre-Independence judicial practices that persisted after 1924. Judges passing sentence of death donned the black cap.[88] Gavan Duffy J dispensed with it when sentencing Thomas Kelly in 1937, leading to an inconsistency of practice that was publicly deprecated by Hanna J in the *Irish Times*.[89] The presentation of white gloves to the judges of the assize courts in the event that there was no criminal business to be heard continued in the Circuit Courts.[90] In 1956 the Circuit Court judges decided collectively that this practice should be discontinued.[91] Another echo of the assizes was discernible in the provision of police guards of honour to greet judges arriving on circuit.[92]

The removal of royal symbols from courthouses occurred on an ad hoc basis, probably because the buildings were the responsibility of individual county councils rather than central government. The emblems were sometimes removed without action on the part of the council, such as when Free State soldiers destroyed the coat of arms on the façade of Roscommon courthouse by firing 'well directed shots' at them.[93] The external emblems

---

85 Mark Coen, Niamh Howlin, Colette Barry and John Lynch, 'Respect, reform and research: an empirical insight into judge-jury relations', *Irish Judicial Studies Journal*, 4:2 (2020), 116–33, at 123.
86 Mark Coen, Niamh Howlin, Colette Barry and John Lynch, *Judges and juries in Ireland: an empirical study* (Dublin, 2020), p. 155.
87 Ibid., p. 28.
88 Ian O'Donnell, *Justice, mercy and caprice: clemency and the death penalty in Ireland* (Oxford, 2017), pp 102–5.
89 Ibid., p. 103.
90 See, e.g., 'Mayo's fine record: white gloves three times in succession', *Ballina Herald*, 10 June 1950, 'Crimeless city and county: white gloves again for judge Roe', *Munster Express*, 2 Nov. 1955.
91 'No more "white gloves" for judges', *Irish Press*, 14 June 1956.
92 See, e.g., 'High Court in Monaghan', *Northern Standard*, 28 July 1950; 'Judge welcomed', *Roscommon Herald*, 20 Mar. 1954.
93 'Coat of arms gone', *Westmeath Independent*, 14 Oct. 1922.

were removed later from the court buildings at Cavan and Galway city. The latter's 'vigorously amateurish sculptures'[94] were relocated to a discreet location in the grounds of University College Galway, where they can still be found today. At the Four Courts, the royal emblems that formerly surmounted the archways on each side of the main block were subtly erased; where previously there were crowns, now there are balls.[95] A notable example of a royal coat of arms retained on the outside of a courthouse may be seen at Monaghan.[96]

Royal coats of arms in courtrooms were ultimately replaced by the harp, but the process took time and was not prioritised. The presence of such a symbol over the judge's bench in the Central Criminal Court provided a propaganda coup to members of Cumann na mBan in 1926. Following the conviction of Sighle Humphreys, Máire Comerford and Helena Molony for the common law offence of embracery (interfering with jurors), Molony made a speech: 'There is an English emblem', she said, pointing to the representation of the lion and unicorn over the bench. 'You have the same old English law, only that it is administered now by people presumably Irish. We are loyal to Ireland, and not to any English colony.'[97] It is difficult to refute the logic of Molony's position. She was being prosecuted for an offence contrary to common law in a court bedecked with all the trappings and signifiers of English legal authority.[98] In time the old coats of arms disappeared and were replaced by the harp. The *Longford Leader* observed proudly of Longford courthouse in 1927: 'The court has been renovated and looks bright and cheery in its new colours, the lion and unicorn and dull red having disappeared before the painter's brush.'[99] In Naas some years later Judge Fawsitt thanked the county council for erecting 'the Irish coat of arms – the harp' in the courtroom there.[100]

It took almost a full century for the courts to shed much of their colonial 'paraphernalia.'[101] Wigs and lordly modes of address were long-lived. While these may seem like trivial issues, their impact on popular perceptions of the

94 Richard Butler, *Building the Irish courthouse and prison: a political history, 1750–1850* (Cork, 2020) p. 30.
95 J. O'Brien and D. Guinness, *Dublin: a grand tour* (Dublin, 1994), p. 181.
96 A newspaper report indicates that the county council decided to remove it in 1950. See 'Emblem to be removed', *Belfast Newsletter*, 18 Sept. 1953.
97 'Circulars to jurors', *Irish Times*, 10 Dec. 1926. A gold harp on a blue background with the words 'Saorstát Éireann' underneath had been erected in each of the courts located in Dublin Castle in Jan. 1926: 'High Court's emblem', *Irish Times*, 28 Jan. 1926. However, the Central Criminal Court was located in Green Street courthouse.
98 On the organised campaign of jury intimidation conducted by Cumann na mBan, see Mark Coen, '"The work of some irresponsible women": jurors, ghosts and embracery in the Irish Free State', *Law and History Review*, 38:4 (2020), 777–810.
99 'Longford Circuit Court', *Longford Leader*, 8 Oct. 1927.
100 'The harp above the bench', *Leitrim Observer*, 18 Dec. 1943.
101 Ua Cadhain, *Law Courts in Éire*, p. 70.

legal system was sizeable. They contributed significantly to the image of an archaic and foreign transplant and undermined the decolonising aims of the Courts of Justice Act. They may also have reinforced traditional attitudes and stifled new ways of thinking about substantive issues. Mohr argues persuasively that the painting of the postboxes green, though 'often presented as a symbol of frivolous and superficial change',[102] was of real importance. It made visible the state's political transformation. The courts system suffered from the absence of similarly potent indigenous symbols.

CONCLUSION

The creation of the new courts was a very important statement of separate Irish identity and was intended to be viewed as such by its architects. They did not want the legitimacy of the new state to be tainted by association with the colonial courts system and were acutely conscious of the expressivist potential of legal systems. The speed with which the new administration moved to change the system indicated the priority they accorded to this aspect of nation-building.

To the trained legal eye, the changes were significant. However, to the observer untrained in the law, the degree to which these new courts differed from their predecessors was much more difficult to quantify. Postcolonial mimicry was strongly in evidence, 'posing the question of whether colonialism [was] being subverted or reinstated'.[103] The failure to underscore the major restructuring of the courts system contained in the Courts of Justice Act 1924 with strong visual symbolism meant that the extent of the changes was masked from the population at large. The new courts did not succeed in looking new to the lay observer. While the reorganisation of the courts was very successful, the image of those courts remained essentially British. The decolonising reforms of the 1924 Act were obscured by the countervailing symbols beloved of a conservative legal community.

---

102 Thomas Mohr, 'The political significance of the coinage of the Irish Free State', *Irish Studies Review*, 23:4 (2015), 451–7, at 452.
103 Enrique Galvan-Alvarez et al., 'Decolonising the state: subversion, mimicry and criminality', *Postcolonial Studies*, 23:2 (2020), 161–9, at 164.

APPENDIX 1

Applications for appointment under the Courts of Justice Act 1924[1]

Applicant	Current position	Position sought	Date of call to Bar	Additional information[2]		
				Preferment subsequent	Education and family background	Career to June 1924
Judge Charles F. Doyle	County Court judge	High Court (subsequently Circuit Court)	1894	See Circuit Court appointments		
Judge Lionel Henry Rosenthal	Deputy County Court judge		1893		BA TCD (scholar) 1879 English Bar	1893 Irish Bar 1913 First Jewish KC, aged 57. 1923 Deputy Recorder, Galway and Deputy County Court Judge, Cork. obit. *I.L.T.&S.J.* (1932) and *Jewish Chronicle*, 22 July 1932
Judge William H. Brown	County Court judge	High Court	1887		BSc London MA RUI	1887 Irish Bar 1911 KC 1914 County Court judge, Cavan and Leitrim obit. *I.L.T.&S.J.* (1927)
Alexander Alfred Dickie KC			1893		Dundalk Institute BA QUB	1893 Irish Bar 1914 KC obit. *I.L.T.&S.J.* (1933)
Serjeant Henry Hanna KC			1896	See appendix 3		
Eugene Sheehy BL	Puisne commissioner under Dáil Éireann Winding Up Commission		1910	See appendix 4		
Edward Little	District justice, Bray, Co. Wicklow	Circuit Court	1895		Father a former premier and uncle a former Supreme Court judge of Newfoundland Clongoweswood College BA Dublin. Also attended UCD	1895 Irish Bar 1910 junior Crown prosecutor, Cork 1924 appointed district justice obit. *I.L.T.&S.J.* (1952)

1 Compiled by Robert D. Marshall. Applications for appointment S 12130, circulated to Executive Council, May 1924, NAI CAB 2/96.
2. These additional details and comments are not contained in the Cabinet paper, but are the work of Robert D. Marshall. See his chapter in this volume.

APPENDIX 1 (continued)

Applicant	Current position	Position sought	Date of call to Bar	Additional information[2]		
				Preferment subsequent	Education and family background	Career to June 1924
James McLoone KC			1893		Father a JP St Patrick's College, Armagh	1893 Irish Bar 1911 KC 1908–13 revising barrister Belfast, and 1914, Co. Dublin; 1907–9 Crown counsel Co. Westmeath 1909–22 senior Crown counsel, Tyrone 1922 resigned obit. *I.L.T.&S.J.* (1934)
Thomas Joseph Campbell KC			1900		St Malachy's College, Belfast MA LLB. Queen's RUI	1895–1906 editor *Irish News*. 1900 Irish Bar 1918 KC 1918 Contested South Monaghan for IPP 1924 Bencher obit. *I.L.T.&S.J.* (1946)
Dudley White KC		Circuit Court	1897		White and Kennedy were the sons of surgeons Belvedere College, Dublin Sch. and Mod., 1892 BA Dublin	1897 Irish Bar 1909 KC 1909 Crown counsel, Wicklow then Green Street obit. *I.L.T.&S.J.* (1930)
Cooper Mark Bloxham KC	A Dublin magistrate		1885	Appointed District Court 1924	Father a JP Official – Ulster Bank	1885 Irish Bar 1897 Crown prosecutor at Assizes: Nenagh; 1903 Clonmel 1916 senior Crown prosecutor, Wexford 1919 police magistrate, Dublin 1919 KC obit. *I.L.T.&S.J.* (1929)

APPENDIX 2

Appointments to the Supreme Court, 1924–5

	Year & place of birth	University	Year of call & age	Year of taking silk & age	Year appointed bencher	Offices held pre-1922	Offices held post-1922	Obituary
Hugh Boyle Kennedy	1879 Dublin	BA, UCD RUI	1902 23	1920 40			1923–4 Fine Gael TD 1921–4 attorney general 1923 Judiciary Committee	I.L.T. & S.J. (1935)
Charles Andrew O'Connor	1854 Roscommon	BA, TCD Dublin	1876 21	1891 39	1896	1907–9 Sergeant 1909–11 Solicitor General 1911–12 Attorney General 1911 Privy Councillor for Ireland 1912–24 Master of the Rolls	1923 Judiciary Committee	I.L.T. & S.J. (1928)
Gerald FitzGibbon	1866 Dublin	Sch. BA, TCD Dublin	1891 25	1908 41	1912	1917–24 King's advocate Admiralty 1921 Unionist MP Southern Ireland (Father lord justice of Appeal 1878–1909)	1921–3 Independent TD, Dublin University 1924 Army Mutiny Enquiry	I.L.T. & S.J. (1942)
James Augustine Murnaghan	1881 Missouri	MA, Ll.B. UCD RUI	1903 22			Father MP (Nat) Mid Tyrone	Constitution Committee 1921	

APPENDIX 3

Appointments to the High Court, 1924–5[1]

	Year & place of birth	University	Year of call & age	Year of taking silk & age	Year appointed bencher	Offices held to June 1924 based upon pre-1922 appointments	Irish Free State offices held 1922–4	Obituary
Timothy Sullivan	1874 Dublin		1895 21	1918 43	1921	Father MP (Nat. APN) 1880–1900		I.L.T. & S.J. (1949)
James Creed Meredith	1875 Dublin	BA TCD Dublin MA UCD RUI D Litt. TCD Dublin 1912	1901 25	1918 43		1914 revising barrister, Down 1	President Dáil Éireann Supreme Court 1923 chief judicial commissioner Dáil Courts Winding Up Commission 1923 Judiciary Committee 1924 Army Enquiry Committee	I.L.T. & S.J. (1942)
Thomas Lopdell O'Shaughnessy	1850 Dublin	QCG	1874 24 1894 English Bar Middle Temple	1889 39	1895	1905–24 Recorder of Dublin 1912 Privy councillor, Ireland 1920 Lord Justice		I.L.T. & S.J. (1933)
William Evelyn Wylie	1881 Dublin Grew up in Coleraine	BA TCD Dublin	1905 24	1914 32	Ex Officio 1920	1916 prosecutor at courts martial 1919–20 law advisor to government 1920–4 judicial commissioner, Irish Land Commission	1922 Chairman Irish Civil Service Compensation Commission	
William John Johnston	1868 Belfast	MA, LLB. QCB RUI	1892 24	1911 43		1910 (Dec.) Liberal candidate, Londonderry South 1911–21 County Court judge Monaghan and Fermanagh 1921–4 Monaghan and Louth	1923 Judiciary Committee	I.L.T. & S.J. (1940)

1 Compiled by Robert D. Marshall.

APPENDIX 3 (*continued*)

	Year & place of birth	University	Year of call & age	Year of taking silk & age	Year appointed bencher	Offices held to June 1924 based upon pre-1922 appointments	Irish Free State offices held 1922-4	Obituary
James Augustine Murnaghan	1881 Missouri Grew up in Omagh	MA, Ll.B. UCD RUI.	1903 22	N/A		Father MP (Nat.) Mid Tyrone 1895–Jan 1910	1921 Constitution Committee	
Henry Hanna	1874 Belfast	BA QCB RUI Ll.B. London	1894 22 1913 Eng. Bar.	1911 39	1915	1918 Unionist Candidate, St Stephen's Green 1919 3rd Serjeant		*I.L.T. & S.J.* (1946)
John O'Byrne	1884 Wicklow	MA UCD NUI	1911 27	1924 40			1921 Constitution Committee 1924–6 attorney general	*I.L.T.R.* (1954)
Appointment Declined:								
Patrick Gregory Lynch	1866 Clare	BA UCD RUI	1888 22	1906 40	1921	1917 Crown prosecutor, Kerry 1917 Nationalist candidate East Clare by-election		*I.L.T. & S.J.* (1947)

APPENDIX 4

Appointments to the Circuit Court, 1924–6[1]

Year and place of birth	University	Year of call & age	Year & age taking silk	Year appointed Bencher	Offices held to Aug. 1924 based upon pre-1922 appointments	Irish Free State offices held post-1922 to August 1924	Obituary
Henry Daniel Conner	1859 Cork	BA TCD Dublin	1882 23	1899 40	1910	Father BA (Oxon.) 1819, a JP and owner of 4,194 acres valued at £1,587 Ballineen, West Cork Justice of the peace	1924 appointed to Circuit Court, Dublin	I.L.T.& S.J. (1925)
St. Lawrence Ernest Joseph Devitt	1873 Ballina, Co. Mayo	Ll.B. RUI	1898 25			1917 junior counsel to James O'Connor KC while attorney general	1921 senior Crown prosecutor, Kilkenny 1923 judicial commissioner Dáil Courts Winding Up Commission 1923 1924 appointed to Circuit Court, Cavan and Monaghan	I.L.T.& S.J. (1936)
Charles Francis Doyle	1863 Limerick	Sch. TCD BA Dublin MA RUI	1888 25	1906 43		1910 County Court judge, Mayo		I.L.T.& S.J. (1928)
Charles Drumgoole	1865 Newry, Co. Down	MA Ll.D. RUI	1893 29	1910 45		1913 County Court judge, Kerry 1920–4 Cork W		I.L.T.& S.J. (1927)
Matthew Joseph Kenny	1861 Clare		1886 Grays Inn, English Bar 25 1889 Irish Bar 28	1914 53		1882–5 (Anti-Parnellite) MP Ennis 1885–95 MP Mid-Tyrone 1917 Crown prosecutor, Kerry		I.L.T.& S.J. (1942)

1 Compiled by Robert D. Marshall.

APPENDIX 4 (continued)

	Year and place of birth	University	Year of call & age	Year & age taking silk	Year appointed Bencher	Offices held to Aug. 1924 based upon pre-1922 appointments	Irish Free State offices held post-1922 to August 1924	Obituary
Edward J. McElligott	1874 Listowel Co. Kerry	St Vincent's Castleknock and TCD	1896 22	1911 37		1913 senior Crown prosecutor, Cork 1914 Treasury Council Valuation Department 1915 chairman of Munitions Tribunal Ireland		*I.L.T. & S.J.* (1946)
Charles Wyse Power	1892 Dublin	TCD BA Dublin	1913 21				1923 Judicial Commissioner Dáil Courts Winding Up Commission	
James Sealy	1876 Dublin	Sch. TCD BA Dublin	1902 26	1918 42		Selection Board Inns of Court Officer Training Corps	1921–4 deputy County Court judge, Tipperary	*I.L.T. & S.J.* (1949)
John Wakely	1861 Edenderry Co. Offally	TCD BA Dublin	1885 24	1899 38	1902	JP and DL, Co Offaly. (Father also a JP & DL) Lord of the manor of Ballyburley, Edenderry, Co. Offaly, comprising 1,722 acres valued at £1,462 1896 Crown prosecutor 1904–24 County Court judge, Roscommon and Sligo		*I.L.T. & S.J.* (1942)

Approved June 1924 but not appointed in June or August 1924

	Date & location of birth	University	Date of call & Age	Date of taking silk & age	Bencher	Offices held to August 1924 based upon pre-1922 appointments	Irish Free State offices held 1922–24	Obituary
Daniel J. O'Brien	1866 Kingstown, Dublin		1898 22	1914 48		1912 Crown prosecutor, Carlow 1917 Crown prosecutor, Co. Kilkenny 1918 Standing Counsel GPO 1920 County Court judge, Kilkenny and Waterford		*I.L.T. & S.J.* (1949)
John Henry Pigot	1863 Dundrum, Co. Dublin	BA Ll.B. TCD Dublin	1890 27	1909 46		Father master of the exchequer 1920–4 County Court judge, Co. Limerick		*I.L.T. & S.J.* (1928)

APPENDIX 5

Judicial office-holders[1]

Former chief justices

- (i) Hugh Kennedy (1924–1936)
- (ii) Timothy Sullivan (1936–1946)
- (iii) Conor Maguire (1946–1961)
- (iv) Cearbhall Ó Dálaigh (1961–1973)
- (v) William FitzGerald (1973–1974)
- (vi) Tom O'Higgins (1974–1985)
- (vii) Thomas Finlay (1985–1994)
- (viii) Liam Hamilton (1994–2000)
- (ix) Ronan Keane (2000–2004)
- (x) John L. Murray (2004–2011)
- (xi) Susan Denham (2011–2017)
- (xii) Frank Clarke (2017–2021)
- (xiii) Donal O'Donnell (2021–present)

Former presidents of the Circuit Court

- (i) William George Shannon (1947–1959)
- (ii) Barra Ó Briain (1959–1973)
- (iii) John Charles Conroy (1973–1975)
- (iv) John James Durcan (1975–1977)
- (v) Thomas Neylon (1977–1986)
- (vi) Thomas Francis Roe (1986–1990)
- (vii) Peter O'Malley (1990–1991)
- (viii) Francis Spain (1991–1997)
- (ix) Diarmuid Sheridan (1998)
- (x) Esmond Smyth (1998–2005)
- (xi) Matthew Deery (2005–2012)
- (xii) Raymond Groarke (2012–2019)
- (xiii) Patricia Ryan (2019–present)

Former presidents of the High Court

- (i) Timothy Sullivan (1924–1936)
- (ii) Conor Maguire (1936–1946)
- (iii) George Gavan Duffy (1946–1951)
- (iv) Cahir Davitt (1951–1966)
- (v) Aindrias Ó Caoimh (1966–1974)
- (vi) Thomas A. Finlay (1974–1985)
- (vii) Liam Hamilton (1985–1994)
- (viii) Harry Whelehan (1994)
- (ix) Declan Costello (1995–1998)
- (x) Frederick Morris (1998–2001)
- (xi) Joseph Finnegan (2001–2006)
- (xii) Richard Johnson (2006–2009)
- (xiii) Nicholas Kearns (2009–2015)
- (xiv) Peter Kelly (2015–2020)
- (xv) Mary Irvine (2020–2022)
- (xvi) David Barniville (2022–present)

Former presidents of the District Court

- (i) Cathal Ó Floinn (1961–1979)
- (ii) Thomas Donnelly (1979–1985)
- (iii) Oliver Macklin (1985–1990)
- (iv) Peter Smithwick (1990–2005)
- (v) Miriam Malone (2005–2012)
- (vi) Rosemary Horgan (2012–2019)
- (vii) Colin Daly (2019–2021)
- (viii) Paul Kelly (2021–present)

---

1 Compiled with the assistance of Daire Hogan.

Bibliography

ARCHIVAL SOURCES

DUBLIN
Irish Military Archives
Bureau of Military History
Military Service Pensions Collection

King's Inns
King's Inns Benchers' Minutes

National Archives of Ireland
Cabinet Committee Minutes
Constitution Committee
Government Meeting Minutes
North Eastern Boundary Bureau
Office of Public Works
Office of the Taoiseach
Civil bill books and papers
District Court order books
Department of Justice
Office of the Attorney General
Prisons Board

National Library of Ireland
Bryce papers
Sheehy-Skeffington papers
Ceannt papers
Richard Bartlett collection

TCD Archives
FitzGibbon papers
Johnston papers

UCD Archives
Eoin MacNeill papers
Ernest Blythe papers
Gavan Duffy papers
Kathleen Barry Moloney papers

Kevin O'Higgins papers
Hugh Kennedy papers
Éamon de Valera papers

UNITED KINGDOM
Bodleian Library (Asquith papers)
Cadbury Research Library (Austin Chamberlain papers)
House of Lords Record Office (Lloyd George papers)
The National Archives (UK) (Cabinet meetings)
University of Edinburgh (Arthur Berriedale Keith papers)

OFFICIAL PUBLICATIONS

Calendar of District Courts (Dublin, 1924)
Central Statistics Office, *Census 2022 summary of results* (Dublin, 2023)
Courts Service of Ireland, *Annual report 2020* (Dublin, 2020) and *2022* (Dublin, 2023)
Dáil Éireann and Seanad Éireann Debates
Department of Industry and Commerce, *Census of population Saorstát Éireann* (Dublin, 1926)
Department of Justice, *Report of the judicial planning working group* (Dublin, 2022)
Documents on Irish foreign policy, vol. 1 (Dublin, 1998)
Hansard's parliamentary debates
High Court practice directions
Iris Oifigiúil
Joint Oireachtas Committee on Justice and Equality, *Report on the reform of family law* (Dublin, 2019)
Joint Oireachtas Committee, *Report on courts and courthouses* (Dublin, 2022)
Jury trial in civil actions. Jury challenges: third and fourth interim reports of the Committee on Court Practice and Procedure (Dublin, 1966)
Law Reform Commission, *Breach of promise of marriage* (LRC 4-1978)
Law Reform Commission, Consolidation and reform of the Courts Acts (LRC CP 46-2007)
Law Reform Commission, *Consultation paper on consolidation and reform of the Courts Acts* (LRCCP 46–2007)
Law Reform Commission, *First report on family law* (LRC 1-1980)
OECD, *Modernising staffing and court management practices in Ireland* (Paris, 2023)
Official yearbook of the Commonwealth of Australia (Melbourne, 1920)
Proceedings of the Joint Committee on the Rules of the Circuit Court
Programme for government: our shared future (Dublin, 2020)
Report from the commission to the Council on whether the Union institutions have sufficient available capacity for the Irish language (21 June 2021)
Report of Committee on reformatory and industrial schools (Dublin, 1970) (Kennedy report)
Report of the Committee on the Courts of Justice Act 1924 (Dublin, 1930)

Report of the Committee on the Criminal Law Amendment Acts (1880–85) and Juvenile Prostitution (Dublin, 1931) (Carrigan report)
Report of the Joint Oireachtas Committee (Dublin, 1930)
Report of the Judiciary Committee (Dublin, 1923)
Report of the Select Committee on judicial salaries, expense allowances and pensions (Dublin, 1953)
Revenue Commissioners of Saorstát Éireann, *First annual report – Year ended 31 March 1924* (Dublin, 1926); *Second annual report Year ended 31 March 1925* (Dublin, 1927)
Statistical abstract 1931
The constructive work of Dáil Éireann No. 1 – the national police and courts of justice (Dublin, 1921)

LEGISLATION

Statutes of Kilkenny (1366)
An Act for the English Order, Habit, and Language 1537 (28 Hen. VIII, c. 15) [Ir.]
Administration of Justice (Language) Act (Ireland) 1737 (11 Geo. II, c. 6)
An Act for Securing the Independency of the Judges and the Impartial Administration of Justice 1782 (21 & 22 Geo. III, c. 50) (Ir.)
Act of Union (Ireland) Act 1800 (40 Geo. III, c. 38)
Crown Cases Act 1848 (11 & 12 Vic., 78)
Lunacy Regulation (Ireland) Act 1871 (30 & 31 Vic., c. 118)
Licensing Act 1872 (35 & 36 Vic., c. 94)
Appellate Jurisdiction Act 1876 (39 & 40 Vic., c. 59)
Elementary Education Act 1876 (39 & 40 Vic., c. 79)
County Officers Act 1877 (40 & 41 Vict., c. 56)
Supreme Court of Judicature Act (Ireland) 1877 (40 & 41 Vic., c. 57)
Explosive Substances Act 1883 (46 & 47 Vic., c. 3)
Statute Law Revision Act 1894 (57 & 58 Vic., c. 56)
Court of Criminal Appeal Act 1907
Supreme Court of Judicature (Ireland) Act 1907
Universities Act 1908
Government of Ireland Act 1920
Restoration of Order in Ireland Act 1920
(UK) Irish Free State (Consequential Provisions) Act 1922
1922 Constitution
Dáil Éireann Courts (Winding-Up) Act 1923
District Justices (Temporary Provisions) Act 1923
Land Act 1923
Land Law (Commission) Act 1923
Courts of Justice Act 1924
Criminal Justice (Administration) Act 1924
Dáil Éireann Courts (Winding-Up) (Amendment) Act 1924

Juries (Amendment) Act 1924
Ministers and Secretaries Act 1924
Dáil Éireann Courts (Winding-Up) Act 1925
Courts of Justice Act 1926
Agricultural Credit Act 1927
An Act to amend the Supreme Court Act, 1927 (Canada)
Courts of Justice Act 1928
Legal Practitioners (Qualification) Act 1929
Constitution (Removal of Oath) Act 1933
Courts of Justice Act 1936
Constitution of Ireland 1937
Courts of Justice (District Court) Act 1946
Criminal Justice Act 1951
Courts of Justice Act 1953
Solicitors Act 1954
Judicial Pensions Act 1959
Sea Fisheries Acts 1959–2005
Administration of Justice Act 1960
Solicitors (Amendment) Act 1960
Courts (Establishment and Constitution Act) 1961
Courts (Supplemental Provisions) Act 1961
Lands Tribunal and Compensation Act (NI) 1964
Succession Act 1965
Administration of Justice Act 1969
Courts Act 1971
Judicature (NI) Act 1978
Criminal Appeal (NI) Act 1980
County Courts (NI) Order 1980
Family Law Act 1981
Magistrates' Courts (NI) Order 1981
Magistrates' Courts Rules (NI) 1984
Dentists Act 1985
Courts Act 1988
Criminal Justice Act 1988
Data Protection Act 1988
Police and Criminal Evidence (NI) Order 1989
Child Care Act 1991
Courts Act 1991
Social Security Administration (NI) Act 1992
Courts and Court Officers Act 1995
Criminal Appeal Act 1995
Family Law Act 1995
Industrial Tribunals (NI) Order 1996
Waste Management Act 1996
Fisheries (Amendment) Act 1997
Hepatitis C Compensation Tribunal Act 1997

Irish Takeover Panel Act 1997
Courts Service Act 1998
Northern Ireland Act 1998
Planning and Development Act 2000
Aviation Regulation Act 2001
Children Act 2001
Mental Health Act 2001
Teaching Council Act 2001
Transport (Railway Infrastructure) Act 2001
Solicitors (Amendment) Act 2002
Criminal Justice Act 2003
European Arrest Warrant Act 2003
Fisheries (Amendment) Act 2003
Official Languages Act 2003
Personal Injuries Assessment Board Act 2003
Criminal Justice (NI) Order 2004
Civil Liability and Courts Act 2004
Residential Tenancies Act 2004
Health and Social Care Professionals Act 2005
Veterinary Practitioners Act 2005
Planning and Development (Strategic Infrastructure) Act 2006
Justice and Security (NI) Act 2007
Medical Practitioners Act 2007
Pharmacy Act 2007
Tribunals, Courts and Enforcement Act 2007
Legal Practitioners (Irish Language) Act 2008
National Asset Management Agency Act 2009
Civil Partnership and Certain Rights and Obligations of Cohabitants Act 2010
Planning and Development (Amendment) Act 2010
Civil Law (Miscellaneous Provisions) Act 2011
Environment (Miscellaneous Provisions) Act 2011
Nurses and Midwives Act 2011
Property Services (Regulation) Act 2011 (as amended)
Protected Disclosures Act 2011
Directive 2012/29/EU
Courts and Civil Law (Miscellaneous Provisions) Act 2013
Court of Appeal Act 2014
Employment Permits (Amendment) Act 2014
Assisted Decision Making (Capacity) Act 2015
Justice Act (NI) 2015
Legal Services Regulation Act 2015
Workplace Relations Act 2015
General Data Protection Regulations and the Data Protection Act 2018
Courts Act 2019
Judicial Council Act 2019
Residential Tenancies (Amendment) Act 2019

Official Languages (Amendment) Act 2021
Personal Insolvency (Amendment) Act 2021
Assisted Decision-Making (Capacity) (Amendment) Act 2022
Criminal Justice (Committal Reform) Act (NI) 2022
Courts Act 2023

Bills

Courts of Justice bill 1923
Public Safety (Emergency Provisions) bill 1923
Juries bill 1927
The Constitution Amendment (Retirement of Judges) bill 1977
Family Courts bill 2022
Defamation (Amendment) bill 2023
Planning and Development bill 2023

Secondary legislation

County Courts (Ireland) Orders 1890
The Provisional Government (Transfer of Functions) Order 1922
Customs (Land Frontier) Regulations 1923
Courts of Justice Act 1924 (Commencement) (No. 4) Order 1924
Rules of the Superior Courts 1926
Rules of the Circuit Court 1926
Circuit Court Rules 1930
Circuit Court (New Circuits) Order 1937
Circuit Court (New Circuits) Order 1960
Rules of the High Court and Supreme Court Mode of Address Rules 1961
Rules of the Court of Judicature (NI) 1980
Criminal Appeal (Prosecution Appeals) Rules (NI) 2005
Official Languages (Amendment) Act 2021 (Commencement) (No.2) Order 2022
Official Languages Act 2003 (Establishment Day) Order 2022
Official Languages (Amendment) (Commencement) Order 2022
Official Languages (Amendment) Act 2021 (Commencement) Order 2023

CASES

A, B and C v. Ireland (2011) 53 EHRR 13
A.C. v. Cork University Hospital [2019] IESC 73, [2019] 2 IR 38
Airey v. Ireland [1981] 3 EHRR 592
AM v. HSE [2019] IESC 3, [2019] 2 IR 115
An Stát (MacFhearraigh) v MacGamhna [1998] IRSR 29
An Stát (MacFhearraigh) v. Breitheamh Dúiche Neilan [1984] IRSR 38
Application of Sir James O'Connor [1930] IR 62
Attorney General (Fahy) v. Bruen (No.2) [1937] IR 125
Attorney General v. Joyce and Walsh [1929] IR 526

Attorney General v. McBride [1928] IR 451
Attorney General v. Murray (No. 2) [1926] IR 300
B.S. v. Director of Public Prosecutions [2017] IESCDET 134
Balc v. Minister for Justice and Equality [2018] IECA 76
Boggan v. Motor Union Insurance Co [1923] 2 IR 136
Braun v. Roche Irish Times, 22 June 1972
Buckley v. Finnegan (1906) ILTR 76
Byrne v. Ireland [1972] IR 241
C.C. v. Minister for Justice and Equality [2016] 2 IR 680
Callaghan v. An Bord Pleanála [2015] IESCDET 60
Callaghan v. An Bord Pleanála [2017] IESC 60
Case of Tanistry (1607) Dav. 28
Clinton v. An Bord Pleanála [2007] 1 IR 272
Criminal Law (Jurisdiction) Bill, 1975 [1977] IR 129
Cronin v. Youghal Carpets (Yarns) Ltd. [1985] IR 312
Curren v. Connolly (1931) Galway cause book in civil cases 1929–33
De Búrca and Anderson v. Attorney General [1976] IR 38
Delap v. Minister for Justice [1990] IRSR 116
Dellway v. National Asset Management Agency [2010] IEHC 375
Department of Finance, Land and Property Services v. Foster [2022] NICA 19
Director of Public Prosecutions v. O'R [2016] 3 IR 322
DMcA v. A Health and Social Services Trust [2017] NICA 3
DPP v. Avadenei [2018] 3 IR 215
DPP v. Billings [2019] IECA 149
Egan v. Macready [1921] 1 IR 265
Ellis v. Irish Land Commission (1925) Galway civil bill papers 1923 to 1927, NAI IC/91/120 1925/7677
Fegan v. Great Northern Railway Co., 19 Mar. 1937
Financial Conduct Authority v. Arch Insurance (UK) Ltd [2021] UKSC 1
Fitzpatrick v. An Bord Pleanála [2018] IESC 60
Flynn v. Power [1985] IR 648
Fox v. Mahon [2015] IESCDET 2
Gaughran v. Chief Constable of the PSNI [2015] UKSC 29, [2016] AC 345
Gaughran v. UK App 45245/15, judgment of 13 Feb. 2020.
Glann Mór Céibh Teoranta v. Minister for Housing [2022] IESC 40
Grace v. An Bord Pleanála [2020] 3 IR 286
Hosie v. Lawless [1927] IR 464
In Re D [1987] IR 449
In Re FD [2015] IESC 83; [2015] 1 IR 741
In Re JJ [2021] IESC 1
In Re Solicitors Act 1954 [1960] IR 239
In Re Francis Dolan [2008] IEHC 264, [2008] 1 ILRM 19
In Re. KK (No. 1) [2023] IEHC 306
Irish Asphalt Ltd v. An Bord Pleanála [1996] 2 IR 179
Irish Hardware Ltd v. South Dublin County Council [2001] 2 ILRM 291
Kinloch v. HM Advocate [2012] UKSC 62, [2013] 2 AC 93

L.O'S. v. Minister for Health and Children [2015] IESC 6
Law Society of Ireland v. Coleman [2018] IESC 71
Lee v. Ashers Baking Company Ltd [2016] NICA 39
Lee v. Ashers Baking Company Ltd [2018] UKSC 49, [2020] AC 413
Lynham v. Butler (No. 2) [1933] IR 74
Mac Giolla Bhríde v. Mac Gamhna (McBride v. McGovern) [1906] 1 IR 181
MacAodháin v. Coiste Rialacha na nUaschúirteanna [2010] 2 IR 678
MacCarthaigh v Éire [1999] IR 200
Mahon v. Powell (1932) Galway cause book in civil cases 1932–1934, NAI ID/73/60
McCord's (Raymond) Application [2016] NIQB 85
McGee v. The Attorney General [1973] IR 284
McKenna v. An Taoiseach (No. 2) [1995] 2 IR 10
Minister for Justice, Equality and Law Reform v. Adach [2010] 3 IR 402
Minister for Justice, Equality and Law Reform v. Connolly [2014] 1 IR 720
Moore v. attorney general of the Irish Free State [1935] IR 472
Ó Gribín v. An Comhairle Mhúinteoireachta [2007] IEHC 454
Ó Gríofáin v. Éire [2009] IEHC 199
Ó'Beoláin v. Fahy [2001] 2 IR 279
O'Byrne v. Minister for Finance [1959] IR 1
Ó'Cadhla v. An tAire Dlí agus Cirt [2019] IEHC 503
O'Conaire v. MacGruairc [2010] 3 IR 30
O'Donoghue v. Minister for Health [1996] 2 IR 20
Ó'Foghludha v. McClean [1934] IR 469
O'Keeffe v. Ireland [2014] 59 EHRR 15
Ó'Maicín v. Éire [2014] 4 IR 583
Ó'Monacháin v. An Taoiseach [1986] ILRM 660
Ó'Murchú v. An Taoiseach [2010] 4 IR 484
O'Reilly v. Gleeson [1975] IR 258
Odum v. Minister for Justice and Equality [2023] IESC 3
Open Door and Dublin Well Woman v. Ireland [1992] ECHR 68
Parker v. Chief Constable of the PSNI [2018] NICA 17
People (AG) v. Conmey [1975] IR 341
People (AG) v. Giles [1974] IR 422
People (DPP) v. Littlejohn [1978] ILRM 147
People (DPP) v. Lynch [1982] IR 64
People (DPP) v. O'Shea [1982] 1 IR 384
People (DPP) v. Shaw [1982] IR 1
Public Prosecution Service of Northern Ireland v. Elliott and McKee [2011] NICA 61,
    [2012] NI 154; [2013] UKSC 32; [2013] 1 WLR 1611
Quinn and White v. Stokes [1931] IR 588
Quinn Insurance Ltd v. PricewaterhouseCoopers [2017] 3 IR 812
Quinn Insurance Ltd v. PricewaterhouseCoopers [2021] 2 IR 70
R (Childers) v. Adjutant General of the Provisional Forces [1923] 1 IR 5
R (Cooney) v. Clinton, R (Corcoran) v. Clinton and R (O'Connell) v. Military Governor
    of Hare Park Camp [1935] IR 245
R (Garde) v. Strickland [1921] 2 IR 317

R (Johnstone) v. O'Sullivan [1923] 2 IR 13
R (Kelly) v. Maguire & O'Sheil [1923] 2 IR 58
R (Miller) v. Secretary of State for Exiting the European Union [2017] UKSC 5, [2018] AC 61
R (Murphy) v. Military Governor, Mountjoy Prison (1924) 58 ILTR 1
R (O'Brien) v. Military Governor of NDU Internment Camp [1924] 1 IR 32
R (Ó'Coileáin) v. Crotty (1927) 61 ILTR 81
R (O'Connell) v. Military Governor of Hare Park Camp [1924] 2 IR 104
R v. Hayes and Palombo [2024] EWCA Crim 304
R v. Adams [2020] UKSC 19, [2020] 1 WLR 2077
R v. Allen [1921] 2 IR 241
R v. JM [2013] NICA 64
R v. Maughan [2022] UKSC 13, [2022] 1 WLR 2820
R v. Z (Attorney General for Northern Ireland's Reference) [2005] UKHL 35, [2005] 2 AC 645
Re Allister's Application for Judicial Review [2023] UKSC 5, [2023] 2 WLR 457
Re Article 26 and the Offences Against the State (Amendment) Bill 1940 [1940] IR 470
Re Earle [1938] IR 485
Re McGuinness's Application for Judicial Review [2020] UKSC 6, [2021] AC 392
Re McLorinan, A Minor [1935] IR 373
Re Westby, Minors (No. 2) [1934] IR 311
Reference by the Attorney General for Northern Ireland – Abortion Services (Safe Access Zones) (Northern Ireland) Bill [2022] UKSC 32, [2023] AC 505
Ryan v. Attorney General [1965] IR 294
S.T.E. v. Minister for Justice and Equality [2019] IECA 332
Sinnott v. Minister for Education [2001] 2 IR 505
State (Buchan) v. Coyne 70 ILTR 185 (1936)
State (Ryan) v. Lennon [1935] IR 170
Talbot v. An Bord Pleanála [2009] 1 IR 375
The King (Kelly) v. Maguire and O'Shiel [1923] 2 IR 58; [1923] 57 ILTR 57
The King (O'Brien) v. The Governor of the Military Internment Camp and Anor [1924] 1 IR 32
The State (Killian) v. Minister for Justice [1954] IR 207
The State (Ryan) v. Lennon [1935] IR 170
Wansboro v. Director of Public Prosecutions [2017] IESCDET
Ward v. Police Service of Northern Ireland [2007] UKSC 50, [2007] 1 WLR 3013
Webb v. Outrim [1907] AC 81 (PC)

ACADEMIC SOURCES

Bacik, I., C. Costello and E. Drew, *Gender injustice* (Dublin, 2003)
Bacik, I., and M. Rogan (eds), *Legal cases that changed Ireland* (Dublin, 2016)
Baker, M.H.C., *Irish railways since 1916* (London, 1972)
Barton, B., 'Runaway jury', *Law Society Gazette* (2023)

Beaumont, C., 'Women, citizenship and Catholicism in the Irish Free State, 1922–1948', *Women's History Review* (1997)

Black, L., '"Women of evil life": Donnybrook Magdalene and the criminal justice system' in Mark Coen, Katherine O'Donnell and Maeve O'Rourke (eds), *A Dublin Magdalene laundry: Donnybrook and Church-State power in Ireland* (Dublin, 2023)

Black, L., *Gender and punishment in Ireland: women, murder and the death penalty, 1922–64* (Manchester, 2022)

Black, L., L. Brangan and D. Healy (eds), *Histories of punishment and social control in Ireland: perspectives from a periphery* (Bradford, 2022)

Boyce, D.G., *The Irish question and British politics, 1868–1996* (2nd edn, London, 1996)

Brennan, K., '"A fine mixture of pity and justice": the criminal justice response to infanticide in Ireland, 1922–1949', *Law and History Review* (2013)

Brennan, K., 'Social norms and the law in responding to infanticide', *Legal Studies* (2018)

Buckley, H., C. Skehill and E. O'Sullivan, 'Protecting children under the Child Care Act 1991 – getting the balance right', *Irish Journal of Family Law* (1999)

Butler, R., *Building the Irish courthouse and prison: a political history, 1750–1850* (Cork, 2020)

Cahillane, L., and D.K. Coffey (eds), *The centenary of the Irish Free State Constitution: constituting a polity?* (London, 2024)

Cahillane, L., *Drafting the Irish Free State Constitution* (Manchester, 2016)

Callanan, F., and T.M. Healy (Cambridge, 1996) in B.M. Walker (ed.), *Parliamentary election results in Ireland, 1801–1922* (Dublin, 1978)

Carrigan, W., *Report of the Joint Committee on the Courts of Justice Act 1924* (Dublin, 1930)

Casey, J., 'Republican courts in Ireland 1919–1922', *Irish Jurist* (1970)

Casey, M., 'The most illustrious Order of Saint Patrick', *Dublin Historical Record* (1991)

Cherry, R.R., and J. Wakely, *The Irish land law and land purchase acts, 1881, 1885, and 1887* (Dublin, 1888)

Choo, A.L.-T., and J. Hunter, 'Gender discrimination and juries in the 20th century: judging women judging men', *International Journal of Evidence and Proof* (2018)

Clancy, C., '50 years later: women in policing', *Communiqué* (Dec. 2009)

Clery, A., H. Kennedy and M. Dawson, *Town Tenants (Ireland) Act, 1906* (Dublin, 1907)

Coen, M., '"The work of some irresponsible women": jurors, ghosts and embracery in the Irish Free State', *Law and History Review* (2020)

Coen, M., 'Through a narrow window: women's jury service in Ireland, 1921–1927', *law & history* (2022)

Coen, M., and N. Howlin, 'The jury speaks: jury riders in the nineteenth and twentieth centuries', *American Journal of Legal History* (2018)

Coen, M., N. Howlin, C. Barry and J. Lynch, 'Respect, reform and research: an empirical insight into judge-jury relations', *Irish Judicial Studies Journal* (2020)

Coen, M., N. Howlin, C. Barry and J. Lynch, *Judges and juries in Ireland: an empirical study* (Dublin, 2020)

Coffey, D.K., 'British, Commonwealth and Irish responses to the abdication of King Edward VIII', *Irish Jurist* (2009)

Coffey, D.K., 'The judiciary of the Irish Free State', *Dublin University Law Journal* (2011)

Cohen, A.P., *The symbolic construction of community* (Abingdon, 2001)

Conner, H.D., *The Fisheries (Ir.) Acts, 1842 to 1901* (Dublin, 1892; 2nd edn, 1907)

Coonan, G., K. O'Toole and M. O'Toole, *Criminal procedure in the District Court* (2nd edn, Dublin, 2022)

Costello, C. (ed.), *The Four Courts: 200 years: essays to commemorate the bicentenary of the Four Courts* (Dublin, 1996)

Costello, J.A., 'The leading principles of the Brehon laws', *Studies: An Irish Quarterly Review* (1913)

Costello, R.Á., 'The Barbarian and the cart: law, citizenship and linguistic identity in Irish macaronic verse', *Law and Humanities* (2021)

Coulter, C., *Family law in practice: a study of cases in the Circuit Court* (Dublin, 2009)

Crooks, P., and T. Mohr (eds), *Law and the idea of liberty in Ireland: from Magna Carta to the present* (Dublin, 2023)

Crowley, T., 'Language, politics and identity in Ireland: a historical overview' in Ray Hickey (ed.), *Socio linguistics in Ireland* (Basingstoke, 2016)

Crowley, T., *The politics of language in Ireland, 1366–1922: a sourcebook* (Dublin, 2000)

Curran, C.P., *Under the receding wave* (Dublin, 1970)

Daly, T.G., 'Hugh Kennedy: Ireland's (quietly) towering nation-maker' in Rehan Abeyratne and Iddo Porat (eds), *Towering judges: a comparative study of constitutional judges* (Cambridge, 2021)

Davies, J., *A discovery of the true causes why Ireland was never subdued and brought under obedience to the Crown of England until the beginning of his majesty's happy reign*, ed. James P. Myers, Jr (Washington, 1969)

Davitt, C., 'The civil jurisdiction of the courts of justice of the Irish Republic, 1920–1922', *Irish Jurist* (1968)

De Blacam, M., 'Official language and constitutional interpretation', *Irish Jurist* (2014)

Delany, V.T.H., *The administration of justice in Ireland* (Dublin, 1962)

Delany, V.T.H., 'The Constitution of Ireland: its origin and development', *University of Toronto Law Journal* (1957)

Denton, G., and T. Fahy, *The Northern Ireland land boundary, 1923–1992* (Belfast, 1993)

Derham, W., '(Re)making majesty: the throne room at Dublin Castle, 1911–2011' in Myles Campbell and William Derham (eds), *Making majesty: the throne room at Dublin Castle, a cultural history* (Kildare, 2017)

Derham, W., 'Chapel Royal, Dublin Castle', *History Ireland* (2017)

Dickson, B., *The Irish Supreme Court: historical and comparative perspectives* (Oxford, 2019)

Donlan, S.P., '"Little better than cannibals": Sir John Davies and Edmund Burke on property and progress', *Northern Ireland Legal Quarterly* (2003)

Donnelly, M., and F. White, *Consumer law: rights and regulation* (Dublin, 2014)
Dougherty, J.I., '"Ocular demonstration" or "tremendous treasure"', *History Ireland* (2010)
Dowling, K., and S. Mullalley, *Civil procedure in the District Court* (Dublin, 2014)
Duffy, S., J. Montague, K. Mulligan & Michael O'Neill, *Dublin Castle: from fortress to palace, vol. 1* (Dublin, 2022)
Elgenius, G., 'National museums as national symbols' in Peter Aronsson and Gabriella Elgenius (eds), *National museums and nation-building in Europe 1750–2010* (Abingdon, 2004)
Enright, M., J. McCandless and A. O'Donoghue, *Northern/Irish feminist judgments: judges' troubles and the gendered politics of identity* (Oxford, 2017)
Ewart, W., *A journey in Ireland* (London, 1922)
Fanning, R., *A history of the Department of Finance* (Dublin, 1978)
Fanning, R., *Independent Ireland* (Dublin, 1983)
Ferguson, K., *King's Inns barristers 1868–2004* (Dublin, 2005)
Ferriter, D., *A nation of extremes: the Pioneers in twentieth-century Ireland* (Dublin, 1999)
Ferriter, D., *The Border: the legacy of a century of Anglo-Irish politics* (London, 2019)
Ferriter, D., *The transformation of Ireland, 1900–2000* (London, 2004)
Fewer, M., *The battle of the Four Courts* (London, 2018)
Fitzgerald, J., and J. Kenny, '"Till debt do us part": financial implications of the divorce of the Irish Free State from the United Kingdom, 1922–1926', *European Review of Economic History* (2020)
FitzGibbon, H.M., and W.J. Johnston, *The law of local government in Ireland: including the Local Government Act, 1898, the orders in council* (Dublin, 1899)
Forrester, M., *Michael Collins: the lost leader* (Dublin, 2006)
Foster, G., *The Irish Civil War and society: politics, class and conflict* (London, 2015)
Foxton, D., *Revolutionary lawyers: Sinn Féin and Crown courts in Ireland and Britain, 1916–1923* (Dublin, 2008)
Foy, M., *Michael Collins's intelligence war* (Gloucestershire, 2008)
Galloway, P., *The most illustrious order: the Order of St Patrick and its knights* (London, 1999)
Galvan-Alvarez, E., et al., 'Decolonising the state: subversion, mimicry and criminality', *Postcolonial Studies* (2020)
Garvin, T., *1922: the birth of Irish democracy* (Dublin, 2005)
Garvin, T., *The evolution of Irish nationalist politics* (Dublin, 1981)
Gaughan, A., *At the coalface: recollections of a city and country priest, 1950–2000* (Dublin, 2000)
Gibbons, I., 'The first British Labour government and the Irish Boundary Commission 1924', *Studies: An Irish Quarterly Review* (2009)
Gibney, J., and K. O'Malley, *The handover: Dublin Castle and the British withdrawal from Ireland, 1922* (Dublin, 2022)
Greer, D., 'A security against illegality? The reservation of Crown cases in nineteenth-century Ireland' in Norma Dawson (ed.), *Reflections on law and history* (Dublin, 2006)
Gwynn, D.R., *The Irish Free State, 1922–1927* (London, 1928)

Hall, E., *The superior courts of law: 'official' law reporting in Ireland, 1866–2006* (Dublin, 2007)
Hallett, T., 'Eoin MacNeill and the Irish Boundary Commission' in Conor Mulvagh and Emer Purcell (eds), *Eoin MacNeill: the pen and the sword* (Dublin, 2022)
Hanna, H., 'Saorstát Éireann (Irish Free State) 1922–1924', *Journal of Comparative Legislation and International Law* (1926)
Hanna, H., *The law of workmen's compensation* (Dublin, 1907)
Hanna, H., *The statute law of the Irish Free State 1922 to 1928* (Dublin, 1929)
Hart, A., *A history of the inn of court of Northern Ireland* (Belfast, 2013)
Healy, M., *The old Munster circuit* (Dublin, 1939 and London, 2001)
Healy, T.M., *Letters and leaders of my day* (London, 1928)
Heuston, R.F.V., *Lives of the lord chancellors, 1885–1940* (Oxford, 1964)
Hogan et al., *Kelly: The Irish Constitution* (5th edn, Dublin, 2018)
Hogan, G., 'Chief Justice Kennedy and Sir James O'Connor's application', *Irish Jurist* (1988)
Hogan, G., 'Irish nationalism as a legal ideology', *Studies: An Irish Quarterly Review* (1986)
Hogan, G., 'Mr Justice Brian Walsh: the legacy of experiment and the triumph of judicial imagination', *Irish Jurist* (2017)
Hogan, G., 'The Count Plunkett *habeas corpus* application and the end of the Dáil Supreme Court', *Irish Jurist* (2022)
Holland, A., 'The papers of Hugh Kennedy: a research legacy for the foundation of the state', *Irish Jurist* (1989)
Hopkinson, M. (ed.), *The last days of Dublin Castle the Mark Sturgis diaries* (Kildare, 1999)
Horan, G., *The Courts of Justice Act, 1924 (Saorstát Éireann)* (Dublin, 1924)
Howlin, N., and K. Costello (eds), *Law and the family in Ireland, 1800–1950* (London, 2017)
Howlin, N., and F. Larkin (eds), *Confluences of law and history: Irish Legal History Society discourses and other papers, 2011–2021* (forthcoming, Dublin)
Howlin, N., 'Compensation for malicious injuries' in Oonagh Breen and Noel McGrath (eds), *Palles: the legal legacy of the last lord chief baron* (Dublin, 2022)
Howlin, N., 'The Irish courts system and the court houses' in Colum O'Riordan, Paul Burns and Ciaran O'Connor (eds), *Ireland's court houses* (Dublin, 2019)
Howlin, N., 'The prehistory of the Offences Against the State Act' in Mark Coen (ed.), *The Offences Against the State Act 1939 at 80: a model counter-terrorism act?* (Oxford, 2021)
Howlin, N., *Barristers in Ireland: an evolving profession since 1921* (Dublin, 2023)
Jacobson, D.S., 'The political economy of industrial location: the Ford Motor Company at Cork, 1912–26', *Irish Economic and Social History* (1977)
Johnson, D.S., 'Cattle smuggling on the Irish Border, 1932–38', *Irish Economic and Social History* (1979)
Johnston, W.J., 'Ireland in the medieval law courts', *Studies: An Irish Quarterly Review* (1923)
Johnston, W.J., 'The first adventure of the common law', *Law Quarterly Review* (1920)
Johnston, W.J., 'The parliament of the Pale', *Law Quarterly Review* (1918)

Johnston, W.J., *Handbook of land purchase in Ireland* (2nd edn, Dublin, 1903)
Johnston, W.J., *Handbook on the Labourers Act* (Dublin, 1907)
Jones, T., *Whitehall diary, vol. iii: Ireland 1918–1925*, ed. Keith Middlemas (Oxford, 1971)
Keane, R., '"The will of the general": martial law in Ireland 1535–1924', *Irish Jurist* (1990)
Keane, R., 'The Irish courts system in the 21st century: planning for the future', *Bar Review* (2001)
Keane, R., 'The voice of the Gael: Chief Justice Kennedy and the emergence of the new Irish court system, 1921–1936', *Irish Jurist* (1996)
Keating, A., 'The demise of Brehon law', *Irish Law Times* (2012)
Keith, A.B., 'Notes on imperial constitutional law', *Journal of Comparative Legislation and International Law* (1932)
Kelly, B., *Asylum: inside Grangegorman* (Dublin, 2020)
Kelly, J.M., *Fundamental rights in the Irish law and Constitution* (Dublin, 1961)
Kennedy, F., 'The suppression of the Carrigan Report: a historical perspective on child abuse', *Studies: An Irish Quarterly Review* (2001)
Kennedy, H., 'Judicial reorganisation in the Irish Free State', *Law Journal* (1924)
Kennedy, H., Editorial, *St Stephen's: a record of university life* (1901)
Kennedy, P., *Hugh Kennedy: the great but neglected chief justice* (Limerick, 2005)
Kennedy, R., *Dublin Castle art* (Dublin, 2010)
Kenny, C., 'Legible letters: the cases of Patrick Pearse and the "English" alphabet' in Adam Hanna and Eugene McNulty (eds), *Law and literature: the Irish case* (Liverpool, 2022)
Kenny, C., 'The Four Courts in Dublin before 1796', *Irish Jurist* (1986)
Khorakiwala, R., *From the colonial to the contemporary: images, iconography, memories, and performances of law in India's High Courts* (Oxford, 2021)
Kleinman, S., and A. O'Raghailligh, 'Scenes of gaiety now filled with beds', *History Ireland* (2016)
Kohn, L., *The Constitution of the Irish Free State* (London, 1932)
Kotsonouris, M., *'Tis all lies, your worship': tales from the District Court* (Dublin, 2011)
Kotsonouris, M., *Retreat from revolution – the Dáil courts, 1920–1924* (Dublin, 1994 and 2020)
Kotsonouris, M., *The winding up of the Dáil courts, 1922–1925: an obvious duty* (Dublin, 2004)
Krause, D., *Seán O'Casey and his world* (New York, 1976)
Kumar, K., 'Empire and English nationalism', *Nations & Nationalism* (2006)
Kyte, E., 'Sighle Humphreys: a case study in Irish socialist feminism, 1920s–1930s', *Saothar* (2011)
Larkin, F.M., and N.M. Dawson (eds), *Lawyers, the law and history* (Dublin, 2013)
Leary, P., 'Bicycles, 'barrows, and donkeys: pinning a tale on the Irish Border', *Folklore* (2018)
Leary, P., *Unapproved routes: histories of the Irish Border 1922–1972* (Oxford, 2016)
Lee, J.J., *Ireland 1912–1985: politics and society* (Cambridge, 1989)
Luddy, M., 'Sex and the single girl in 1920s and 1930s Ireland', *The Irish Review* (2007)

Lyall, A., *The Irish House of Lords: a court of law in the eighteenth century* (Dublin, 2013)
Mac Cárthaigh, D., and S. Ó'Conaill, 'Aguisíní le breithiúnas Hardiman BRMH in Ó'Maicín v. Éire', *Irish Judicial Studies Journal* (2020)
MacCormaic, R., *The Supreme Court* (Dublin, 2016)
Macardle, D., *The Irish republic* (Dublin, 1951)
MacCarthaigh, D., *An Ghaeilge sa Dlí* (Dublin, 2020)
Maguire, C.A., 'The Republican Courts', *Capuchin Annual* (1969)
Maguire, J.B., 'Seventeenth-century plans of Dublin Castle', *The Journal of the Royal Society of Antiquaries of Ireland* (1974)
Maine, H., 'Theories of primitive society' in Henry Maine, *Dissertations on early law and custom* (London, 1883)
Maine, H.S., *The early history of institutions* (7th edn, London, 1914)
Maine, H.S., *Lectures on the early history of institutions* (London, 1875)
Manning, C., '"But you are first to build a tower" – the Bermingham Tower, Dublin Castle', *Ulster Journal of Archaeology* (2017)
Mansergh, N., *The Irish Free State: its government and politics* (London, 1934)
Marshall, R.D., 'The constitution of the Church of Ireland in action' in Kevin Costello and Niamh Howlin (eds), *Law and religion in Ireland, 1700–1970* (London, 2021)
Martin, K., and Dowling, S., *Civil procedure in the Circuit Court* (Dublin, 2020)
McBride, L.W., *The greening of Dublin Castle* (Washington DC, 1991)
McCabe, D., 'Open court: law and the expansion of magisterial jurisdiction at Petty Sessions in nineteenth-century Ireland' in N.M. Dawson (ed.), *Reflections on law and history* (Dublin, 2006)
McCarthy, J.P., *Kevin O'Higgins, builder of the Irish State* (Dublin, 2006)
McCormick, C., and B. Dickson, *The Court of Appeal in Northern Ireland* (Bristol, 2024, forthcoming)
McGarry, F., 'Independent Ireland' in Richard Bourke and Ian McBride (eds), *The Princeton history of modern Ireland* (Princeton, 2016)
McGarry, F., 'Southern Ireland, 1922–32: a free state?' in Alvin Jackson (ed.), *The Oxford handbook of modern Irish history* (Oxford, 2014)
McMahon, B., *Judge or jury? The jury trial for personal injury cases in Ireland* (Cork, 1985)
McMahon, D., 'The politician: a reassessment', *Studies: An Irish Quarterly Review* (1998)
McMahon, R., 'The Court of Petty Sessions and society in pre-Famine Galway' in Raymond Gillespie (ed.), *The remaking of modern Ireland, 1750–1950: Beckett prize essays in Irish history* (Dublin, 2004)
McNally, G., 'Probation in Ireland: a brief history of the early years', *Irish Probation Journal* (2007)
Meenan, F., *Employment law* (2nd edn, Dublin, 2023)
Meenan, J., *George O'Brien: a biographical memoir* (Dublin, 1986)
Meredith, J.C., *Kant's critique of aesthetic judgement* (Oxford, 1911)
Moeller, E.v., 'Die Enstehung des Dogmas von dem Ursprung des Rechts aus dem Volksgeist' in *Mitteilungen des Instituts für Österreichische Geschichtsforschung* (Innsbruck, 1909)

Mohr, T., 'Irish newspapers and the creation of the 1922 Constitution of the Irish Free State', *Comparative Legal History* (2023)
Mohr, T., 'Law in a Gaelic utopia: perceptions of Brehon law in nineteenth and early twentieth century Ireland' in Oliver Brupbacher et al. (eds), *Remembering and forgetting* (Oxford, 2007)
Mohr, T., 'British involvement in the creation of the Constitution of the Irish Free State', *Dublin University Law Journal* (2008)
Mohr, T., 'Religious minorities under the Constitution of the Irish Free State, 1922–1937', *American Journal of Legal History* (2021)
Mohr, T., 'The "provisional period" – law and the birth of the Irish Free State', *Irish Jurist* (2023)
Mohr, T., 'The influence of Chief Justice Hugh Kennedy on Irish legal scholarship and publishing', *Irish Jurist* (2020)
Mohr, T., 'The political significance of the coinage of the Irish Free State', *Irish Studies Review* (2015)
Mohr, T., 'The rights of women under the Constitution of the Irish Free State', *Irish Jurist* (2006)
Mohr, T., *Guardian of the Treaty: the Privy Council appeal and Irish sovereignty* (Dublin, 2016)
Moore, C., *Birth of the Border: the impact of partition in Ireland* (Dublin, 2019)
Morgan, J.H., *The new Irish Constitution* (London, 1912)
Morris, E., *Our own devices: national symbols and political conflict in twentieth-century Ireland* (Dublin, 2005)
Mulcahy, L., *Legal architecture: justice, due process and the place of law* (Oxford, 2011)
Mulcahy, L., 'Watching women: what illustrations of courtroom scenes tell us about women and the public sphere in the nineteenth century', *Journal of Law and Society* (2015)
Murnaghan, J.A., 'The development of supreme judicature in Ireland', *Studies: An Irish Quarterly Review* (1912)
Murnaghan, J.A., 'The lordship of Ireland and the counties palatine', *Studies: An Irish Quarterly Review* (1913)
Murray, C.R.G., and D. Wincott, 'Partition by degrees: routine exceptions in border and immigration practice between the UK and Ireland, 1921–1972', *Journal of Law and Society* (2020)
Murray, P., *The Irish Boundary Commission and its origins, 1886–1925* (Dublin, 2011)
Nash, C., and B. Reid, 'Border crossings: new approaches to the Irish Border', *Irish Studies Review* (2010)
Nash, C., B. Reid and B. Graham, *Partitioned lives: the Irish Borderlands* (Abingdon, 2013)
Neligan, D., *The spy in the Castle* (London, 1999)
Nic Shuibhne, N., 'State duty and the Irish language', *Dublin University Law Journal* (1997)
Norris, M., 'Social housing' in Declan Redmond and Michelle Norris (eds), *Housing contemporary Ireland: policy, society and shelter* (Dublin, 2005)
Ó Beacháin, D., *From partition to Brexit: the Irish government and Northern Ireland* (Manchester, 2019)
O'Brien, J., and D. Guinness, *Dublin: a grand tour* (Dublin, 1994)

Ó Broin, L., *W.E. Wylie and the Irish Revolution 1916–1921* (Dublin, 1989)
Ó Cruadhlaoich, D., *The oath of allegiance* (Dublin, 1925)
Ó Gráda, C., '"The greatest blessing of all": the old age pension in Ireland', *Past and Present* (2002)
Ó hAnluain, R., 'Tuairiscí speicialta 1980–1998', *Tuairiscí Éireann / The Irish Reports* (1999)
Ó Tuathaigh, G., 'Foreword' in Mary Kotsonouris, *'Tis all lies, your worship': tales from the District Court* (Dublin, 2011)
O'Brien, M., *The fourth estate: journalism in twentieth-century Ireland* (Manchester, 2017)
O'Callaghan, M., 'Religion and identity: the Church and Irish independence', *The Crane Bag* (1983)
O'Casey, S., *Juno and the Paycock and The plough and the stars* (Dublin, 1969)
O'Conaill, S., 'The Irish language and the Irish legal system, 1922 to present' (PhD, University of Cardiff, 2013)
O'Connor, J., *A history of Ireland* (London, 1929)
O'Connor, J., *History of Ireland, 1798–1924* (London, 1925)
O'Donnell, D., 'A partial or uneven administration of the law: lawyers, the law and the importation of arms into Ireland, 1914', *Irish Jurist* (2015)
O'Donnell, D., 'Irish legal history of the twentieth century', *Studies: An Irish Quarterly Review* (2016)
O'Donnell, D., 'The sleep of reason', *Dublin University Law Journal* (2017)
O'Donnell, I., *Coercive confinement* (Manchester, 2012)
O'Donnell, I., *Justice, mercy and caprice: clemency and the death penalty in Ireland* (Oxford, 2017)
O'Hanlon, R., 'The sacred cow of trial by jury', *Irish Jurist* (1990)
O'Leary, B., *A treatise on Northern Ireland: volume II, control* (Oxford, 2019)
O'Malley, E., *On another man's wound* (Dublin, 2002)
O'Nolan, C., *The Irish District Court: a social portrait* (Cork, 2013)
O'Síocháin, P.A., *The criminal law of Ireland* (3rd edn, Dublin, 1952)
Osborough, W.N., 'Law in Ireland, 1916–1926', *Northern Ireland Legal Quarterly* (1972)
Osborough, W.N., 'The title of the last lord chief justice of Ireland' in W.N. Osborough, *Studies in Irish legal history* (Dublin, 1999)
Osborough, W.N., 'The title of the last lord chief justice of Ireland', *Irish Jurist* (1974)
Osborough, W.N., *An island's law: a bibliographical guide to Ireland's legal past* (Dublin, 2013)
Osborough, W.N., *Studies in Irish legal history* (Dublin, 1999)
Osborough, W.N., *The law school of University College Dublin* (Dublin, 2014)
Oxford dictionary of national biography
Pakenham, F., *Peace by ordeal* (London, 1935)
Paul-Dubois, L., *Contemporary Ireland* (Dublin, 1908)
Pearce, D.R., *The Senate speeches of W.B. Yeats* (London, 1961)
Pearse, P., 'The sovereign people' in Richard Bourke and Niamh Gallagher (eds), *The political thought of the Irish Revolution* (Cambridge, 2022)
Phelan, M., *Irish speakers, interpreters and the courts, 1754–1921* (Dublin, 2019)

Poser, N.S., *Lord Mansfield: justice in the age of reason* (Montreal, 2013)
Prager, J., *Building democracy in Ireland* (Cambridge, 1986)
Rackley, E., and R. Auchmuty (eds), *Women's legal landmarks: celebrating the history of women and law in the UK and Ireland* (Oxford, 2019)
Rainey, H.W., *Handbook on the jurisdiction and practice of the Circuit Court* (Dublin, 1906)
Rattigan, C., '"Done to death by father or relatives": Irish families and infanticide cases, 1922–1950', *The History of the Family* (2008)
Rattigan, C., *'What else could I do?' single mothers and infanticide, Ireland, 1900–1950* (Dublin, 2012)
Redmond, M., 'The emergence of women in the solicitors' profession in Ireland' in Eamonn Hall and Daire Hogan (eds), *The Law Society of Ireland 1852–2002: portrait of a profession* (Dublin, 2002)
Regan, J.M., *The Irish counter-revolution 1921–1936: Treatyite politics and settlement in independent Ireland* (Dublin, 1999)
Requa, M., 'Revisiting the past: miscarriages of justice, the courts and transition' in Anne-Marie McAlinden and Clare Dwyer (eds), *Criminal justice in transition: the Northern Ireland context* (Oxford, 2015)
Robinson, H.A., *Memories wise and otherwise* (London, 1923)
Ruane, B., 'Régime change: the fate of the senior Crown judiciary following the Anglo-Irish Treaty', *Irish Jurist* (2015)
Ruane, B., 'The challenge of creating a new judiciary 1922–1924' in Eoin Carolan (ed.), *Judicial power in Ireland* (Dublin, 2018)
Ryan, L., '"Furies" and "Die-hards": women and Irish republicanism in the early twentieth century', *Gender & History* (1999)
Ryan, M., *Michael Collins and the women who spied for Ireland* (Cork, 1996)
Savigny, F.C.v., 'Über den Zweck dieser Zeitschrift', *Zeitschrift für Geschichtliche Rechtswissenschaft* (1815)
Savigny, F.C.v., *Of the vocation of our age for legislation and jurisprudence*, tr. Abraham Hayward (London, 1831)
Savigny, F.C.v., *Vom Beruf unsrer Zeit für Gesetzgebung und Rechtswissenschaft* (Heidelberg, 1814)
Skehill, C., *The nature of social work in Ireland: a historical perspective* (New York, 1999)
Smith, Z., *The Fraud* (London, 2023)
Spenser, E., *A view of the present state of Ireland* (Dublin, 1633)
Stephen, E.M., 'The Constitution' in *Saorstát Éireann / Irish Free State: official handbook* (Dublin, 1932)
Towey, T., 'Hugh Kennedy and the constitutional development of the Irish Free State, 1922–1923', *Irish Jurist* (1977)
Tuathail, S.Ó., *Gaeilge agus an Bunreacht* (Baile Átha Cliath, 2002)
Ua Cadhain, Liam, *The law courts in Éire* (Dublin, 1943)
Urquhart, D., 'Ireland's criminal conversations', *Études Irlandaises* (2012)
Valiulis, M., 'Neither feminist nor flapper: the ecclesiastical construction of the ideal Irish woman' in Mary O'Dowd and Sabine Wichert (eds), *Chattel, servant or citizen: women's status in church, state and society* (Belfast, 1995)

Valiulis, M., 'Virtuous mothers and dutiful wives: the politics of sexuality in the Irish Free State' in Maryann Valiulis (ed.), *Gender and power in Irish history* (Dublin, 2008)

Valiulis, M., *The making of inequality in the Irish Free State, 1922–37; women, power and gender ideology* (Dublin, 2019)

Valiulis, M., 'Defining their role in the new state: Irish women's protest against the Juries Act 1927', *Canadian Journal of Irish Studies* (1992)

Valiulis, M., *Almost a rebellion: the Irish Army mutiny of 1924* (Cork, 1985)

Vaughan, W.E., *Murder trials in Ireland, 1836–1914* (Dublin, 2009)

Veach, C., and T. O'Keeffe, 'King John and the origins of colonial rule in Ireland', *History Ireland* (2016)

Ward, M., *Maud Gonne: Ireland's Joan of Arc* (London, 1990)

Ward, M., *Unmanageable revolutionaries: women and Irish nationalism* (London, 1983)

Ward, Margaret, *Hanna Sheehy Skeffington, suffragette and Sinn Féiner: her memoirs and political writings* (Dublin, 2017)

Waterhouse, K., *Ireland's District Court: language, immigration and consequences for justice* (Manchester, 2014)

Wheeler-Bennett, J., *John Anderson Viscount Waverly* (London, 1962)

White, T.D.V., *The story of the Royal Dublin Society* (Tralee, 1955)

Whyte, G., G. Hogan, D. Kenny and R. Walsh, *Kelly: The Irish Constitution* (Dublin, 2018)

Wylie, W.E., 'Memoir' in Léon Ó Broin, *W.E. Wylie and the Irish Revolution* (Dublin, 1989)

NEWSPAPERS AND PERIODICALS

Anglo Celt
Connacht Tribune
Cork Examiner
Dublin Evening Herald
Dundalk Democrat
Evening Echo
Evening News (Sydney)
Irish Jurist (o.s.)
Law Journal
Law Times
Leitrim Observer
Meath Chronicle
Morning Post
Munster Express
Nationalist and Leinster Times
Nationality
Nenagh Guardian
New English Weekly
Northern Standard
Other Clare
Poblacht na hÉireann (Scottish Edition)
Poblacht na hÉireann (Southern Edition)
Poblacht na hÉireann (War News)
Prospectus
Republic of Ireland (Scottish)
Republic of Ireland (Southern)
Republic of Ireland (War News)
Roscommon Herald
Round Table
Scotsman
Solicitors' Journal
Solicitors' Journal and Weekly Reporter
Sunday Independent
Sunday Pictorial
Times
Tipperary Star
Watchword
Weekly Freeman's Journal
Weekly Irish Times
Westmeath Independent
Wicklow People

Web Sources

Borderlands: www.irishborderlands.com
Central Statistics Office: www.cso.ie/en/releasesandpublications/ep/p-1916/1916irl/.
Dictionary of Irish biography www.dib.ie
National Folklore Schools Collection: www.duchas.ie
Rozenberg: A lawyer writes https://rozenberg.substack.com/p/who-has-the-last-word.
RTÉ Brainstorm, 9 Nov. 2023: www.rte.ie/radio/podcasts/22340870-how-a-kiss-in-public-in-devaleras-ireland-caused/
Ruth Cannon: https://ruthcannon.com/2021/11/11/the-unopened-doors-of-the-supreme-court-1937-73/
YouTube: www.youtube.com/playlist?list=PLHKVjBSDqMB6aa4LcEkJCa73CeuGB_305

Table of statutes

CONSTITUTION OF THE IRISH FREE STATE

Constitution of the Irish Free State 1922 .... 1, 4, 6, 10, 28, 30–1, 33, 35–6, 37, 38, 44–5, 46–7, 48–9, 62, 65–9, 66–9, 68–9, 79, 81, 92, 93, 94, 168, 191, 235, 241, 247, 249, 273, 275, 285
- Article
- 2A 47
- 4 .... 235, 238, 245
- 6 .... 39, 42, 43
- 24 42
- 35 68
- 42 235
- 47 .... 39, 40, 41
- 50 .... 43, 45, 46, 47
- 60 68
- 64 .... 36, 42, 166, 194
- 64–72 3
- 65 167
- 66 .... 167, 210, 250
- 68 204
- 69 191
- 70 .... 42, 43
- 72 .... 42, 43
- 75 .... 3, 36, 191, 193

CONSTITUTION OF IRELAND

Constitution of Ireland 1937 .... 5, 47, 120, 168, 249
- Article
- 8 .... 235, 239, 245, 246
- 12.8 198
- 14 198
- 25.5 239
- 31 198
- 31.2 181
- 34 .... 168, 204
- 34.4.1 .... 210, 250
- 34.5.2 198

34.5.3 . . . . 250, 253
34.5.4 . . . . 249, 250, 253, 254
34.6.1 198
38 246
38.4.5 120
42A 125
47 40
58 168

ACTS OF THE OIREACHTAS

Acquisition of Land (Reference Committee) Act 1925 181
Adaptation of Enactments Act 1922 277
Arbitration Act 2010 180
    s. 9 180
Assisted Decision-Making (Capacity) Act 2015 . . . . 158, 162, 176
    s. 4 162
    s. 8 163
    s. 55A 163
Assisted Decision-Making (Capacity) (Amendment) Act 2022 . . . . 162, 164
Child Care Act 1991 122
    s.18 126
Children Act 2001 . . . . 125, 126
    s. 96 126
Companies (Miscellaneous Provisions) Act 2013 162
Constitution of the Irish Free State (Saorstát Éireann) Act 1922 35–6
Constitution (Amendment No. 1) Act 1925 44
Court of Appeal Act 2014 167
    s. 28 167
Courts Act 1964 156
Courts Act 1991 99
Courts Act 2023
    s. 6 120
Courts and Court Officers Act 1995 199
    s. 8 199
Courts and Court Officers (Amendment) Act 2007 157
Courts (Establishment and Constitution) Act 1961 . . . . 120, 204
    s. 1A 168
    s. 2 168
    s. 4 157
    s. 7 168
    s. 10 (3) 168–9
    s. 11 168

Table of statutes

Courts (Supplemental Provisions) Act 1961 .... 120, 158
    s. 7 (3) 212
    s. 9 .... 166, 176
    s. 10 198
    s. 10 (4) 198–9
    s. 56 .... 181, 199
Courts of Justice Act 1924 .... 3–10, 22, 25–8, 27–8, 28–31, 32,
    33, 43, 45, 62, 69, 72–3, 76, 105, 116, 118–20, 147, 152, 155, 156, 197,
        201, 236–40, 245, 247, 249–57, 269–77, 281–4, 287, 291
    s. 5 197
    s. 9 167
    s. 19 .... 165, 168, 177, 197, 202
    s. 20 198
    s. 29 249–57
    s. 44 .... 238, 240
    s. 71 .... 238, 240, 245
    s. 77B (iii) 224
    s. 83 210
    s. 88 (2) 238
    s. 99 195
Courts of Justice Act 1925 .... Plate 12
Courts of Justice Act 1936 .... 118, 167, 168, 177
    s. 4 .... 198, 208
    s. 5 208
    s. 9 .... 165, 166, 171, 176, 198
    s. 67 198
Courts of Justice (District Court) Act 1946 198
Courts of Justice (District Court) Act 1949 199
Courts Service Act 1998 199
    s.11 (1) 199
    s.11 (4) 199–200
Criminal Evidence Act 1992 288
Criminal Justice (Administration) Act 1924 284
Criminal Justice (Enforcement Powers) (Covid-19) Act 2020 162
Dáil Éireann Courts (Winding Up) Act 1923 .... 34n
Data Protection Act 2018 161
    s. 117 161
    s. 150 161
District Court (Temporary Provisions) Act 1923 117
District Justices (Temporary Provisions) Act 1923 .... 106, 107
Domestic Violence Act 2018 159
Equal Status Acts 2000 to 2018 .... 158, 160
Equality (Miscellaneous Provisions) Act 2015 160

European Communities Act 1972
    s. 3 243
Family Law Act 1995 159
Family Law (Protection of Spouses and Children) Act 1976 122
Gender Recognition Act 2015 159
Housing (Building Facilities) Act 1924 13
Illegal Immigrants (Trafficking) Act 2000
    s. 5 (3) 252
Indemnity Act 1923 . . . . 43, 44
Intoxicating Liquor Act 1927
    s. 15 (1) 210
Intoxicating Liquor Act 1960 211
Irish Legal Terms Act 1945 240
Judicial Appointments Commission Act 2023 200
    s. 9 (1)(a) 200
    s. 9 (4) 200
    s. 10 200
    s. 16 (3) 200
Judicial Council Act 2019
    s. 8 (4) 200
    s. 44 200
Juries (Amendment) Act 1924 220
Juries (Protection) Act 1929 227
Land Act 1923 72
Land and Conveyancing Law Reform Act 2009 121
Legal Practitioners Qualification Act 1929 239–40
Legal Services Regulation Act 2015 . . . . 179, 200
    s. 86 179
    s. 172 200
Licensing Act 1924 20
Ministers and Secretaries Act 1924 72
Offences Against the State Act 1939 222
Official Languages Act 2003 . . . . 239, 243, 247
    s. 8 (6) 244
Personal Insolvency Act 2012 . . . . 157, 159, 160
Personal Insolvency (Amendment) Act 2015 159
Personal Insolvency (Amendment) Act 2021 160
Planning and Development Act 2000 158
    s. 50 (4)(f) 252
    s. 50A (11) 253
    s. 105 181
Planning and Development (Strategic Infrastructure) Act 2006 253

Prosecution of Offences Act 1974 199
    s. 2 (7) 199
Protected Disclosures Act 2014 .... 158, 160–1
Protected Disclosures (Amendment) Act 2022 161
Public Safety Act 1927 47
Public Safety (Emergency Powers) Act 1923 .... 39–40, 41, 42, 45, 113
Public Safety (Emergency Powers) (No. 2) Act 1923 40–1
Public Safety (Powers of Arrest and Detention) Temporary
    Act 1924 .... 42, 44
Residential Tenancies Act 2004 .... 158, 162
    ss. 88 and 189 158
Road Traffic Act 1961
    s. 49 122
Sex Disqualification (Removal) Act 1919 213
Solicitors Act 1954 177
Solicitors (Amendment) Act 1960 178
Statute of Limitations 1957 158
Unfair Dismissals Acts 1977 to 2015 160
Workmen's Compensation Act 1934 160
Workplace Relations Act 2015 160

STATUTORY INSTRUMENTS, RULES AND ORDERS

Circuit Court Rules 1928
    Order 1, rule 4 238
Planning and Development Regulations 2001–2023 181
Provisional Government (Transfer of Functions) Order 1922 105
Rules of the Superior Courts
    Order 120 (2) and (3) 244

BILLS OF THE OIREACHTAS

Courts of Justice Bill 1923 .... 3, 9, 21, 270, 274, 277, 281
Courts of Justice Bill 1934 .... 165, 168, 170–1, 207
Courts of Justice Bill 1935 207
Family Courts Bill 2022 .... 123, 124, 159
Planning and Development Bill 2023 257
    s. 259 (1) 253, 256

BRITISH AND UK LEGISLATION

Acquisition of Land (Assessment of Compensation) Act 1919 181
Act of Union 186, 187
    Article 8 187

Administration of Justice (Language) Act (Ireland) 1737 234
Children Act 1908 122
   s. 111 218
Constabulary (Ireland) Act 1836 117
Customs Consolidation Act 1876 136–7
Finance (1909–10) Act 1910 198
Government of Ireland Act 1920 .... 33, 45, 90, 128, 189, 190
   s. 38 189
   s. 44 (2) 189
Housing Act 1908 13
Judicature (NI) Act 1978 258
Labourers (Ireland) Act 1906 13
Labourers Acts 77
Land Purchase Acts 1881–1923* 75, 77
Licensing Act 1872 113
Northern Ireland Act 1998 267
Statute Law Revision Act 1894 188
Summary Jurisdiction Act 1851 210
Summary Jurisdiction Act 1857
   s. 2 210
Superannuation Acts 1834 to 1919 103
Supreme Court of Judicature Act (Ireland) 1877 .... 33, 187, 190
   s. 1 188
   s. 3 .... 187, 188
   s. 6 187
   s. 18 188
   s. 22 188
   s. 50 210
Town Tenants (Ireland) Act 1906 77

INTERNATIONAL TREATIES

Anglo-Irish Treaty 1921 .... 4, 11, 16–17, 23, 34, 42, 43,
                                  53, 65–6, 67, 68, 128, 276, 279
   article 10 .... 34, 95, 196
   article 12 17

EUROPEAN LEGISLATION

Victims Rights Directive 125

Index

Compiled by Julitta Clancy

Abbey Theatre, 13
Aberdeen, Lord, 87
access to justice, 8, 124, 146, 149, 154
Access to Justice Working Group, 200–1
Act of Union, 186, 187
Admiralty Court, 79
Advisory Committee on the Grant of Patents of Precedence, 181
Agricultural Credit Corporation, 154
Aiken, Frank, 12, 38
Airey, Johanna, 231
alcohol abuse, 20, 113
Allberry, Harry, 55–6, 60
Allen, John, 41, 65
An Post: commemorative stamp, *Plate 18*
Anderson, John, 81
Andrews, William Drennan, 87, 88, 90
Anglo-Irish bench, 93, 191–2; *see also* Crown judiciary
Anglo-Irish Treaty (1921), 4, 11, 16–17, 23, 34, 42, 43, 53, 65–6, 67, 68, 73, 95, 128, 196, 276, 279
   opposition to, *see* anti-Treaty Republicans; Civil War
anti-Treaty Republicans, 11, 19, 30, 32, 34, 65, 74, 280, 286
   habeas corpus applications, 24, 35, 38–9, 41–2, 66, 196
   IRA, 12, 38, 54, 74
   judicial office, barriers to, 69, 70–1, 74
   opposition to 1924 Act, 4, 22, 28–31
   women, 12, 226–8, 232–3
appeals; *see also* case stated procedure; criminal appeals; planning appeals
   certification process (s. 29, 1924 Act), legacy of, 249–57
   jurisdiction of courts, 249, 250, 253–7; *see also* Circuit Court; Court of Appeal; High Court; Supreme Court
   'leapfrog' appeal procedures, 8, 249–56, 253, 264
   new structures and procedures (1924 Act), 8–9
   Northern Ireland appeal routes, 258–68
   Privy Council, *see* Privy Council appeal
arbitration courts, 22, 31
arbitration matters, 180–1, 198
Ardfert, Co. Kerry, 186
Army Council, 16
Army Inquiry Committee, 15–16, 79, 81
army mutiny (1924), 15–16, 75, 79, 81
Arnott, Lady, 214
Asquith, Herbert, 64, 87
assisted decision-making, 162–3, 164, 176
assize courts, 26, 156, 279, 285, 289
Association of the Councils of State and Supreme Administrative Jurisdictions of the European Union, 201
Attorney General, office of, 199, 247
Attorney General v. Joyce and Walsh, 240
Attorney General v. McBride, 41, 47, 48
Attorney General (Fahy) v. Bruen (No. 1), 210
Attorney General (Fahy) v. Bruen (No. 2), 208–11
Australia, 8, 86, 206, 269, 270, 273, 277

Bailieborough, Co. Cavan, 278
Ballybay District Court: 1923 cases, 106–14, 135
Ballyshannon District Court, 138
Bangor, Co. Down, 190

Bank of Ireland, 74
Bar Council, 146, 147, 199, 288
Bar of Ireland, 75, 76, 124, 201, 285
    decentralisation policy, opposition to, 4, 146, 151, 152, 153, 154, 155
Barniville, David, 5, 300
Barrett, Dick, 37
barristers, 8, 23, 74, 75, 76, 79, 118, 140, 146, 152, 153, 155, 179, 279
    women, 126, 213–14, 219; *see also* legal practitioners
Barry, Charles, 87, 88
Barry, Kathleen, 215, 217
Barry, Kevin, 217
Barry, Redmond, 89
Barton, Dunbar Plunkett, 89
Beattie, Lady Rachel, 214
Beirne, Patrick, 16
Belfast, 74, 76, 79, 131
Belfast County Court, 82
Belfast Telegraph, 282
Bell, Michael, 288
Belturbet courthouse, 279
Bennett, James, 139
Bennett, Louie, 217
Bewley, Edmund, 89
Biehler, Hilary, 8, 9
Birkenhead, Lord (F.E. Smith), 159
Black, Lynsey, 4, 7
Blackrock Urban District Council, 214
Bloxham, Cooper Mark, 294
Blythe, Ernest, 14, 80–1, 98
Boland, Gerald, 222
An Bord Pleanála, 181
Border, 128–9, *129* (map), 130, 133–4; *see also* cross-border smuggling
Boundary Commission, 16–18, 75, 128–9
Boyce, D.G., 17
Boyd, Walter, 87, 88, 89–90
Boyd Barrett, Fr Edward, 13
Boylan, Francis, 142
Boylan, Patrick, 229–30
Bracken, Mary, 216–17
Brady, Sir Francis, 88

Brehon law, 183, 184, 185, 197, 273, 274–5
Brennan, Karen, 225
Brennan, Lena, 216
Brennan, Lily, 216
Brewster, Gordon, '*Man Overboard*,' Plate 12
Bridewell Garda station, 122
Britain, 228; *see also* Crown; England and Wales
British Army, 113
British courts system (in Ireland), *see* Crown courts; Crown judiciary
British government, 17–18, 64, 68, 78, 196
British press, 282–3, 287–8
Brown, Thomas, 14
Brown, William H., 293
Bryce, James, 87
B.S. v. Director of Public Prosecutions, 254
Buckley, Margaret, 215
Buckmaster, Stanley, lord chancellor, 87
Burke, Seamus, 14
Burnfoot District Court, 138, 142
Butt, Isaac, 82
Byrne, Edward, archbishop of Dublin, 19
Byrne, Kathleen, 231

Cabinteely Petty Sessions, 214
Cadden, Mamie, 229
Cahillane, Laura, 7, 75, 106
Callaghan v. An Bord Pleanála, 255–6
Callanan, Frank, 80
Campbell, James H. *see* Glenavy, Lord
Campbell, Thomas Joseph, 79, 80–1, 294
Campion, Frances, 216
Canada, 8, 86, 206
Carrick-on-Shannon Circuit Court, 230
Carrigan, William, 79, 220
Carrigan committee, 223
Carroll, Eugene, 278
Carroll, Evelyn, 223
Carson, Sir Edward, 17, 64, 67

Case of Tanistry, 185
case stated procedure, 210, 258–9, 263
Castleblayney, Co. Monaghan, 106, 113, 114
Castleblayney District Court, 135, 139, 142
Catholic Church, 18–20, 232
Catholic judges, 78, 195
Cavan County Council, 278
Cavan courthouse, 278, 290, *Plate 17*
C.C. v. Minister for Justice and Equality, 255
Ceannt, Áine, 215
Central Criminal Court, 165, 168, 169, 221, 226, 290
 judicial robes, design for, *Plate 7*
Century of Courts conference: logo, *Plate 14*
Chancery Division, 186, 187
Chatterton, Hedges Eyre, 87, 88
Cherry, Richard Robert, 64, 77, 89, 188
chief justice, 167, 168, 181, 194–201, 204; *see also* Kennedy, Hugh
 appointments, 205; list of office-holders, 300 (Appendix 5)
 establishment of office, 5, 197–8
 remuneration, 102
 role and functions, 5–6, 197–201; non-statutory functions, 200–201; solicitors, 177–8, 197–8; wardship jurisdiction, 167, 168, 169–70
 seal of, *Plate 11*
Chief Place, court of, 202
child neglect, 110–11
child welfare, 122–3, 124, 125, 126
Childers, Erskine, 205
Children's Court, 61, 126, 218
children's rights, 125
Chotah, 80
Christ Church Cathedral, Dublin, 52
Church of Ireland, 78
Church of Ireland Gazette, 19
Churchill, Winston, 24

Circuit Court, 5, 8, 9, 60, 121, 145, 156, 165, 244
 appeals from, 9, 168
 business of (1924–33), 153–5
 decentralisation, and opposition to, 145–53, 154, 155
 judges, *see* Circuit Court judges
 jurisdiction, 8, 9, 119, 146–63, 284, 286; appellate, 158, 160, 161, 162; civil, 157–61; employment law, 160–1; family law, 158–9; financial matters, 159–60; growth and development, 161–3
 legal aid, 153
 reorganisation of circuits, 156
 stenographers, 9, 221
Circuit Court judges, 26, 69, 156–7, 164, 289; *see also* president of the Circuit Court
 appointments, 76, 79, 298–9 (Appendix 4)
 expanding role of, 156–64
 Irish language, knowledge of, 237, 238
 judicial address, 288
 judicial robes, design for, *Plate 5*
 remuneration, 99, 100, 101, 102, 103
 retirement age, 85, 91
Circuit Court Rules, 9, 148–9, 150–1, 151–3, 238
Circuit Family Court, 159
Civic Guard, 105, 111; *see also* An Garda Síochána
civil actions
 jurisdiction of courts, *see* Circuit Court; District Court
 Northern Ireland appeal routes, 263–4
 women in, 231–2
civil legal aid, 153
Civil War, 11–12, 13, 15, 19, 20, 24, 28, 37–41, 50, 62–63, 74, 82–8, 105, 108, 120, 191, 194, 205, 269
 anti-Treatyites, *see* anti-Treaty Republicans
 challenges in aftermath of, 279–80
 executions, 37, 78

Clare, county, 173, 214, 216
Clarke, Frank, 255, 300
Clarke, Kathleen, 66, 215
Clery, Arthur, 23, 79
Clinton v. An Bord Pleanála, 252–3
Clones, Co. Monaghan, 113
Clones District Court, 135–6, 138–9, 140
Coen, Mark, 6, 7, 9
Coffey, Donal K., 8
Cohen, Anthony, 281
An Coimisinéir Teanga, 239
Cole, Brigid, 11
Coleman, Edward, 139
Collins, Maurice, 3
Collins, Michael, 15, 53, 54, 55, 65, 68, 81
Collins, Patrick, 139
Comerford, Máire, 227, 290
commissioners of oaths, 198, 202
commissioners of Public Works, 21; *see also* Office of Public Works
common law, 6, 48, 117, 184–7, 197, 273–4, 277, 285
Common Pleas, court of, 185–6, 187, 202
Common Pleas Division, 187, 188
Commonwealth, 273
company law, 162
compulsory acquisition, 198
Comyn, Michael, 79
Congested Districts Board, 154
Conlon, J.H., 112
Connaught, 76
Conner, Henry Daniel, 76, 77, 78, 80, 298
Connolly, James, 38
Connolly, Mary Catherine, 110
Connolly O'Brien, Nora, 38–40
Conroy, John Charles, 300
Constitution Committee (1922), 66
Constitution of Ireland 1937, 5, 40, 47, 120, 125, 168, 181, 198, 204, 210, 235, 239, 245, 246, 249, 250, 253, 254, 276–277; *see also* Table of Statutes

Constitution of the Irish Free State 1922, 1, 3, 4, 6, 10, 28, 33, 35–6, 37, 38, 39, 40, 41, 42, 43, 45, 46, 47, 48, 65, 68, 92, 94, 166, 167, 168, 191, 193, 194, 204, 210, 235, 238, 245, 249, 250, 273, 275, 285; *see also* Table of Statutes
 amendment, 47; doctrine of implied amendment, 44–5, 46–7, 48
 drafting, 1, 9–10, 62, 65–9, 79, 81, 93, 277
 Irish language, status of, 235, 241, 247
 judicial appointments, 68–9
 judicial independence, 66–9, 92, 191
 opposition to, 30–1
constitutional cases, 231
constitutional law, 192, 277
constitutional statutes, 72–3
Coogan, Michael, 142
Cooper, Major Bryan, 236
Cork, county, 75, 216
Cork Chamber of Commerce, 151
Cork Circuit Court, 156
Cosgrave, William T., 2, 3, 16, 17, 18, 26, 45, 53, 54, 58, 69–70, 78, 79, 85, 93, 95, 145–6, 147, 151, 194, 236, 272, 287
 and judicial appointments, 73, 78, 81
 and new courts system, 2, 3, 37, 281, 282, 284
Costello, Declan, 170, 300
Costello, John A., 165, 166, 168, 170–1, 182, 195, 275
Costello, Kevin, 4, 5, 9, 106, 159
Costello, Róisín, 7, 222
Coulson, Edith, 139
Council of State, 181, 198
County Courts, 5, 36, 37, 64, 145, 146, 147, 149, 150, 156
 judges, 75, 79, 83, 87–88, 99; *see also* Crown judiciary
County Courts (Northern Ireland), 258–9, 263
county registrars, 181, 199

Court of Appeal, 9, 38–40, 41, 43–4, 45, 46, 167, 186–7, 188, 194, 205, 206, 249
  appellate jurisdiction, 250, 252–3; limitations, 253–7
  judges, 167; appointments, 73; deaths in office (1897–1923), 88
Court of Appeal (Northern Ireland), 258–60, 261–2, 265, 266–7
Court of Appeal in Southern Ireland, 33, 37, 189
Court of Criminal Appeal, 47, 165, 206, 238, 240, 284
  appeals from: certification process (s. 29), 9, 249–57
  establishment, 8–9
Court of Justice of the European Union, 200
courthouses, 121
  royal symbols, 278, 279, 289–90
Courtney, Agnes, 110
courts, 21, 36, 269–70; *see also* judiciary
  1924 Act, established under, 4–5, 47, 48–9, 58, 62, 273, 274; *see also* individual courts; British reactions, 282–3; Republican opposition, 28–31, 286
  decentralization, *see* decentralisation of justice
  decolonisation, symbolism and nation-building, *see* decolonisation; symbolism
  independence, *see* judicial independence
  judicial interregnum (1922–4), 36–49
  partitioning of, 33
courts of first instance, 1, 166
Courts of Justice Act 1924, 3–10, 33, 43, 45, 62, 197, 270–1; *see also* Table of Statutes
  and Bunreacht na hÉireann (1937), 276–7
  centenary commemorations, 201; An Post stamp, *Plate 18*
  comparative perspective, 269–77
  constitutional statute, as, 72–3

courts and judiciary, *see* courts; judiciary; *individual courts*
criminal justice, changes to, 284
  and Dáil courts, 22, 25–8, 32
  decentralised justice, *see* decentralisation of justice
  decolonising intentions, 281–4, 287, 291
  drafting (1923 bill), 26, 30, 31, 84–5, 91, 195, 197, 235–7, 257, 270, 277, 281
  Irish language, 236–40, 245, 247
  judicial independence, 62, 69
  opposition to, 28–31
Courts Service, 5, 166, 181, 199–200
Covid-19 pandemic, 124, 127
Craig, Sir James, 17, 18, 64, 131
criminal appeals, 8–9
  certification process (s. 29, 1924 Act), 9, 249–52
  jurisdiction of courts, *see* individual courts
  leapfrog appeals, 8, 253–5, 264
  new structures and procedures, 8–9, 49
  Northern Ireland, 258–62
Criminal Cases Review Commission (Northern Ireland), 266
criminal conversation, 232
criminal prosecutions, 113, 122, 199, 284
  smuggling, *see* cross-border smuggling
criminal trials, 42–3, 284–5; *see also* criminal appeals; jury trial
  Ballybay District Court: 1923 cases, 111–13
  death sentences, 226, 229–30, 289
  Irish language hearings, 244–7; *see also* Irish language
  jurisdiction of courts, *see* individual courts
  Northern Ireland appeal routes, 258–62, 265
  public gallery, 228–30
  stenographers, 221–2
  women and, 224–7

cross-border smuggling, 4, 7, 128–43, 144
Crotty, J.F., 244
Crowe, Christopher, 229
Crowley, Jeremiah (Diarmaid), 23, 24, 29, 66, 79
Crown, symbols of, 7, 278–9, 289–90
Crown courts, 3, 22, 23, 24–5, 27, 28, 33, 62–3, 193, 276, 278–9, 281, 282; *see also* assize courts; County Courts
   judges, *see* Crown judiciary
   judicial interregnum (1922–4), continuance during, 3, 33, 34, 35–8, 48, 65–6, 193–4
Crown courts (Northern Ireland)
   appeals from, 261–2, 263
Crown judiciary, 27–8, 63–4, 70, 71
   antipathy towards, 63, 64–5, 92–4, 191–2, 269, 270, 275, 281, 283
   appointments to new judiciary, 75, 79, 219, 279
   remuneration, 94–5, 97, 196–7
Cumann na mBan, 4, 12, 290
Cumann na nGaedheal, 13–14, 17, 73, 205, 224, 279–80, 281
Cumann na Saoirse, 217
Curley, Ross, 111
Curran, Constantine, 195–6
Cussen, G.P., 288
Customs and Excise, 132
customs barrier, 4, 129, 130–5, 144; *see also* cross-border smuggling

Dáil courts, 4, 7, 22–3, 24, 31, 33–4, 36, 62, 65, 71, 117, 120, 145, 197, 274–5
   and 1924 Act, 22, 25–8, 32
   abolition, 23–8, 29, 32, 34, 66, 194; review of decisions, 27
   Circuit Court, 117
   District and Parish Courts, 22, 25, 26, 32, 117, 215
   judges, 22–3, 25, 26, 70, 79, 80, 81, 84, 142, 205, 214–16, 217; appointments to new judiciary, 27–8; independence, 65–6

   jurisdictional deficits, 65–6
   Land courts, 23, 34, 217
   Supreme Court, 23, 24, 26, 34, 66, 84, 117, 205
   women, involvement of, 22–3, 214–17, 219
Dáil Courts Winding Up Commission, 27, 29, 79, 80, 83, 194–5, 197
Dáil Department of Home Affairs, 214, 215
Dáil Éireann, 17, 22, 28, 29, 35, 45, 64–5, 71, 165, 166, 170, 194, 204, 207, 218, 221–2, 270, 288
Daily Mail, 288
Daily Mirror, 287–8
Dalton, Colonel Charles, 15
Daly, Colin, 300
Daly, Tom, 192
Dargan, Miss, 223
data protection, 158, 161
Data Protection Commission, 158, 161
Davies, Sir John, 1
Davin, William, 59
Davitt, Cahir, 23, 27, 81, 228, 229, 300
Davitt, Michael, 228
de Búrca, Máirín, 231
de Búrca and Anderson v. Attorney General, 221
de Búrca, Tomás, district justice, 288
de Exeter, Richard, 185–6
de Valera, Éamon, 12, 28, 38, 39, 64, 65, 126, 193, 204, 205, 276
Decade of Centenaries Committee, 201
decentralisation of justice, 8, 145–7
   opposition to, 4, 146, 147–53, 154, 284
decolonisation, 279, 280, 281–4, 286, 287, 291
Deeney, Edward, 142–3
Deery, Matthew, 300
Delany, V.T.H., 277
Delap v. Minister for Justice, 243
Denham, Susan, 252–3, 300
dentists, 180
Department of External Affairs, 60
Department of Finance, 20; *see also* Ministry of Finance

Department of Justice, 20, 60, 61, 154
Derham, William, 51
Derry, 134, 138, 142
Despard, Charlotte, 227
Devane, Fr Richard, 21
Devaney, Kathleen (later O'Doherty), 217
Deverell, Averil, 126, 214
Devitt, St Lawrence Ernest, 76, 298
Dickie, Alexander Alfred, 293
Dickson, Brice, 8
Dillon, John, 82, 196
Dillon, Nellie, 216
Dillon-Leetch, Mollie, 213
Director of Public Prosecutions (Northern Ireland), 266
Director of Public Prosecutions, office of, 199
Disciplinary Committee of the Law Society, 178
District Court, 3, 4, 8, 105, 121, 123, 156, 158, 193, 210, 227; *see also* Children's Court; Dáil courts
    Ballybay: 1923 cases, 106–14
    century (1924–2024), 116–27
    courthouses, 121
    evolution and reform, 120–6, 127
    jurisdiction, 5, 118–20; civil, 119, 121; criminal, 119–20, 121, 122, 125, 284; expansion, 8, 121–6, 127; family law, 122–3, 123–4, 125; licensing, 119; sexual cases, 224–5
    justices, *see* District judges
    new technology and remote hearings, 124
    smuggling cases, *see* cross-border smuggling
    women, involvement of, 125–6
District Court judges, 26, 27, 140–2, 144, 193, 284
    chief justice and, 198–199
    eligibility for office, 117–18, 140
    and Irish language, 236, 237, 238, 245–6
    judicial robes, 287–8, *Plate 7*, *Plate 9*
    number, 120–1
    removal, 69
    remuneration, 99–100, 100–3
    retirement age, 91, 199
    status, 98, 103, 104
    temporary assistant justices, 3, 25, 105–6, 107, 118
    women, 126
Dixon, Beatrice, 221
Dockrell, Lady Margaret, 214
doctors, 179–80
Dodd, William H., 42, 89, 220
domestic violence, 122, 159
Donaghadee, 190
Donegal District Court, 245
Donnelly, Thomas, 300
Donnybrook, Dublin, 226
Dowling, Karl, 121
Dowling, Sighle, 216
Doyle, Charles Francis, 76, 77, 79, 139–40, 293, 298
Drug Treatment Court, 125
Drumgoole, Charles, 76, 79, 298
Dublin, 214, 215, 217
Dublin Castle, 4, 50–2, 57–8, 59, 60, 61, 192, *Plate 4*
    'handover' to Irish Free State (1922), 34, 55, 81
    law courts (medieval period), 51, 52
    law courts (1923–31), 4, 47, 50–61, 74, 90, 269; inaugural ceremony, 58, 283, 287, *Plates 2–3*; relocation to Four Courts, 50, 60–1
Dublin Circuit Bar Association, 151
Dublin Circuit Court, 156
Dublin Metropolitan Children Court, 126
Dublin Metropolitan Police District, 223
Dublin University, 76, 78, 270
Duggan, Éamonn, 66
Duggan, Marion, 216, 222
Dún Aonghusa, 275
Dun Emer Guild: designs for judicial robes, 224, *Plates 5–6*

Dundalk Circuit Court, 139
Dundalk Democrat, 132
Dundalk District Court, 133
Dundalk Gaol, 110, 111, 113, 114
Dunleavy, Betty, 111–12
Dunleavy, Catherine, 112
Durcan, John James, 300

Earle, Re, 211
Early, Helena, 125
Earner-Byrne, Lindsay, 232
Easter Rising (1916), 22, 78, 79, 142
Eastern circuit, 214
Economist, 131
Egan v. Macready, 64, 70
Éire – The Irish Nation, 29–30
embracery, 227, 290
employment law, 160–161
England and Wales, 95, 96, 183, 186, 187, 197, 259, 264, 284
English and Empire Digest, 77
English Bar, 77
English language, 234–5
English law, 2, 184–5; *see also* common law
Ennis Circuit Court, 230
enrolled bill rule, 40
equality, 158, 160
Eucharistic Congress (1932), 61
European Court of Human Rights, 200, 201
European Union, 121, 201, 243, 244, 247–8, 267
EU–UK Withdrawal Agreement Ireland/Northern Ireland Protocol, 264
Evening Herald, 229
examinership, 162
Exchequer, court of, 186, 187, 188

family courts, 122, 123, 124, 159
family law, 122–7, 158–9
Fanning, Ronan, 15, 287
Farmers Party, 59
Farrell, Patrick, 278
Fawsitt, Diarmaid, 290

Feetham, Richard, 18
Fenianism, 73
Fennelly, Nial, 253
Ferriter, Diarmaid, 3–4, 7
Fianna Fáil, 59, 71, 203, 205, 276, 278
Figgis, Darrell, 192
financial crisis (2008), 159
financial matters, 159–60
Fine Gael, 165
Finlay, James, 140
Finlay, Thomas, 300
Finnegan, Joseph, 300
First World War, 55, 56, 61
Fisher, Joseph Robert, 18
FitzAlan-Howard, Edmund, Viscount, 55, 81
FitzGerald, William, 300
FitzGerald-Kenney, James, 50, 150, 151, 153
FitzGibbon, Gerald, 46–7, 78, 79, 87, 88, 173–4, 192, 208, 209, 211, 270, 276, 295
FitzGibbon, James, 27
Flight of the Earls, 185
Ford plant, Cork, 131
Four Courts, 16, 35, 54, 145, 146, 154, 185, 290
    occupation and destruction (1922), 4, 50–1, 52, 63, 74, 193–4, 269
    reconstruction and reopening, 50–1, 60–1
Fox v. Mahon, 250
Freeman's Journal, 41, 131, 133
Frost, Georgina, 214
Fry, J.S., 154

Gaelic law, *see* Brehon law
Gaelic Romantic norms, 73
Gaeltacht, 118, 237, 238
Galway city courthouse, 290
An Garda Siochána, 223; *see also* Civic Guard
Gardiner, David, 138
Gaughan, Fr Anthony, 226
Gavan Duffy, George, 24, 26–7, 44, 78, 92, 94, 191, 192, 289, 300

GDPR (General Data Protection Regulations), 158, 161
Geoghegan, Bridget, 112
Geoghegan, James, 205, 208, 210, 221, 222
George IV, king, 55
George V, king, 59
Germany, 271
Gibson, John George, 87, 88, 90
Glann Mór Céibh Teoranta v. Minister for Housing, 243, 244
Glenavy, Lord (James H. Campbell), 9, 21, 30, 64, 85, 87, 188, 190, 270–1, 277, 281, *Plate 1*
  chair of Judiciary Committee, 2, 9, 37, 147
  and Circuit Court, 9, 147, 148–51, 153
Goff, Bartholomew, 106–7, 108, 110–11, 112, 113, 133, 139–40, 141–2
Gonne MacBride, Maud, 215, 227–8
Good, John, 218
Goodman, Michael, 113
Gordon, John, 80, 88
Gorey, Denis, 59
governor general, 68, 81, 117, 204
Grace v. An Bord Pleanála, 255
grand juries, 6, 284
Great Northern Railway Company, 130
Green Street courthouse, Dublin, 226, 229
Grenville, George, marquis of Buckingham, 57
Griffin, Lawrence, 229
Griffith, Arthur, 65, 68
Groarke, Raymond, 300
Guinness, Henry Seymour, 74
Gwynn, Denis, 194

Hamill, J.B. (state solicitor), 133, 140
Hamilton, Liam, 300
Hanna, Henry, 41, 77, 80, 152, 203, 210, 211, 276–7, 286, 289, 293, 297
Hannan, M.J., 137, 138, 139, 140
Hanratty, Frank, 137
Hanratty, John and Patrick, 111

Hanson, Sir Philip, 55, 58, 59, 60, 61
Hardiman, Adrian, 242–3, 246
Harmon, Kathleen, 229
Hayes, Michael, 80
health professionals, 180
Healy, T.M., 81–2
Henchy, Séamus, 281
Henn, Thomas Rice, 87–8
Henry II, king, 184, 273
Henry III, king, 185
Henry VIII, king, 184
Herlihy, Mary, 216
Heron, Áine, 215
Heron, Dorothea, 125
Heuston, R.F.V., 191
Hewart, Gordon, Viscount Hewart, 68, 86
High Court, 36, 41, 46, 145, 146, 147, 148, 155, 162, 210; *see also* Central Criminal Court
  appeals from, 210, 250; certification mechanism (s. 29), 250–2; certification mechanism (s. 29), legacy of, 253–6
  composition, 168, 203, 207, 208
  establishment (1924), 47, 166–7, 194
  Irish language, 238, 245, 246
  judges, *see* High Court judges
  jurisdiction, 5, 166–7, 180–1; appellate, 168; legal practitioners and other professions, 179–80; solicitors, 5, 178–9; wardship, 166, 168, 176
  lists, 169
High Court (Northern Ireland), 263, 264
High Court judges, 26, 90–1, 166, 167, 207, 208; *see also* president of the High Court
  additional judges, 168
  appointments, 76, 79, 83, 195, 203, 296–7 (Appendix 3)
  assignment, 169
  deaths in office (1897–1923), 88
  judicial robes, design for, *Plate 8*

High Court judges (*continued*)
　remuneration, 95, 96, 97, 100, 102
　retirement age, 91
　travelling judges, 284–5
High Court of Appeal, 90, 189
High Court of Justice, 187–8
High Court of Justice in Southern
　Ireland, 33, 189
historical context, 3–4, 11–21
Hoey, Jennie, 216
Hoey, Lawrence, 133, 141
Hoey, Patricia, 216
Hogan, Daire, 7, 8, 76, 106
Hogan, Gerard, 5, 10, 174, 243, 244,
　285
Holmes, Hugh, 89
Home Rule, 79, 190, 195, 196
Horan, Gerald, 5, 6, 286
Horgan, Rosemary, 300
Hosie v. Lawless, 148–9
House of Commons, 63
House of Lords (Dublin), 83
House of Lords (Westminster), 63, 67,
　83, 88, 187, 190, 205
housing, 13
Howlin, Niamh, 51, 117
Howth gun-running (1914), 189
Hughes, Douglas, 133
Hughes, Michael, 140
human rights, 125
Humphreys, Madeleine, 20
Humphreys, Sighle, 12, 227, 290
Hunter, Dr, 109
Hynes, John William, 75

immigration law, 252, 257
Incorporated Council for Law
　Reporting, 222
industrial schools, 110, 115, 126
infanticide, 225, 226
Inland Revenue Department, 53, 59
insolvency judges, 157
interest reipublicae ut sit finis litium,
　263
Irish Asphalt Ltd v. An Bord Pleanála,
　252

Irish Bar, *see* Bar of Ireland
Irish Civil Service Compensation
　Committee, 81
Irish Enlightenment, 73
Irish Free State, 4, 11–21, 28, 29, 31, 92,
　120, 128, 189, 269, 271, 272–3
　central fund, 100
　decolonisation and nation building,
　　see decolonisation; symbolism
　financial security, 74–5
　legal elite, 81
　new courts system, *see* courts
　and Northern Ireland, 128–34; *see
　　also* cross-border smuggling;
　　customs barrier
Irish Independent, 54, 61, 229, 230–1
Irish language, 7–8, 10, 118, 234–48
　case law following 1924 Act, 240–2,
　　243–4
　hearings in court, 244–7
　interpreters, 222–3
　legal sources, 242–4
Irish Law Times and Solicitors' Journal,
　56, 208, 209
Irish Legal Terms Advisory Committee,
　240
Irish Parliamentary Party, 74, 83, 205
Irish Reports, 209
Irish Republican Army (IRA), 12, 16,
　216; *see also* anti-Treaty
　Republicans
Irish Republican Army Organisation
　(IRAO), 15, 16
Irish Republican Brotherhood (IRB),
　15, 16
Irish Society (Oxford University), 11–12
Irish Statesman, 151
Irish Times, 14, 58, 96, 97, 131, 195, 289
Irish Trade Union Congress, 153
Irish Volunteers, 16, 189
Irish White Cross, 12
Irish Women Citizens Association, 221
Irish Women Workers' Union (IWWU),
　217–18
Irvine, Mary, 300
ISPCC, 110

James I, king, 185
Jameson, Andrew, 74
Jefferis, Danielle, 4, 7
John, king of England, 51
Johnson, David S., 134
Johnson, Richard, 300
Johnson, Thomas, 46, 98, 100–1, 149, 224, 270
Johnson, William, 87, 88, 90
Johnston, Francis, 55
Johnston, Joseph, 131–2
Johnston, William, 27, 70, 76, 77, 79, 80, 81, 85, 184, 185, 186, 273–4, 296
Joint Oireachtas Committee, *Report on courts and courthouses*, 124
Joint Oireachtas Committee on Justice and Equality, 123–4
Joint Oireachtas Committee on Temporary Accommodation for the Oireachtas, 59
Joint Oireachtas Committee on the Courts of Justice 1930, 167, 169, 170, 171
Jones, Tom, 17
Jordan family, 185
Joyce, James, 195
Judicature Acts, 183, 202
judicial address, mode of, 69–70, 286, 288–9
judicial appointments, 84, 199, 200, 204; *see also* chief justice; Circuit Court judges; High Court judges; Supreme Court judges
   1924 Act, under, 70–1, 72–83, 295–300; age, 76; applications, 293–4; educational background, 76–7; former Dáil court and Crown court judges, 27–8, 75, 79, 219; legal qualifications, 75, 76; personal relationships, 81–2; political background, 70, 75, 79–80, 219; religious profession, 78–9
   Constitution of 1922, 68–9
   Crown courts, 63–64

sectarianism, allegations of, 30
   women, 219–20
Judicial Appointments Advisory Board, 5, 166, 181, 199
judicial attire, 69–70, 287–8, 289, 290–1
   robes, 10, 21, 224, 285, 287–8;
   designs, *Plates 5–9*
judicial behaviour, 289
judicial careers, 87–90
Judicial Committee of the Privy Council, appeal to, *see* Privy Council appeal
Judicial Council, 5, 166, 181, 200
judicial independence, 4, 62, 63–71, 191
   Constitution of 1922, 66–9, 92
   Dáil courts, 65–6
   and remuneration, 93, 94, 96, 100, 101, 103
judicial interregnum (1922–4), 3, 33–49, 65, 193–4
   habeas corpus applications, 35, 38–49, 66
Judicial Network of the European Union, 201
judicial remuneration, 7, 67–8, 75, 92–104
   bonuses, 99–100
   British system, 94–5
   Oireachtas debates, 94–102
   pensions, 102, 103
   source of salaries, 100–3
judicial retirement, 7, 8, 63–4, 67, 69, 76, 86, 91, 199
   introduction of retirement age, 8, 84–91
   retirements (1897–1923), 88
judicial review
   certification mechanism (s. 29), legacy of, 251–3
   Northern Ireland, 260–1
judiciary, 2, 6–7, 27–8, 29, 92, 167, 289; *see also* judicial appointments; judicial independence; judicial remuneration; judicial retirement
   British system, *see* Crown judiciary

judiciary (*continued*)
    declaration/oath, 31, 69, 70–1, 198
    inauguration (1924), 47, 58, 287, *Plates 2–3*
    individual courts, *see* Circuit Court judges; District Court judges; High Court judges; Supreme Court judges
    interregnum (1922-24), during, *see* judicial interregnum
    Irish language, knowledge of, 236–7
    legal training, requirement for, 7, 26, 69
    precedence between, 167
    status, 98–9, 101, 104
    tenure, 84
    women judges, 4, 219–20
Judiciary Committee (1923–4), 1–3, 4, 6, 9, 10, 21, 37, 72, 74, 79, 81, 93, 118, 145, 197, 205, 224, 270, 272, 277, 281, 285
    and Circuit Court, 146–7
    and Dáil courts, 25–6
    and judicial independence, 69
    and judicial remuneration, 95, 99
    and judicial retirement age, 84–7, 90–1
    proposals from public, 25–6; women, 217–19
    report, 2–3, 146
    terms of reference and instructions, 2, 37, 282
Judiciary Committee (1930), 205, 207
jury trial, 6, 42, 58, 227, 284
    intimidation of jurors, 227, 233, 290
    Irish-language jury, 246–7
    women jurors, 220–1
justices of the peace, 117, 118, 214
juvenile courts, 217–19
juvenile justice, 125, 126

Kavanagh, James and Bernard, 110
Keane, Ronan, 86, 277, 285, 288, 300
Kearns, Nicholas, 300
Keenan, John Joseph (state solicitor), 139
Keith, Arthur Berriedale, 276
Kelly, John, 183

Kelly, Paul, 5, 8, 115, 159, 300
Kelly, Peter, 181, 300
Kelly, Thomas, 289
Kennedy, Eileen, 126
Kennedy, Finola, 223
Kennedy, Hugh, 9–10, 18, 20, 27, 35, 37, 45, 47, 48, 50, 51, 61, 68, 69–70, 80, 84, 85, 192–3, 195–6, 217, 218, 224–5, 272, 275, 281, 285, 295, 300, *Plate 1, Plate 10, Plate 13*
    and Circuit Court jurisdiction, 147, 149–50, 153
    and Constitution of 1922, 81, 93
    and courts system, 2, 10, 21, 192–3, 195, 274, 277, 281, 282, 283, 284, 286, 287
    and Crown judiciary, 75, 92, 93–4, 191–2, 283
    death (1936), 10, 204, 205, 209
    and Irish language, 234, 236, 239–40, 241, 247, 248
    and judicial appointments, 73, 75, 81
    and relocation of courts to Dublin Castle, 52–4, 55–6, 58, 59, 60
    and Supreme Court composition, 205–7, 212
    wardship cases, 169–70, 171–6
Kennedy, John, 110
Kenny, Matthew J., 76–7, 80, 82, 83, 298
Kenny, Patrick W., 237
Kenny, William, 88, 90
Keogh, William, 281
Kerry, county, 215
Kettle, Tom, 196
Kilcoole gun-running (1914), 80, 205
Kildare, county, 216
King's Bench, court of, 83, 90, 186, 187
King's Inns, 35, 54, 76, 90, 194, 197, 239
Kinsale courthouse, 279
Kirwan, Bernard, 229
Kirwan, Laurence, 229
Kohn, Leo, 191
Kotsonouris, Mary, 105, 117, 122, 126, 140, 275, 281
Kyle, Frances, 126, 213

Index

La Mancha, Malahide, 229
labour activists, 13
Labour Court, 158
Labour Party, 46, 59, 149, 224, 270
Land Commission, 23, 79, 89, 90, 154
Land Courts (Dáil courts), 23, 34, 217
Land Settlement Commission, 23
Laois, county, 216
Larne gun-running (1914), 190
Lavelle, Patrick, 110–11
Laverty, Mr, 139
Law Journal, 93, 283
law library, 76, 146
Law Quarterly Review, 184
Law Reform Commission, 232
Law Society, 152, 178, 179, 199
Law Students Debating Society, 275
Law Times, 89, 285, 287
Lawrence, Alfred Tristram, 86
leapfrog appeals, *see* appeals
Leary, Peter, 130, 133
Lee, Joe, 18, 287
Lee v. Ashers Baking Company Ltd, 263
legal aid, 153
legal practitioners, 179, 239–40; *see also* barristers, solicitors
Legal Practitioners Disciplinary Tribunal, 179
legal services, regulation of, 179, 200
Legal Services Regulatory Authority, 179
Leinster House, Dublin, 59
Lemass, Seán, 38
Letterkenny, Co. Donegal, 142
Leyland and Birmingham Rubber Company, 154
licensing, 20, 113, 119, 210–11
Lifford Circuit Court, 223
Lifford District Court, 138
Limerick, 214
Limerick County Council, 151
Little, Edward, 288, 293
Lloyd George, David, 64, 68
Logue, Cardinal Michael, 19, 20
London University, 76
Longford courthouse, 290

Longford Leader, 290
lord chancellor, 63, 167, 187, 188, 189, 191, 197
lord chief justice, 186, 187–9, 197, 202
  of Northern Ireland, 190
  of Southern Ireland, 189–94, 196
Loughran, James, 110
Loyalist gun-running, 190
Lucy, Mary, 226
lunacy matters, *see* wardship jurisdiction
lunatic asylums, 110
Lupton, Edmond, 148
Lyall, Andrew, 187
Lynch, Mary, 216
Lynch, Patrick, 71, 76, 78, 79, 297
Lynham v. Butler (No. 2), 46–7
Lynn, Alex, 39
Lyons, Sarah, 138

McAllister, Annie, 138
Mac Aodháin v Coiste Rialacha na nUaschúirteanna, 244
McAuley, Edward, 138
McBrien, Michael, 138
McCabe, Desmond, 117
McCabe, Henry, 229
McCann, Thomas S., 79
MacCarthaigh v. Éire, 246
McCarthy, Florence, 227
McConville, Elizabeth, 111
McConville, John, 111
MacDonald, Ramsay, 17
McDonnell, Ernest, 278
McElligott, Edward J., 76–7, 230, 299
McElligott, James John, 20
McEntee, Mary Ellen, 110
MacEoin, Sean, 211–12
MacEoin, Tomás, 45
McGarry, Fearghal, 280, 287
McGee, Mary, 231
McGeehan, Brigid, 216
McGilligan, Patrick, 101, 170
McGinety, James, 112–13
McGoldrick, Patrick, 236–7
McGovern, James, Anne and Mary, 111
McGovern, John, 111

McGovern, Margaret, 111
McGuigan, Evan, 4
McGuinness, Catherine, 242–3
McGuirk, Mary, 112
MacHale, Kate, 216
McKean, Mrs, 215
McKelvey, Joe, 37
McKenna, Patricia, 231
McKenna v. An Taoiseach (No. 2), 40
Macklin, Oliver, 300
McLoone, James, 79, 294
McLorinan, A Minor, Re, 175–6
McMahon, Deirdre, 19
McMahon, James, 81
McMahon, Richard, 117
McMenamin, Daniel, 221–2
McNally, Gerry, 223
MacNeill, Eoin, 18
Macnie, Isa, '*Kennedy Chief Justice*,' Plate 13
McQuillan, Thomas, 113
McWilliam, Mr, 113
Madden, Dodgson Hamilton, 87, 88
Magdalene laundries, 225–6
Magennis, William, 31, 95–6, 218
Magistrates' Courts (Northern Ireland) appeals from, 258–61, 263
Maguire, Conor A., 166, 170, 178, 203, 205, 217, 300
Maguire, Paul Richard, 267
Magwood, Annie, 137
Maher, Mrs, 229
Maine, Henry, 184, 273, 275
malicious injuries, 64–5, 111
Mallon, Bernard, 110
Malone, Miriam, 300
Mangan, Frederick, 230–1
Mansergh, Nicholas, 193
Mansfield, Lord, 86
Markey, Bridget, 112
Marshall, Robert, 3, 6, 7
Marsh's Library, 202
Martin, Samuel, 137
May, George Augustus Chichester, 188
Maynooth seminary, Co. Kildare, 20
Mayo, county, 216

Mellows, Liam, 37
Meredith, Arthur Carew, 84–5
Meredith, James Creed, 15, 16, 23, 26, 27, 60, 70, 77, 80, 81, 84, 145, 194–5, 205, 208, 210, 211, 296
Meredith, Richard E., 84, 89
Miller, David, 109
Ministry of Finance, 53, 54, 59; *see also* Department of Finance
Ministry of Labour, 53
Ministry of Munitions, 55
Model Law, 180
Mohr, Thomas, 4, 7, 34, 117, 272, 291
Molony, Helena, 215–16, 227, 290
Molony, Thomas F., 34, 38–9, 40, 41, 42, 54–5, 56, 59, 188, 189–90, 193–4, 195–6, 197, 202
Monaghan, county, 135–7, 216
Monaghan asylum, 110
Monaghan Circuit Court, 155
Monaghan courthouse, 290, *Plate 16*
Monaghan District Court, 136, 139, 140
Montreal Convention 1999, 158
Moore, William, 74, 90
Morgan, John Hartman, 190
Moriarty, John Francis, 88
Morning Post, 274, 282
Morris, Ewan, 279, 280
Morris, Frederick, 300
Morris, Sir Michael, 87, 88, 188
Morrissey, Daniel, 152, 224
Morrissey Committee, 152–3
*Moult v. Manga*n, 57
Mountjoy Prison, 37, 110
Mulcahy, Linda, 228
Mulcahy, Richard, 15, 16, 39
Muldoon, John, 79
Mullalley, Suzanne, 121
Mulligan, James, 112–13
Munster, 76
Murnaghan, James, 46, 76, 77, 81, 82, 173, 174, 192, 203, 208, 209, 210, 295, 297
Murphy, Bridget, 223
Murphy, James, 88
Murray, John L., 300

Naas courthouse, 290
Nash, Lady Agnes, 214
National Army, 14–15, 16; *see also* army mutiny (1924)
National Council of Women of Ireland, 221
National Land Commission, 23
National University of Ireland, 80
Nenagh, Co. Tipperary, 288
Nenagh Circuit Court, 153–4
Nenagh Guardian, 230
Network of Presidents of Supreme Judicial Courts of the European Union, 201
New South Wales, 146, 270
New Zealand, 86
Newry, Co. Down, 133–4, 142
Neylon, Thomas, 300
Ní Raifeartaigh, Úna, 7, 222, 246
Nolan, Martin, 16
North Eastern Boundary Bureau, 17, 131–2, 134, 141
Northern circuit, 213
Northern Ireland, 74, 86, 90, 128, 189; *see also* Border; cross-border smuggling
  appeal routes, 8, 258–68; civil cases, 263, 264; criminal cases, 258–62; judicial review, 260–1; leapfrog appeals, 264
  and Boundary Commission, 17, 18
  devolution issues, 266, 267
  references, 266–7
Northern Ireland Assembly, 263, 266, 267
Northern Ireland Protocol, 264
Northern Standard, 111
notaries public, 198, 202
nurses, 180

Ó Beoláin v. Fahy, 242–3
Ó Briain, Barra, 300
O'Brien, Daniel J., 299
O'Brien, George, 76
O'Brien, Miss, 223
O'Brien, Peter, Lord O'Brien, 87, 89, 188, 281

O'Brien, William, 88
O'Byrne, John, 76, 81, 98, 195, 203, 229–30, 275, 282, 297
Ó Cadhla v. An tAire Dlí agus Cirt, 245, 246
O'Callaghan, Margaret, 19
Ó Caoimh, Aindrias, 300
O'Casey, Seán, *Juno and the Paycock*, 13
O'Connor, Sir Charles, 27, 35, 38, 42, 43–4, 64, 70, 76, 77, 79, 81, 85, 295
O'Connor, Sir James, 43, 64, 68, 80, 85–6, 90, 96–7, 203, 286
O'Connor, Rory, 37, 194
Ó Dálaigh, Cearbhall, 300
O'Donnell, Donal, 5, 6, 10, 254–5, 300
O'Donoghue, Marie, 231
Odum v. Minister for Justice and Equality, 254–5
Offaly, county, 217
Office of Arms, 57
Office of Public Works (OPW), 50, 51, 53, 54, 55–56, 59, 60–1; *see also* Commissioners of Public Works, 21
Official handbook of the Free State, 273
Official yearbook of Australia, 273
Ó Floinn, Cathal, 300
Ó Foghludha v. McClean, 234, 240, 241, 247
Ó Gráda, Cormac, 14
O'Hanlon, Rory, 243
O'Hanrahan, Sean, 138
O'Higgins, Kevin, 1, 11–12, 15, 17, 20, 36, 54, 81, 105, 106, 107, 148–9, 150, 220, 221
O'Higgins, Tom, 300
Oireachtas, 18, 36, 41, 42, 43, 46–7, 59, 207, 276, 281; *see also* Joint Oireachtas Committee; Judiciary Committee (1930)
  judges prohibited from sitting in, 67
  judicial remuneration, debates on, 94–102
O'Kelly, Sarah, 217
old age pension, 14, 75
O'Leary, Catherine, 216

Omagh, Co. Tyrone, 82
Ó Maicín v. Éire, 246–7
O'Malley, Ernie, 12, 32
O'Malley, Iseult, 255
O'Malley, Peter, 300
Ó Monacháin v. An Taoiseach, 245
Ó Murchú v. An Taoiseach, 243
Order of St Patrick, 57
Orpen, William, 197
Osborough, Nial, 189, 270, 286
O'Shaughnessy, Thomas L., 70, 76–7, 79, 82, 91, 203, 296
O'Shiel, Kevin, 17, 18, 217
O'Siocháin, Pádraig Augustine, 286
Ó Tuathaigh, Gearóid, 115
Oxford University, 11

Palles, Christopher, 87, 88, 89, 90, 188
Palles, Miss, 214
Parish Courts (Dáil courts), 22, 25, 26, 32
Parnell, Charles Stewart, 80, 82
partition of Ireland, 33, 74, 82, 90, 128, 131, 142, 189; *see also* Border; cross-border smuggling
patents of precedence, 200
Paul-Dubois, Louis, 52
peace commissioners, 118, 237, 238
Pearse, Patrick, 272, 275
People (AG) v. Conmey, 251, 253
personal insolvency, 159–60
Petty Sessions courts, 24–5, 106, 117, 120, 121, 214, 284
pharmacists, 180
Phelan, Kathleen, 213–14
Phillimore, Lord, 190
An Phoblacht, 29, 31, 228, 286
Phoenix Park, Dublin, 21
Pigot, John Henry, 299
Pim, Jonathan, 42, 43
planning appeals
    judicial review, 252–3, 256, 257
planning law, 158, 181
Plunkett, George, 66
Porter, Andrew Marshall, 89
Porter, Samuel Clarke, 86, 87
Portrane Asylum, 13

Post Office, 53
Powell, John Blake, 88, 90
Power, Charles Wyse, 76, 80, 299
Power, Jenny Wyse, 215
Prager, Jeffrey, 73
Presbyterians, 78
president of Ireland, 198
president of the Circuit Court, 5, 156–7, 167, 168, 300 (Appendix 5)
president of the Court of Appeal, 167, 168, 199
president of the District Court, 5, 120, 159, 300 (Appendix 5)
president of the High Court, 167, 199, 205
    establishment of office, 5
    office-holders, 300 (Appendix 5)
    remuneration, 95, 102
    role of, 5, 165–82, 198; solicitors and other professions, in relation to, 5, 177–80; wardship matters, 167, 168, 170, 176–7, 198
president of the Supreme Court, 95; *see also* chief justice
presidential commission, 198
Privy Council (Ireland), 52, 55, 63, 79
Privy Council appeal, 6, 31, 66–7, 71, 269, 276
Probate and Matrimonial Division (High Court), 188
probation officers, 223
professionals, regulation of, 179–80; *see also* legal practitioners; solicitors
property arbitrators, 181, 198
property service providers, 180
prosecution of offences, 199
protected disclosures, 158, 160–1
Protestants, 19, 29, 30, 78, 172, 174
Provisional Government, 3–4, 35, 55, 105, 116, 193
    abolition of Dáil courts, 24–7, 28, 34, 66
    and judicial independence, 67–9
    and 'judicial interregnum' (1922–4), 34, 35–49, 65

relocation of courts to Dublin Castle, 51, 52, 53–4
public dancing, 119
Public Prosecution Service of Northern Ireland v. Elliott and McKee, 260
Public Safety legislation, 39–41, 42, 44, 45, 47, 113

Quarter Sessions courts, 36, 117, 156
Queen's Bench, 187, 202
Queen's University Belfast, 77
Queensland (Australia), 270
Quinn and White v. Stokes, 153
Quinn Insurance Ltd v. PricewaterhouseCoopers, 254, 256–7
Quirke, Dr, 152

R v. Allen, 41, 64, 191
R (Childers) v. Adjutant General of the Provisional Forces, 35, 70
R (Cooney) v. Clinton, 38, 42, 43–4, 46, 47, 48
R (Corcoran) v. Clinton, 43, 44
R (Johnstone) v. O'Sullivan, 35
R (Murphy) v. Military Governor, Mountjoy Prison, 42
R (Ó Coileáin) v. Crotty, 244–5
R (O'Brien) v. Military Governor of North Dublin Union Internment Camp, 38–40, 41, 196
R (O'Connell) v. Military Governor of Hare Park Camp, 42–3, 44, 48
railways, 130
Rathmines and Rathgar Dáil District Court, 215–16
Reddin, John, 288
Redmond, John, 196
Redmond, Lady, 214
Redmond, William, 96, 98, 147
Reference Committee, 181
Registrar of Wards of Court, 177
Reilly, James Laurence, 112
remote hearings, 124
Republican courts, *see* Dáil courts
Republicans, 8, 11, 65, 66, 142; *see also* anti-Treaty Republicans

resident magistrates (RMs), 105, 106, 117, 281
residential law, 158, 162
Residential Tenancies Board, 162
restorative justice, 117
Revenue Commissioners
and cross-border smuggling, 7, 134, 137, 140, 143
Richmond Asylum, 13
road traffic offences, 122
Rock, Francis, 137
Roe, Thomas Francis, 300
Roebuck Castle, Co. Dublin, 172
Ronan, Stephen, 38, 39, 40, 43, 89, 196
Rooney, Joseph, 16
Roscommon courthouse, 289
Rosenthal, Lionel Henry, 293
Ross, Sir John, 84, 90
The Round Table, 283
Royal Commission of Inquiry into shooting of Sheehy Skeffington (1916), 196
Royal Commission on the Landing of Arms at Howth (1914), 189–90
Royal Courts of Justice (Northern Ireland), 74
Royal Dublin Society (RDS), 77
Royal University of Ireland, 76
Ruane, Bláthna, 4, 7, 48, 92
rule of law, 4, 7, 105, 146
rules of court, 69, 106; *see also* Circuit Court Rules; Superior Courts Rules
Rutland, duke of, 86
Ruttledge, P.J., 170, 207–8
Ryan, Gladys, 231
Ryan, Mary E., 223
Ryan, Patricia, 5, 8, 300

St Martha's industrial school, 110
Samuels, Arthur, 57
Savigny, Friedrich Carl von, 271–5
Sealy, James, 299
Seanad Éireann, 9, 38, 42, 159
Seanad Éireann (Senate), 70, 74, 85
Second Vatican Council, 288
Senate, *see* Seanad Éireann

separation of powers, 7, 66, 71, 73, 92, 94, 231
Shannon, Charles: designs for judicial robes, Plates 7–8
Shannon, George William, 156, 300
Sharkey, A.M., 223
Sheehy, Eugene, 80, 230, 293
Sheehy Skeffington, Francis, 196
Sheehy Skeffington, Hanna, 214–15, 223, 227, 228
Sheridan, Diarmuid, 300
Sherlock, Lorcan, 220
Sherry, Thomas, 112
Sinn Féin, 11, 12, 64, 65, 94, 142, 145, 195
Sinn Féin courts, see Dáil courts
Sinnott, Kathryn, 231
Sisters of Charity, 226
Sligo, 210
Smith, F.E., Lord Birkenhead, 190
Smith, Zadie, 183
Smithwick, Peter, 300
smuggling, see cross-border smuggling
Smyth, Esmond, 300
social care professionals, 180
Society of Chartered Surveyors Ireland, 181
Society of St Vincent de Paul, 110
solicitors, 5, 8, 118, 140, 152, 153, 166, 197–8, 202; see also legal practitioners
    regulation of, 177–8, 179
Solicitors Act 1954, In re, 178, 179
Solicitors Disciplinary Tribunal, 178
South Africa, 206
Southern circuit, 214
Southern Ireland, 74, 128, 189
Southern Law Association, 151
Southern Unionists, 9, 68, 70, 71, 74, 147
Spain, Francis, 300
Special Criminal Court, 222
Spenser, Edmund, 184–5
Stack, Austin, 65, 145
'state courts' (1922–4), 25, 31
State (Ryan) v. Lennon, 42–3, 46, 47, 48, 192, 276

statutory instruments, 243, 244
stenographers, 221–2, 236
Stewart, Mr, 108
Strabane, Co. Tyrone, 132, 133–4
Sullivan, Kathleen, 223
Sullivan, Timothy, 76–7, 81, 82, 173, 174, 205, 208, 210, 245, 296, 300
Sunday Independent, 132, 192
Sunday Pictorial, 282
Superior Courts Network, 201
Superior Courts Rules, 69, 70, 181, 198, 244
Superior Courts Rules Committee, 70
Supreme Court, 5, 9, 10, 36, 40, 166, 201, 276
    appellate jurisdiction, 167, 249, 250, 253; certification process (s. 29), legacy of, 249–57
    composition, 5; and winter of 1936–7, 203–12
    establishment, 1, 47, 194, 197–8
    finality of decisions, 6
    and Irish language, 238, 242
    judges, see chief justice; Supreme Court judges
    Privy Council appeal, right of, see Privy Council appeal
    wardship jurisdiction, 171–6
Supreme Court (Northern Ireland), 259–61, 263, 264, 267
Supreme Court judges, 26, 192, 198; see also chief justice
    additional judges, 208
    appointments, 69, 76, 203, 205; (1924–5), 295 (Appendix 2)
    declaration, 198
    ranking, 167
    remuneration, 95, 96, 97, 100, 102
    retirement age, 91
    robes, design for, Plate 6
Supreme Court of Judicature, 33, 36, 37, 187, 189
Supreme Court of Judicature of Northern Ireland, 189
Supreme Court of Judicature of Southern Ireland, 189

Supreme Court of the United
    Kingdom, 183
Surveyors Institution, 198
Swanton, Kathleen, 221
symbolism, 6, 7, 279, 287–91
    Crown symbols, removal of, 278–9,
        289–90
    harp, 285

teachers, 180
Thomas, James Henry, 17
Thurles, Co. Tipperary, 288
Tichborne case, 183
Times (London), 228, 282
Tobin, Major-General Liam, 15
Tone, Wolfe, 227
Towey, T., 93
Tralee courthouse, *Plate 15*
Treasury, 196–7
Trickett, J.M., 197
Trinity College Dublin, 77, 192, 195,
    196, 197
Trinity College OTC, 78
Tyrell, justice, 139

Ua Cadhain, Liam, 288
UCD, *see* University College Dublin
Ulster, 76
Ulster plantation, 185
Ulster Unionists, 17, 18
Ulysses (Joyce), 195
unfair dismissals, 160
UNCITRAL Model Law, 180
Unionists, 30, 64, 80, 128, 190; *see also*
    Southern Unionists
United Kingdom, 8, 86, 128, 129, 132,
    183, 267, 281, 282
United States, 8, 67, 206, 217
University College Dublin, 31, 77, 195,
    196
    UCD Archives, 11, 12, 18, 81
University College Galway, 290
Urquhart, Diane, 232

Venice Commission: Joint Council on
    Constitutional Justice, 201

veterinary practitioners, 180
victims, 125, 224–5
Victoria, queen, 55
Volksgeist, 271

Wakely, John, 76, 77, 78, 79, 149, 299
Waldre, Vincenzo, 57
Walker, Samuel, 88
Walsh, Annie, 226
Walsh, Brian, 251
Walsh, Louis, 21, 138, 142, 143
War of Independence, 11, 53, 56, 62,
    120, 128, 142, 191, 194, 196, 279,
    286
Ward, Margaret, 214
Wards of Court, office of, 177
wardship jurisdiction, 5, 115, 163, 165,
    166, 167, 168, 169–77, 188, 198,
    202
    abolition, 176–7
Warren, R.R., 87, 88
The Watchword, 153
Waterford, county, 216
Waterford District Court, 229
Watson, Thomas, 52
Webb v. Outrim, 269
Webster, Charles, 111–12
welfare provision, 13–14
Westby, Frances Valentine, 173
Westby (Minors) (No. 2), Re, 171–4
Western circuit, 213
Whelan, Norah, 229–230
Whelehan, Harry, 300
White, Dudley, 79, 294
White, John, 110
Willoughby, Penelope, 229
women, 4, 8, 21, 213–33
    anti-treatyites, *see* anti-Treaty
        Republicans
    in civil litigation, 231–2
    in criminal courts, 224–7
    in Dáil courts, 22–3, 214–17
    dress and appearance, 230–231
    Judiciary Committee (1923),
        submissions to, 217–19
    justices of the peace, 214

women (*continued*)
   in legal profession: barristers and solicitors, 125–6, 213–14, 219; judges, 4, 22–3, 126, 214–16, 219–20, 232
   other roles, 8, 221–4, 233; jurors, 220–1; public gallery, 228–30; stenographers, 221–2
Women's Independent Association, 225
Women's Prisoners' Defence League, 227

World Conference on Constitutional Justice, 201
Wright, George, 88
Wylie, James, 88, 90
Wylie, William E., 70, 75, 76, 77, 78, 79, 81–2, 90, 203, 296
Wyndham, George, 55

Yeats, W.B., 18
Young, James, 139

IRISH LEGAL HISTORY SOCIETY SERIES*

1 Daire Hogan and W.N. Osborough (eds), *Brehons, serjeants and attorneys: studies in the history of the Irish legal profession* (1990)
2 Colum Kenny, *King's Inns and the kingdom of Ireland: the Irish 'inn of court', 1541–1800* (1992)
3 Jon G. Crawford, *Anglicizing the government of Ireland: the Irish Privy Council and the expansion of Tudor rule, 1556–1578* (1993)
4 W.N. Osborough (ed.), *Explorations in law and history: Irish Legal History Society discourses, 1988–1994* (1995)
5 W.N. Osborough, *Law and the emergence of modern Dublin: a litigation topography for a capital city* (1996)
6 Colum Kenny, *Tristram Kennedy and the revival of Irish legal training, 1835–1885* (1996)
7 Brian Griffin, *The Bulkies: police and crime in Belfast, 1800–1865* (1997)
8 Éanna Hickey, *Irish law and lawyers in modern folk tradition* (1999)
9 A.R. Hart, *A history of the king's serjeants at law in Ireland: honour rather than advantage?* (2000)
10 D.S. Greer and N.M. Dawson (eds), *Mysteries and solutions in Irish legal history: Irish Legal History Society discourses and other papers, 1996–1999* (2000)
11 Colum Kenny, *King's Inns and the battle of the books, 1972: cultural controversy at a Dublin library* (2002)
12 Desmond Greer and James W. Nicolson, *The factory acts in Ireland, 1802–1914* (2003)
13 Mary Kotsonouris, *The winding-up of the Dáil courts, 1922–1925: an obvious duty* (2004)
14 Paul Brand, Kevin Costello and W.N. Osborough (eds), *Adventures of the law: proceedings of the 16th British Legal History Conference, Dublin 2003* (2005)
15 Jon G. Crawford, *A Star Chamber court in Ireland: the Court of Castle Chamber, 1571–1641* (2005)
16 A.P. Quinn, *Wigs and guns: Irish barristers and the Great War* (2006)
17 N.M. Dawson (ed.), *Reflections on law and history: Irish Legal History Society discourses and other papers, 2000–2005* (2006)
18 James Kelly, *Poynings' Law and the making of law in Ireland, 1660–1800* (2007)
19 W.E. Vaughan, *Murder trials in Ireland, 1836–1914* (2009)
20 Kevin Costello, *The Court of Admiralty of Ireland, 1575–1893* (2011)
21 W.N. Osborough, *An island's law: a bibliographical guide to Ireland's legal past* (2013)
22 Felix M. Larkin and N.M. Dawson (eds), *Lawyers, the law and history: Irish Legal History Society discourses and other papers, 2005–2011* (2013)
23 Daire Hogan and Colum Kenny (eds), *Changes in practice and law: a selection of essays by members of the legal profession to mark twenty-five years of the Irish Legal History Society* (2013)
24 W.N. Osborough, *The Irish stage: a legal history* (2015)
25 Thomas Mohr, *Guardian of the Treaty: the Privy Council appeal and Irish sovereignty* (2016)
26 Joseph C. Sweeney, *The life and times of Arthur Browne in Ireland and America, 1756–1805* (2017)
27 Niamh Howlin, *Juries in Ireland: laypersons and law in the long nineteenth century* (2017)
28 Patrick Hyde Kelly (ed.), *The case of Ireland's being bound by acts of parliament in England, stated, Dublin 1698* (2018)
29 Mary Phelan, *Irish speakers, interpreters and the courts, 1754–1921* (2019)
30 Coleman A. Dennehy (ed.), *Law and revolution in seventeenth-century Ireland* (2020)
31 Daire Hogan and Patrick Maume (eds), *The reminiscences of Ignatius O'Brien, lord chancellor of Ireland 1913–18: a life in Cork, Dublin and Westminster* (2021)
32 Peter Crooks and Thomas Mohr (eds), *Law and the idea of liberty in Ireland: from Magna Carta to the present* (2023)
33 Bríd McGrath, *The operations of the Irish House of Commons, 1613–48* (2023)
34 Niamh Howlin (ed.), *A century of courts: the Courts of Justice Act 1924* (2024)

ALSO AVAILABLE
The Irish Legal History Society (1989)
*Volumes 1–7 are published by Irish Academic Press

Irish Legal History Society

Established in 1988 to encourage the study and advance the knowledge of the history of Irish law, especially by the publication of original documents and of works relating to the history of Irish law, including its institutions, doctrines and personalities, and reprinting or editing of works of sufficient rarity or importance.

PATRONS 2022–3

The Right Honourable Dame Siobhán Keegan Lady Chief Justice of Northern Ireland	The Honourable Donal O'Donnell Chief Justice of Ireland

COUNCIL 2022–3

President

John G. Gordon DL

Vice Presidents

John Larkin KC	Dr Thomas Mohr

Honorary Treasurers

R.D. Marshall	Kevin Neary

Honorary Secretaries

Dr David Capper BL	Paul Egan SC

Web editor

Dr Coleman Dennehy

Council members

Ex officio: Professor Patrick M. Geoghegan, President 2018–21

Dr Lynsey Black	Dr Sparky Booker
Dr Kevin Costello	Dr Coleman Dennehy
Dr Kenneth P. Ferguson BL	Professor Robin Hickey
Dr Niamh Howlin	The Hon. Mr Justice Ian Huddleston
Professor Colum Kenny BL	Felix M. Larkin FRHistS
Professor Irene Lynch Fannon	James I. McGuire MRIA
Mark Orr KC	Dr Bláthna Ruane SC
Mark Tottenham BL	

www.ilhs.eu